Discovery and Exploration of the Mississippi Valley
by John Gilmary Shea

Address:
HardPress
8345 NW 66TH ST #2561
MIAMI FL 33166-2626
USA
Email: info@hardpress.net

302 SHEA, JOHN GILMARY. Discovery and Exploration of **The Mississippi Valley**, with the original narratives of Marquette, Allouez, Membré, Hennepin, and Anastase Douay, and a fac-simile of the original map of Marquette. 8vo. cl. map. pp. 348. N. Y., 1853. Scarce. $7.00

A volume of rare interest to those concerned to know the history of this great western land.

Mon Reverend Pere.

Pax X.

Ayant este contrainct de demeurer a St. François
tout l'este, acause de quelque incommodité, en ayant este
guery du 8 mois de Septembre J'y attendois l'arrivée
de nos gens ou retour de la bas pour sçavoir ceque
ie ferois pour mon hyuernement, lesquels m'ont apporté
les ordres pour mon voyage a la mission de la
Conception des Ilinois, ayant satisfait aux sentiments
de S'R pour les copies de mon iournal touchant la
Riviere de Missilipi, Je partis auec Pierre Porteret et
Jacque le 25 oct 1674 Sur les midy la nuit nous
contraignit de coucher a la sortie de la Riviere, ou
les Pouteatamis s'assembloient les vieux n'ayant
pas voulu qu'on allast du costé des Ilinois, de peur
que la ieunesse n'allant des robbes auec les
marchandises qu'ils ont apporter de la bas, et chassant
au castor ne voulut descendre le printemps qu'ils
voient auoir hiet de craindre les nadoessi.

1 Lettre et Journal
du feu P. marquette +

† Mon Reverend Pere
Le P. Claude Dablon
Superieur des Missions
de la Compagnie de Jesus
en la nouvelle france

Jacque marquette

Claude Allouez

DISCOVERY AND EXPLORATION

OF THE

MISSISSIPPI VALLEY:

WITH

THE ORIGINAL NARRATIVES OF MARQUETTE, ALLOUEZ, MEMBRÉ, HENNEPIN, AND ANASTASE DOUAY.

BY

JOHN GILMARY SHEA.

WITH A FACSIMILE OF THE NEWLY-DISCOVERED MAP OF MARQUETTE.

REDFIELD,
CLINTON HALL, NEW YORK.
1852.

STEREOTYPED BY C. C. SAVAGE,
13 Chambers Street, N. Y.

TO

JARED SPARKS, LL.D.

PRESIDENT OF HARVARD UNIVERSITY,

𝕿𝖍𝖎𝖘 𝖁𝖔𝖑𝖚𝖒𝖊 𝖎𝖘 𝖎𝖓𝖘𝖈𝖗𝖎𝖇𝖊𝖉,

AS A MARK OF PERSONAL REGARD,

BY THE AUTHOR.

PREFACE.

It has long been a desideratum to have in English the early narratives of the discovery and exploration of the Mississippi. Marquette's map and voyage have indeed appeared, but the narrative varies in no small degree from the authentic manuscript, and the map is not at all a copy of that still preserved, as it came from the hand of the great explorer. These published from original manuscripts, and accompanied by the narratives of the missionaries in La Salle's expedition, are now first presented in an accessible shape, and complete the annals of the exploration.

The life of Marquette, and the history of the exploration itself, are the result of many years study of the early Spanish and French authorities, both printed and manuscript, some of which have never before been consulted.

Besides my own researches, I have been aided by those of the President of St. Mary's College, and of the Hon. James Viger, of Montreal, and I trust that the volume will be found to be as faithful as the subject is interesting.

New York, *Sept.*, 1852.   J. G. S.

CONTENTS.

HISTORY

DISCOVERY OF THE MISSISSIPPI RIVER.

ON glancing at a map of America, we are at once struck
by the mighty river Mississippi, which, with its countless branches, gathers the waters of an immense valley, and
rolls its accumulated floods to the gulf of Mexico, affording a
line of uninterrupted communication for thousands of miles,
which has in our day peopled its banks with flourishing
towns and cities. So large a stream, so important a means
of entering the heart of the continent, could not, it would be
supposed, long remain unknown—or, known, remain unap-
preciated : yet so, in fact, it was.

Columbus himself entered the gulf of Mexico, but the
southern coast only was explored by the discoverer of the
New World. By whom the northern shore was first explored
we do not know ; but it is laid down with considerable accuracy in an edition of Ptolemy printed at Venice in 1513.
This map is the more remarkable as the delta of a river cor-
responding to the Mississippi is traced upon it more distinctly
than in the maps of the next century. Several adventurers
now sailed along the northern or Florida shore, till it was

completely examined by Garay in 1518. Three years later, a map was drawn up by the arbitrator appointed to decide between the claims of rival discoverers, and on it we find the Mississippi again traced on the part assigned as peculiarly Garay's, and on it the name it subsequently bore, Rio del Espiritu Santo, or River of the Holy Ghost.*

Several expeditions were now fitted out to explore and reduce the realms of Florida. Brilliant, daring, and adventurous attempts they were, and give the time that hue of chivalry which almost makes us forget the crimes which marked it—crimes, magnified and distorted indeed by foreign writers, but still coolly and dispassionately examined crimes that we must condemn.† It was the last age of the political freedom, of the nicely-poised balance between the

---

* These facts and the maps are to be found in an English version of the "Shipwrecks of Alvar Nuñez Cabeza de Vaca," printed for private distribution at Washington, in 1851, for Geo. W. Riggs, jr. The translator is Mr. Buckingham Smith.

† It is not so much the cruelty here as the wantonness of it that shocks our modern taste. That was an age of cruelty. The Spaniard, from his long guerilla wars with the early Moors, was necessarily a man used to blood: and when the Reformation came, and the new religionists sprang at the rich plunder of the churches, those who adhered to old ideas clung to them with desperation; and when deprived of them, unable to retaliate on the church property of their antagonists who had none, vented their rage on their spoilers themselves. In countries where the advocates of the new ideas had not entered, the example of what had occurred elsewhere taught the old-idea party to prevent their entrance at all hazard, if they wished to worship at the shrines raised by their ancestors. Had they been angels, they might have been mild; but they were men, and necessarily cruel, and the retaliations were so too. The sixteenth century, then, is marked by constant scenes of blood, not only in America, but in Europe, and only bigots would attempt to represent any one case as isolated and build a theory on it. In this age, and from this very cruelty, the English and French navies rose; both were in their origin piratical flotillas, which lived by plundering the Spanish main and the rich argosies which were crossing to Cadiz. Even these bore a religious appearance, for the mariners, not only of England but of France, at the time professed a horror of the religion of the Spaniard, equalled only by their love for his gold. In fact, it is not easy to express now all that a Spaniard, on terra firma or the Spanish main, comprised in that fearful word "herege."

ruler and the ruled. Not yet had the world been startled by the extremes of a claim of divine right in the person of the monarch, and annual revolutions in the name of the people. The Spaniard was the freest man in Europe : the various powers of the state, still unbroken, maintained on each other that salutary check which prevents all tyranny. The time was yet when the tutor of the heir-apparent of the Spanish crown could inculcate on his pupil the doctrine that a tyrant might be put to death ; while, at the same time, the people were taught that religion required their obedience to the ruling powers, with submission and support from which only extreme cases could absolve them.*

Besides this, " many circumstances concurred at this epoch of overwrought excitement, violence, and a mania for discovery by land and sea, to favor individuality of character, and enable some highly-gifted mind to develop noble germs drawn from the depth of feeling. They err," says Humboldt, " who believe that the Spanish adventurers were incited by mere love of gold and religious fanaticism. Perils always exalt the poetry of life ; and besides, this remarkable age, unfolding as it did new worlds to men, gave every enterprise and the natural impressions awakened by distant travels, the charm of novelty and surprise."

Leon, Cordova, and Ayllon, had successively found death on the shores of Florida ; but the spirit of the age was not damped : in 1528, Pamphilus de Narvaez undertook to conquer and colonize the whole northern coast of the gulf. He landed, and, after long and fruitless marches, returned to the coast, and in wretched boats endeavored to reach Tampico. Almost all perished : storms, disease, and famine, swept them

---

* Mariana's De Rege Tyranno was written for a Spanish prince,

away, and the coast was whitened with their bleaching
bones. A few with Cabeza de Vaca were thrown on an
island on the coast of Mississippi. After four years' slavery,
De Vaca escaped and struck inland with four companions.
Taken for supernatural beings, they became the medicine-
men of the tribes through which they passed, and, with as
little difficulty as the Indian jugglers, established their reputation. With lives thus guarded by superstitious awe, they
rambled across to the gulf of California, traversing the bison-
plains and the adobe towns of the half-civilized natives of
New Mexico, perched on their rocky heights. De Vaca is the
first known to have traversed our territory from sea to sea.
In this long wandering, he must have reached and crossed
the Mississippi; but we in vain examine his narrative for
something to distinguish it from any other large river that he
met. He remains then in history, in a distant twilight, as
the first European known to have stood on the banks of the
Mississippi, and to have launched his boat upon its waters;
but his "shipwrecks" shed no new light on its history.*

When he and his companions suddenly appeared amid
their countrymen in Mexico, their strange accounts, and an
air of mysterious secrecy which they affected, gave a new
impulse to the adventurous spirit of the age. In the spring
of 1539, two attempts were made to reach the realm in the
interior, which De Vaca had protested to be "the richest
country in the world." One of these expeditions started from
the Pacific, the other from the Atlantic. The former was led
by the Franciscan friar Mark, a native of Nice in Italy, who,
burning with a desire of conquering for Christ the many
tribes within, set out with a negro companion of De Vaca's

---

* De Vaca's narrative in Spanish is in Barcia's collection, and in French in
that of Ternaux-Compans.

from Culiacan, and crossing the desert wastes, reached the Colorado; but after gazing from a commanding height on the embattled towers of Cibola, with its houses rising story above story, and its gateways so well glazed that they seemed masses of turquoise, returned with baffled hopes, for the natives had refused him entrance, and actually cut off his negro guide and a large party of friendly Indians. Friar Mark, on his return, raised the hopes of the Spanish authorities still higher, and his statements, apparently true in themselves, were so understood by the excited imaginations of all, as to leave impressions far from the reality. An ideal kingdom rose into existence, and a new expedition was projected. This reached the valley of the Mississippi; but before we trace its course, we must go back to the Atlantic expedition of 1539.*

It was commanded by the successful Ferdinand de Soto, who had risen by the conquest of Peru to rank and wealth, and was now governor of the rich island of Cuba. With a force far superior to any that had yet landed on the continent, he entered Florida, and, with his gallant array, struck into the unknown interior. The Mississippi, under the name of Espiritu Santo, was not unknown to him; for, after proceeding westward and turning slightly northeast to Hurripacuxi — after striking westward to Eteocale, whose heroes wore (the natives said) helmets of burnished gold — after carrying, by stubborn fight, the gallant town of Napetuca — after pressing on through Ivetachuco, fired like another Moscow by its dauntless people — after reaching Anaica Apalache, — he sent Maldonado back to Havana, with orders to meet him in six months at the mouth of the Mississippi.†

---

* The narrative of Friar Mark is in the Appendix to the Narrative of Casta-fiedo de Najera, published by Ternaux. It deserves to be read, for it is not so much a fiction as is generally supposed.

† Historical Coll. of Louisiana, vol. ii., p. 99.

Here began his second campaign; lured by the glittering promises of an Indian guide, he marched to the northeast, crossing the Altamaha, and perhaps entered the territory of Carolina, a land full of remembrances of Ayllon. Weary with a march of twelve hundred miles, his men were fain to settle there; but no, on they must go, and turning northward, he traversed unconsciously the golden sands of the Chalaques, with a heavy heart, for it was poor in maize. At last he reached a great river by the western course, and with his mind still full of great hopes from the river of Espiritu Santo, he took the Coosa for the Mississippi, and traced it to its source,* then following down its gentle current, crossing as villages invited him, he reached Mavila to waste the lives and property of his men in a terrible contest with the gigantic Tuscalosa, the chieftain of the land. Here any but the resolute Soto would have renounced his schemes, and joined his vessels in Pensacola bay; but no, though winter was coming on, he marched north, fighting his way across river after river to the heart of the Chickasaw country, and wintered there, although they, too, burned their village in which the invaders were quartered; thence he marched northwest to the country of the Alibamons, who threw up a palisade entrenchment to prevent his passage. With considerable loss De Soto carried it, and captured corn enough to carry him across the desert land to Quizquiz, and here at last he really came to the long-sought Rio del Espiritu Santo. It was the Mississippi. Here all doubt vanishes. Listen to the characteristic description of the most detailed narrative. "The river," says the unknown Portuguese, "was almost half a league broad; if a man stood still on the other side, it could not be discerned whether he was a man or no. The

---

* *Historical Coll. of Louisiana,* vol. ii., p. 101.

river was of great depth, and of a strong current; the water was always muddy; there came down the river continually many trees and timber, which the force of the water and stream brought down."[*] And the inhabitants were not unworthy of the great river. "The cacique came with two hundred canoes full of Indians with their bows and arrows, painted, with great plumes of white and many-colored feathers, with shields in their hands, wherewith they defended the rowers on both sides, and the men of war stood from the head to the stern, with their bows and arrows in their hands. The canoe wherein the cacique sat, had a canopy over the stern, and he sat beneath it, and so were the other canoes of the principal Indians. And from under the canopy where the chief man sat, he commanded and governed the other people.

From the frequent mention of the river in Biedma's narrative we may infer that allusion to it was suppressed, or at most, mysteriously made by De Vaca, and that it was supposed to be the key to his land of gold. Certain it is, that their hopes seem here to brighten; they build boats, the first European craft to traverse the river, and crossed to the western side some twenty or thirty miles, as modern investigators tell us, below the mouth of the Arkansas.[†]

The country now reached by the Spaniards, was one of large and populous towns, well defended by walls and towers, pierced with regular loop-holes, and surrounded by well-made ditches. De Soto ascended the river, and striking on a higher, drier, and more champaign country than he had yet seen, proceeded onward to Pacaha, a place it would not be easy now to locate. The Mississippi was thus explored

[*] *Historical Coll. of Louisiana,* vol. ii., p. 168.
[†] See the opinions collected in Bancroft, vol. i., p. 51.

for a considerable distance; but far other than commercial
or colonial projects filled the mind of De Soto; he stood by
what he knew an outlet to the sea, a great artery of the continent, but his splendid array had dwindled down, and the
rich realm of De Vaca had not yet rewarded his many toils.
Nerved by despair, he marched northeast till he found himself
among the wandering Indians of the plains, with their portable
cabins. This was his highest point, and could not have been
far from the Missouri. He then turned southwest again to the
Arkansas, at the large town of Quigata, to seek guides to lead
them to the southern sea; but Coligoa beyond the mountains
tempted him to the northwest again; yet Coligoa ill-repaid their
toil; it was poorer than the well-built towns they had left
behind. Striking west and southwest again, he seems to have
once more reached the Arkansas at Cayas, and ascended it
to the town of Tanico, with its lake of hot water and saline
marshes. Turning then to the south and east, he again reached
Vicanque also on the Arkansas, and wintering there, descended it in the spring of 1542 to die on the banks of the Mississippi; after having thus explored the valley of the Arkansas,
and examined its inhabitants, who, from the scanty notices
we have, seem quite different from those afterward found
there, and apparently an offshoot of the New Mexican tribes.*

De Soto was now dead, the expedition was abandoned,
the only object was to leave the fatal country. Muscoso,
their new leader, despaired of reaching the gulf by the
Mississippi, and struck westward in hopes of reaching New
Spain, as De Vaca had done. In this western march of over
seven hundred miles, he explored a considerable part of the
valley of the Red river, passing by the tribes which were not

---

* In confining these rambles of De Soto to the valley of the Arkansas, I am
not alone; see *M'Culloch's Researches*, pp. 529, 531, cited by Bancroft.

expelled or exterminated when the country was ultimately explored by the French. Nazacahoz, in the province of Guasco, was the most westerly town in their march. Here they found turquoises, pottery, and cotton mantles from New Mexico, and even an Indian woman who had escaped from the Pacific expedition, of which we shall next speak. From her statement, and the account given by the Indians of the large river of Daycao to the west, they marched ten days more, and crossing this river, probably the Pecos branch of the Rio Grande, found themselves in the country of the roving tribes. Disheartened at the prospect before him, Muscoso returned to the Mississippi, and ascending above Guachoya where De Soto had died, entered at Aminoya, and working up all their chains and iron into nails, began to build vessels to navigate the Mississippi. The place where these first brigantines were built, has not been clearly settled, its Indian name Aminoya has left no trace. Here "seven brigantines were constructed, well made, save that the planks were thin, because the nails were short, and were not pitched, nor had any decks to keep the water from coming in. Instead of decks, they laid planks, whereon the mariners might run to trim their sails, and the people might refresh themselves above and below." They were finished in June, and "it pleased God that the flood came up to the town to seek the brigantines, from whence they carried them by water to the river." Thus three hundred and twenty-two Spaniards sailed from Minoya on the 2d of July, 1543, and passing Guachoya, were attacked by the people of Quigalta, who pursued them for many days, and did considerable harm to the little fleet. At last, however, on the eighteenth day they reached the gulf of Mexico, after having sailed, as they computed, two hundred and fifty leagues down the river. Thence, after many dangers and hardships, the survivors coasting along reached Tampico, " whereat the viceroy and all the inhabitants of Mexico wondered," says the chronicle.*

Such is, in brief, the history of the Mississippi as explored by De Soto, and his successor, Muscoso, the first who sailed " Down the great river to the opening gulf."

The account they gave received additional confirmation from the second expedition of Father Mark's from the Pacific coast. This expedition commanded by Coronado, and guided by the adventurous missionary, reached and took Cibola, which proved of little value. Ascending the Colorado, the commander left its valley and crossed the Rio Grande in search of Quivira; a faithless guide promised him gold in all abundance, and others as faithless now led him up and down the prairies watered by the upper branches of the Arkansas and Platte. He was thus on the upper waters of the former river, in 1542, at the time when Muscoso heard of him by his runaway slave; but neither trusted the accounts which he received and they did not meet. At Tiguex before he reached the Rio Grande, Coronado had found a " Florida Indian" whose description of the Mississippi tallies quite well with with that of the gentleman of Elvas. " This river in his country," he said, " was two leagues wide, and that they found fish in it as large as horses, and that they had on it canoes which could hold twenty rowers on each side : and that the lords sat at the stern under a canopy."† At the Rio Grande, too, Coronado heard from the Querechos, or roving Indians of the plains, " that marching toward the rising sun, he should meet a very great river, the banks of which he could

---

* For an account of De Soto's expedition, see Biedma's narrative, and that of the gentleman of Elvas, in *Historical Collections of Louisiana*, vol. ii. La Florida del Inca, is a romance.

† *Castanedo de Nagera in Ternaux*, p. 77.

follow ninety days without leaving inhabited country. They added that the first village was called Haxa, that the river was more than a league wide, and that there was a great number of canoes."[*]

Such clear accounts of a great river, which the party of De Soto had found navigable for at least a thousand miles, would naturally have drawn attention to it; but we find no notice of any Spanish vessels entering the river to trade in furs or slaves, or simply to explore. Accident occasionally brought some to its banks, but these visits are few and brief, and they led to no result. Thus, in 1553, a rich argosy from Vera Cruz, after stopping at Havana, was wrecked on the Florida coast, and a few survivors reached Tampico by land, escaping from the constant and terrible attacks of the natives.[†] In consequence of this and other disasters the king, in 1557, ordered the reduction of Florida, and an army of 1,500 men was fitted out two years after under Don Tristan de Luna, who carried with him every survivor of any expedition or shipwreck in Florida, who could be found.

De Luna reached St. Mary's bay in safety, and had sent back two vessels to announce his arrival in Florida, when a sudden storm came on, and all his vessels were dashed to pieces. Thus left in as miserable a state as any shipwrecked party before, Tristan was not disheartened; he advanced to an Indian town Nanipacna, which had been taken and wasted by De Soto.[‡] Hearing very flattering accounts of the rich country of Coosa, he despatched a party of two hundred there, under his sargente mayor accompanied by two Dominicans. The party reached Coosa in safety, entered into an alliance offensive and defensive with the cacique, who was

---

[*] *Castanedo de Nagera in Ternaux*, p. 117. [†] *Ensayo Crono. ad ann.*
[‡] It must be the Napetuca of the Portuguese relation. For De Luna, see *Ens. Cron.* 1559.

then at war with the Napŏchies (probably the Natchez), who
lay on the Ochechiton, or great water, which the Spaniards
took to be the sea.   An expedition was soon set on foot
against the Natchez, and the cacique went at the head as
chief of Coosa never went before, on a gallant Arabian steed,
with a negro groom at his horse's head.   Defeating the enemy, they reached the Ochechiton which proved to be a
mighty river, the Rio del Espiritu de Santo, in other words,
the Mississippi, thus reached again by the Spanish adventurers and missionaries.   Revolts had meanwhile arisen in De
Luna's camp, and vessels soon came to bear the survivors
back to Mexico, and none now looked in hope to that fatal
quarter.

The entrance of some missionaries into New Mexico in
1580, though fatal to themselves, led to new expeditions, and
to the final establishment of Spanish colonies there ; here as
before, they heard continually of the Mississippi, or Rio
Grande del Espiritu Santo, and some seem actually to have
reached it ;* but no steps were taken to explore it, and the Rio
Grandee is so called merely because some one mistook it for
the great river of De Soto.†

A work published in 1630,‡ has indeed an account of a
Portuguese captain, Vincent Gonzalez, who is said to have
sailed up a large river between Apalache and Tampico, and
to have approached quite near the kingdom of Quivira, but
though this is supposed by the author to be the Espiritu
Santo, the notice is too vague to found any inference.

The Mississippi was now forgotten, and although explored
for at least a thousand miles, known to have at least two

* See *Ensayo Chronologico*, p. 170 ; and tit *Bonilla Torquemada*, vol. iii., p. 358.
† I have seen this fact stated, but can not now state the work.
‡ Benavides Memorial.

branches equal in size to the finest rivers of Spain, to be nearly a league wide and perfectly navigable, it is laid down on maps as an insignificant stream, often not even distinguished by its name of Espiritu Santo, and then we are left to conjecture what petty line was intended for the great river of the west.*

The Spaniards had thus abandoned the valley of the Mississippi, and a few years after the French at the north began to hear of it, and it was finally reached and explored by the Jesuit missionaries, the great pioneers of the north and west. Quebec was founded by Champlain, in 1608. He was soon joined by Recollect friars, and while he entered the Seneca country with his Huron allies, the intrepid Father Le Caron had ascended the Ottawa and reached the banks of Lake Huron. Subsequently others joined him there; they invited the Jesuits to aid them, and the tribes in the peninsula were visited from Detroit to Niagara, and from Lake Nipissing to Montreal. The capture of Canada by the English, in 1629, defeated any further missionary efforts for a time; but it was restored in 1632, and the Jesuits sent out to continue the missions alone. They " now became the first discoverers of the greater part of the interior of this continent. They were the first Europeans who formed a settlement on the coast of Maine, and among the first to reach it from the St. Lawrence. They, it was, who thoroughly explored the Saguenay, discovered Lake St. John, and led the way overland from Quebec to Hudson's bay. It is to one of them that we owe the discovery of the rich and inexhaustible salt springs of Onon-

---

* An English voyage up in 1648, or thereabouts, and a Spanish one up into New York by the Mississippi and Ohio, in 1669, have found advocates; but I confess my skepticism. That a ship may have occasionally entered the Delta, is not improbable, and Indian report seems to fix one somewhere near 1669. See *Sparks's Life of La Salle, Life of Marquette, Denton's New-York.*

daga. Within ten years of their second arrival, they had
completed the examination of the country from Lake Superior
to the gulf, and founded several villages of Christian neophytes on the borders of the upper lakes. While the intercourse of the Dutch was yet confined to the Indians in the
vicinity of Fort Orange, and five years before Elliott of New-
England had addressed a single word to the Indians within
six miles of Boston harbor the French missionaries planted
the cross at Sault Ste. Marie, whence they looked down on
the Sioux country and the valley of the Mississippi. The
vast unknown west now opened its prairies before them.

"Fortunately the early missionaries were men of learning
and observation. They felt deeply the importance of their
position, and while acquitting themselves of the duties of
their calling, carefully recorded the progress of events around
them."* Year after year these accounts reached Europe,
and for a long time were regularly issued from the press, in
the same epistolary form in which they were written.

In the history of the French colonies, they are a source
such as no other part of the country possesses. For our present purpose, they have been invaluable; from them we can
trace step by step, the gradual discovery of the Mississippi.

As early as 1639, the adventurous and noble hearted sieur
Nicolet,† the interpreter of the colony had struck west of the

---

* O'Callaghan, Jesuit Relations.

† As we are perhaps the first to advance the claim of the sieur Nicolet, it
may not be amiss to give a menger sketch of a man too much unknown, though
he occupied an important place in the early history of Canada. He came out to
Canada in 1618, and was never from that time unemployed. Almost immediately after his coming, he was sent to the plundering Honqueronons, or Indians
of the island, above the Chaudiere falls on the Ottawa. Here he remained two
years, often suffering from hunger and their brutality, but finally acquired a
great knowledge of the Algonquin. After this, he was sent with four hundred
Algonquins to make peace with the Iroquois, and completely succeeded in his
mission. He was then for eight or nine years stationed among the Ninissings,
and became almost as Indian as they. After the restoration of Canada to France,

Hurons, and, reaching the last limit of the Algonquins, found himself among the Ouinipegou (Winnebagoes), " a people called so, because they came from a distant sea, but whom some French erroneously called Puants," says this early account. Like the Nadѕeѕis they spoke a language distinct from the Huron and Algonquin. With these Nicolet entered into friendly relations, and exploring Green bay, ascended Fox river to its portage, and embarked on a river, flowing west ; and says Father Vimont, " the sieur Nicolet who had penetrated furthest into those distant countries, avers that had he sailed three days more on a great river which flows from that lake [Green bay], he would have found the sea." This shows that Nicolet like De Luna's lieutenant mistook for the sea, the Indian term *Great Water*, applied to the Mississippi. It is certain then, that to Nicolet is due the credit of having been the first to reach the waters of the Mississippi. The hope of reaching the Pacific now aroused the courage of the missionaries, some fathers invited by the Algonquins were to be sent to " those men of the other sea," but, adds Vimont prophetically, " Perhaps this voyage will be reserved for one of us who have some little knowledge of the Algonquin."*

he was made interpreter and commissary of the colony, which office he filled till he was sent, about 1639, to Green Bay, and the *Men of the sea*, where he met an assembly of four or five thousand men, and concluded peace with them. It must have been at this time that he ascended the Fox river to the Wisconsin. Returning to Quebec, he succeeded Olivier as commissary, and retained this office till his death. In 1641, we find him with F. Ragueneau, negotiating a peace with the Iroquois, at Three-Rivers. In 1642, sent from Quebec to Three-Rivers, to rescue a poor Abenaqui from the hands of some pagan Algonquins, he set out in a small boat on the 31st of October, at sunset with Savigni, but a storm came on, and their little craft capsized near Sillery. Savigni swam to the shore, Nicolet, unable to swim, sank to rise no more. Thus perished, in a work of Christian charity, the sieur Nicolet, the first Frenchman who reached the waters of the Mississippi. See *Rel.* 1639–'40, p. 135. *Rel.* 1640–'41, ch. ix. *Rel.* 1642–'43, p. 8. *Creuxius*, p. 359.

* *Rel.* 1639–'40, pp. 132, 135, &c. The Lac des Puans is laid down on Champlain's map of 1632 ; but in all probability, only from report, as it is placed

In 1641, two Jesuits from the Huron mission, the illustrious Isaac Jogues and Charles Raymbout were actually sent to Sault St. Mary's, and they too heard of the Sioux and the river on which they lay, and they burned to enter those new realms and speak that language yet unknown, which fell so strangely on their ears now used to Huron and Algonquin sounds.[*]

The next year the Iroquois war broke out in all its fury; and the missionaries had to abandon all hopes of extending to the west. The war proved fatal to the allies of the French; by 1650, all Upper Canada was a desert, and not a mission, not a single Indian was to be found, where but a few years before the cross towered in each of their many villages, and hundreds of fervent Christians gathered around their fifteen missionaries. The earth still reeked with the blood of the pastor and his flock; six missionary fathers had fallen by the hands of the Iroquois, another had been fearfully mutilated in their hands. But scarce was there a ray of peace when the survivors, were again summoned to the west. A field opened on Lake Superior. Father Garreau was sent in 1656, but was killed ere he left the St. Lawrence. De Groseilles and another Frenchman, more fortunate, wintered on the shores of the lake in 1658; they too visited the Sioux, and from the fugitive Hurons among them heard still clearer tidings of a great river on which they had struck, as, plunging through unknown wood and waste, over cliffs and mountains, they had sought to escape the destructive hand of the pursuing Iroquois. "It was a beautiful river," writes the annalist, "large, broad, and deep, which would bear comparison, they say, with our St. Lawrence." On its banks they found the Abimi8ec, the Ilinois of later days.

north of Lake Superior, unless it is meant for Lake Winnipeg, which, like Green bay, got its name from the Algonquin epithet for the Dacotahs, as coming from the Pacific.   [*] *Rel.* 1642, p. 166.

From other quarters, too, they began to hear of this great river. The missionaries on the Saguenay heard of the Winnipegouek, and their bay whence three seas could be reached, the north, the south, and the west.* The missionaries in New York saw Iroquois war-parties set out against the Ontoagannha whose towns " lay on a beautiful river [Ohio], which leads to the great lake as they called the sea, where they traded with Europeans, who pray to God as we do, and have rosaries and bells to call men to prayers." This sea the missionaries judged must be the gulf of Mexico, or that of California.†

Meanwhile Ménard, an old Huron missionary, proceeded, in 1660, to Lake Superior, and founded an Ottawa mission on the southern shore. He, too, heard of the Mississippi, and had resolved to reach the nations on its banks, undeterred by the difficulties of the way; but a work of charity called him to another quarter, and a death in the wilderness arrested his projects, before which one of half his years would have recoiled.‡

His successor, Father Allouez, also heard of the great river, " which empties," says he, " as far as I can conjecture, into the sea by Virginia." He heard, too, of the Ilimouek, and the Nadouessiouek; and here, for the first time, we find the

---

* *Rel.* 1659–'60, p. 61.   † *Rel.* 1661–'62, p. 9.

‡ See his letter in *Rel.* 1663–'64, ch. i. Recent publications have put a Jesuit mission on the lake, and even on the Mississippi, as early as 1658; but the Relations have not the slightest allusion to the fact, and speak of Ménard as the first. The Jesuits named as being concerned, are not mentioned either in the journal of the superior of the mission, nor in any printed Relations, nor in Ducreux, nor in Le Clercq. The fact of a missionary at Tamaroa prior to Marquette's voyage, is perfectly irreconcilable with the Relations, and if established, would destroy their authority. In this view, I will pay the most exorbitant price for any letter to or from F. Louis de Guerre, or Charles Drocoux, or any act of theirs at Tamaroa during the period in question, or any manuscript of the 17th century showing their existence there.

river bear a name. "They live," says he, "on the great river called Messipi."*

The western mission now received new accessions, and their hopes of entering the great river became more and more sanguine. The distinguished Father Dablon was sent out as superior of the Ottawa missions. A station among the Illinois was determined upon, Father Marquette named to begin it, and the study of the Illinois language actually begun by that missionary. From the accounts of a young man who was his master in that language, he formed new conjectures as to its mouth, and was apparently the first who heard of the Missouri. As to his intended voyage, he says, " If the Indians who promise to make me a canoe do not break their word, we shall go into this river as soon as we can with a Frenchman and this young man given me, who knows some of these languages, and has a readiness for learning others ; we shall visit the nations that inhabit them in order to open the passage to so many of our fathers, who have long awaited this happiness. This discovery will give us a complete knowledge of the southern or western sea."†

Meanwhile Allouez, on the 3d of November, 1669, left Sault St. Mary's to visit Green bay ; with great danger and hardship he reached it, and spent the winter preaching to the Pottawatomies, Menomonees, Sacs, Foxes, and Winnebagoes, whom he found mingled there. On the 16th of April, 1670, he began to ascend Fox river, and passing two rapids, reached Winnebago lake, and crossing it, came to a river "from a wild-oat lake." He was now, however, in search of the Outagamis, or Foxes, and turned up their river. He found them dejected by the loss of several families carried off by the Senecas on the banks of Lake Machihiganing (our

---

* *Rel.* 1666–'67, p. 106.   † *Rel.* 1669–'70, p. 157.

Lake Michigan). After consoling them as he could, he explained the object of his coming, and after given them his first general instruction in Christianity, sailed down their river again, and continued to the town of the Machkoutench, whom, says he, the Hurons call Assistacctaeronnous, or Fire nation. To reach them, he traversed the lake or marsh at the head of the Wisconsin, for they lay on that river. "It was," he says, "a beautiful river running southwest without any rapid. It leads," he says, further on, "to the great river named Messi-sipi, which is only six days' sail from here." Thus had Allouez at last reached the waters of the Mississippi, as Nicolet had done thirty years before.*

There was now no difficulty in reaching it; an easier way lay open than that from Chagoimegon. Father Dablon wished himself to visit the spot, and in company with Allouez, he returned to Green bay, and as early as September, in the same year, both were again at Maskoutens.†

Father Dablon had meanwhile been named superior-general of the Canada missions, and seems to have taken the more interest in the exploring of the Mississippi by the Wisconsin, as the projected Illinois mission of Father Marquette was, for a time at least, defeated. The peace on which they relied was suddenly destroyed; the Sioux provoked by the rash insolence of the Hurons and Ottawas, declared war, and

---

* *Rel.* 1669-'70, p. 92.

† *Rel.* 1670-'71, p. 169. At the time of drawing my notice on F. Allouez, p. 67 post, I had some doubts as to these visits of Allouez and Dablon. The former, Allouez, is the first missionary who reached the waters of the Mississippi; he twice ascended the Fox river in 1670, and twice overthrew the idol at Kakalin rapid. Fortunately Mr. Squier knows but little of the French missionaries at the north, or he would not have called the good fathers *infamous* for thus unseating the *sacred* object of the worship of the aborigines to substitute what with whimsical archæology he calls the *fictions of their own religion.* Allouez is the first to use a term at all like Michigan for the lake, and confirms my conjecture of the identity of the Maskoutens and Assistagueronons.

sent back to the missionary the pictures which he had given them. Stratagem enabled them to neutralize the advantage which firearms gave their enemies; the Hurons and Ottawas were completely defeated, and fugitives already before the face of the Iroquois, they now fled again from a more terrible foe in the west. All hopes of his Illinois mission being thus dashed, the dejected Marquette followed his fugitive flocks, and as the Ottawas proceeded apart to Manitoulin, he accompanied the Hurons to Mackinaw.* Here, doubtless, a hope of reaching the Mississippi by the Wisconsin, again roused him, as we soon find it the burthen of his thoughts.

Father Dablon published the Relations of 1670–'71, and its map of Lake Superior. In his description of the map he at once alludes to the Mississippi. "To the south flows the great river, which they call the Missisipi, which can have its mouth only in the Florida sea, more than four hundred leagues from here."† Further on he says, " I deem it proper to set down here all we have learnt of it. It seems to encircle all our lakes, rising in the north and running to the south, till it empties in a sea, which we take to be the Red sea (gulf of California), or that of Florida ; as we have no knowledge of any great rivers in those parts which empty into those two seas.‡ Some Indians assure us that this river is so beautiful that more than three hundred leagues from its mouth, it is larger than that which flows by Quebec, as they make it more than a league wide. They say, moreover, that all this vast extent of country is nothing but prairies, without trees or woods, which obliges the inhabitants of those parts to use turf and sun-dried dung for fuel, till you come about twenty leagues from the sea. Here the forests begin to ap-

---

* *Rel.* 1670–'71, p. 147.   † *Rel.* 1670–'71, p. 89.

‡ There is probably a misprint here, and it should be, " we have some knowledge" or else he held a theory that every sea must have its great river.

pear again. Some warriors of this country (Maskoutens), who say that they have descended that far, assure us that they saw men like the French, who were splitting trees with long knives, some of whom had their house on the water, thus they explained their meaning, speaking of sawed planks and ships. They say besides, that all along this great river are various towns of different nations, languages, and customs, who all make war on each other; some are situated on the river side, but most of them inland, continuing thus up to the nation of the Nadouessi who are scattered over more than a hundred leagues of country."*

The course of the Mississippi, its great features, the nature of the country, were all known to the western missionaries and the traders, who alone with them carried on the discovery of the west. Among the latter was Jolliet, who in his rambles also penetrated near the Mississippi.† As the war seemed an obstacle to so hazardous an undertaking, the missionaries, it would appear, urged the French court to set on foot an expedition. Marquette held himself in readiness to leave Mackinaw at the first sign of his superior's will, and at last on the 4th of June, 1672, the French minister wrote to Talon, then intendant of Canada : " As after the increase of the colony, there is nothing more important for the colony than the discovery of a passage to the south sea, his majesty wishes you to give it your attention."‡ Talon was then about to return to France, but recommended Jolliet to the new governor Frontenac, who had just arrived. The latter approved the choice, and Jolliet received his proper instructions from the new intendant. "The Chevalier de Grand Fontaine," writes Frontenac, on the 2d of November, " has deemed expedient

* *Rel.* 1670–'71, p. 175.
† *Mem. of Frontenac,* N. Y. Paris Doc., vol. i., p. 274.   ‡ Ibid, vol. i., p. 267.

for the service to send the sieur Jolliet to discover the south
sea by the Maskoutens country, and the great river Mississippi, which is believed to empty in the California sea.   He
is a man of experience in this kind of discovery, and has already been near the great river, of which he promises to see
the mouth."*

Of the missionaries, two seemed entitled to the honor of
exploring the great river, Allouez, the first to reach its waters,
and Marquette named for some years missionary to the Illinois.   The latter was chosen, and since his departure from
Chegoimegon, he had constantly offered up his devotions to
the blessed Virgin Immaculate, to obtain the grace of reaching the Mississippi.   What was his joy when on the very
festival dearest to his heart, that of the Immaculate Conception, Jolliet arrived bearing the letters of his superiors which
bid him embark at last, in his company to carry out the design so long, and so fondly projected.

"The long-expected discovery of the Mississippi was now
at hand, to be accomplished by Jolliet of Quebec, of whom
there is scarce a record but this one excursion that gives him
immortality and by Marquette, who, after years of pious assiduity to the poor wrecks of Hurons, whom he planted near
abundant fisheries, on the cold extremity of Michigan, entered, with equal humility, upon a career which exposed his
life to perpetual danger, and by its results affected the des-
tiny of nations."†

The winter was spent in preparation, in studying over all
that had yet been learned of the great river, in gathering
around them every Indian wanderer, and amid the tawny
group drawing their first rude map of the Mississippi, and
the water courses that led to it.   And on this first map traced

* *Mem. of Frontenac*, N. Y. Paris Doc., vol. i., p. 274.   † Bancroft.

doubtless kneeling on the ground they set down the names of each tribe they were to pass, each important point to be met. The discovery was dangerous, but it was not to be rash ; all was the result of calm, cool investigation, and never was chance less concerned than in the discovery of the Mississippi.

In the spring they embarked at Mackinaw in two frail bark canoes, each with his paddle in hand, and full of hope, they soon plied them merrily over the crystal waters of the lake. All was new to Marquette, and he describes as he went along the Menomonies, Green bay, and Maskoutens, which he reached on the 7th of June, 1673. He had now attained the limit of former discoveries, the new world was before them ; they looked back a last adieu to the waters, which great as the distance was, connected them with Quebec and their countrymen ; they knelt on the shore to offer, by a new devotion, their lives, their honor, and their undertaking, to their beloved mother the Virgin Mary Immaculate ; then launching on the broad Wisconsin, sailed slowly down its current amid its vine-clad isles, and its countless sand-bars. No sound broke the stillness, no human form appeared, and at last, after sailing seven days, on the 17th of June, they happily glided into the great river. Joy that could find no utterance in words filled the grateful heart of Marquette. The broad river of the Conception, as he named it, now lay before them, stretching away hundreds of miles to an unknown sea. Soon all was new ; mountain and forest had glided away ; the islands, with their groves of cotton-wood, became more frequent, and moose and deer browzed on the plains ; strange animals were seen traversing the river, and monstrous fish appeared in its waters. But they proceeded on their way amid this solitude, frightful by its utter absence

of man. Descending still further, they came to the land of
the bison, or pisikiou, which, with the turkey, became sole
tenants of the wilderness; all other game had disappeared.
At last, on the 25th of June, they descried foot-prints on the
shore. They now took heart again, and Jolliet and the missionary leaving their five men in the canoes, followed a little
beaten path to discover who the tribe might be. They travelled on in silence almost to the cabin-doors, when they halted,
and with a loud hallao proclaimed their coming. Three villages lay before them; the first, roused by the cry, poured
forth its motley group, which halted at the sight of the new-
comers, and the well-known dress of the missionary. Old
men came slowly on, step by measured step, bearing aloft
the all-mysterious calumet. All was silence; they stood at
last before the two Europeans, and Marquette asked, "Who
are you?" "We are Illinois," was the answer, which dispelled all anxiety from the explorers, and sent a thrill to the
heart of Marquette; the Illinois missionary was at last amid
the children of that tribe which he had so long, so tenderly yearned to see.

After friendly greetings at this town of Pewaria, and the
neighboring one of Moing-wena, they returned to their canoes,
escorted by the wondering tribe, who gave their hardy visi-
tants a calumet, the safeguard of the West. With renewed
courage and lighter hearts, they sailed on, and passing a high
rock with strange and monstrous forms depicted on its rugged
surface, heard in the distance the roaring as of a mighty cataract, and soon beheld Pekitanoui, or the muddy river, as the
Algonquins call the Missouri, rushing like some untamed
monster into the calm and clear Mississippi, and hurrying in
with its muddy waters the trees which it had rooted up in its
impetuous course. Already had the missionaries heard of

the river running to the western sea to be reached by the branches of the Mississippi, and Marquette, now better informed, fondly hoped to reach it one day by the Missouri. But now their course lay south, and passing a dangerous eddy, the demon of the western Indians, they marked the Waboukigou, or Ohio, the river of the Shawnees, and still holding on their way, came to the warm land of the cane, and the country which the musquitoes might call their own. While enveloped in their sails as a shelter from them, they came upon a tribe who invited them to the shore. They were wild wanderers, for they had guns bought of Catholic Europeans to the east.

Thus far all had been friendly, and encouraged by this second meeting, they plied their oars anew, and amid groves of cotton-wood on either side, descended to the 33d degree, where, for the first time, a hostile reception seemed promised by the excited Metchigameas. Too few to resist, their only hope on earth was the mysterious calumet, and in heaven the protection of Mary, to whom they sent up those fervent prayers, which none but one who has called on her in the hour of need can realize. At last the storm subsided, and they were received in peace; their language formed an obstacle, but an interpreter was found, and after explaining the object of their coming, and announcing the great truths of Christianity, they embarked for Akamsea, a village thirty miles below on the eastern shore.

Here they were well received, and learned that the mouth of the river was but ten days sail from this village; but they heard, too, of nations there trading with Europeans, and of wars between the tribes, and the two explorers spent a night in consultation. The Mississippi, they now saw, emptied into the gulf of Mexico, between Florida and Tampico, two Spanish points ; they might by proceeding fall into their hands. They resolved to return. Thus far only Marquette traced the map, and he put down the names of other tribes of which they heard. Of these in the Atotchasi, Matora, and Papihaka, we recognise Arkansas tribes ; and the Akoroas and Tanikwas, Pawnees and Omahas, Kansas and Apiches, are well known in after days.

They accordingly set out from Akensea on the 17th of July to return. Passing the Missouri again, they entered the Illinois, and meeting the friendly Kaskaskias at its upper portage, were led by them in a kind of triumph to Lake Michigan, for Marquette had promised to return and instruct them in the faith. Sailing along the lake, they crossed the outer peninsula of Green bay, and reached the mission of St. Francis Xavier, just four months after their departure from it.

Thus had the missionaries achieved their long-projected work. The triumph of the age was thus completed in the discovery and exploration of the Mississippi, which threw open to France, the richest, most fertile, and accessible territory in the new world. Marquette, whose health had been severely tried in this voyage, remained at St. Francis to recruit his strength before resuming his wonted missionary labors, for he sought no laurels, he aspired to no tinsel praise.

Jolliet, who had, like Marquette, drawn up a journal and map of his voyage, set out (probably in the spring) for Quebec, to report to the governor of Canada the result of his expedition, and took with him an Indian boy, doubtless the young slave given them by the great chief of the Illinois. Unfortunately, while shooting the rapids above Montreal, his canoe turned, and he barely escaped with his life, losing all his papers and his Indian companion. What route he had followed from Mackinaw, we do not know ; but he seems to have descended by Detroit river, Lake Erie, and Niagara, as Frontenac announcing his return to the government in France, says, "he has found admirable countries, and so easy a navigation by the beautiful river which he found, that from Lake Ontario and Fort Frontenac, you can go in barks to the gulf of Mexico, there being but one discharge to be made at the place where Lake Erie falls into Lake Ontario."

Separated as he was from Marquette, and deprived of his papers by the accident, Jolliet drew up a narrative of his voyage from recollection, and also sketched a map which Frontenac transmitted to France in November, 1674, three months after Jolliet's arrival at Quebec.* The loss of Jolliet's narrative and map now gave the highest importance to those

---

* As Frontenac's memoir completely refutes the assertion of Hennepin, that Jolliet made no report to the government, and is a monument of no little importance, as substantiating the voyage of Marquette and Jolliet we insert it in the original, from vol. i., p. 258, of the Paris Documents at Albany.

"QUEBEC LE 14 NOVEMB., 1674.

"§ VI. Retour du Sr. Joliet de son voyage à la découverte de la mer du sud.

"Le Sr. Joliet que M. Talon m'a conseillé d'envoyer à la découverte de la mer du sud, lorsque j'arrivai de France, en est de retour depuis trois mois et a découvert des pays admirables et une navigation si aisie par les belles rivières qu'il a trouvées que du lac Ontario et du fort Frontenac on pourrait aller en barque jusque dans le golfe du Mexique, n'y ayant qu'une seule décharge a faire dans l'endroit ou le Lac Erie tombe dans le Lac Ontario.

"Ce sont des projets a quoi l'on pourra travailler lorsque la paix sera bien établie et quand il plaira au roi de pousser ces découvertes.

"Il a été jusqu'à dix journées du golfe du Mexique et croit que les rivières que du coté de l'ouest tombent dans la grande rivière qu'il a trouvée, qui va du nau S . . . et qu'on trouveroit des communications d'eaux qui méneroient à la mer Vermeille et de la Californie.

"Ie vous envoie par mon secrétaire la carte qu'il en a faite et les rémarques dont il s'est pu souvenir, ayant perdu tous ses memoires et ses journaux dans la naufrage qu'il fit à la vue de Montreal, où il pensa se noyer, apres avoir fait un voyage de douze cents lieues et perdit tous ses papiers et un petit sauvage qu'il ramenoit de ces pays là.

"Il avoit laisseé dans le Lac Superieur au Sault Ste. Marie chez les Peres des copies de ses journaux, que nous ne saurions avoir que l'année prochaine, par où vous apprendrez plus de particularités de cette découverte, dont il s'est très bien acquitté.   'FRONTENAC."

C

in the hands of the missionaries ; these Frontenac promised to send, and Father Marquette, as we find by his autograph letter, transmitted copies to his superior at his request, prior to October; and the French government was, undoubtedly, possessed, in 1675, of Marquette's journal and map, and fully aware of the great advantage to be derived from the discoveries made, either for communicating direct with France from Illinois, or of seeking the nearest road to the gulf of California and the Pacific, by the western tributaries of the Mississippi. " These," says Frontenac, " are projects we can take in hand when peace is well established, and it shall please his majesty to carry out the exploration."

The court allowed the whole affair to pass unnoticed. Marquette's narrative was not published, and the Jesuit Relations apparently prohibited ; so that it would not, perhaps, have seen the light to our days, had not Thevenot obtained a copy of the narrative and a map which he published in 1681.* France would have derived no benefit from this discovery, but for the enterprise and persevering courage of Robert Cavalier de la Salle. When Jolliet passed down Lake Ontario, in 1674, he stopped at Fort Frontenac where La Salle was then commander under Frontenac. He was thus one of the first to know the result of Jolliet's voyage, and, perhaps, was one of the few that saw his maps and journal which were lost before he reached the next French post. At the time it does not seem to have made much impression on La Salle ; his great object then was to build up a fortune, and the next year he obtained a grant of Fort Frontenac and the monopoly of the lake trade and a patent of nobility. His plans failed, and instead of acquiring wealth, he found himself embarrassed by immense debts. He now looked for

---

* There is a copy of this original edition in the library of Harvard College. An exact copy was printed by Mr. Rich, a few years ago.

some new field, and by reading the accounts of the Spanish adventurers, seems to have been the first to identify the great river of Marquette, and Jolliet with the great river of De Soto. The vast herds of bison seemed to him to afford an easy means of realizing all that he could hope, by enabling him to ship from the banks of the Missouri and Illinois direct to France by the gulf of Mexico, cargoes of buffalo-skins and wool. In 1677, he repaired again to France, and by the help of Frontenac's recommendation, obtained a patent for his discovery, and a new monopoly in the following May, and by September was in Canada with Tonty and a body of mechanics and mariners, with all things necessary for his expedition. The plan traced by Jolliet in Frontenac's despatch of 1674, seems to have been followed by him without further investigation. As it would be necessary to unload at the falls of Niagara, the Ongbiara, of the old missionaries, he resolved to build a new fort there, and construct vessels above the cataract to ply on the upper lakes, and thus connect his trading-houses on the Mississippi with Fort Frontenac, his chief and most expensive establishment. Such was his celerity that, by the 5th of December, the first detachment of his party entered the Niagara river, and a site was soon selected for a fort, and for the construction of a vessel above the falls. Difficulties with the Senecas finally compelled him to relinquish the fort, and a mere shed or storehouse was raised. The vessel, however, went on, and he at last saw it glide down into the rapid current of Niagara in August, 1679, amid the admiring crowd of Indians who had gathered around the French.

There was now no obstacle to his further progress, but we must here regret that he had not studied former discoveries more narrowly. One of his clear and comprehensive mind

would have seized at once the great western branch of the
Mississippi, already known to the missionaries and the Iroquois.   By his present plans he had to build one vessel above
the falls of Niagara, and a second on the Illinois river; one
on the Ohio, so easily reached by the Alleghany would have
carried him to the gulf, and he would thus have avoided the
various troubles which so long retarded his reaching the
mouth of the Mississippi.   He sailed to Green bay, but found
that he had arrayed against him all the private traders of
the west, by sending men to trade, contrary to his patent,
which expressly excepted the Ottawa country.   Of this he
soon felt the effects, his men began to desert, and to crown
all his misfortunes, his new vessel, the Griffin, was lost on her
way back to Niagara.   Before this catastrophe he had set out
to descend Lake Michigan.   He built a kind of fort at the
mouth of the St. Joseph's and sounded its channel, and, at
last, in December, proceed to enter the Kankakee, a branch
of the Illinois, by a portage from the St. Joseph's.   Disheartened by the desertion and disaffection of his men, and by the
want of all tidings of his vessel, he began the erection of
Fort Crevecœur, and of a vessel near the Illinois camp below
Lake Peoria.   The vessel he had finally to abandon for want
of proper materials to complete it, and he set out almost
alone for Fort Frontenac by land, after sending Father Hennepin to explore the Illinois to its mouth.   That missionary
went further; voluntarily or as a prisoner of the Sioux, he
seems to have ascended as far as St. Anthony's falls, which
owe their name to him.   His exploration of the Mississippi
between the Illinois river and St. Anthony's falls, took place
in 1680, between the months of March and September, when,
delivered by De Luth, he returned to Mackinaw, and thence
in the spring almost direct to Quebec and Europe.   By

1683, he published, at Paris, an account of his voyage under the title of Description de la Louisiane, which after the Relations, and Marquette's narrative, is the next work relative to the Mississippi, and contains the first printed description of that river above the mouth of the Wisconsin, from actual observation.

La Salle returned to Illinois in 1681, and, to his surprise, found his fort deserted. He soon after met the survivors of his first expedition at Mackinaw, and set about new preparations for his great work. In January, 1682, he was again with his party at the extremity of Lake Michigan, and entering the Chicago river, followed the old line of Father Marquette, reached Fort Crevécœur once more, and at last began in earnest his voyage down the Mississippi. He had abandoned the idea of sailing down in a ship, and resolved to go in boats, ascertain accurately the position of its mouth, and then return to France and sail direct with a colony for the mouth, and ascend to some convenient place. On the 6th of February, the little expedition, apparently in three large boats or canoes, conducted by La Salle and his lieutenants, Tonty and Dautray, with Father Zenobius Membré, as their chaplain, and Indians as hunters and guides, entered the wide waters of the Mississippi, which henceforward, in the narratives of La Salle's companions assumes the name of Colbert. They passed the mouth of the muddy Missouri, and further on, the deserted village of the Tamaroas, and next the Ohio, where the marshy land began that prevented their landing. Detained soon after by the loss of one of his men, La Salle encamped on the bluff, and fell in with some Chickasaws, then proceeding on, at last, on the 3d of March, was roused by the war-cries, and the rattling drums of an Arkansas village. He had reached the limit of Jolliet's voyage; henceforward, he was to be the first French explorer. Warlike as the greeting was, La Salle soon entered into friendly relations with them, and several days were spent in their village. Here a cross was planted with the arms of the French king, and the missionary endeavored, by interpreters and signs to give some idea of Christianity.

On the 17th, La Salle embarked again, and passing two more Arkansas towns, reached the populous tribe of the Taensas, in their houses of clay and straw, with roofs of cane, themselves attired in mantles, woven of white pliant bark, and showing Eastern reverence for their monarch, who in great ceremony visited the envoys of the French.

Pursuing his course, the party next came to the Natchez, where another cross was planted, and visiting the Koroas proceeded on till the river divided into two branches. Following the westerly one, they sailed past the Quinipissas, and the pillaged town of another tribe, till they reached the delta, on the 6th of April. La Salle and his two lieutenants, each taking a separate channel, advanced, full of hope; the brackish water, growing salter as they proceeded, being a sure index of the sea, which they reached at last on the 9th of April, 1682, sixty-two days after their entering the Mississippi.

The French had thus, at last, in the two expeditions of Jolliet and La Salle, completely explored the river from the falls of St. Anthony to the gulf of Mexico. La Salle now planted a cross with the arms of France amid the solemn chant of hymns of thanksgiving, and in the name of the French king took possession of the river, of all its branches, and the territory watered by them; and the notary drew up an authentic act, which all signed with beating hearts, and a leaden plate with the arms of France, and the names of the discoverers was amid the rattle of musketry deposited in the earth.

La Salle now ascended again to Illinois, and despatched Father Zenobius Membré to France to lay an account of his voyage before the government. He sailed from Quebec on the 15th of November with Frontenac, and the course of the Mississippi was known in France before the close of 1682.*

The next year La Salle himself reached France, and set out by sea to reach the mouth of the Mississippi; he never again beheld it; but Tonty seeking him, had again descended to the mouth, and it was soon constantly travelled by the adventurous trader, and still more adventurous missionary. A Spanish vessel under Andrew de Pes, entered the mouth soon after; but, on the 2d of March, 1699, the Canadian Iberville, more fortunate than La Salle, entered it with Father Anastasius Douay, who had accompanied that unfortunate adventurer on his last voyage.† Missionaries from Canada soon came to greet him, and La Sueur ascended the Mississippi to St. Peter's river, and built a log fort on its blue-earth tributary.

Henceforward all was progress; we might now trace the labors of those who explored each mighty tributary, and watch the progress of each rising town; we might follow down the first cargo of wheat, or look with the anxiety of the day at the first crop of sugar and of cotton; but this were to write the history of the Mississippi valley, and we undertook only that of its discovery. Our work is done. We turn now to trace the life of its first French explorers.

* The works on La Salle's voyages, besides Hennepin already noticed, are, 1. *Etablissement de la Foi*, &c., par le P. Chretien Le Clercq, Paris, 1691. 2. *Der nieres découvertes*, &c., par le Chev. de Tonty, Paris, 1697. 3. *Journal Historique*, &c., par M. Joutel, Paris, 1713.

† *Historical Collections of Louisiana*, vol. iii., p. 14.

LIFE

OF

FATHER JAMES MARQUETTE,

OF THE SOCIETY OF JESUS,

FIRST EXPLORER OF THE MISSISSIPPI.

NEAR a little branch of the river Oise, in the department of Aisne, the traveller finds perched on the mountain-side the small but stately city of Laon. Strong fortifications without, and a vast cathedral within, show that in former days it was one of those cities which were constantly replete with life and movement in the endless contests between noble and noble, and not unfrequently between the suzerain himself and his more powerful vassal.

The most ancient family in this renowned city, is that of Marquette, and in its long annals we find the highest civic honors borne almost constantly by members of that illustrious race. It already held an important place in the reign of Louis the young, and its armorial bearings still commemorate the devotedness of the sieur James Marquette, sheriff of Laon, to the cause of his royal master, the unfortunate John of France, in 1360.

A martial spirit has always characterized this citizen family, and its members have constantly figured in the daz-

zling wars of France. Our own republic is not without its
obligations to the valor of the Marquettes, three of whom died
here in the French army during the Revolutionary war.

Yet not their high antiquity nor their reckless valor would
ever have given the name of Marquette to fame; the un-
sought tribute which it has acquired among us, is due to the
labors of one who renounced the enjoyments of country and
home to devote his days to the civilization and conversion of
our Indian tribes; who died in the bloom of youth, worn
down by toil, in a lonely, neglected spot, whose name every
effort was made to enshrine in oblivion, but who has been at
last, by the hand of strangers, raised on a lofty pedestal
among the great, the good, and the holy, who have honored
our land ; the family is known to us only as connected with
Father James Marquette of the Society of Jesus, the first explorer of the Mississippi.

Born at the ancient seat of his family, in the year 1637, he
was, through his pious mother Rose de la Salle, allied to the
venerable John Baptist de la Salle, the founder of the insti-
tute known as the Brothers of the Christian Schools, whose
services in the cause of gratuitous education of the poor had
instructed thousands before any of the modern systems of
public schools had been even conceived.* From his pious
mother the youthful Marquette imbibed that warm, generous,
and unwavering devotion to the mother of God, which makes
him so conspicuous among her servants. None but a mother
could have infused such a filial affection for Mary.

At the age of seventeen his heart, detached from this world
and all its bright allurements, impelled him to enter the Society of Jesus, as he did in the year 1654. When the two

---

* Devisme Histoire de la Ville de Laon. A member of his family, Francis
Marquette, founded similar schools for girls, in 1685, and the religious were commonly called Sœurs Marquette.

years of self study and examination had passed away, he was as is usual with the young Jesuits, employed in teaching or study, and twelve years glided away in the faithful performance of the unostentatious duties assigned him. No sooner, however, was he invested with the sacred character of the priesthood, than his ardent desire to become in all things an imitator of his chosen patron, St. Francis Xavier, induced him to seek a mission in some land that knew not God, that he might labor there to his latest breath, and die unaided and alone.

The province of Champagne in which he was enrolled contained no foreign mission: he was transferred to that of France, and, in 1666, sailed for Canada. On the 20th of September he landed, buoyant with life and health, at Quebec, and amid his brethren awaited the new destination on which his superiors should decide.*

The moment of his arrival was one of deep interest in the religious history of a colony, which had in its early settlement so nobly represented the purest Catholicity, neither hampered by civil jealousy, nor unhearted by the cold and selfish policy of a pagan age. The halcyon days of the Canadian church were passing away, but God had raised up one to guide and guard his church, that is, in fact, his poor and little ones, in the coming struggle with worldliness and policy. This was Francis de Laval, who landed at Quebec in 1659, with the title of bishop of Petrea, and vicar apostolic of New France. Gradually he gathered around him a few secular priests and began to settle the ecclesiastical affairs of the French posts, till then mere missions in the hands of the Jesuits. At the period of Marquette's arrival, he had already begun to see his diocese assume a regular shape, his clergy had increased, his

* Jour. Sup. Jes.

cathedral and seminary were rapidly rising. The war with the Iroquois which had so long checked the prosperity of the colony, and the hopes of the missionaries, was at last brought to a successful issue by the efforts of the viceroy de Tracy, and a new field was opened for the missions.

These had always been an object of his deep solicitude; the wide west especially was a field which he sighed to penetrate himself, cross in hand, but this could not be. As early as 1660, from the new impulse thus given, an Ottawa mission was resolved upon, and the veteran Ménard, one of the last survivors of the old Huron mission, cheered by the parting words of his holy bishop, embarked to raise the cross of Sault St. Mary's, which his companions Jogues and Raymbaut had planted twenty years before. He bore it on to Keweena bay in Lake Superior, and while full of projects for reaching the Sioux on the upper Mississippi, died in the woods, a victim to famine or the hatchet of the roving Indian. At the time of Marquette's arrival, Father Allouez was there exploring parts which no white man had yet visited, and as he saw a wide field opening before his view, earnestly imploring a new missionary reinforcement.

Such was the Ottawa mission; but there were others also. Father Jogues thus associated with the earliest western discoveries, had penetrated into New York, and reddening the Mohawk with his life's blood, brought it within the bounds of catholicity. From this moment New York was a land which each missionary ambitioned; visited successively by two more as prisoners, their sufferings and blood confirmed the title of the missionaries, and, in 1654, Father Simon le Moyne visited Onondaga, and gave the first account of western New York. A mission was established the next year, and the missionaries explored the whole state from the Hud-

son to the Niagara; but a sudden change took place — a plot
was formed against the French colony at Onondaga, and this
first mission was crushed in its infancy, after a brief existence
of three years. The war which ensued made Canada itself
tremble, and a new mission in New York was not even
thought of; the attempt to renew that in Michigan is, indeed,
one of the hardiest undertakings in the annals of the Jesuit
missions, and a noble monument of their fearless zeal. But
now the tree of peace was planted, the war-parties had
ceased, and missionaries hastened to the Iroquois cantons,
which, for nearly twenty years, were to be so well instructed
in the truths of Christianity, that even now the catholic Iroquois almost outnumber the rest of their countrymen.

Another great mission of the time was that of the Abnakis,
in Maine, founded by Druillettes in 1647, and continued by
him at intervals until it became at last the permanent residence of several zealous men.

Besides these were the missions of the wandering Algonquins of the river, which centred at Sillery and Three Rivers,
but had been almost entirely destroyed by the Iroquois after
the destruction of the Huron missions and depopulation of
Upper Canada. These expiring missions the Jesuits still
maintained; but another and a harder field was that of the
Montagnais, of which Tadoussac was the centre. Here at the
mouth of that strange river, the Saguenay, which pours its
almost fathomless tide into the shallower St. Lawrence, is the
oft-mentioned post of Tadoussac. For a few weeks each year,
it was a scene of busy, stirring life; Indians of every petty
tribe from the Esquimaux of Labrador, to the Micmac of
Nova Scotia, came to trade with the French. Here, then, a
missionary was always found to instruct them as much as time
permitted, and when found sufficiently acquainted with the

mysteries of our faith, to baptize them. The Christian Indian always repaired to this post to fulfil the obligations of the church, to lay down the burthen of sin, to receive the bread of life, and then depart for the wilderness with his calendar and pin to be able to distinguish the Sundays and holydays; and thus amid the snows and crags join in the prayers and devotions of the universal church. When the trade was over, a new field lay before the missionary; the country was to be traversed in every direction to carry the light of faith from cabin to cabin, to exhort, instruct, confirm. These adventurous expeditions through parts still a wilderness, are full of interest, and, strange as it may seem, are rife with early notices of our western country; they reached from the Saguenay to Hudson's bay, and stretching westward, almost reached Lake Superior.

This mission required one full of life, zeal, and courage, and to it Father Marquette was in the first instance destined. The Montagnais was the key language to the various tribes, and as early as the tenth of October,* we find him starting for Three Rivers to begin the study of that language under Father Gabriel Druilletes. While thus engaged, his leisure hours were of course devoted to the exercise of his ministry, and here he remained until April, 1668, when the first project was abandoned, and he was ordered to prepare for the Ottawa mission, as that of Lake Superior was then called. He had by this time acquired also a knowledge of the Algonquin, and thus fitted for his new mission, he left Quebec on the 21st of April with three companions for Montreal, where he was to await the Ottawa flotilla, which was to bear him westward. A party of Nezpercés came at last, bearing Father Nicholas Louis, the companion of Allouez, and with

* Jour. Sup. Jes.

them Father Marquette embarked. The journey up the Ottawa river, and through French river to Lake Huron, and then across that inland sea to Sault St. Mary's, has been too often and too vividly described to need repetition here. Its toil and danger are associated with the accounts of all the early Huron missionaries.

When he reached Lake Superior, Marquette found that the tribes whom fear of the Iroquois had driven to the extremity of the lake, were now returning to their former abodes. New missions were thus required, and it was resolved to erect two, one at Sault St. Mary's, the other in Green Bay. The former was assigned to Father Marquette, and planting his cabin at the foot of the rapid on the American side, he began his missionary career. Here, in the following year, he was joined by Father Dablon, as superior of the Ottawa missions, and by their united exertion, a church was soon built; and thus, at last, a sanctuary worthy of the faith raised at that cradle of Christianity in the west.

The tribes to which he ministered directly here were all Algonquin, and numbered about two thousand souls. They showed the greatest docility to his teaching, and would all gladly have received baptism, but caution was needed, and the prudent missionary contented himself for a time with giving them clear, distinct instructions, and with efforts to root out all lurking superstitions, conferring the sacrament only on the dying. The missionary's first lesson was, " to learn to labor and to wait."*

His stay at the Sault among the Pahwitting-dach-irini, Outchibous, Maramegs, &c., was not, however, to be of long duration. Father Allouez departed for Green Bay, and a missionary was to be sent to Lapointe to continue the dis-

* *Rel.* 1668–'69, p. 102.

heartening labors of that ungrateful field. Marquette was chosen. Without repugnance he set out for his new station in the autumn of 1669. We can not better depict his labors than by inserting at length the letter descriptive of his mission, which he addressed to Father Francis Le Mercier, the superior of the missions in the following year.

" Reverend Father,
        " The Peace of Christ.†

" I am obliged to render you an account of the mission of the Holy Ghost among the Ottawas, according to the orders I received from you and again from Father Dablon on my arrival here, after a month's navigation on snow and through ice which closed my way, and kept me in constant peril of life.

" Divine Providence having destined me to continue the mission of the Holy Ghost begun by Father Allouez, who had baptized the chiefs of the Kiskakonk, I arrived there on the thirteenth of September, and went to visit the Indians who were in the clearings which are divided into five towns. The Hurons to the number of about four or five hundred, almost all baptized, still preserve some little Christianity. A number of the chiefs assembled in council, were at first well pleased to see me; but I explained that I did not yet know their language perfectly, and that no other missionary was coming, both because all had gone to the Iroquois, and because Father Allouez, who understood them perfectly, did not wish to return that winter, as they did not love the prayer enough. They acknowledged that it was a just punishment, and during the winter held talks about it, and resolved to amend, as they tell me.

---

† For the benefit of investigators of manuscripts I would remark that these words, or the letters P. C. and a cross at the top of the page, are alone almost sufficient to show a paper to be written by one of the Jesuit missionaries.

"The nation of the Outaouaks Sinagaux is far from the kingdom of God, being above all other nations addicted to lewdness, sacrifices, and juggleries. They ridicule the prayer, and will scarcely hear us speak of Christianity. They are proud and undeveloped, and I think that so little can be done with this tribe, that I have not baptized healthy infants who seem likely to live, watching only for such as are sick. The Indians of the Kinouché tribe declare openly that it is not yet time. There are, however, two men among them formerly baptized. One now rather old, is looked upon as a kind of miracle among the Indians, having always refused to marry, persisting in this resolution in spite of all that had been said. He has suffered much even from his relatives, but he is as little affected by this as by the loss of all the goods which he brought last year from the settlement, not having even enough left to cover him. These are hard trials for Indians, who generally seek only to possess much in this world. The other, a new-married young man, seems of another nature than the rest. The Indians extremely attached to their reveries had resolved that a certain number of young women should prostitute themselves, each to choose such partner as she liked. No one in these cases ever refuses, as the lives of men are supposed to depend on it. This young Christian was called ; on entering the cabin he saw the orgies which were about to begin, and feigning illness immediately left, and though they came to call him back, he refused to go. His confession was as prudent as it could be, and I wondered that an Indian could live so innocently, and so nobly profess himself a Christian. His mother and some of his sisters are also good Christians. The Ottawas, extremely superstitious in their feasts and juggleries, seem hardened to the instructions given them, yet they like to have their children

D

baptized. God permitted a woman to die this winter in her sin; her illness had been concealed from me, and I heard it only by the report that she had asked a very improper dance for her cure. I immediately went to a cabin where all the chiefs were at a feast, and some Kiskakonk Christians among them. To these I exposed the impiety of the woman and her medicine-men, and gave them proper instructions. I then spoke to all present, and God permitted that an old Ottawa rose to advise, granting what I asked, as it made no matter, he said, if the woman did die. An old Christian then rose and told the nation that they must stop the licentiousness of their youth, and not permit Christian girls to take part in such dances. To satisfy the woman, some child's play was substituted for the dance; but this did not prevent her dying before morning. The dangerous state of a sick young man caused the medicine-men to proclaim that the devil must be invoked by extraordinary superstitions. The Christians took no part. The actors were these jugglers and the sick man, who was passed over great fires lighted in every cabin. It was said that he did not feel the heat, although his body had been greased with oil for five or six days. Men, women, and children, ran through the cabins asking as a riddle to divine their thoughts, and the successful guesser was glad to give the object named. I prevented the abominable lewdness so common at the end of these diabolical rites. I do not think they will recur, as the sick man died soon after.

"The nation of Kiskakons,* which for three years refused to receive the gospel preached them by Father Allouez, re-

---

* Father Allouez, in the *Relation* of 1668–'69, does not use the term Kiskakon He calls them Queues coupés, and states that they had formerly lived on Lake Huron, where they had been visited by the old Huron missionaries, and had been first visited by Menard on Lake Superior. I add this to my subsequent note on them, as it may throw some new light on their original position.

solved, in the fall of 1668, to obey God. This resolution was adopted in full council, and announced to that father who spent four winter months instructing them. The chiefs of the nation became Christians, and as Father Allouez was called to another mission, he gave it to my charge to cultivate, and I entered on it in September, 1669.

"All the Christians were then in the fields harvesting their Indian corn; they listened with pleasure when I told them that I came to Lapointe for their sake and that of the Hurons; that they never should be abandoned, but be beloved above all other nations, and that they and the French were one. I had the consolation of seeing their love for the prayer and their pride in being Christians. I baptized the new-born infants, and instructed the chiefs whom I found well-disposed. The head-chief having allowed a dog to be hung on a pole near his cabin, which is a kind of sacrifice the Indians make to the sun, I told him that this was wrong, and he went and threw it down.

"A sick man instructed, but not baptized, begged me to grant him that favor, or to live near him, as he did not wish medicine-men to cure him, and that he feared the fires of hell. I prepared him for baptism, and frequently visited his cabin. His joy at this partly restored his health; he thanked me for my care, and soon after saying that I had recalled him to life, gave me a little slave he had brought from the Ilinois two or three months before.

"One evening, while in the cabin of the Christian where I sleep, I taught him to pray to his guardian-angel, and told him some stories to show him the assistance they give us, especially when in danger of offending God. 'Now,' said he, 'I know the invisible hand that struck me when, since my baptism, I was going to commit a sin, and the voice that bid

me remember that I was a Christian ; for I left the companion
of my guilt without committing the sin.' He now often
speaks of devotion to the angels, and explains it to the other
Indians.

"Some young Christian women are examples to the tribe,
and are not ashamed to profess Christianity. Marriages
among the Indians are dissolved almost as easily as they are
made, and then it is no dishonor to marry again. Hearing
that a young Christian woman abandoned by her husband
was in danger of being forced to marry by her family, I encouraged her to act as a Christian ; she has kept her word.
Not a breath has been uttered against her. This conduct,
with my remonstrances, induced the husband to take her
back again at the close of winter, since which time she has
come regularly to the chapel, for she was too far off before.
She has unbosomed her conscience to me, and I admired
such a life in a young woman.

"The pagans make no feast without sacrifices, and we have
great trouble to prevent them. The Christians have now
changed these customs, and to effect it more easily, I have
retained some, suppressing only what is really bad. The
feast must open with a speech ; they then address God, asking him for health and all they need, as they now give food
to men. It has pleased God to preserve all our Christians in
health except two children whom they tried to hide, and for
whom a medicine-man performed his diabolic rites, but they
died soon after my baptizing them.

Having invited the Kiskakons to come and winter near the
chapel, they left all the other tribes to gather around us so as
to be able to pray to God, be instructed, and have their
children baptized. They call themselves Christians ; hence,
in all councils and important affairs, I address them, and

when I wish to show them that I really wish what I ask, I need only address them as Christians; they told me even that they obeyed me for that reason. They have taken the upper hand, and control the three other tribes. It is a great consolation to a missionary to see such pliancy in savages, and thus live in such peace with his Indians, spending the whole day in instructing them in our mysteries, and teaching them the prayers. Neither the rigor of the winter, nor the state of the weather, prevents their coming to the chapel; many never let a day pass, and I was thus busily employed from morning till night, preparing some for baptism, some for confession, disabusing others of their reveries. The old men told me that the young men had lost their senses, and that I must stop their excesses. I often spoke to them of their daughters, urging them to prevent their being visited at night. I knew almost all that passed in two tribes near us, but though others were spoken of, I never heard anything against the Christian women, and when I spoke to the old men about their daughters, they told me that they prayed to God. I often inculcated this, knowing the importunities to which they are constantly exposed, and the courage they need to resist. They have learned to be modest, and the French who have seen them, perceive how little they resemble the others, from whom they are thus distinguished.

"One day instructing the old people in my cabin, and speaking of the creation of the world, and various stories from the Old Testament, they told me what they had formerly believed, but now treat as a fable. They have some knowledge of the tower of Babel, saying that their ancestors had related that they had formerly made a great house, but that a violent wind had thrown it down. They now despise all the little gods they had before they were baptized: they often ridicule

them, and wonder at their stupidity in sacrificing to these
subjects of their fables.

"I baptized an adult after a long trial. Seeing his assiduity at prayer, his frankness in recounting his past life, his
promises especially with regard to the other sex, and his assurance of good conduct, I yielded to his entreaty. He has
persevered, and since his return from fishing, comes regularly
to chapel. After Easter, all the Indians dispersed to seek
subsistence; they promised me that they would not forget
the prayer, and earnestly begged that a father should come in
the fall when they assemble again. This will be granted,
and if it please God to send some father, he will take my
place, while I, to execute the orders of our father superior,
will go and begin my Ilinois mission.

"The Ilinois are thirty days' journey by land from Lapointe
by a difficult road; they lie south-southwest of it. On the
way you pass the nation of the Ketchjgamins, who live in
more than twenty large cabins; they are inland, and seek to
have intercourse with the French, from whom they hope to
get axes, knives, and ironware. So much do they fear them
that they unbound from the stake two Ilinois captives, who
said, when about to be burned, that the Frenchman had declared he wished peace all over the world. You pass then to
the Miamiwek, and by great deserts reach the Ilinois, who
are assembled chiefly in two towns, containing more than
eight or nine thousand souls. These people are well enough
disposed to receive Christianity. Since Father Allouez spoke
to them at Lapointe, to adore one God, they have begun to
abandon their false worship, for they adored the sun and
thunder. Those seen by me are of apparently good disposition; they are not night-runners like the other Indians. A
man kills his wife, if he finds her unfaithful; they are less

prodigal in sacrifices, and promise me to embrace Christianity, and do all I require in their country. In this view, the Ottawas gave me a young man recently come from their country, who initiated me to some extent in their language during the leisure given me in the winter by the Indians at Lapointe. I could scarcely understand it, though there is something of the Algonquin in it; yet I hope by the help of God's grace to understand, and be understood if God by his goodness leads me to that country.

"No one must hope to escape crosses in our missions, and the best means to live happy is not to fear them, but in the enjoyment of little crosses, hope for others still greater. The Ilinois desire us, like Indians, to share their miseries, and suffer all that can be imagined in barbarism. They are lost sheep to be sought amid woods and thorns, especially when they call so piteously to be rescued from the jaws of the wolf. Such really can I call their entreaties to me this winter. They have actually gone this spring to notify the old men to come for me in the fall.

"The Ilinois always come by land. They sow maize which they have in great plenty; they have pumpkins as large as those of France, and plenty of roots and fruit. The chase is very abundant in wild-cattle, bears, stags, turkeys, duck, bustard, wild-pigeon, and cranes. They leave their towns at certain times every year to go to their hunting-grounds together, so as to be better able to resist, if attacked. They believe that I will spread peace everywhere, if I go, and then only the young will go to hunt.

"When the Ilinois come to Lapointe, they pass a large river almost a league wide. It runs north and south, and so far that the Ilinois, who do not know what canoes are, have never yet heard of its mouth; they only know that there are very great nations below them, some of whom raise two crops of maize a year. East-south-east of the country is a nation they call Chawanon, which came to visit them last summer. The young man given me who teaches me the language saw them; they wear beads, which shows intercourse with Europeans; they had come thirty days across land before reaching their country. This great river can hardly empty in Virginia, and we rather believe that its mouth is in California. If the Indians who promise to make me a canoe do not fail to keep their word, we shall go into this river as soon as we can with a Frenchman and this young man given me, who knows some of these languages, and has a readiness for learning others; we shall visit the nations which inhabit it, in order to open the way to so many of our fathers, who have long awaited this happiness. This discovery will give us a complete knowledge of the southern or western sea.

"Six or seven days below the Ilois (sic) is another great river (Missouri), on which are prodigious nations, who use wooden canoes; we can not write more till next year, if God does us the grace to lead us there.

The Ilinois are warriors; they make many slaves whom they sell to the Ottawas for guns, powder, kettles, axes, and knives. They were formerly at war with the Nadouessi, but having made peace some years since, I confirmed it, to facilitate their coming to Lapointe, where I am going to await them, in order to accompany them to their country.

The Nadouessi are the Iroquois of this country beyond Lapointe, but less faithless, and never attack till attacked. They lie southwest of the mission of the Holy Ghost, and are a great nation, though we have not yet visited them, having confined ourselves to the conversion of the Ottawas. They fear the Frenchman, because he brings iron into their country. Their language is entirely different from the Huron and Algonquin; they have many towns, but they are widely scattered; they have very extraordinary customs; they principally adore the calumet; they do not speak at great feasts, and when a stranger arrives, give him to eat with a wooden fork as we would a child. All the lake tribes make war on them, but with small success; they have false oats, use little canoes, and keep their word strictly. I sent them a present by an interpreter, to tell them to recognise the Frenchman everywhere, and not kill him or the Indians in his company; that the black-gown wished to pass to the country of the Assinipoüars, to that of the Kilistinaux; that he was already at Outagamis, and that I was going this fall to the Ilinois, to whom they should leave a free passage. They agreed; but as for my present waited till all came from the chase, promising to come to Lapointe in the fall, to hold a council with the Ilinois and speak to me. Would that all these nations loved God, as much as they fear the French! Christianity would soon flourish.

"The Assinipoüars, whose language is almost that of the Nadouessi, are toward the west from the mission of the Holy Ghost; some are fifteen or twenty days off on a lake where they have false oats and abundant fishery. I have heard that there is in their country a great river running to the western sea, and an Indian told me that at its mouth he saw Frenchmen, and four large canoes with sails.*

'The Kilistinaux are a nomad people, whose rendezvous we do not yet know. It is northwest of the mission of the Holy Ghost; they are always in the woods, and live solely by their bow. They passed by the mission where I was last fall in two hundred canoes, coming to buy merchandise and

---

* This is not the first indication of the Columbia.

corn, after which they go to winter in the woods; in the spring I saw them again on the shore of the lake."*

Such is the substance of his letter as it has reached us, and shows us the hopes which Marquette entertained of reaching in the fall of that year, the Ilinois mission to which he had been appointed and for which he was now prepared by his knowledge of their language. If the Sioux and Ilinois met him at Lapointe in the fall, nothing was concluded; and the missionary did not begin his overland journey to the lodges of the Ilinois. It is not, however, probable that the meeting took place; for early in the winter the Sioux, provoked by the insolence of the Hurons and Ottawas, declared war, and first sent back to the missionaries the pious pictures which he had sent them as a present. Their war parties now came on in their might, and the Indians of Lapointe trembled before the fierce Dahcotah with his knives of stone stuck in his belt, and in his long, black hair. In the spring both Huron and Ottawa resolved to leave so dangerous a neighborhood; the latter were the first to launch upon the lake, and they soon made their way to Ekaentouton island. Father Marquette, whose missionary efforts had been neutralized by the unsettled state of his neophytes, and the concentration of their thoughts on the all-engrossing war, was now left alone with the Hurons. With both he had more to suffer than to do; and now he was at last compelled to leave Lapointe, and turn his back on his beloved Ilinois to accompany his Hurons in their wanderings and hardships. The remnant of a mighty nation resolved once more to commit themselves to the waves and seek a new home: with their faithful missionary they all embarked in their frail canoes, and now for the first time

* *Rel.* 1669'–70, Ottawa part.

turned toward their ancient home. Fain would they have
revisited the scenes of Huron power, the land of the fur-lined
graves of their ancestors; fain too would the missionary have
gone to spend his surviving years on the ground hallowed by
the blood of Daniel, Brebeuf, Lalemant, Garnier, and Chaba-
nel, but the power of the Iroquois was still too great to justify
the step, and the fugitives remembering the rich fisheries of
Mackinaw, resolved to return to that pebbly strand.

But who, the reader may ask, were the Hurons with whom
the missionary's career seems thus linked, yet who at first
were not the special object of his care. It is a tale worthy
of an historian.

The Wendats, whom the French called Hurons and the
English Wyandots, are a nation of the same stock as the Iroquois.* They were one of the first tribes known to the
French, to whom they always remained closely united. They
were a trading people, and their many fortified towns lay in
a very narrow strip on Georgian Bay, a territory smaller than
the state of Delaware. Between the west and southwest lay
in the mountains the kindred tribe of the industrious Tionon-
tates, whose luxuriant fields of tobacco, won them from the
early French the name of Petuns, while south of both, from
Lake St. Claire to Niagara and even slightly beyond were the
allied tribes, which from the connection between their language and that of the Hurons, were called by the latter Attiwandaronk, but Neutral by the French, from their standing
aloof in the great war waged by the Iroquois against the
Hurons and Algonquins.

No sooner had the French founded Quebec than the Franciscan missionaries attempted the conversion of the Hurons.

---

* Champlain (Ed. 1613, p. 238), calls the Hurons les bons Yroquois, as distinguished from the other Yroquois enemies.

Father Joseph Le Caron, the founder of that mission, win
tered among them in 1615, and in subsequent years other
recollects did their best to prepare them for the faith. The
Jesuits were at last called in by the recollects to aid them,
and laboring together in harmony, they looked forward with
sanguine hope to the speedy conversion of the Hurons and
Neuters, for they, too, were visited, when all their prospects
were blasted by the English conquest of Canada, in 1629.
On its restoration the French court offered the Canada missions to the Capucins, but, on their recommendation, committed it to the Jesuits alone. Brebeuf, for the second time,
reached Upper Canada, and labored zealously on till the Huron nation was annihilated by the Iroquois. Twenty-one missionaries at different times came to share his toils, and of
these eight like himself perished by hostile hands, martyrs to
their faith and zeal, a nobler body of heroes than any other
part of our country can boast. On the deaths of Brebeuf and
Garnier, in 1650, the ruin of the Hurons and Petuns was con-
summated. The survivors fled and blended into one tribe,
soon divided into two great parties, one composed entirely of
Christians, repairing to Quebec to settle on Orleans island,
whose descendants are still lingering at Lorette ; the other,
part Christians, part pagans, fled at last to Mackinaw, but
pursued constantly by the Iroquois, they next settled on some
islands at the mouth of Green Bay, where they seem to have
been in Ménard's time ; later still, after roaming to the lodges
of the Sioux on the Mississippi, they came to pitch their
cabins by the mission cross planted by Allouez, at Chegoimegon,* and here Marquette had found them. Such is the tale
of their wanderings, till the period of our narrative.†

* *Rel.* 1671-'72.
† Their subsequent wanderings are to Detroit, Sandusky, and at last to Indian
territory, where the descendants of Marquette's flock still exist, the smallest but
wealthiest band of deported Indians.

Mackinaw, where they now rested, was indeed a bleak spot to begin a new home; it was a point of land almost encompassed by wind-tossed lakes, icy as Siberian waters. The cold was intense, and cultivation difficult; but the waters teemed with fish, and the very danger and hardships of their capture gave it new zest. Besides this, it was a central point for trade, and so additionally recommended to the Huron, who still, as of old, sought to advance his worldly prospects by commerce.

Stationed in this new spot, Father Marquette's first care was to raise a chapel. Rude and unshapely was the first sylvan shrine raised by catholicity at Mackinaw; its sides of logs, its roof of bark had nothing to impress the senses, nothing to win by a dazzling exterior the wayward child of the forest; all was as simple as the faith he taught. Such was the origin of the mission of St. Ignatius, or Michilimackinac, already in a manner begun the previous year by missionary labors on the island of that name.* The Hurons soon built near the chapel a palisade fort, less stout and skilful indeed than the fortresses found in among their kindred Iroquois by Cartier and Champlain, but in their declining state sufficient for their defence.

No details of Marquette's labors during the first year have reached us; he wrote no letters to recount his wanderings,* but of the second year we are better informed. An unpublished manuscript gives us the following letter addressed to Father Dablon : —

"REV. FATHER : —

"The Hurons, called Tionnontateronnons or Petun nation, who compose the mission of St. Ignatius at Michilimakinong began last year near the chapel a fort enclosing all their

* *Rel.* 1670–'71, p. 144.

cabins. They have come regularly to prayers, and have listened more readily to the instructions I gave them, consent-
ing to what I required to prevent their disorders and abominable customs. We must have patience with untutored
minds, who know only the devil, who like their ancestors have
been his slaves, and who often relapse into the sins in which
they were nurtured. God alone can fix these fickle minds,
and place and keep them in his grace, and touch their hearts
while we stammer at their ears.

"The Tionnontateronnons number this year three hundred
and eighty souls, and besides sixty Outaouasinagaux have
joined them. Some of these came from the mission of St.
Francis Xavier, where Father André wintered with them
last year; they are quite changed from what I saw them at
Lapointe; the zeal and patience of that missionary have
gained to the faith those hearts which seemed to us most
averse to it. They now wish to be Christians; they bring
their children to the chapel to be baptized, and come regularly to prayers.

"Having been obliged to go to St. Marie du Sault with
Father Allouez last summer, the Hurons came to the chapel
during my absence as regularly as if I had been there, the
girls singing what prayers they knew. They counted the days
of my absence, and constantly asked when I was to be back;
I was absent only fourteen days, and on my arrival all assembled at chapel, some coming even from their fields, which
are at a very considerable distance.

"I went readily to their pumpkin-feast, where I instructed
them, and invited them to thank God, who gave them food
in plenty, while other tribes that had not yet embraced
Christianity, were actually struggling with famine. I ridi-
culed dreams, and urged those who had been baptized to ac-

knowledge Him, whose adopted children they were. Those who gave the feast, though still idolaters, spoke in high terms of Christianity, and openly made the sign of the cross before all present. Some young men, whom they had tried by ridicule to prevent from doing it, persevered, and make the sign of the cross in the greatest assemblies, even when I am not present.

"An Indian of distinction among the Hurons, having invited me to a feast where the chiefs were, called them severally by name and told them that he wished to declare his thoughts, that all might know it, namely, that he was a Christian; that he renounced the god of dreams and all their lewd dances; that the black-gown was master of his cabin; and that for nothing that might happen would he forsake his resolution. Delighted to hear this, I spoke more strongly than I had ever yet done, telling them that my only design was to put them in the way of heaven; that for this alone I remained among them; that this obliged me to assist them at the peril of my life. As soon as anything is said in an assembly, it is immediately divulged through all the cabins, as I saw in this case by the assiduity of some in coming to prayers, and by the malicious efforts of others to neutralize my instructions.

"Severe as the winter is, it does not prevent the Indians from coming to the chapel. Some come twice a day, be the wind or cold what it may. Last fall I began to instruct some to make general confessions of their whole life, and to prepare others who had never confessed since their baptism. I would not have supposed that Indians could have given so exact an account of all that had happened in the course of their life; but it was seriously done, as some took two weeks to examine themselves. Since then, I have perceived a marked change, so that they will not go even to ordinary feasts without ask-ing my permission.

"I have this year baptized twenty-eight children, one of which had been brought from Ste. Marie du Sault, without having received that sacrament as the Rev. F. Henry Nouvel informed me, to put me on my guard. Without my knowing it, the child fell sick, but God permitted that while instruct-ing in my cabin two important and sensible Indians, one asked me, whether such a sick child was baptized. I went at once, baptized it, and it died the next night. Some of the other children too are dead, and now in heaven. These are the consolations which God sends us, which make us esteem our life more happy as it is more wretched.

"This, rev. father, is all I give about this mission, where minds are now more mild, tractable, and better disposed to receive instructions, than in any other part. I am ready, however, to leave it in the hands of another missionary to go on your order to seek new nations toward the south sea who are still unknown to us, and to teach them of our great God whom they have hitherto unknown."*

Such was the laborious post to which this talented, yet humble missionary condemned himself, daily subjected to the caprices of some, the insults and petty persecution of others, looking only to another world for the reward of labors which, crowned with the most complete success, would in the eyes of the world seem unimportant; but "motives are the test of merit," and convinced by the studies of riper years, no less than by the early teachings of a mother, that the baptismal promises were a reality, he sought to open by that sacrament the doors of bliss to the dying infant, or more aged but re-

MS. Rel. 1672–'73.

penting sinner. To him the salvation of a single soul was more grand and noble than the conquest of an empire, and thus borne up, he labored on.

This letter of which the date is not given, nor the closing words, must have been written in the summer of 1672, and transmitted to Quebec by the Ottawa flotilla. The same conveyance, doubtless, brought him back the assurance that his prayers had been heard, that the government had at last resolved to act in the matter, and that he was the missionary selected to accompany the expedition. His heart exulted at the prospect, though he foresaw the danger to which he was exposed, a health already shaken by his toils and hardships, a difficult and unknown way, the only nation known — the fierce Dahcotah — now hostile to the French and their allies, with many another tribe noted in Indian story for deeds of blood, closed up their path. But this did not alarm him. The hope of a glorious martyrdom while opening the way to future heralds of the cross, buoyed him up, though in his humility he never spoke of martyrdom. To him it was but "a death to cease to offend God."

This now engrossed his thoughts, and he waited with anxiety the coming of Jolliet, named to undertake the expedition. At last he arrived, and by a happy coincidence on the feast of the Immaculate Conception of the blessed Virgin, "whom," says the pious missionary, "I had always invoked since my coming to the Ottawa country, in order to obtain of God the favor of being able to visit the nations on the Missisipi river."

The winter was spent in the necessary arrangements, regulating the affairs of his mission, which he left, it would seem, in the hands of Father Pierson, and in drawing up the maps and statements which Indian narrators could enable them to

E

form. At last, on the 17th of May, 1673, they embarked
in two canoes at Mackinaw, and proceeded to Green Bay,
whence ascending the Fox river they at last reached the
Wisconsin by its portage, and glided down to the Mississippi.
We need not here detail this remarkable voyage, the first
down the great river, as his whole narrative is contained in
the volume. Sufficient to say, that with Jolliet he descended
to the Arkansas, and having thus ascertained the situation of
the mouth, and the perfect navigability of the river, reas-
cended it as far as the mouth of the Ilinois, into which they
turned, and by a portage reached Lake Michigan, and in September arrived without accident at the mission in Green Bay.

In this voyage he twice met the Peoria tribe of the Ilinois,
and baptized one dying child at the water's edge, as he left
them finally. He also passed the Kaskaskia tribe of the
same nation on the upper waters of the Ilinois, and having
been already named an Ilinois missionary, he yielded to their
earnest entreaties, and promised to return and begin a mission among them.* He had now reached Green Bay, but
his health had given way; he was prostrated by disease, and
was not completely restored before the close of the following
summer. By the Ottawa flotilla of that year he transmitted
to his superior copies of his journal down the Mississippi, and
doubtless the map which we now publish. The return of the
fleet of canoes brought him the necessary orders for the establishment of the Ilinois mission; and as his health was now
restored, he set out on the 25th of October, 1674, for Kaskaskia. The line of travel at that time was to coast along to the
mouth of Fox river, then turn up as far as the little bay
which nearly intersects the peninsula, where a portage was
made to the lake. This was the route now taken by Mar-

---

* See his narrative in this volume.

quette with two men to aid him, accompanied by a number of Pottawotamies and Illinois. Reaching the lake, the canoes coasted along slowly, the missionary often proceeding on foot along the beautiful beach, embarking only at the rivers. He represents the navigation of the lake as easy; " there being," says he, " no portage to make, and the landing easy, provided you do not persist in sailing when the winds and waves are high." The soil except in the prairies was poor, but the chase was abundant, and they were thus well supplied.

In spite of all his courage, he was at last unable to proceed; by the 23d of November his malady had returned, and though he continued to advance, exposed to the cold and snows, when he reached Chicago river on the 4th of December, he found the river closed, and himself too much reduced to be able to attempt that winter march by land. There was no alternative but to winter there alone, and accordingly instructing his Indian companions as far as time allowed, they went their way, and he remained with his two men at the portage. Within fifty miles of them were two other Frenchmen, trappers and traders, one of whom was a surgeon at least in name, and still nearer an Illinois village. The former had prepared a cabin for the missionary, and one came now to visit him, being informed of his ill health; the Indians who had also heard it, wished to send a party to carry him and all his baggage, fearing that he might suffer from want. The good missionary, charmed at their solicitude, sent to reassure them on that head, although he was forced to tell them that if his malady continued, he would find it difficult to visit them even in the spring.

Alarmed at this, the sachems of the tribe assembled and deputed three to visit the blackgown, bearing three sacks of corn, dried meat and pumpkins, and twelve beaver-skins;

first, to make him a mat; second, to ask him for powder; third, to prevent his being hungry; fourth, to get some merchandise. "I answered them," says Marquette in his last letter, "first, that I came to instruct them by speaking of the prayer; second, that I would not give them powder, as we endeavor to make peace everywhere, and because I did not wish them to begin a war against the Miamis; third, that we did not fear famine; fourth, that I would encourage the French to bring them merchandise, and that they must make reparation to the traders there for the beads taken from them, while the surgeon was with me." The missionary then gave them some axes, knives, and trinkets, in return for their presents, and as a mark of his gratitude for their coming twenty leagues to visit him. Before he dismissed them, he promised to make every effort to reach the village, were it but for a few days. "On this," says he, "they bid me take heart and stay and die in their country, as I had promised to remain a long time," and they returned to their winter-camps.

Despairing now of being able to reach his destined goal without the interposition of Heaven, the missionary turned to the patroness of his mission, the blessed Virgin Immaculate, and with his two companions began a novena in her honor. Nor was his trust belied; God heard his prayer, his illness ceased, and though still weak, he gradually gained strength, and when the opening of the river and the consequent inundation compelled them to remove, he again resumed his long interrupted voyage to Kaskaskia, then on the upper waters of the Illinois river.

During this painful wintering, which for all his expressions of comfort, was one of great hardship and suffering, his hours were chiefly spent in prayer. Convinced that the term of his existence was drawing rapidly to a close, he consecrated this period of quiet to the exercises of a spiritual retreat, in which his soul overflowed with heavenly consolations, as rising above its frail and now tottering tenement, it soared toward that glorious home it was so soon to enter.

The journal of his last voyage* comes down to the sixth of April, when the weather arrested his progress; two days after he reached Kaskaskia, where he was received as an angel from heaven. It was now Monday in holy week, and he instantly began his preliminary instructions, assembling for that purpose the chiefs and old men, and going from cabin to cabin where new crowds constantly gathered. When he had thus prepared all to understand his meaning and object, he convoked a general assembly in the open prairie on Maunday-Thursday, and raising a rustic altar, adorned it with pictures of the blessed Virgin, under whose invocation he had placed his new mission; he turned to the assembled chiefs and warriors, and the whole tribe seated or standing around, and by ten presents declared the object of his coming, and the nature of the faith he bore, explaining the principal mysteries of religion, and especially the mystery of redemption, the incarnation and death of the Son of God, which the church then commemorated. He then celebrated mass for the first time in his new mission, and during the following days renewed his separate instructions. After celebrating the great festival of Easter, his malady began to appear once more, and he felt that the period granted to his earnest prayers was ended. The sole object to which he had for years directed all the aspirations of his heart was now attained. He had actually begun his Illinois mission; he had given them the first rudiments of instruction in public and in private; he had twice in their midst offered up the adorable

* Printed in the appendix of this volume.

sacrifice; there was no more to be asked on earth; he was
content to die.

In hopes of reaching his former mission of Mackinaw to
die with his religious brethren around him, fortified by the
last rites of the church, he set out escorted to the lake by the
Kaskaskias, to whom he promised that he, or some other missionary should soon resume his labors.

He seems to have taken the way by the St. Joseph's river,
and reached the eastern shore of Lake Michigan, along which
he had not yet sailed. His strength now gradually failed,
and he was at last so weak that he had to be lifted in and
out of his canoe when they landed each night. Calmly and
cheerfully he saw the approach of death, for which he prepared by assiduous prayer; his office he regularly recited to
the last day of his life; a meditation on death, which he had
long since prepared for this hour, he now made the subject
of his thoughts; and as his kind but simple companions
seemed overwhelmed at the prospect of their approaching
loss, he blessed some water with the usual ceremonies, gave
his companions directions how to act in his last moments, how
to arrange his body when dead, and to commit it to the earth,
with the ceremonies he prescribed. He now seemed but to
seek a grave; at last perceiving the mouth of a river which
still bears his name, he pointed to an eminence as the place
of his burial.

His companions, Peter Porteret and James ———, still hoped
to reach Mackinaw, but the wind drove them back, and they
entered the river by the channel, where it emptied then, for
it has since changed. They erected a little bark cabin, and
stretched the dying missionary beneath it, as comfortably as
their want permitted them. Still a priest, rather than a man,
he thought of his ministry, and, for the last time, heard the

confessions of his companions, and encouraged them to rely with confidence on the protection of God, then sent them to take the repose they so much needed. When he felt his agony approaching he called them, and taking his crucifix from around his neck, he placed it in their hands, and pronouncing in a firm voice his profession of faith, thanked the Almighty for the favor of permitting him to die a Jesuit, a missionary and alone. Then he relapsed into silence, interrupted only by his pious aspirations, till at last, with the names of Jesus and Mary on his lips, with his eyes raised as if in ecstacy above his crucifix, with his face all radiant with joy, he passed from the scene of his labors to the God who was to be his reward. Obedient to his directions his companions, when the first outbursts of grief were over, laid out the body for burial, and to the sound of his little chapel-bell, bore it slowly to the point which he had pointed out. Here they committed his body to the earth, and raising a cross above it, returned to their now desolate cabin.

Such was the edifying and holy death of the illustrious explorer of the Mississippi, on Saturday, the 18th of May, 1675. He was of a cheerful, joyous disposition, playful even in his manner, and universally beloved. His letters show him to us a man of education, close observation, sound sense, strict integrity, a freedom from exaggeration, and yet a vein of humor which here and there breaks out, in spite of all his self-command.

But all these qualities are little compared to his zeal as a missionary, to his sanctity as a man. His holiness drew on him in life the veneration of all around him, and the lapse of years has not even now destroyed it in the descendants of those who knew him.* In one of his sanctity, we naturally

---

* It led to the romantic tales which have even found their way into sober history. The missionaries in the west now hear the same account as that which Charlevoix believed and inserted.

find an all-absorbing devotion to the mother of the Savior, with its constant attendants, an angelical love of purity, and a close union of the heart with God. It is, indeed, characteristic of him. The privilege which the church honors under the title of the Immaculate Conception, was the constant object of his thoughts; from his earliest youth, he daily recited the little office of the Immaculate Conception, and fasted every Saturday in her honor. As a missionary, a variety of devotions directed to the same end still show his devotions and to her he turned in all his trials. When he discovered the great river, when he founded his new mission, he gave it the name of the Conception, and no letter, it is said, ever came from his hand that did not contain the words, "Blessed Virgin Immaculate," and the smile that lighted up his dying face, induced his poor companions to believe that she had appeared before the eyes of her devoted client.

Like St. Francis Xavier, whom he especially chose as the model of his missionary career, he labored nine years for the moral and social improvement of nations sunk in paganism and vice, and as he was alternately with tribes of varied tongues, found it was necessary to acquire a knowledge of many American languages; six he certainly spoke with ease; many more he is known to have understood less perfectly. His death, however, was as he had always desired, more like that of the apostle of the Indies; there is, indeed, a striking resemblance between their last moments, and the wretched cabin, the desert shore, the few destitute companions, the lonely grave, all harmonize in Michigan and Sancian.

He was buried as he had directed on a rising ground near the little river, and a cross raised above his grave showed to all the place of his rest. The Indians soon knew it, and two years after his death, and almost on the very anniversary his own flock, the Kiskakons, returning from their hunt stopped there, and with Indian ideas, resolved to disinter their father, and bear his revered bones to their mission. At once they did so; the bones were placed in a neat box of bark, and the flotilla now become a funeral convoy, proceeded on its way; the missionary thus accomplishing in death the voyage which life had not enabled him to terminate. A party of Iroquois joined them, and as they advanced to Mackinaw, other canoes shot out to meet them with the two missionaries of the place, and there upon the waters rose the solemn De Profundis, continued till the body reached the land. It was then borne to the church with cross, and prayer, and tapers burning like his zeal, and incense rising like his aspirations to heaven; in the church a pall had been arranged in the usual form for a coffin, and beneath it was placed the little box of bark, which was next, after a solemn service, deposited in a little vault in the middle of the church, "where," says our chronicler, "he reposes as the guardian-angel of our Ottawa missions."

There he still reposes, for I find no trace of any subsequent removal; vague tradition, like that of his death as given by Charlevoix and others, would indeed still place him at the mouth of his river; but it is certain that he was transferred to the church of old Mackinaw, in 1677. This church was, as I judge from a manuscript Relation (1675), erected subsequent to the departure of Marquette from Mackinaw, and probably about 1674. The founding of the post of Detroit drew from Mackinaw the Christian Hurons and Ottawas, and the place became deserted. Despairing of being able to produce any good among the few pagan Indians, and almost as pagan coureurs-de-bois who still lingered there, the missionaries resolved to abandon the post, and set fire to their church in or about the year 1706. Another was subsequently erected, but this too has long since disappeared.*

The history of his narrative and map are almost as curious as that of his body. We have seen that he transmitted copies to his superior, and went to his last mission. Frontenac had promised to send a copy to the government, and in all probability he did. At this moment the publication of the Jesuit Relations ceases; though not from choice on their part as the manuscript of the year 1672–'73 prepared for the press by Father Dablon, still exists; it could not have been from any difficulty on the part of the printer, as the announcement of the expedition to the Mississippi would have given it circulation, even though the journal itself were reserved for the next year. To the French government then we must attribute the non-publication of further relations, the more so, as they neglected to produce the narrative of Marquette in their possession. The whole might have fallen into perfect oblivion, had not the narrative come into the hands of Thevenot who had just published a collection of travels; struck with the importance of this, he issued a new volume in 1681, called Receuil de Voyages, in which the journal of Father Marquette as commonly known, appeared with a map of the Mississippi. The narrative is evidently taken from a manuscript like that in my hands, in the writing of which I can see the cause of some of the strange forms which Indian names have assumed. The opening of the narrative was curtailed, and occasional omissions made in the beginning, few at the end. The map is so different from that which still exists in the hand-writing

---

* In La Hontan there is a plan of Mackinaw, with the site of the church in which Marquette was buried. As to its fidelity, I can not speak; but with that of Bellin in 1744, showing the sites of the second church at old Mackinaw, and the third one in new Mackinaw, the place of the original one, and of Marquette's grave, may perhaps be determined.

of Father Marquette, that it is not probable that it was taken from it. With greater likelihood we may believe it to be Jolliet's map drawn from recollection, which Frontenac, as his despatch tells us, transmitted to France in 1674. If this be so, it has a new value as an original map, and not a blundering copy. Sparks, in his life of Father Marquette, observes truly of this first-published map of the Mississippi, "It was impossible to construct it, without having seen the principal objects delineated;" and he adds, "It should be kept in mind that this map was published at Paris, in the year 1681, and consequently the year before the discoveries of La Salle on the Mississippi, and that no intelligence respecting the country it represents, could have been obtained from any source subsequently to the voyage of Marquette."[*]

Of the narrative itself, he says, "It is written in a terse, simple, and unpretending style. The author relates what occurs, and describes what he sees without embellishment or display. He writes as a scholar, and as a man of careful observation and practical sense. There is no tendency to exaggerate, nor any attempt to magnify the difficulties he had to encounter, or the importance of his discovery. In every point of view, this tract is one of the most interesting of those, which illustrate the early history of America."

In spite of all this it was overlooked and nearly forgotten; all the writers connected with La Salle's expedition except the first edition of Hennepin, published in 1683, speak of Jolliet's voyage as a fiction. Marquette they never mention;

---

[*] The map in Thevenot had an addition of the editor in the words chemin de l'allée, and chemin du retour. The latter is incorrect, but it came from his endeavor to make Father Marquette meet the Peorias on his return. He did not know that the villages went into a body to hunt, and that the two explorers might thus have met them below the Ilinois river, or on it. Other errors on the map are easily rectified. The change of the letter gives us Misscousing, Cachkachkia, Démon (des monts), Pewarea, Allini-wek, &c.

but in Le Clercq and those whom he cites, in the second
Hennepin, in Joutel, in all in fact, except the faithful Tonty,
the narrative of Marquette is derided, called a fable, or narrative of a pretended voyage ; and one actually goes so far as
to say that, sailing up the river with the book in his hand, he
could not find a word of truth in it.   As a necessary result
of these assertions which few examined, most writers in
France and elsewhere passed over it, and in works on the
Mississippi, no discovery prior to that of La Salle is mentioned.   Even Harris, who cites Marquette by name as describing the calumet, and calls him a man of good sense and fair
character, does not give him due credit as the first explorer.*

"Indeed the services and narrative would hardly have escaped from oblivion, had not Charlevoix brought them to
light in his great work on Canada, nearly seventy years after
the events."†

As to the charges themselves, they are clearly refuted by
Frontenac's despatches.   Hennepin, in his Description de la
Louisiane, (p. 13), and F. Anastasius in Le Clercq (p. 364),
admit that Jolliet descended the Mississippi below the mouth
of the Missouri.   Membré evidently alludes to his work (p.
259).   Thus even his maligners admit that he was on the
river, and without the despatches, without the force of its publication prior to La Salle's voyage, we need only weigh the
respective writers by their works.   We find in Marquette
simple narrative, in the others, the declamation of partisans,
and the disposition to deprive Jolliet and Marquette of the
honor of reaching the Mississippi at all, though they are
forced to admit it.

* Vol ii., p. 351.   On the preceding page he has a summary, but just condem-
nation of Hennepin and Lahontan.

† And even he misdates the time of its publication.   Thevenot's edition, of
which Harvard possesses a copy, was issued in 1681, not 1687.

Meanwhile one of the copies, after having been prepared for publication by Father Claude Dablon, superior of the mission, with the introductory and supplementary matter in the form in which we now give it, lay unnoticed and unknown in the archives of the Jesuit college at Quebec. It did not even fall into the hands of Father Charlevoix when collecting material for his history, for he seems to have made little research if any into the manuscripts at the college of Quebec. A few years after the publication of his work, Canada fell into the hands of England, and the Jesuits and Recollects, as religious orders, were condemned, the reception of new members being positively forbidden. The members of each order now formed Tontints, the whole property, on the death of the last survivor, to go to the British government, or to the law knows whom, if situated in the United States.

The last survivor of the Jesuits, Father Cazot, after beholding that venerable institution, the college of Quebec closed for want of professors, and Canada deprived of its only and Northern America of its oldest collegiate seat of learning, felt at last that death would soon close with him the Society of Jesus in Canada. A happy forethought for the historic past induced him to wish to commit to other than to state hands, some objects and documents regarded as relics by the members of his society. Of these he made a selection, unfortunately too moderate and too rapid, and these papers he deposited in the Hotel Dieu, or hospital at Quebec, an institution destined to remain, as the nuns who directed it had not fallen under the ban of the government. They continued in their hands from shortly before 1800 till 1844, when the faithful guardians of the trust presented them to the Rev. F. Martin, one of the Jesuit fathers who returned in 1842 to the scene of the labors and sacrifices of their society. On the

application of Mr. B. F. French to publish the narrative of
Marquette in his Historical Collections, and apply the proceeds, and such other sums as might be received, to the erection of a monument to the great discoverer of the Mississippi,
the manuscript journal and map were committed to the hands
of the writer of these sketches.

This narrative is a very small quarto, written in a very
clear hand, with occasional corrections, comprising in all,
sixty pages.   Of these, thirty-seven contain his voyage down
the Mississippi, which is complete except a hiatus of one leaf
in the chapter on the calumet; the rest are taken up with the
account of his second voyage, death and burials, and the
voyage of Father Allouez.   The last nine lines on page 60,
are in the hand-writing of Father Dablon, and were written
as late as 1678.

With it were found the original map in the hand-writing
of Father Marquette, as published now for the first time, and
a letter begun but never ended by him, addressed to Father
Dablon, containing a journal of the voyage on which he died,
beginning with the twenty-sixth of October, (1674), and running down to the sixth of April.   The endorsements on it,
in the same hand as the direction ascribe, the letter to
Father Marquette; and a comparison between it, the written
parts of the map, and a signature of his found in a parish
register at Boucherville, would alone, without any knowledge
of its history, establish the authenticity of the map and letter.

NOTICE ON THE SIEUR JOLLIET.

AFTER so extended a notice on Father Marquette, it would seem unjust to say nothing of his illustrious companion in his great voyage. It would be doubly interesting to give a full account of Jolliet, as he was a native of the country, but unfortunately our materials are scanty and our notices vague.

Neither his birthplace nor its epoch has, as far as the present writer knows, been ascertained. His education he owed to the Jesuit college of Quebec, where, unless I am mistaken, he was a class-mate of the first Canadian who was advanced to the priesthood. Jolliet was thus connected with the Jesuits, and apparently was an assistant in the college. After leaving them, he proceeded to the west to seek his fortune in the fur-trade. Here he was always on terms of intimacy with the missionaries, and acquired the knowledge and experience which induced the government to select him as the explorer of the Mississippi.

This choice was most agreeable to the missionaries, and he and Marquette immortalized their names. They explored the great river, and settled all doubts as to its course. On his return Jolliet lost all his papers in the rapids above Montreal, and could make but a verbal report to the government. This, however, he reduced to writing, and accompanied with a map drawn from recollection. On the transmission of these to France, he, doubtless, expected to be enabled to carry out such plans as he had conceived, and to profit to some extent by his great discovery. But he was thrown aside by more flattered adventurers. The discoverer of Mississippi was rewarded as if in mockery with an island in the gulf of St. Lawrence. This was Anticosti, and here Jolliet built a fort and a dwelling for his family, and houses for trade. They were not, however, destined to be a source of emolument to him. His labors were devoted also to other fields. Thus we find him, in 1689, in the employment of the government, rendering essential services in the west.

Two years after his island was taken by the English fleet, and he himself, with his wife and mother-in-law, probably while attempting to reach Quebec, fell into the hands of Phipps, the English commander. His vessel and property were a total loss, but his liberty he recovered when the English retired from the walls of Quebec.

Of his subsequent history there are but occasional traces, and we know only that he died some years prior to 1737.

Authorities: *Charlevoix, La Hontan*, vol. i., p. 323; ii., p. 10. *MS. Journal of the Superior of the Jesuits. Bouchett's Topograph. Dic. Canada.* Titles: *Anticosti and Jolliet.*

RELATION

OF THE

VOYAGES, DISCOVERIES, AND DEATH,

OF

FATHER JAMES MARQUETTE,

AND

THE SUBSEQUENT VOYAGES OF FATHER CLAUDIUS ALLOUEZ,

BY

FATHER CLAUDIUS DABLON,

SUPERIOR OF THE MISSIONS OF THE SOCIETY OF JESUS, IN NEW FRANCE.

PREPARED FOR PUBLICATION IN 1678.

NOTICE ON FATHER DABLON.

FATHER CLAUDIUS DABLON came to Canada in 1655, and was immediately sent to Onondaga, where he continued with but one short interval of absence till the mission was broken up in 1658. Three years after, he and the hardy Druilletes attempted to reach Hudson's bay, by the Saguenay, but were arrested at the sources of the Nekouba by Iroquois war-parties. In 1668, he followed Father Marquette to Lake Superior, became superior of the Ottawa mission, founded Sault St. Mary's, visited Green bay, and reached the Wisconsin with Allouez. then returned to Quebec to assume his post as superior of all the Canada missions. This office he held with intervals for many years, certainly till 1693, and he was still alive, but not apparently superior in the following year. As the head of the missions, he contributed in no small degree to their extension, and above all, to the exploration of the Mississippi, by Marquette. He published the Relations of 1670–'71, and '72, with their accurate map of Lake Superior, and prepared for press those of 1672–'73 and 1673–'79, which still remain in manuscript, and the following narratives of Marquette and Allouez. The period of his death is unknown.

His writings are the most valuable collection on the topography of the north-west, which have come down to our days.

THE

VOYAGES AND DISCOVERIES

OF

FATHER JAMES MARQUETTE,

IN

THE VALLEY OF THE MISSISSIPPI.

CHAPTER I.

OF THE FIRST VOYAGE MADE BY FATHER MARQUETTE TOWARD NEW MEXICO, AND HOW THE DESIGN WAS CONCEIVED.

FATHER MARQUETTE had long projected this enterprise, impelled by his ardent desire of extending the kingdom of Jesus Christ, and of making him known and adored by all the nations of that country. He beheld himself, as it were, at the door of these new nations, when, in 1670, he was laboring at the mission of Lapointe du St. Esprit,* which is at the extremity of the upper Lake of the Ottawas. He even saw at times many of those new tribes, concerning whom he gathered all the information that he could. This induced him to make several efforts to undertake the enterprise, but always in vain; he had even given

* This place is now called simply Lapointe, as the lake is called Superior, retaining only the first word of its former name, Lac Superieur aux Outaoüacs.

up all hopes of succeeding, when the Almighty presented him the following opportunity :—

In 1673, the Comte de Frontenac,* our governor and Mr. Talon then our intendant, knowing the importance of this discovery, either to seek a passage from here to the China sea by the river which empties into the California or Red sea,† or to verify what was afterward said of the two kingdoms of Theguaïo and Quivira, which border on Canada, and where gold mines are, it is said abundant,‡ these gentlemen,

* Louis de Buade, Comte de Frontenac, succeeded M. de Courcelles in the government of Canada, in 1672.   M. Talon, the wise and energetic intendant of the colony, seeing the advantages to be derived to France from the discovery of the Mississippi river, immediately, on the arrival of Comte de Frontenac, laid before him his plan for exploring that river, which was adopted, and the administration of Frontenac is signalized by the first exploration of the Mississippi by Marquette and Jollyet, between the Wisconsin and Arkansas, and by the subsequent voyage of La Salle, who continued the survey to the gulf, while his companion, Hennepin, visited the portion between the Wisconsin and St. Anthony's falls. But before the return of La Salle, Comte de Frontenac's term had expired, and he was, in 1682, succeeded by M. Lefebore de la Barre.   But he was afterward re-instated governor of Canada in 1689, and died at the age of seventy-seven. He was a brave and ambitious man, and to his wise administration may be attributed the consolidation of French power in North America.—F.

† The gulf of California was called by the Spaniards Mar de Cortes, or more commonly Mar Bermejo, from its resemblance in shape and color to the Red sea.   Gomara His de las Indias, p. 12.   Cluvier Introductio.   Venegas Historia de la California.   Clavigero, Storia della California, p. 29.   In ignorance of this fact, the French translated Bermejo by Vermeille, and English writers Vermillion.

‡ Theguaïo, or commonly Tiguex, and sometimes apparently Tejas, and Quivira, were two kingdoms as to which the imagination of the Spaniards, and especially of the Mexicans, had become so aroused that Feijoo in his Teatro Critico includes them in the category of fabled lands, St. Brandon's Isle, the Eldorado, &c., although he admits that he hesitated as he found Quivira mentioned by every geographer.   These two kingdoms which lay east of the country north of the river Gila, and are probably the present New Mexico and Texas, were first made known by the attempt of a Franciscan missionary to reach the rich countries of the interior which had been spoken of by Cabeza de Vaca.   The missionary in question, Fray Marc, a native of Nice in Italy, crossed the Gila, and from the well-built houses and cotton dresses of the people, easily gave credit to the accounts of more wealthy tribes.   A subsequent expedition showed that he had been mistaken, and none but hardy missionaries sought to penetrate to the fabled

I say, both at the same time selected for the enterprise the Sieur Jollyet, whom they deemed competent for so great a design, wishing to see Father Marquette accompany him.*

They were not mistaken in their choice of the Sieur Jollyet, for he was a young man, born in this country, and endowed with every quality that could be desired in such an enterprise. He possessed experience and a knowledge of the languages of the Ottawa† country, where he had spent several years; he had the tact and prudence so necessary for the success of a voyage equally dangerous and difficult; and, lastly, he had courage to fear nothing where all is to be feared. He accordingly fulfilled the expectations entertained of him, and if, after having passed through dangers of a thousand kinds, he had not unfortunately been wrecked in the very harbor — his canoe having upset below the Saut St. Louis, near Montreal, where he lost his men and papers, and only escaped by a kind of miracle with his life — the success of his voyage had left nothing to be desired.

land. The belief of its mineral wealth was, however, too deeply rooted to be easily shaken, and the discovery of California's resources in our days has justified it, and shown that Talon in seeking to reach California from Canada, attempted no chimerical project.

* It would seem by this wording that Marquette was not officially chosen for the expedition. The troubles at the time between the civil and ecclesiastical authorities will account for this, while the researches made by Marquette as to the river, and his knowledge of the Indians and their dialects, rendered it important that he should be one of the party. That his account alone survived, and that it was published in his name, was something neither expected nor intended by any of those concerned, as M. Jollyet had prepared an account of the expedition, the loss of which, as stated in the text, alone raised the journal of Father Marquette to its present degree of importance. (In 1680, the French government rewarded the Sieur Jollyet for this eminent service by a grant of the island of Anticosti, in the gulf of St. Lawrence; and, in 1697, by the seignory of Jollyet, in Beauce county, Canada, which is now the property of the Hon. T. Taschereau, one of the judges of the court of King's bench.)

† The Ottawas, or Outaouacs, were first called by the French, Cheveux Relevés, and placed on Great Manitouline.—*Champlain*, 262, *Segard*, 201. Their Indian name is then given in the form, Andatahouats. The earlier Jesuit Rela-

SECTION I.

DEPARTURE OF FATHER JAMES MARQUETTE FOR THE DISCOVERY OF THE GREAT RIVER, CALLED BY THE INDIANS MISSISIPI, WHICH LEADS TO NEW MEXICO.

THE day of the Immaculate Conception of the Blessed Virgin, whom I had always invoked since I have been in this Ottawa country, to obtain of God the grace to be able to visit the nations on the river Missisipi,* was identically that on which M. Jollyet arrived with orders of the Comte de Frontenac, our governor, and M. Talon, our intendant, to make this discovery with me. I was the more enraptured at this good news, as I saw my designs on the point of being accomplished, and myself in the happy necessity of exposing my life for the salvation of all these nations, and particularly for the Ilinois, who had, when I was at Lapointe du St. Esprit, very earnestly entreated me to carry the word of God to their country.

We were not long in preparing our outfit, although we

tions call them Ondatawawak, and Bressani, Ondawawat. Under the form Outaoüacs (Uttawax), it was applied as a general term to all the Algonquin tribes on Lake Superior and Michigan who traded with the French. The English in the same way applied to them the name of the tribe which they called Chippeways, and the French, Outchibouee, which is still more diversified by the new spelling Ojibwa, introduced by Schoolcraft.

* The name of this river is derived from the Algonquin language one of the original tongues of our continent. It was spoken by every tribe from the Chesapeake to the gulf of St. Lawrence, and running westward to the Mississippi and Lake Superior. The Abnakis, Montagnais, Algonquins proper, Ottawas, Nipissings, Nezperces, Illinois, Miamis, Sacs, Foxes, Mohegans, Delawares, Shawnees and Virginia Indians, as well as the minor tribes of New England, all spoken dialects of this widespread language. The only exception in this vast strip of territory, was the Huron-Iroquois language, spoken by the Hurons, Petuns, Neuters, and Iroquois, which is distinct from the Algonquin. The word Mississippi is a compound of the word *Missi*, signifying great, and *Sepe*, a river. The

were embarking on a voyage the duration of which we could not foresee. Indian corn, with some dried meat, was our whole stock of provisions. With this we set out in two bark canoes,* M. Jollyet, myself, and five men, firmly resolved to do all and suffer all for so glorious an enterprise.

It was on the 17th of May, 1673, that we started from the mission of St. Ignatius at Michilimakinac,† where I then was. Our joy at being chosen for this expedition roused our courage, and sweetened the labor of rowing from morning till night. As we were going to seek unknown countries, we took all possible precautions, that, if our enterprise was hazardous, it should not be foolhardy: for this reason we gathered all possible information from Indians who had frequented those parts, and even from their accounts traced a map of all the new country, marking down the rivers on which we were to sail, the names of the nations and places through which

---

former is variously pronounced *Missil*, or *Michil*, as in Michilimackinac; *Michi*, as in Michigan; *Missu*, as in Missouri; and *Missi*, as in Mississippi. The word *Sipi* may be considered as the English pronunciation, derived through the medium of the French, of *Sepe*, and affords an instance of an Indian term of much melody, being corrupted by Europeans, into one that has a harsh and hissing sound.—F.

* The two frail canoes which bore these adventurous travellers from the snows of Canada to the more genial clime of the Arkansas, were constructed entirely different from those wood canoes with which the Indians navigated the Hudson, and the Delaware, and which we still occasionally see in use among our western tribes. The Canadian canoe made use of in this expedition, was built of birch-bark, cedar splints, and ribs of spruce roots, covered with yellow pine pitch, so light and so strong, that they could be carried across portages on the shoulders of four men, and paddled at the rate of four miles per hour in smooth water. For river navigation, where there are no rapids or portages, nothing could be better adapted for explorations; and they were used in subsequent expeditions to explore the Missouri, St. Peter's, Columbia, and Mackenzie rivers.—F.

† This is not the island, but the point north of it in the present county of that name. (*Charlevoix.*) The mission was subsequently on the south, if we credit Charlevoix's maps, and finally on the island of that name.

we were to pass, the course of the great river, and what direction we should take when we got to it.

Above all, I put our voyage under the protection of the Blessed Virgin Immaculate, promising her, that if she did us the grace to discover the great river, I would give it the name of Conception; and that I would also give that name to the first mission which I should establish among these new nations, as I have actually done among the Ilinois.*

SECTION II.

THE FATHER VISITS BY THE WAY THE WILD-OATS TRIBES.—WHAT THESE WILD OATS ARE.—HE ENTERS THE BAY OF THE FETID.—SOME PARTICULARS AS TO THIS BAY.—HE REACHES THE FIRE NATION.

WITH all these precautions, we made our paddles play merrily over a part of Lake Huron and that of the Ilinois into the Bay of the Fetid.

The first nation that we met was that of the Wild Oats.† I entered their river to visit them, as we have preached the

* The name which the pious missionary gave to the Mississippi, is found only here, and on the accompanying map, which corresponds perfectly with his narrative. The name of the Immaculate Conception, which he gave to the mission among the Kaskaskias, was retained as long as that mission lasted, and is now the title of the church in the present town of Kaskaskia. Although his wish was not realized in the name of the great river, it has been fulfilled in the fact that the Blessed Virgin, under the title of the Immaculate Conception, has been chosen by the prelates of the United States assembled in a national council, as the patroness of the whole country, so that not only in the vast valley of the Mississippi, but from the Atlantic to the Pacific, the Blessed Virgin *Immaculate* is as dear to every American Catholic, as is Our Lady of Guadaloupe to our Mexican neighbors.

† This plant, the *Zizania Aquatica*, of Linn., is perennial and forms the principal food of most of the northwestern tribes. It is called in English, wild rice; and in French, *Folles-Avoine*, or wild oats. It was first accurately described in the *Rel.* 1662–'63, apparently from Ménard's Letters. The tribe here alluded to are the Oumalouminik, Malhominies or Menomonees, whose river still shows their locality.—*Rel.* 1672–'73. MS.

gospel to these tribes for some years past, so that there are many good Christians among them.

The wild oats, from which they take their name, as they are found in their country, are a kind of grass which grows spontaneously in little rivers with slimy bottoms, and in marshy places; they are very like the wild oats that grow up among our wheat. The ears are on stalks knotted at intervals; they rise above the water about the month of June, and keep rising till they float about two feet above it. The grain is not thicker than our oats, but is as long again, so that the meal is much more abundant.

The following is the manner in which the Indians gather it and prepare it for eating. In the month of September, which is the proper time for this harvest, they go in canoes across these fields of wild oats, and shake the ears on their right and left into the canoe as they advance; the grain falls easily if it is ripe, and in a little while their provision is made. To clear it from the chaff, and strip it of a pellicle in which it is enclosed, they put it to dry in the smoke on a wooden lattice, under which they keep up a small fire for several days. When the oats are well dried, they put them in a skin of the form of a bag, which is then forced into a hole made on purpose in the ground; they then tread it out so long and so well, that the grain being freed from the chaff is easily winnowed; after which they pound it to reduce it to meal, or even unpounded, boil it in water seasoned with grease, and in this way, wild oats are almost as palatable as rice would be when not better seasoned.

I informed these people of the Wild Oats of my design of going to discover distant nations to instruct them in the mysteries of our Holy Religion; they were very much surprised, and did their best to dissuade me. They told me, that I

would meet nations that never spare strangers, but tomahawk
them without any provocation; that the war which had
broken out among various nations on our route, exposed us
to another evident danger——that of being killed by the war-
parties which are constantly in the field; that the Great
River is very dangerous, unless the difficult parts are known;
that it was full of frightful monsters who swallowed up men
and canoes together; that there is even a demon there who
can be heard from afar, who stops the passage and engulfs
all who dare approach; lastly, that the heat is so excessive in
those countries, that it would infallibly cause our death.

I thanked them for their kind advice, but assured them
that I could not follow it, as the salvation of souls was concerned; that for them, I should be too happy to lay down
my life; that I made light of their pretended demon, that
we would defend ourselves well enough against the river-
monsters; and, besides, we should be on our guard to avoid
the other dangers with which they threatened us. After
having made them pray and given them some instruction, I
left them, and, embarking in our canoes, we soon after reached
the extremity of the Bay of the Fetid, where our Fathers
labor successfully in the conversion of these tribes, having
baptized more than two thousand since they have been there.

This bay bears a name which has not so bad a meaning
in the Indian language, for they call it rather Salt Bay
than Fetid Bay, although among them it is almost the same,
and this is also the name which they give to the sea. This
induced us to make very exact researches to discover
whether there were not in these parts some salt springs, as
there are among the Iroquois, but we could not find any.*

---

* The tribe called by the French, Puants, were the Ouenibegouc, our Winnebagoes. Rel. 1672–'73. MS. Dela Potherie, vol. ii., p. 48. In the Relation of

We accordingly concluded that the name has been given on account of the quantity of slime and mud there, constantly exhaling noisome vapors which cause the loudest and longest peals of thunder that I ever heard.

The bay is about thirty leagues long, and eight wide at its mouth; it narrows gradually to the extremity, where it is easy to remark the tide which has its regular flow and ebb, almost like that of the sea. This is not the place to examine whether they are real tides, whether they are caused by the winds, or by some other age; whether there are winds, out-riders of the moon, or attached to her suite, who consequently agitate the lake and give it a kind of flow and ebb, whenever the moon rises above the horizon. What I can certainly aver is, that when the water is quite tranquil, you can easily see it rise and fall with the course of the moon, although I do not deny that this movement may be caused by distant winds,

1636, they are called Aweatsiwaenrrhonons, which, as the termination shows was their name among the Hurons. Charlevoix, on what ground I know not, calls them Otchagras. As Marquette justly remarks, their name signified salt, rather than Fetid, and they are undoubtedly the *Gens de mer* discovered by the adventurous Nicolet three hundred leagues west of the Hurons, several years prior to his death, in 1642.—*Rel.* 1642-'43, p. 8. Indeed, the dislike of the Indians to salt was so great, that they confounded the two terms. When Father Le Moyne visited Onondaga, he heard of a spring in which there was a devil that made it fetid; it was, in fact, a salt spring. So too the accounts of the death of the heroic missionaries Brebeuf and Lalemant shows that the Iroquois detected in the flesh of the latter, who had recently left European food, traces of salt which they disliked, and they showed their disgust in the additional torture they inflicted. All this establishes the identity of the terms fetid and salt, and confirms what is stated in the Relation of 1653-'54, and by Bressani in his Breve Relatione, that the Winnebagoes were so called, because they came from the fetid water or ocean, which was then said to be nine days' journey to the west. In point of fact, the Winnebagoes are a branch of the Dahcota family, which advancing further east than the rest, became cut off from them and surrounded by Algonquins. Hence, the very name comes in to confirm the philological researches which connect them with the Tartars. The bay called formerly Baie des Puants, or La Grande Baie, has now become Green Bay, and the town of that name is near the site of the old mission of St. Francis Xavier, founded in 1670.

which pressing on the centre of the lake, make it rise and fall on the shore in the way that meets our eyes.*

We left this bay to enter a river† emptying into it. It is very beautiful at its mouth, and flows gently; it is full of bustards, duck, teal, and other birds, attracted by the wild oats of which they are very fond; but when you have advanced a little up this river, it becomes very difficult, both on account of the currents and of the sharp rocks which cut the canoes and the feet of those who are obliged to drag them, especially when the water is low. For all that we passed the rapids safely, and as we approached Machkoutens, the Fire nation, I had the curiosity to drink the mineral waters of the river which is not far from this town. I also took time to examine an herb, the virtue of which an Indian, who possessed the secret, had, with many ceremonies, made known to Father Allones. Its root is useful against the bite of serpents, the Almighty having been pleased to give this remedy against a poison very common in the country. It is very hot, and has the taste of powder when crushed between the teeth. It must be chewed and put on the bite of the serpent. Snakes have such an antipathy to it, that they fly from one rubbed with it. It produces several stalks about a foot long, with pretty long leaves, and a white flower, much like the gillyflower.‡ I put some into my

---

* The last opinion now prevails, and the tides of the lake which have been so much discussed, are now ascribed to the action of the winds, although Charlevoix supposed it was owing to the springs at the bottom of the lakes, and to the shock of their currents, with those of the rivers, which fall into them from all sides, and thus produce those intermitting motions.

† The Fox river, of Green bay, is about 260 miles in length. The portage between the head waters of this river and the Wisconsin (Meskonsing), is over a level plain, and during high water, canoes frequently pass over the lowest parts of the prairie from one river to the other.—F.

‡ This plant is called by the French "Serpent-à-Sonnettes," and is an infallible remedy against the poison of snakes. The root is commonly reduced to a

canoe to examine it at leisure, while we kept on our way toward Maskoutens, where we arrived on the 7th of June.

SECTION III.

DESCRIPTION OF THE VILLAGE OF MASKOUTENS. — WHAT TRANSPIRED BETWEEN THE FATHER AND THE INDIANS. — THE FRENCH BEGIN TO ENTER A NEW AND UNKNOWN COUNTRY, AND REACH THE MISSISIPI.

HERE we are then at Maskoutens. This word in Algonquin, may mean Fire nation,* and that is the name given to them. This is the limit of the discoveries made by the French, for they have not yet passed beyond it.

This town is made up of three nations gathered here, Miamis, Maskoutens, and Kikabous. The first are more civil, liberal, and better made; they wear two long ear-locks, which give them a good appearance; they have the name of being warriors and seldom send out war parties in vain; they

---

powder, which the Indians chew, or make a poultice of, which prevents the poison from taking effect. It may be taken in water with the same effect. It has a nauseous smell, and is always avoided by snakes. If two or three drops are put into a snake's mouth, it immediately dies.—F.

* Father Marquette who was a good Algonquin scholar, does not speak positively as to the meaning of Maskoutens, though from his use of the common interpretation, he evidently favored it. Charlevoix, indeed, treats this as an error, and says, that Mascoutenec means a prairie, but on the meaning of an Indian name a traveller is more apt to err than one habituated to the country and its dialects. Certain it is that, from the earliest times, there dwelt on Lake Michigan a tribe known to the Indians of Canada by the name of Fire Indians. Their Huron name was Asistagueronons, from *asista* (fire). They lay beyond the Puants, says the early historian, Brother Sagard (p. 201). Under the same name, Atsistaehronons, they are mentioned by Father Brebeuf (Rel. 1640–'41, p. 48,) as the enemies of the tribes called by the French the Neutral Nation, who lay chiefly north of Lake Erie, between Ontario and Lake St. Clair. Now as the peninsula between Detroit and Lake Michigan was not inhabited by any Indian tribe, the Assistae must have dwelt beyond Lake Michigan, in the territory where we afterward find a tribe called by the Algonquins, Maskoutench, or Nation of Fire.

are very docile, listen quietly to what you tell them, and showed themselves so eager to hear Father Allouez when he was instructing them, that they gave him little rest, even at night. The Maskoutens and Kikabous are ruder and more like peasants, compared to the others.

As bark for cabins is rare in this country, they use rushes, which serve them for walls and roof, but which are no great shelter against the wind, and still less against the rain when it falls in torrents. The advantage of this kind of cabins is that they can roll them up, and carry them easily where they like in hunting-time.

When I visited them, I was extremely consoled to see a beautiful cross planted in the midst of the town, adorned with several white skins, red belts, bows and arrows, which these good people had offered to the Great Manitou (such is the name they give to God) to thank him for having had pity on them during the winter, giving them plenty of game when they were in greatest dread of famine.

I felt no little pleasure in beholding the position of this town; the view is beautiful and very picturesque, for from the eminence on which it is perched, the eye discovers on every side prairies spreading away beyond its reach, interspersed with thickets or groves of lofty trees.* The soil is very good, producing much corn; the Indians gather also quantities of plums and grapes, from which good wine could be made, if they chose.

No sooner had we arrived that M. Jollyet and I assembled the sachems; he told them that he was sent by our governor to discover new countries, and I, by the Almighty, to illumine them with the light of the gospel ;† that the Sovereign Master of our

---

* This narrative abounds with sketches of scenery and Indian localities that would grace the artist's pencil.—F.

† The missionaries were careful to avoid all appearance of a worldly or na-

lives wished to be known by all nations, and that to obey his will, I did not fear death, to which I exposed myself in such dangerous voyages; that we needed two guides to put us on our way, these, making them a present, we begged them to grant us. This they did very civilly, and even proceeded to speak to us by a present, which was a mat to serve us as a bed on our voyage.

The next day, which was the tenth of June, two Miamis whom they had given us as guides, embarked with us, in the sight of a great crowd, who could wonder enough to see seven Frenchmen alone in two canoes, dare to undertake so strange and so hazardous an expedition.

We knew that there was, three leagues from Maskoutens, a river emptying into the* Missisipi; we knew too, that the point of the compass we were to hold to reach it, was the west-south-west; but the way is so cut up by marshes and little lakes, that it is easy to go astray, especially as the river leading to it is so covered with wild oats, that you can hardly discover the channel. Hence, we had good need of our two guides, who led us safely to a portage of twenty-seven hundred paces, and helped us to transport our canoes to enter this river, after which they returned, leaving us alone in an unknown country, in the hands of Providence.

We now leave the waters which flow to Quebec, a distance of four or five hundred leagues, to follow those which will henceforth lead us into strange lands. Before embarking, we all began together a new devotion to the Blessed Virgin Immaculate, which we practised every day, addressing her par-

tional mission. Most of those in our northern parts were French; but though they planted the cross on many a mountain and valley, history can not tell us the place where they carved the "Lilies of the Bourbons." In fact, they never did.

* Father Marquette, however, never uses the article with Missisipi, Pekita-noüi, and other names of rivers.

ticular prayers to put under her protection both our persons and the success of our voyage. Then after having encouraged one another, we got into our canoes. The river on which we embarked is called Meskousing; it is very broad, with a sandy bottom, forming many shallows, which render navigation very difficult. It is full of vine-clad islets. On the banks appear fertile lands diversified with wood, prairie, and hill. Here you find oaks, walnut, whitewood, and another kind of tree with branches armed with long thorns. We saw no small game or fish, but deer and moose* in considerable numbers.

Our route was southwest, and after sailing about thirty leagues, we perceived a place which had all the appearances of an iron mine, and in fact, one of our party who had seen some before, averred that the one we had found was very good and very rich. It is covered with three feet of good earth, very near a chain of rock, whose base is covered with fine timber. After forty leagues on this same route, we reached the mouth of our river, and finding ourselves at $42\frac{1}{2}°$ N., we safely entered the Missisipi† on the 17th of June, with a joy that I can not express.

* The French word here is *vaches*, which has been generally translated bison, or buffalo. This is clearly a mistake; they had not yet reached the buffalo ground and the missionary afterward describes the animal when he meets it. The animal called by the Canadian French, *vache sauvage*, was the American elk, or moose.—*Rel.* 1656–'57. *Boucher, Hist. Nat. Canada.*—*Nat. Hist. of N. Y., Art.* "Moose." Boucher expressly states, that buffaloes were found only in the Ottawa country, that is, in the far west, while the *vache sauvage*, or orignal, and *ane sauvage*, or caribou, were seen in Canada.

† This latitude is nearly correct. Prairie du Chien is in north latitude 43° 3'. The mouth of the Wisconsin or, as he writes it, Meskousing, is distant one hundred and eighty miles from the portage. Above this it can be ascended ninety miles, and is then connected by short portages with the Ontonagon and Montreal rivers of Lake Superior. The Wisconsin country was subsequently inhabited by the Sacs and Foxes, but they were afterward driven away by the Chippeways and French.—F.

SECTION IV.

*OF THE GREAT RIVER CALLED MISSISIPI.—ITS MOST STRIKING PECULIARI-
TIES.—VARIOUS ANIMALS, AND PARTICULARLY THE PISIKIOUS OR WILD
CATTLE.—THEIR FORM AND DISPOSITION.—THE FIRST ILINOIS VILLAGES
REACHED BY THE FRENCH.*

HERE then we are on this renowned river, of which I
have endeavored to remark attentively all the peculiarities.
The Missisipi river has its source in several lakes* in the
country of the nations to the north; it is narrow at the mouth
of the Miskousing; its current, which runs south, is slow and
gentle; on the right is a considerable chain of very high mountains, and on the left fine lands; it is in many places studded
with islands. On sounding, we have found ten fathoms of
water. Its breadth is very unequal: it is sometimes three
quarters of a league, and sometimes narrows in to three *arpents*
(220 yards). We gently follow its course, which bears south
and southeast till the forty-second degree. Here we perceive
that the whole face is changed; there is now almost no wood
or mountain, the islands are more beautiful and covered with
finer trees; we see nothing but deer and moose, bustards and
wingless swans, for they shed their plumes in this country.
From time to time we meet monstrous fish, one of which
struck so violently against our canoe, that I took it for a large
tree about to knock us to pieces.† Another time we perceived on the water a monster with the head of a tiger, a
pointed snout like a wild-cat's, a beard and ears erect, a

* It would appear from this remark, that the source of the Mississippi river
which is now ascertained to be in Itasca lake, and more than three thousand
miles from the gulf of Mexico, was then perfectly well-known to the northwestern tribes.—F.

† This was probably the cat fish of the Mississippi (*Silurus Mississippiensis*).
They sometimes grow enormously large, and strike with great force any object
that comes in their way.—F.

grayish head and neck all black.* We saw no more of them. On casting our nets, we have taken sturgeon and a very extraordinary kind of fish;† it resembles a trout with this difference, that it has a larger mouth, but smaller eyes and snout. Near the latter is a large bone, like a woman's busk, three fingers wide, and a cubit long; the end is circular and as wide as the hand. In leaping out of the water the weight of this often throws it back.

Having descended as far as 41° 28′, following the same direction, we find that turkeys have taken the place of game, and the pisikious,‡ or wild cattle, that of other beasts. We

---

* Probably an American tiger-cat, the "*pichou du sud*" of Kalm. They differ from those of Africa and South America, because they have no spots.——F.

† The "*polyodon spatula*" of Linn. It is now very rare, and but seldom found in the Mississippi. It is also called by the French, "*le spatule.*"——F.

‡ This animal was first made known by Coronado's expedition to Cibola, in 1540. That commander proceeded as far as the Rio Grande from the gulf of California, in search of the realms of Quivira. His greatest discovery was that of the bison plains, and this peculiarly American animal. From the first object of his expedition Cibola, a town on the Gila, the animal received among Spanish writers the same name. Boucher, in his natural history of Canada, calls it the buffalo, and Father Marquette, who was the first Frenchman to reach the bison range, gives here its Indian name pisikiou, but I do not find that the name was ever adopted. The term wild-cattle, *bœufs sauvages*, was generally used by the French, as buffalo, was later by the English settlers, till the term bison, used by Pliny, was applied exclusively to this species. The buffalo has a clumsy gait like the domestic ox. Unlike the ox, however, it exhibits no diversity of color, being a uniform dark brown, inclining to dun. It is never spotted with black, red, or white. It has short, black horns, growing nearly straight from the head, and set at a considerable distance apart. The male has a hunch upon its shoulders covered with long flocks of shaggy hair, extending to the top of the head from which it falls over the eyes and horns, giving him a very formidable appearance. The hoofs are cloven like those of the cow. The tail is naked, toward the end, where it is tufted, in the manner of the lion. The Indians employ both the rifle and the arrow to hunt it, and in the prairies of Missouri and Arkansas, they pursue them on horseback; but on the upper Mississippi, where they are destitute of horses, they make use of several ingenious stratagems. One of the most common of these, is the method of hunting them with fire. The buffaloes have a great dread of fire, and retire toward the centre of the prairie as they see it approach, then being pressed together in great numbers, the Indians rush in with their arrows and musketry, and slaughter immense numbers in a few

call them wild cattle, because they are like our domestic cattle; they are not longer, but almost as big again, and more corpulent; our men having killed one, three of us had considerable trouble in moving it. The head is very large, the forehead flat and a foot and a half broad between the horns, which are exactly like those of our cattle, except that they are black and much larger. Under the neck there is a kind of large crop hanging down, and on the back a pretty high hump. The whole head, the neck, and part of the shoulders, are covered with a great mane like a horse's; it is a crest a foot long, which renders them hideous, and falling over their eyes, prevents their seeing before them. The rest of the body is covered with a coarse curly hair like the wool of our sheep, but much stronger and thicker. It falls in summer, and the skin is then as soft as velvet. At this time the Indians employ the skins to make beautiful robes, which they paint of various colors; the flesh and fat of the Pisikious are excellent, and constitute the best dish in banquets. They are very fierce, and not a year passes without their killing some Indian. When attacked, they take a man with their horns, if they can, lift him up, and then dash him on the ground, trample on him, and kill him. When you fire at them from a distance with gun or bow, you must throw yourself on the ground as soon as you fire, and hide in the grass; for, if they perceive the one who fired, they rush on him and attack him. As their feet are large and rather short, they do not

hours. Few animals of the American forest contribute more to the comforts of savage life. The skin is dressed to supply them with clothing and blankets. The tallow is an article of commerce. The tongue is a delicate article of food. and the flesh, when dried after their manner, serves them for bread and meat. The buffalo is generally found between 31° and 49° north latitude, and west of the Mississippi. South of 31° north latitude, the buffalo is not found; but its place is supplied in Mexico by the wild-ox, without a hunch, which is considered of European origin.

generally go very fast, except when they are irritated. They are scattered over the prairies like herds of cattle. I have seen a band of four hundred.

We advanced constantly, but as we did not know where we were going, having already made more than a hundred leagues without having discovered anything but beasts and birds, we kept well on our guard. Accordingly we make only a little fire on the shore at night to prepare our meal, and after supper keep as far off from it as possible, passing the night in our canoes, which we anchor in the river pretty far from the bank. Even this did not prevent one of us being always as a sentinel for fear of a surprise.

Proceeding south and south-southwest, we find ourselves at 41° north; then at 40° and some minutes, partly by southeast and partly by southwest, after having advanced more than sixty leagues since entering the river, without discovering anything.

At last, on the 25th of June, we perceived footprints of men by the water-side, and a beaten path entering a beautiful prairie. We stopped to examine it, and concluding that it was a path leading to some Indian village, we resolved to go and reconnoitre; we accordingly left our two canoes in charge of our people, cautioning them strictly to beware of a surprise; then M. Jollyet and I undertook this rather hazardous discovery for two single men, who thus put themselves at the discretion of an unknown and barbarous people. We followed the little path in silence, and having advanced about two leagues, we discovered a village on the banks of the river, and two others on a hill, half a league from the former.*

* These villages are laid down on the map on the westerly side of the Mississippi, and the names of two are given, Peouarea and Moingwena, whence it is generally supposed that the river on which they lay, is that now called the Desmoines. The upper part of that river still bears the name Moingonan, while the

Then, indeed, we recommended ourselves to God, with all our hearts; and, having implored his help, we passed on undiscovered, and came so near that we even heard the Indians talking. We then deemed it time to announce ourselves, as we did by a cry, which we raised with all our strength, and then halted without advancing any further. At this cry the Indians rushed out of their cabins, and having probably recognised us as French, especially seeing a black gown,* or at least having no reason to distrust us, seeing we were but two, and had made known our coming, they deputed four old men to come and speak with us. Two carried tobacco-pipes well-adorned, and trimmed with many kinds of feathers. They marched slowly, lifting their pipes toward the sun, as if offering them to him to smoke, but yet without uttering a single word. They were a long time coming the little way from the village to us. Having reached us at last, they stopped to consider us attentively. I now took courage, seeing these ceremonies, which are used by them only with friends, and still more on seeing them covered with stuffs, which made me judge them to be allies. I, therefore, spoke to them first, and asked them, who they were; "they answered that they were Ilinois and, in token of peace, they presented their pipes to smoke. They then invited us to their village where all the tribe awaited us with impatience. These pipes for smoking are called in the country calumets,† a word that is so much in use, that I shall be obliged to employ it in order to be understood, as I shall have to speak of it frequently.

latitude of the mouth seems to establish the identity. It must, however, be admitted that the latitude given at that day differs from ours generally from 80′ to a degree, as we see in the case of the Wisconsin and Ohio. This would throw Moingwena somewhat higher up.

* This is the well-known Indian name for the Jesuits.

† We are probably indebted to Father Marquette for the addition to our language of this word.

SECTION V.

HOW THE ILINOIS RECEIVED THE FATHER IN THEIR VILLAGE.

AT the door of the cabin in which we were to be received, was an old man awaiting us in a very remarkable posture; which is their usual ceremony in receiving strangers. This man was standing, perfectly naked, with his hands stretched out and raised toward the sun, as if he wished to screen himself from its rays, which nevertheless passed through his fingers to his face. When we came near him, he paid us this compliment: "How beautiful is the sun, O Frenchman, when thou comest to visit us! All our town awaits thee, and thou shalt enter all our cabins in peace." He then took us into his, where there was a crowd of people, who devoured us with their eyes, but kept a profound silence. We heard, however, these words occasionally addressed to us: "Well done, brothers, to visit us!"

As soon as we had taken our places, they showed us the usual civility of the country, which is to present the calumet. You must not refuse it, unless you would pass for an enemy, or at least for being impolite. It is, however, enough to pretend to smoke. While all the old men smoked after us to honor us, some came to invite us on behalf of the great sachem of all the Ilinois to proceed to his town, where he wished to hold a council with us. We went with a good retinue, for all the people who had never seen a Frenchman among them could not tire looking at us: they threw themselves on the grass by the wayside, they ran ahead, then turned and walked back to see us again. All this was done without noise, and with marks of a great respect entertained for us.

Having arrived at the great sachem's town, we espied him at his cabin-door, between two old men, all three standing naked, with their calumet turned to the sun. He harangued us in few words, to congratulate us on our arrival, and then presented us his calumet and made us smoke; at the same time we entered his cabin, where we received all their usual greetings. Seeing all assembled and in silence, I spoke to them by four presents which I made: by the first, I said that we marched in peace to visit the nations on the river to the sea: by the second, I declared to them that God their Creator had pity on them, since, after their having been so long ignorant of him, he wished to become known to all nations; that I was sent on his behalf with this design; that it was for them to acknowledge and obey him: by the third, that the great chief of the French informed them that he spread peace everywhere, and had overcome the Iroquois. Lastly, by the fourth, we begged them to give us all the information they had of the sea, and of the nations through which we should have to pass to reach it.

When I had finished my speech, the sachem rose, and laying his hand on the head of a little slave, whom he was about to give us, spoke thus: "I thank thee, Blackgown, and thee, Frenchman," addressing M. Jollyet, "for taking so much pains to come and visit us; never has the earth been so beautiful, nor the sun so bright, as to-day; never has our river been so calm, nor so free from rocks, which your canoes have removed as they passed; never has our tobacco had so fine a flavor, nor our corn appeared so beautiful as we behold it to-day. Here is my son, that I give thee, that thou mayst know my heart. I pray thee to take pity on me and all my nation. Thou knowest the Great Spirit who has made us all; thou speakest to him and hearest his word: ask him to give me life and health, and come and dwell with us, that we may know him." Saying this, he placed the little slave near us and made us a second present, an all-mysterious calumet, which they value more than a slave; by this present he showed us his esteem for our governor, after the account we had given of him; by the third, he begged us, on behalf of his whole nation, not to proceed further, on account of the great dangers to which we exposed ourselves.

I replied, that I did not fear death, and that I esteemed no happiness greater than that of losing my life for the glory of Him who made all. But this these poor people could not understand.

The council was followed by a great feast which consisted of four courses, which we had to take with all their ways; the first course was a great wooden dish full of sagamity, that is to say, of Indian meal boiled in water and seasoned with grease. The master of ceremonies, with a spoonful of sagamity, presented it three or four times to my mouth, as we would do with a little child; he did the same to M. Jollyet. For the second course, he brought in a second dish containing three fish; he took some pains to remove the bones, and having blown upon it to cool it, put it in my mouth, as we would food to a bird; for the third course, they produced a large dog,* which they had just killed, but learning that we did not eat it, it was withdrawn. Finally, the fourth course was a piece of wild ox, the fattest portions of which were put into our mouths.

After this feast we had to visit the whole village, which

---

* The dog among all Indian tribes is more valued and more esteemed than by any people of the civilized world. When they are killed for a feast, it is considered a great compliment, and the highest mark of friendship. If an Indian sees fit to sacrifice his faithful companion to give to his friend, it is to remind him of the solemnity of his professions.—F.

consists of full three hundred cabins. While we marched through the streets, an orator was constantly haranguing, to oblige all to see us without being troublesome; we were everywhere presented with belts, garters, and other articles made of the hair of the bear and wild cattle, dyed red, yellow, and gray. These are their rareties; but not being of consequence, we did not burthen ourselves with them.

We slept in the sachem's cabin, and the next day took leave of him, promising to pass back through his town in four moons. He escorted us to our canoes with nearly six hundred persons, who saw us embark, evincing in every possible way the pleasure our visit had given them. On taking leave, I personally promised that I would return the next year to stay with them, and instruct them. But before leaving the Ilinois country, it will be well to relate what I remarked of their customs and manners.

SECTION VI.

CHARACTER OF THE ILINOIS.—THEIR MANNERS AND CUSTOMS.—THEIR ESTEEM OF THE CALUMET, OR TOBACCO-PIPE, AND THEIR DANCE IN ITS HONOR.

To say Ilinois is, in their language, to say "the men," as if other Indians compared to them were mere beasts. And it must be admitted that they have an air of humanity* that

---

* "The Ilinois," as described by Father Marest in a letter to Father Germon, from the village "of the Immaculate Conception of the Holy Virgin, Cascasquias, November 9, 1712," "are much less barbarous than the other Indians. Christianity, and their intercourse with the French, have by degrees somewhat civilized them. This is particularly remarked in our village, of which the inhabitants are almost all Christians, and has brought many French to establish themselves here, three of whom we have recently married to Ilinois women. These Indians are not at all wanting in wit; they are naturally curious, and are able to use raillery in a very ingenious way. The chase and war are the sole occupa-

we had not remarked in the other nations that we had seen
on the way. The short stay I made with them did not permit

tions of the men, while the rest of the labor falls upon the women and girls. They
are the persons who prepare the ground for sowing, do the cooking, pound the
corn, build the wigwams, and carry them on their shoulders in their journeys.
These wigwams are constructed of mats made of platted reeds, which they have
the skill to sew together in such a way that the rain can not penetrate them
when they are new. Besides these things, they occupy themselves in manufac-
turing articles from buffaloes' hair, and in making bands, belts, and sacks; for
the buffaloes here are very different from our cattle in Europe. Besides having
a large hump on the back by the shoulders, they are also entirely covered with
a fine wool, which our Indians manufacture instead of that which they would
procure from sheep, if they had them in the country.

"The women, thus occupied and depressed by their daily toils, are more docile to the truths of the gospel. This, however, is not the case at the lower end
of the Missisipi, where the idleness which prevails among persons of that sex
gives opportunity for the most fearful disorders, and removes them entirely from
the way of safety.

"It would be difficult to say what is the religion of our Indians. It consists
entirely in some superstitions with which their credulity is amused. As all their
knowledge is limited to an acquaintance with brutes, and to the necessities of
life, it is to these things also that all their worship is confined. Their medicine-
men, who have a little more intellect than the rest, gain their respect by their
ability to deceive them. They persuade them that they honor a kind of spirit,
to whom they give the name of Manitou, and teach them that it is this spirit
which governs all things, and is master of life and of death. A bird, a buffalo,
a bear, or rather the plumage of these birds, and the skin of these beasts — such
is their manitou. They hang it up in their wigwams, and offer to it sacrifices
of dogs and other animals.

"The braves carry their manitous in a mat, and unceasingly invoke them to
obtain the victory over their enemies. Their medicine-men have in like manner
recourse to their manitous when they compose their remedies, or when they
attempt to cure the diseased. They accompany their invocations with chants,
and dances, and frightful contortions, to induce the belief that they are inspired
by their manitous; and at the same time they thus aggravate their diseases, so
that they often cause death. During these different contortions, the medicine-
man names sometimes one animal, and sometimes another, and at last applies
himself to suck that part of the body in which the sick person perceives the pain.
After having done so for some time, he suddenly raises himself and throws out
to him the tooth of a bear, or of some other animal, which he had kept concealed
in his mouth. 'Dear friend,' he cries, 'you will live. See what it was that was
killing you!' After which he says, in applauding himself: 'Who can resist my
manitou? Is he not the one who is the master of life?' If the patient happens
to die, he immediately has some deceit ready prepared, to ascribe the death to
some other cause which took place after he had left the sick man. But if, on

me to acquire all the information I would have desired. The following is what I remarked in their manners.

the contrary, he should recover his health, it is then that the medicine-man receives consideration, and is himself regarded as a manitou; and after having well rewarded his labors, they procure the best that the village produces to regale him.

"The influence which these kinds of jugglers have places a great obstacle in the way of the conversion of the Indians. By embracing Christianity, they expose themselves to their insults and violence. It is only a month ago that a young Christian girl experienced this treatment. Holding a rosary in her hand, she was passing before the wigwam of one of these impostors. He had imagined that the sight of a similar chaplet had caused the death of his father; and being transported with fury, he took his gun, and was on the point of firing at this poor neophyte, when he was arrested by some Indians who happened to be present.

"I can not tell you how many times I have received the like insults from them, nor how many times I should have expired under their blows, had it not been for the particular protection of God, who has preserved me from their fury. On one occasion, among others, one of them would have split my head with his hatchet, had I not turned at the very time that his arm was raised to strike me. Thanks to God, our village is now purged from these impostors. The care which we have ourselves taken of the sick, the remedies we have given them, and which have generally produced a cure, have destroyed the credit and reputation of these medicine-men, and forced them to go and establish themselves elsewhere.

"There are, however, some among them who are not so entirely brutal, and with whom we can sometimes talk, and endeavor to disabuse them of the vain confidence they have in their manitous; but it is not ordinarily with much success. A conversation which one of our fathers had with one of these medicine-men will enable you to understand the extent of their obstinacy on this point, and also what ought to be the condescension of a missionary in attempting even to refute opinions as extraordinary as those with which they are here met.

"The French had established a fort on the river Ouabache: they asked for a missionary, and Father Mermet was sent to them. This father thought that he should also labor for the conversion of the Mascoutens, who had formed a settlement on the banks of the same river, a tribe of Indians who understood the Ilinois language, but whose extreme attachment to the superstitions of their medicine-men rendered them exceedingly indisposed to listen to the instructions of the missionary.

"The course which Father Mermet took was, to confound in their presence one of their medicine-men, who worshipped the buffalo as his grand manitou. After having insensibly led him to confess that it was not by any means the buffalo which he worshipped, but a manitou of the buffalo, which is under the earth —which animates all the buffaloes, and which gives life to their sick—he asked him whether the other beasts, as the bears, for example, which his comrades worshipped, were not equally animated by a manitou which is under the earth.

They are divided into several villages, some of which are quite distant from that of which I speak, and which is called

'Certainly,' replied the medicine-man. 'But if this be so,' said the missionary, 'then men ought also to have a manitou which animates them.' — 'Nothing can be more certain,' said the medicine-man. 'That is sufficient for me,' replied the missionary, 'to convict you of having but little reason on your side; for if man who is on the earth be the master of all the animals — if he kills them, if he eats them — then it is necessary that the manitou which animates the men should also be the master of all the other manitous. Where is, then, your wisdom, that you do not invoke him who is the master of all the others?' This reasoning disconcerted the medicine-man, but this was the only effect which it produced, for they were not less attached than before to their ridiculous superstitions.

"At that same time a contagious disease desolated their village, and each day carried off many of the Indians: the medicine-men themselves were not spared, and died like the rest. The missionary thought that he would be able to win their confidence by his attention to the care of the sick, and therefore applied himself to it without intermission; but his zeal very often came near costing him his life. The services which he rendered to them were repaid only by outrages. There were even some who proceeded to the extremity of discharging their arrows at him, but they fell at his feet; it may be that they were fired by hands which were too feeble, or because God, who destined the missionary for other labors, had wished to withdraw him at that time from their fury. Father Mermet, however, was not deterred from conferring baptism on some of the Indians, who requested it with importunity, and who died a short time after they had received it.

"Nevertheless, their medicine-men removed to a short distance from the fort, to make a great sacrifice to their manitou. They killed nearly forty dogs, which they carried on the tops of poles, singing, dancing, and making a thousand extravagant gestures. The mortality, however, did not cease, for all their sacrifices. The chief of the medicine-men then imagined that their manitou, being less powerful than the manitou of the French, was obliged to yield to him. In this persuasion he many times made a circuit around the fort, crying out with all his strength: 'We are dead; softly, manitou of the French, strike softly — do not kill us all!' Then, addressing himself to the missionary: 'Cease, good manitou, let us live; you have life and death in your possession: leave death — give us life!' The missionary calmed him, and promised to take even more care of the sick than he had hitherto done; but notwithstanding all the care he could bestow, more than half in the village died.

"To return to our Ilinois: they are very different from these Indians, and also from what they formerly were themselves. Christianity, as I have already said, has softened their savage customs, and their manners are now marked by a sweetness and purity which have induced some of the French to take their daughters in marriage. We find in them, moreover, a docility and ardor for the practice of Christian virtues. The following is the order we observe each day in our mission: Early in the morning we assemble the catechumens at the church, where they have prayers, they receive instructions, and chant some can-

Peöuarea.   This produces a diversity in their language which in general has a great affinity to the Algonquin, so that we

ticles. When they have retired, mass is said, at which all the Christians assist, the men placed on one side and the women on the other; then they have prayers, which are followed by giving them a homily, after which each one goes to his labor. We then spend our time in visiting the sick, to give them the necessary remedies, to instruct them, and to console those who are laboring under any affliction.

"After noon the catechising is held, at which all are present, Christians and catechumens, men and children, young and old, and where each, without distinction of rank or age, answers the questions put by the missionary. As these people have no books, and are naturally indolent, they would shortly forget the principles of religion if the remembrance of them was not recalled by these almost continual instructions. Our visits to their wigwams occupy the rest of the day.

"In the evening, all assemble again at the church, to listen to the instructions which are given, to say prayers, and to sing some hymns. On Sundays and festivals we add to the ordinary exercises, instructions which are given after the vespers. The zeal with which these good neophytes repair to the church at all such hours is admirable : they break off from their labors, and run from a great distance, to be there at the appointed time. They generally end the day by private meetings which they hold at their own residences, the men separately from the women, and there they recite the rosary in alternate choirs, and chant the hymns, until the night is far advanced. These hymns are their best instructions, which they retain the more easily, since the words are set to airs with which they are acquainted, and which please them.

"They often approach the sacraments, and the custom among them is to confess and to communicate once in a fortnight. We have been obliged to appoint particular days on which they shall confess, or they would not leave us leisure to discharge our other duties. These are the Fridays and Sundays of each week, when we hear them, and on these days we are overwhelmed with a crowd of penitents. The care which we take of the sick gains us their confidence, and it is particularly at such times that we reap the fruits of our labors. Their docility is then perfect, and we have generally the consolation of seeing them die in great peace, and with the firm hope of being shortly united to God in heaven.

"This mission owes its establishment to the late Father Gravier. Father Marquette was, in truth, the first who discovered the Missisipi, about thirty-nine years ago ; but, not being acquainted with the language of the country, he did not remain. Some time afterward he made a second journey, with the intention of fixing there his residence, and laboring for the conversion of these people; but death, which arrested him on the way, left to another the care of accomplishing this enterprise. This was Father Allouez, who charged himself with it. He was acquainted with the language of the Ouniamis, which approaches very nearly to that of the Ilinois. He, however, made but a short sojourn, having the idea while there that he should be able to accomplish more in a different country, where indeed he ended his apostolic life.

easily understood one another. They are mild and tractable in their disposition, as we experienced in the reception they

"Thus Father Gravier is the one who should properly be regarded as the founder of the mission to the Ilinois. He first investigated the principles of their language, and reduced them to grammatical rules, so that we have since only been obliged to bring to perfection what he began with so great success. This missionary had at first much to suffer from their medicine-men, and his life was exposed to continual dangers; but nothing repulsed him, and he surmounted all these obstacles by his patience and mildness. Being obliged to depart to Michilimakinac, his mission was confided to Father Bineteau and Father Pinet. In company with these two missionaries I labored for some time, and after their death remained in sole charge of all the toilsome duties of the mission, until the arrival of Father Mermet. My residence was formerly in the great village of the Peouarias, where Father Gravier, who had returned thither for the second time, received a wound which caused his death. * * *

"After having remained eight days at the mission of St. Joseph, I embarked with my brother in his canoe, to repair together to Michilimakinac. The voyage was very delightful to me, not only because I had the pleasure of being with a brother, who is very dear, but also because it afforded me an opportunity of profiting for a much longer time by his conversation and example.

"It is, as I have said, more than a hundred leagues from the mission of St. Joseph to Michilimakinac. We go the whole length of Lake Michigan, which on the maps has the name, without any authority, of 'the lake of the Ilinois,' since the Ilinois do not at all dwell in its neighborhood. The stormy weather delayed us, so that our voyage took seventeen days, though it is often accomplished in less than eight.

"Michilimakinac is situated between two great lakes, into which other lakes and many rivers empty. Therefore it is that this village is the ordinary resort of the French, the Indians, and almost all those engaged in the fur-trade of the country. The soil there is far inferior to that among the Ilinois. During the greater part of the year one sees nothing but fish, and the waters which are so agreeable during the summer render a residence there dull and wearisome during the winter. The earth is entirely covered with snow from All-Saints' day even to the month of May.

"The character of these Indians partakes of that of the climate under which they live. It is harsh and indocile. Religion among them does not take deep root, as should be desired, and there are but few souls who from time to time give themselves truly to God, and console the missionary for all his pains. For myself, I could not but admire the patience with which my brother endured their failings, his sweetness under the trial of their caprices and their coarseness, his diligence in visiting them, in teaching them, in arousing them from their indolence for the exercises of religion, his zeal and his love, capable of inflaming their hearts, if they had been less hard and more tractable; and I said to myself that 'success is not always the recompense of the toils of apostolic men, nor the measure of their merit.'

"Having finished all our business during the two months that I remained with gave us. They have many wives, of whom they are extremely jealous; they watch them carefully, and cut off their

my brother, it became necessary for us to separate. As it was God who ordered this separation, he knew how to soften all its bitterness. I departed to rejoin Father Chardon, with whom I remained fifteen days. He is a missionary full of zeal, and who has a rare talent for acquiring languages. He is acquainted with almost all those of the Indians who are on these lakes, and has even learned that of the Ilinois sufficiently to make himself understood, although he has only seen some of those Indians accidentally, when they came to his village; for the Pouteautamis and the Ilinois live in terms of friendship, and visit each other from time to time. Their manners, however, are very different: those are brutal and gross, while these, on the contrary, are mild and affable.

"After having taken leave of the missionary, we ascended the river St. Joseph to where it was necessary to make a portage, about thirty leagues from its mouth. The canoes which are used for navigation in this country are only of bark, and very light, although they carry as much as a large boat. When the canoe has carried us for a long time on the water, we in our turn carry it on the land, over to another river; and it was thus that we did in this place. We first transported all there was in the canoe toward the source of the river of the Ilinois, which they call Haukiki; then we carried thither our canoe, and after having launched it, we embarked there to continue our route. We were but two days making this portage, which is one and a half leagues in length. The abundant rains which had fallen during this season had swelled our little rivers, and freed us from the currents which we feared. At last we perceived our own agreeable country, the wild buffaloes and herds of stags wandering on the borders of the river; and those who were in the canoe took some of them from time to time, which served for our food.

"At the distance of some leagues from the village of the Peouarias, many of these Indians came to meet me, to form an escort to defend me from hostile parties of warriors who might be roaming through the forest; and when I approached the village, they sent forward one of their number to give notice of my arrival. The greater part ascended to the fort, which is situated on a rock on the banks of the river, and, when I entered the village, made a general discharge of their guns in sign of rejoicing. Their joy was, indeed, pictured plainly on their countenances, and shone forth in my presence. I was invited, with the French and the Ilinois chiefs, to a feast which was given to us by the most distinguished of the Peouarias. It was there that one of the principal chiefs addressed me in the name of the nation, testifying to me the deep grief they felt at the unworthy manner in which they had treated Father Gravier, and conjured me to forget it, to have pity on them and their children, and to open to them the gate of heaven, which they had closed against themselves.

"For myself, I returned thanks to God, from the bottom of my heart, that I thus saw that accomplished which I had desired with the utmost ardor. I answered them, in a few words, that I was touched with their repentance; that I always regarded them as my children; and that after having made a short excursion to my mission, I should come to fix my residence in the midst of them,

nose or ears when they do not behave well ; I saw several who
bore the marks of their infidelity.   They are well-formed, nim-
ble, and very adroit in using the bow and arrow ; they use guns
also, which they buy of our Indian allies who trade with the
French ; they use them especially to terrify their enemies by
the noise and smoke, the others lying too far to the west, have
never seen them, and do not know their use.   They are warlike and formidable to distant nations in the south and west,
where they go to carry off slaves, whom they make an article
of trade, selling them at a high price to other nations for
goods.*

The distant nations against whom they go to war, have no
knowledge of Europeans ; they are acquainted with neither

to aid them by my instructions to return into the way of salvation, from which
they had perhaps wandered.   At these words the chief uttered a loud cry of joy,
and each one with emulation testified his gratitude.   During two days that I
remained in the village, I said mass in public, and discharged all the duties of a
missionary.

"It was toward the end of August that I embarked to return to my mission
of the Cascasquias, distant a hundred and fifty leagues from the village of the
Peouarias.   During the first day of our departure, we found a canoe of the
Sioux, broken in some places, which had drifted away, and we saw an encamp-
ment of their warriors, where we judged by the view there were at least one
hundred persons.   We were justly alarmed, and on the point of returning to
the village we had left, from which we were as yet but ten leagues' distance.

"These Sioux are the most cruel of all the Indians, and we should have been
lost if we had fallen into their hands.   They are great warriors, but it is principally upon the water that they are formidable.   They have only small canoes
of bark, made in the form of a gondola, and scarcely larger than the body of a
man, for they can not hold more than two or three at the most.   They row on
their knees, managing the oar now on one side and now on the other; that is,
giving three or four strokes of the oar on the right side, and then as many on
the left side, but with so much dexterity and swiftness, that their canoes seem to
fly on the water.   After having examined all things with attention, we concluded that these Indians had struck their intended blow, and were retiring :
we, however, kept on our guard, and advanced with great caution, that we
might not encounter them.   But when we had once gained the Missisipi, we
sped on by dint of rowing.   At last, on the 10th of September, I arrived at my
dear mission, in perfect health, after five months' absence."— *Kip's Jesuit Miss.*

* It would appear from this remark, that a traffic in Indian slaves was carried
on extensively at a very early period, by the aborigines of North America.

iron or copper, and have nothing but stone knives. When
the Ilinois set out on a war party, the whole village is notified by a loud cry made at the door of their huts the morning and evening before they set out. The chiefs are distinguished from the soldiers by their wearing a scarf* inge-
niously made of the hair of bears and wild oxen. The face
is painted with red lead or ochre, which is found in great
quantities a few days' journey from their village.† They live
by game, which is abundant in this country, and on Indian
corn, of which they always gather a good crop, so that they
have never suffered by famine. They also sow beans and
melons, which are excellent, especially those with a red seed.
Their squashes are not of the best; they dry them in the sun,
to eat in the winter and spring.

Their cabins are very large; they are lined and floored
with rush-mats. They make all their dishes of wood, and
their spoons of the bones of the buffalo, which they cut so
well, that it serves them to eat their sagamity easily.

They are liberal in their maladies, and believe that the
medicines given them operate in proportion to the presents
they have made the medicine-man. Their only clothes are

---

* The scarf or belt has always formed a part of the costume of chiefs. Among
the tribes of the west it is generally made of long hair braided in figures with
shells, beads, &c. Belts of deer and buffalo skins are also worn. These belts
are worn over the left shoulder, and passed around the waist, ending in a
long fringe. In addition to the scarf, they likewise adorn themselves with arm,
knee, and wrist bands; knee-rattles made of deer-hoofs, and arm themselves
with the formidable bow and arrow, war-club, and scalping-knife.—F.

† The custom of painting their bodies is characteristic of all savage tribes. The
native Britons, Germans, and Scandinavians, formerly practised it. The savage
tribes of North and South America continue the custom to the present day, with
a view of rendering themselves more attractive to their friends, or more terrible
to their enemies. The substances usually employed are ochres, clays, native
oxydes of iron, and other minerals, the production of their country. When they
go to war, they paint themselves red; when they mourn for their friends or relatives, with black; at other times they cover their face and body with a variety
of fantastic colors, which they are very skilful in mixing.—F.

3

skins; their women are always dressed very modestly and decently, while the men do not take any pains to cover themselves. Through what superstition I know not, some Ilinois, as well as some Nadouessi, while yet young, assume the female dress, and keep it all their life. There is some mystery about it, for they never marry, and glory in debasing themselves to do all that is done by women :* yet they go to war, though allowed to use only a club, and not the bow and arrow, the peculiar arm of men; they are present at all the juggleries and solemn dances in honor of the calumet; they are permitted to sing, but not to dance; they attend the councils, and nothing can be decided without their advice; finally, by the profession of an extraordinary life, they pass for manitous (that is, for genii), or persons of consequence.

It now only remains for me to speak of the calumet, than which there is nothing among them more mysterious or more esteemed. Men do not pay to the crowns and sceptres of kings the honor they pay to it : it seems to be the god of peace and war, the arbiter of life and death. Carry it about you and show it, and you can march fearlessly amid enemies, who even in the heat of battle lay down their arms when it is shown. Hence the Ilinois gave me one, to serve as my safeguard amid all the nations that I had to pass on my voyage. There is a calumet for peace, and one for war, distinguished only by the color of the feathers with which they are adorned, red being the sign of war. They use them also for settling disputes, strengthening alliances, and speaking to strangers.†

* Others represent this custom to have been to satisfy that unnatural lust which dishonored all paganism, from the vaunted Trajan to the lowest savage. See Hennepin's account of this custom in his "Voyage en un pays plus grand que l'Europe entre mer glaciale, et le Nouveau Mexique."

† The calumet of peace is adorned with the feathers of the white eagle; and the bearer of it may go everywhere without fear, because it is held sacred by all tribes.—F.

It is made of a polished red stone, like marble, so pierced that one end serves to hold the tobacco, while the other is fastened on the stem, which is a stick two feet long, as thick as a common cane, and pierced in the middle; it is ornamented with the head and neck of different birds of beautiful plumage; they also add large feathers of red, green, and other colors, with which it is all covered. They esteem it particularly because they regard it as the calumet of the sun; and, in fact, they present it to him to smoke when they wish to obtain calm, or rain, or fair weather. They scruple to bathe at the beginning of summer, or to eat new fruits, till they have danced it. They do it thus:—

The calumet dance* which is very famous among these Indians, is performed only for important matters, sometimes to strengthen a peace or to assemble for some great war; at other times for a public rejoicing; sometimes they do this honor to a nation who is invited to be present; sometimes they use it to receive some important personage, as if they wished to give him the entertainment of a ball or comedy. In winter the ceremony is performed in a cabin, in summer in the open fields. They select a place, surrounded with trees, so as to be sheltered beneath their foliage against the heat of the sun. In the middle of the space they spread out a large party-colored mat of rushes; this serves as a carpet, on which to place with honor the god of the one who gives the dance; for every one has his own god, or manitou† as

* Besides the calumet dance, these tribes have a great variety of other dances, wholly of their own invention. Twenty-one of these are still in use among the southwestern Indians, to each of which there is a history attached; and many of them, without doubt, have been handed down from generation to generation until their origin is even lost in tradition.—F.

† Manitou is a word employed to signify the same thing by all Indians from the gulf of Mexico to the arctic regions. In the Indian language it signifies "spirit." They have good and bad manitous, great and small manitous; a manitou for every cave, water-fall, or other commanding object in nature, and gene-

they call it, which is a snake, a bird, or something of the
kind, which they have dreamed in their sleep, and in which
they put all their trust for the success of their wars, fishing,
and hunts.   Near this manitou and at its right, they put the
calumet in honor of which the feast is given, making around
about it a kind of trophy, spreading there the arms used by
the warriors of these tribes, namely, the war-club, bow, hatchet,
quiver, and arrows.

Things being thus arranged, and the hour for dancing
having arrived, those who are to sing take the most honorable
place under the foliage.   They are the men and the women
who have the finest voices, and who accord perfectly.   The
spectators then come and take their places around under the
branches; but each one on arriving must salute the manitou,
which he does by inhaling the smoke and then puffing it
from his mouth upon it, as if offering incense.   Each one
goes first and takes the calumet respectfully, and supporting
it with both hands, makes it dance in cadence, suiting himself to the air of the song; he makes it go through various
figures, sometimes showing it to the whole assembly by turning it from side to side.

After this, he who is to begin the dance appears in the
midst of the assembly, and goes first; sometimes he presents
it to the sun, as if he wished it to smoke; sometime he in-

rally make offerings at such places.   Their bad manitou answers to our devil.
All Indians are more or less superstitious, and believe in miraculous transforma-
tions, ghosts, and witchcraft.   They have jugglers and prophets who predict
events, interpret dreams, and perform incantations and mummeries.   In the
true acceptation of the term, the Indians have a religion, for they believe
in a great spirit who resides in the clouds, and reigns throughout the earth.
The French missionaries have been the most successful in planting Christianity
among them; but in general, they prefer "to follow the religion of their fathers."   The savage mind, habituated to sloth, is not easily roused into a state
of moral activity, and therefore, in general, they are incapable of embracing and
understanding the sublime truths and doctrines of the evangelical law.—F.

clines it to the earth ; and at other times he spreads its wings as if for it to fly ; at other times, he approaches it to the mouths of the spectators for them to smoke, the whole in cadence. This is the first scene of the ballet.

The second consists in a combat, to the sound of a kind of drum, which succeeds the songs, or rather joins them, harmonizing quite well. The dancer beckons to some brave to come and take the arms on the mat, and challenges him to fight to the sound of the drums ; the other approaches, takes his bow and arrow, and begins a duel against the dancer who has no defence but the calumet. This spectacle is very pleasing, especially as it is always done in time, for one attacks, the other defends ; one strikes, the other parries ; one flies, the other pursues ; then he who fled faces and puts his enemy to flight. This is all done so well with measured steps, and the regular sound of voices and drums, that it might pass for a very pretty opening of a ballet in France.

The third scene consists of a speech delivered by the holder of the calumet, for the combat being ended without bloodshed, he relates the battles he was in, the victories he has gained ; he names the nations, the places, the captives he has taken, and as a reward, he who presides at the dance presents him with a beautiful beaver robe, or something else, which he receives, and then he presents the calumet to another, who hands it to a third, and so to all the rest, till all having done their duty, the presiding chief presents the calumet itself to the nation invited to this ceremony in token of the eternal peace which shall reign between the two tribes.

The following is one of the songs which they are accustomed to sing ; they give it a certain expression, not easily represented by notes, yet in this all its grace consists :—

> "Ninahani, ninahani, ninahani,
> Naniongo."

We take leave of our Ilinois about the end of June, at three o'clock in the afternoon, and embark in sight of all the tribe, who admire our little canoes, having never seen the like.

We descend, following the course of the river, toward another called Pekitanoüi,* which empties into the Missisipi, coming from the northwest, of which I have something considerable to say, after I have related what I have remarked of this river.

Passing by some pretty high rocks which line the river, I perceived a plant which seemed to me very remarkable. Its root is like small turnips linked together by little fibres, which had the taste of carrots. From this root springs a leaf as wide as the hand, half of a finger thick with spots in the middle; from this leaf spring other leaves like the sockets of chandeliers in our saloons. Each leaf bears five or six bell-shaped yellow flowers.† We found abundance of mulberries, as large as the French, and a small fruit which we took at first for olives, but it had the taste of an orange, and another as large as a hen's egg; we broke it in half and found two separations, in each of which were encased eight or ten seed shaped like an almond, which are quite good when ripe.‡ The tree which bears them has, however, a very bad smell, and its leaf resembles that of the walnut. There are also, in the prairies, fruit resembling our filberts, but more tender; the leaves are larger, and spring from a stalk crowned at the top with a head like a sunflower, in which all these nuts are neatly arranged; they are very good cooked or raw.‖

---

* The name here given by Marquette, Pekitanoüi, that is, muddy water, prevailed till Marest's time, (1712). A branch of Rock river is still called Pekatonica. The *Recollects*, called the Missouri, the river of the Ozages.

† Probably the *Cactus opuntia*, several species of which grow in the western states.—F.

‡ Probably the *Diospyros virginiana*, or persimon-tree.

‖ Probably the *Castanea pumila*, or chincapin.—F.

As we coasted along rocks frightful for their height and length, we saw two monsters painted on one of these rocks, which startled us at first, and on which the boldest Indian dare not gaze long. They are as large as a calf, with horns on the head like a deer, a fearful look, red eyes, bearded like a tiger, the face somewhat like a man's, the body covered with scales, and the tail so long that it twice makes the turn of the body, passing over the head and down between the legs, and ending at last in a fish's tail. Green, red, and a kind of black, are the colors employed. On the whole, these two monsters are so well painted, that we could not believe any Indian to have been the designer, as good painters in France would find it hard to do as well; besides this, they are so high upon the rock that it is hard to get conveniently at them to paint them. This is pretty nearly the figure of these monsters, as I drew it off.*

As we were discoursing of them, sailing gently down a beautiful, still, clear water, we heard the noise of a rapid into which we were about to fall. I have seen nothing more frightful; a mass of large trees, entire, with branches, real floating islands, came rushing from the mouth of the river Pekitanoüi, so impetuously, that we could not, without great danger, expose ourselves to pass across. The agitation was so great that the water was all muddy and could not get clear.

Pekitanoüi† is a considerable river which coming from

---

* The drawing of these figures by Marquette is lost. "The painted monsters," says Stoddard, "on the side of a high perpendicular rock, apparently inaccessible to man, between the Missouri and Ilinois, and known to moderns by the name of *Piesa*, still remain in a good degree of preservation."

† Father Marquette had now reached the junction of the Missouri and the Mississippi, in latititude north 38° 50′. "The Achelous and Teliboas," says Stoddard, "are insignificant rivers when compared with the Mississippi and Missouri; yet Thucydides and Xenophon exerted all their powers to render them immortal. The two great rivers of the west furnish themes still more pregnant with the sublime and beautiful. The great length of them, the variety of scenery as they roll among mountains, or over extensive plains, at once charm the senses

very far in the northwest, empties into the Missisipi.   Many Indian towns are ranged along this river, and I hope, by its means, to make the discovery of the Red, or California sea.

We judged by the direction the Missisipi takes, that if it keeps on the same course it has its mouth in the gulf of Mexico ; it would be very advantageous to find that which leads to the South sea, toward California and this, as I said, I hope to find by Pekitanoüi, following the account which the Indians have given me ; for from them I learn that advancing up this river for five or six days, you come to a beautiful prairie twenty or thirty leagues long, which you must cross to the northwest.   It terminates at another little river on which you can embark, it not being difficult to transport canoes over so beautiful a country as that prairie.   This second river runs southwest for ten or fifteen leagues, after which it enters a small lake, which is the source of another deep river, running to the west where it empties into the sea.*   I have hardly any doubt that this is the Red sea, and I do not despair of one day making the discovery, if God does me this favor and grants me health, in order to be able to publish the gospel to all the nations of this new world who have so long been plunged in heathen darkness.

Let us resume our route after having escaped as best we could, the dangerous rapid caused by the obstacle of which I have spoken.

and warm the imagination.   The facilities they yield to commerce, the superflu- ous wealth of twenty states conveyed to the ocean, the variety of climates, soils, and productions on their borders, the mineral and other subterranean riches of the soil, seem to be designed by Heaven to impress us with their importance and sub- limity."

* Marquette was right in his conjecture, as topographical surveys have since determined, that the gulf of California might be reached by the Platte which is one of the tributaries of the Missouri.   The head waters of the Platte almost in- terlock with the head waters of the Colorado, which latter river flows into the Red sea, or gulf of California, as here stated by Marquette.—F.

SECTION VII.

NEW COUNTRIES DISCOVERED BY THE FATHER.—VARIOUS PARTICULARS.— MEETING WITH SOME INDIANS.—FIRST TIDINGS OF THE SEA AND OF EURO- PEANS.—GREAT DANGER AVOIDED BY THE CALUMET.

AFTER having made about twenty leagues due south, and a little less to the southeast, we came to a river called Oua- boukigou,* the mouth of which is at 36° north. Before we arrived there, we passed by a place dreaded by the Indians, because they think that there is a manitou there, that is, a demon who devours all who pass, and of this it was, that they had spoken, when they wished to deter us from our enter- prise. The devil is this—a small bay, full of rocks, some twenty feet high, where the whole current of the river is whirled ; hurled back against that which follows, and checked by a neighboring island, the mass of water is forced through a narrow channel ; all this is not done without a furious com- bat of the waters tumbling over each other, nor without a great roaring, which strikes terror into Indians who fear everything. It did not prevent our passing and reaching 8ab8kig8. This river comes from the country on the east, inhabited by the people called Chaoúanons,† in such numbers

* The Ohio, or beautiful river, as that Iroquois name signifies. The name given by Marquette, became finally Ouabache, in our spelling Wabash, and is now applied to the last tributary of the Ohio. The letter used a few lines lower down for ou, is the Greek contraction, and was used by the missionaries to ex- press a peculiar Indian sound, which we have often represented by W.

† The Chawanons have become by our substitution of sh, Shawnees. I find the name Chaoüanong in the *Relation* 1671–'72, as another name for the people called Ontoüagannha, which is defined in the *Relation* of 1661–'62, to mean "where they do not know how to speak." This is not then their name, and the name Chaoüanong probably came through the western Algonquins, and was usually translated by the French the Chats, or Cat tribe. I am strongly in- clined to think them identical with the tribe called, by the Huron missionaries, while that nation stood, the Erieehonons, or Cats (*Rel.* 1640–'41). This tribe

that they reckon as many as twenty-three villages in one district, and fifteen in another, lying quite near each other; they are by no means warlike, and are the people the Iroquois go far to seek in order to wage an unprovoked war upon them; and, as these poor people can not defend themselves, they allow themselves to be taken and carried off like sheep, and innocent as they are, do not fail to experience, at times, the barbarity of the Iroquois, who burn them cruelly.

A little above this river of which I have just spoken, are cliffs where our men perceived an iron mine, which they deemed very rich; there are many veins, and a bed a foot thick. Large masses are found combined with pebbles. There is also there a kind of unctuous earth of three colors, purple, violet, and red,* the water in which it is washed becomes blood-red. There is also a very heavy, red sand; I put some on a paddle, and it took the color so well, that the

then occupied western New York, except a little strip on the Niagara river, where there were three or four villages of Attiwandaronk, or Neuters. Morgan in his *League of the Iroquois*, indeed, thinks the Neuters to be Cats; but as the Neuters were incorporated into the Iroquois (*Rel.* 1655, &c.), under the name of Atirhagenret, or Rhagenraka (*Rels.* 1671, '73, '74), while the Eries were gradually expelled; it seems more probable that they retired from their lake to the Ohio, thence to the Tennessee, and turning south, came up again to Pennsylvania. During this period, being known chiefly through Algonquins tribes, they were called by an Algonquin word for the animal of which they bore the name. De Laet giving the names of the tribes from the mouth of the Delaware to Lake Erie, puts the Sawanos one of those nearest the Senecas and the lake; and this name differs from the later French name only in the aspirate, frequently omitted and expressed at random by the same writer, as we find *Missilimakinac*, and *Michilimackinac*, *Maskoutens* and *Machkoutens*, *Kaskaskia* and *Kachkachkia*. This will I think, justify our supposing the Eries, Shawnees, Chaouanons, Ontoüagannha, Sawanas, to be the same unfortunate tribe whom the Iroquois so perseveringly followed. Much confusion has been of late years occasioned by writers utterly unfamiliar with the language, religion, or writings of the early French missionaries. This has gone so far, that in Schoolcraft's ponderous work on the *History, Condition, and Progress of the Indian Tribes*, we are asked, at p. 560, whether the Eries were the Neuters!

* This has always been a favorite spot for the resort of Indians to obtain different colored clays with which they paint themselves.—F.

water did not efface it for fifteen days that I used it in rowing.

Here we began to see canes, or large reeds on the banks of the river; they are of a very beautiful green; all the knots are crowned with long, narrow, pointed leaves; they are very high, and so thick-set, that the wild cattle find it difficult to make their way through them.

Up to the present time we had not been troubled by musquitoes, but we now, as it were, entered their country.* Let me tell you what the Indians of these parts do to defend themselves against them. They raise a scaffolding, the floor of which is made of simple poles, and consequently a mere grate-work to give passage to the smoke of a fire which they build beneath. This drives off the little animals, as they can not bear it. The Indians sleep on the poles, having pieces of bark stretched above them to keep off the rain. This scaffolding shelters them too from the excessive and insupportable heat of the country; for they lie in the shade in the lower story, and are thus sheltered from the rays of the sun, enjoy the cool air which passes freely through the scaffold.

With the same view we were obliged to make on the water a kind of cabin with our sails, to shelter ourselves from the musquitoes and the sun. While thus borne on at the will of the current, we perceived on the shore Indians armed with guns, with which they awaited us. I first presented my feathered calumet, while my comrades stood to arms, ready to fire on the first volley of the Indians. I hailed them in Huron, but they answered me by a word, which seemed to us a declaration of war. They were, however, as much frightened as our-

---

* Marquette had now reached the country of the warlike Chicachas, whose territory extended several hundred miles along the banks of the Mississippi, and far to the eastward, where they carried on a traffic with tribes who traded with Europeans.—F.

selves, and what we took for a signal of war, was an invitation to come near, that they might give us food ; we accordingly landed and entered their cabins, where they presented us wild-beef and bear's oil, with white plums, which are excellent. They have guns, axes, hoes, knives, beads, and double glass bottles in which they keep the powder. They wear their hair long and mark their bodies in the Iroquois fashion ; the head-dress and clothing of their women were like those of the Huron squaws.

They assured us that it was not more than ten days' journey to the sea ; that they bought stuffs and other articles of Europeans on the eastern side ; that these Europeans had rosaries and pictures ; that they played on instruments ; that some were like me, who received them well. I did not, however, see any one who seemed to have received any instruction in the faith ; such as I could, I gave them with some medals.*

This news roused our courage and made us take up our paddles with renewed ardor. We advance then, and now begin to see less prairie land, because both sides or the river are lined with lofty woods. The cotton-wood, elm and white-wood, are of admirable height and size. The numbers of wild cattle we heard bellowing, made us believe the prairies near. We also saw quails on the water's edge, and killed a little parrot with half the head red, the rest, with the neck, yellow, and the body green. We had now descended to near 33° north, having almost always gone south, when on the water's

---

* The missionary gives no name to this tribe or party, but from their dress and language, apparently of the Huron-Iroquois family, they may have been a Tuscarora party, and referred to the Spaniards of Florida with whom they traded in trinkets for skins. That they were not dwellers on the Mississippi seems probable, from the fact that they were spoken of, not by the next tribe, but by those lower down, whom they had doubtless reached on some other foray.

edge we perceived a village called Mitchigamea.* We had recourse to our patroness and guide, the Blessed Virgin Immaculate ; and, indeed, we needed her aid, for we heard from afar the Indians exciting one another to the combat by continual yells. They were armed with bows, arrows, axes, warclubs, and bucklers, and prepared to attack us by land and water; some embarked in large wooden canoes, a part to ascend the rest to descend the river, so as to cut off our way, and surround us completely. Those on shore kept going and coming, as if about to begin the attack. In fact, some young men sprang into the water to come and seize my canoe, but the current having compelled them to return to the shore, one of them threw his war-club at us, but it passed over our heads without doing us any harm. In vain I showed the calumet, and made gestures to explain that we had not come as enemies. The alarm continued, and they were about to pierce us from all sides with their arrows, when God suddenly touched the hearts of the old men on the water-side, doubtless at the sight of our calumet, which at a distance they had not distinctly recognised ; but as I showed it continually, they were touched, restrained the ardor of their youth, and two of the chiefs having thrown their bows and quivers into our canoe, and as it were at our feet, entered and brought us to the shore, where we disembarked, not without fear on our part. We had at first to speak by signs, for not one under-

---

* The Mitchigameas were a warlike tribe, and lived on a lake of that name near the river St. Francis. They finally became fused into the Ilinois nation, as Charlevoix assures us in his journal, where he makes them inhabitants of the villages of the Kaskaskias, in 1721. This brings them near the part which had but shortly before taken the name of Michigan, given also to the lake which the Jesuits called Lake Ilinois. The name Michigan may come from them, though I am informed by the Rev. Mr. Pierz, an Ottawa missionary, that Mitchikan, meaning a *fence*, was the Indian of Mackinaw, and the name under the form Machihiganing was used some years prior by Alloucz.—*Rel.* 69, 70.

stood a word of the six languages I knew; at last an old man was found who spoke a little Ilinois.

We showed them by our presents, that we were going to the sea; they perfectly understood our meaning, but I know not whether they understood what I told them of God, and the things which concerned their salvation. It is a seed cast in the earth which will bear its fruit in season. We got no answer, except that we would learn all we desired at another great village called Akamsea, only eight or ten leagues farther down the river. They presented us with sagamity and fish, and we spent the night among them, not, however, without some uneasiness.

SECTION VIII.

RECEPTION GIVEN TO THE FRENCH IN THE LAST OF THE TOWNS WHICH THEY SAW.—MANNERS AND CUSTOMS OF THESE SAVAGES.—REASONS FOR NOT GOING FURTHER.

We embarked next morning with our interpreter, preceded by ten Indians in a canoe. Having arrived about half a league from Akamsea* (Arkansas), we saw two canoes coming

* It is probable that Akamsea was not far from the Indian village of Guacho-ya, where De Soto breathed his last, one hundred and thirty years before; and Mitchigamea, the village of Aminoya, where Alvarado de Moscoso built his fleet of brigantines to return to Mexico. The historian of that expedition, says "The same day we left Aminoya (July 2d, 1543), we passed by Guachoya, where the Indians tarried for us in their canoes." The Spaniards were attacked in de-scending the river by powerful fleets of Indian canoes, and lost in one of these engagements the brave John de Guzman and eleven men. In sixteen days they reached the mouth of the Mississippi, and on the 10th September, 1543, the rem-nant of this once splendid expedition reached Mexico. It must have been, there-fore, at or near the mouth of the Arkansas, and not Red river, where De Soto died, otherwise it would not have taken Moscoso one half of the time to reach the gulf of Mexico from the latter river, which is but three hundred and fifty miles from the gulf.—F.

toward us. The commander was standing up holding in his hand the calumet, with which he made signs according to the custom of the country; he approached us, singing quite agreeably, and invited us to smoke, after which he presented us some sagamity and bread made of Indian corn, of which we ate a little. He now took the lead, making us signs to follow slowly. Meanwhile they had prepared us a place under the war-chiefs' scaffold; it was neat and carpeted with fine rush mats, on which they made us sit down, having around us immediately the sachems, then the braves, and last of all, the people in crowds. We fortunately found among them a young man who understood Ilinois much better than the interpreter whom we had brought from Mitchigamea. By means of him I first spoke to the assembly by the ordinary presents; they admired what I told them of God, and the mysteries of our holy faith, and showed a great desire to keep me with them to instruct them.

We then asked them what they knew of the sea; they replied that we were only ten days' journey from it (we could have made this distance in five days); that they did not know the nations who inhabited it, because their enemies prevented their commerce with those Europeans; that the hatchets, knives, and beads, which we saw, were sold them, partly by the nations to the east, and partly by an Ilinois town four days' journey to the west; that the Indians with fire-arms whom we had met, were their enemies who cut off their passage to the sea, and prevented their making the acquaintance of the Europeans, or having any commerce with them; that, besides, we should expose ourselves greatly by passing on, in consequence of the continual war-parties that their enemies sent out on the river; since being armed and used to war, we

could not, without evident danger, advance on that river
which they constantly occupy.

During this converse, they kept continually bringing us in
wooden dishes of sagamity, Indian corn whole, or pieces of
dog-flesh; the whole day was spent in feasting.

These Indians are very courteous and liberal of what they
have, but they are very poorly off for food, not daring to go
and hunt the wild-cattle, for fear of their enemies.   It is
true, they have Indian corn in abundance, which they sow
at all seasons; we saw some ripe; more just sprouting, and
more just in the ear, so that they sow three crops a year.
They cook it in large earthern pots,* which are very well
made; they have also plates of baked earth, which they employ for various purposes. The men go naked, and wear
their hair short; they have the nose and ears pierced, and
beads hanging from them.   The women are dressed in
wretched skins; they braid their hair in two plaits, which falls
behind their ears; they have no ornaments to decorate their
persons. Their banquets are without any ceremonies; they
serve their meats in large dishes, and every one eats as much
as he pleases, and they give the rest to one another.   Their
language is extremely difficult, and with all my efforts, I
could not succeed in pronouncing some words. Their cabins,
which are long and wide, are made of bark; they sleep at
the two extremities, which are raised about two feet from the
ground. They keep their corn in large baskets, made of
cane, or in gourds, as large as half barrels. They do not
know what a beaver is; their riches consisting in the hides
of wild cattle. They never see snow, and know the winter

* Indian pottery is one of the most ancient arts of this country. The southern
tribes particularly excelled in the manufacture of various articles for household
use, which, in form and finish, were not unlike the best remains of Roman
art.—F.

only by the rain which falls oftener than in summer.* We eat no fruit there but watermelons; if they knew how to cultivate their ground, they might have plenty of all kinds.

In the evening the sachems held a secret council on the design of some to kill us for plunder, but the chief broke up all these schemes, and sending for us, danced the calumet in our presence, in the manner I have described above, as a mark of perfect assurance; and then, to remove all fears, presented it to me.

M. Jollyet and I held another council to deliberate on what we should do, whether we should push on, or rest satisfied with the discovery that we had made. After having attentively considered that we were not far from the gulf of Mexico, the basin of which is 31° 40′ north, and we at 33° 40′, so that we could not be more than two or three days journey off; that the Missisipi undoubtedly had its mouth in Florida or the gulf of Mexico, and not on the east, in Virginia, whose seacoast is at 34° north, which we had passed, without having as yet reached the sea, nor on the western side in California, because that would require a west, or west-southwest course, and we had always been going south. We considered, moreover, that we risked losing the fruit of this voyage, of which we could give no information, if we should throw ourselves into the hands of the Spaniards, who would undoubtedly, at least, hold us as prisoners. Besides, it was

---

* Marquette had now descended to genial climes, "that knew no winter, but rains, beyond the bound of the Huron and Algonquin tribes," to tribes that claimed descent from the Aztecs, and who still probably spoke a Mexican dialect which compelled Marquette to employ an interpreter. The few words which have been recorded of the Arkansas tribes by early travellers, and the similarity of their institutions and customs to Mexican tribes, seem likewise to confirm their origin. That they came from Mexico by the Rio Colorado and headwaters of the Platte or Arkansas rivers to the Mississippi, is not at all improbable; but when they came is a problem which can not be so easily solved.—F.

clear, that we were not in a condition to resist Indians allied to Europeans, numerous and expert in the use of fire-arms, who continually infested the lower part of the river. Lastly, we had gathered all the information that could be desired from the expedition.* All these reasons induced us to resolve to return; this we announced to the Indians, and after a day's rest, prepared for it.

SECTION IX.

RETURN OF THE FATHER, AND THE FRENCH BAPTISM OF A DYING CHILD.

AFTER a month's navigation down the Missisipi, from the 42d to below the 34th degree, and after having published the gospel as well as I could to the nations I had met, we left the village of Akamsea on the 17th of July, to retrace our steps. We accordingly ascended the Missisipi, which gave us great trouble to stem its currents.† We left it indeed, about the 38th degree, to enter another river, which greatly shortened

* The great object was to discover where the river emptied, and this did not require further progress. Marquette's voyage indeed settled it so completely, that we find no more hopes expressed of reaching the Pacific by the Mississippi. The missionary's fears of the Spaniards were not unnatural, as New Mexico was the avowed object of the expedition, and the authorities there would certainly have prevented their return, for fear of opening a path to French encroachment.

† The Mississippi is remarkable for its great length, uncommon depth, and the muddiness and salubrity of its waters after its junction with the Missouri. Below this river the banks present a rugged aspect; the channel is deep and crooked, and often winds from one side of the river to the other. The strength and rapidity of its current are such in high water, that before steam was used, it could not be stemmed without much labor and waste of time. At high water the current descends at the rate of five or six miles an hour, and in low water at the rate of two or three miles only. Between the Arkansas and the Delta the velocity of the current is diminished nearly one third; and from this to the sea, about one half. In 1727, it took Father du Poisson, missionary to the Arkansas, to make a voyage from New Orleans to that mission, including some stoppages, from the 25th May to the 7th July.—F.

our way, and brought us, with little trouble, to the lake of the Ilinois.*

We had seen nothing like this river for the fertility of the land, its prairies, woods, wild cattle, stag, deer, wildcats, bustards, swans, ducks, parrots, and even beaver; its many little lakes and rivers. That on which we sailed, is broad, deep, and gentle for sixty-five leagues. During the spring and part of the summer, the only portage is half a league.

We found there an Ilinois town called Kaskaskia, composed of seventy-four cabins; they received us well, and compelled me to promise to return and instruct them. One of the chiefs of this tribe with his young men, escorted us to the Ilinois lake, whence at last we returned in the close of September to the bay of the Fetid, whence we had set out in the beginning of June.

Had all this voyage caused but the salvation of a single soul, I should deem all my fatigue well repaid, and this I have reason to think, for, when I was returning, I passed by the Indians of Peoria.† I was three days announcing the faith in all their cabins, after which as we were embarking, they brought me on the water's edge a dying child, which I

---

* Lake Michigan was so called for a long time, probably from the fact that through it lay the direct route to the Ilinois villages, which Father Marquette was now the first to visit. Marest erroneously treats the name as a mistake of geographers, and is one of the first to call it Michigan. The river which Marquette now ascended has been more fortunate, it still bears the name of Ilinois.

† Unfortunately he does not tells us where he met these roving Peorians, who thus enabled him to keep his promise to resist them. As they have left their name on the Ilinois river, he may have found them there, below the Kaskaskias who, no less erratic, left their name to a more southerly river, and to a town at its mouth, on the Mississippi. It must then be borne in mind that Marquette's Peoria, and his and Alloues' town of Kaskaskia are quite different from the present places of the name in situation. The Ilinois seemed to have formed a link between the wandering Algonquin and the fixed Iroquois; they had villages like the latter, and though they roved like the former, they roved in villages.

baptized a little before it expired, by an admirable Providence
for the salvation of that innocent soul.†

† The following table of distances offer the best means of forming some idea
of the whole distance passed over by M. Jollyet and Father Marquette :—

	Miles.
From the mission of St. Ignac to Green bay about.............	218
From Green bay (Puans) up Fox river to the portage..........	175
From the portage down the Wisconsin to the Mississippi........	175
From the mouth of the Wisconsin to the mouth of the Arkansas..	1,087
From the mouth of the Arkansas to the Ilinois river...........	547
From the mouth of the Ilinois to the Chicago.................	305
From the Chicago to Green bay, by the lake shore	260
	2767

Spark's Life of Marquette.

CHAPTER II.

SECTION I.

THE FATHER SETS OUT A SECOND TIME FOR THE ILINOIS.—HE ARRIVES THERE IN SPITE OF HIS ILLNESS AND FOUNDS THE MISSION OF THE CONCEPTION.

FATHER JAMES MARQUETTE having promised the Ilinois, called Kaskaskia, to return among them to teach them our mysteries, had great difficulty in keeping his word. The great hardships of his first voyage had brought on a dysentery, and had so enfeebled him, that he lost all hope of undertaking a second voyage. Yet, his malady having given way and almost ceased toward the close of summer in the following year, he obtained permission of his superiors to return to the Ilinois to found that noble mission.*

* By his last journal, which we publish entire from his autograph, we learn that Father Marquette was detained at the mission of St. Francis Xavier, in Green bay, during the whole summer of 1674. Recovering in September, he drew up and sent to his superiors, copies of his journal down the Mississippi, and having received orders to repair to the Ilinois, set out, on the 25th of October, with two men named Pierre Porteret and Jacques —————. They crossed the peninsula which forms the eastern side of Green bay, and began to coast along the shore of Lake Michigan, accompanied by some Ilinois and Pottawatomies. They advanced but slowly by land and water, frequently arrested by the state of the lake. On the 23d of November, the good missionary was again seized by his malady, but he pushed on, and by the 4th of December, had reached the Chicago, which connects by portage with the Ilinois. But the river was now

He set out for this purpose in the month of November, 1674, from the Bay of the Fetid, with two men, one of whom had already made that voyage with him. During a month's navigation on the Ilinois lake, he was pretty well; but as soon as the snow began to fall, he was again seized with the dysentery which forced him to stop in the river which leads to the Ilinois. There they raised a cabin and spent the winter in such want of every comfort that his illness constantly increased; he felt that God had granted him the grace he had so often asked, and he even plainly told his companions so, assuring them that he would die of that illness, and on that voyage. To prepare his soul for its departure, he began that rude wintering by the exercises of St. Ignatius,* which, in spite of his great bodily weakness, he

frozen, and though they attempted to proceed, the pious missionary submitted to the necessity, and deprived even of the consolation of saying mass on his patronal feast, the Immaculate Conception, resolved at last, on the 14th, to winter at the portage, as his illness increased. His Indian companions now left him, and though aided by some French-traders, he suffered much during the following months. Of this, however, he says nothing. "The Blessed Virgin Immaculate," says his journal, "has taken such care of us during our wandering, that we have never wanted food; we have lived very comfortably; my illness not having prevented my saying mass every day." How little can we realize the faith and self-denial which could give so pleasant a face to a winter passed by a dying man in a cabin open to the winds. The Ilinois aware of his presence so near them, sent indeed; but so gross were their ideas of his object, that they asked the dying missionary for powder and goods. "I have come to instruct you, and speak to you of the prayer," was his answer. "Powder, I have not; we come to spread peace through the land, and I do not wish to see you at war with the Miamis." As for goods, he could but encourage the French to continue their trade. Despairing at last of human remedies, the missionary and his two pious companions began a novena, or nine days' devotion to the Blessed Virgin Immaculate. From its close he began to gain strength, and when the freshet compelled them to remove their cabin, on the 29th of March he set out again on his long interrupted voyage, the river being now open; his last entry is of the 6th of April, when the wind and cold compelled them to halt. He never found time to continue his journal; and his last words are a playful allusion to the hardships undergone by the traders, in which he sympathized, while insensible of his own.

* These are a series of meditation on the great truths of religion — the object

performed with deep sentiments of devotion, and great heavenly consolation; and then spent the rest of his time in colloquies with all heaven, having no more intercourse with earth, amid these deserts, except with his two companions whom he confessed and communicated twice a week, and exhorted as much as his strength allowed. Some time after Christmas, in order to obtain the grace not to die without having taken possession of his beloved mission, he invited his companions to make a novena in honor of the Immaculate Conception of the Blessed Virgin. Contrary to all human expectation he was heard and recovering found himself able to proceed to the Ilinois town as soon as navigation was free; this he accomplished in great joy, setting out on the 29th of March. He was eleven days on the way, where he had ample matter for suffering, both from his still sickly state, and from the severity and inclemency of the weather.

Having at last reached the town on the 8th of April, he was received there as an angel from heaven; and after having several times assembled the chiefs of the nation with all the old men (anciens),* to sow in their minds the first seed of the gospel; after carrying his instructions into the cabins, which were always filled with crowds of people, he resolved to speak to all publicly in general assembly, which he convoked in the open fields, the cabins being too small for the meeting. A beautiful prairie near the town was chosen for the great council; it was adorned in the fashion of the country, being spread with mats and bear skins, and the father having hung on cords some pieces of India taffety, attached to them four large pictures

of man's creation, the work of his redemption, and the means of attaining the former by participating in the latter. To spend a number of days in revolving these serious thoughts is called making a retreat.

* I have my doubts whether *anciens*, in these French accounts, does not mean sachems, the rulers of the tribe.

of the Blessed Virgin, which were thus visible on all sides. The auditory was composed of five hundred chiefs and old men, seated in a circle around the father, while the youth stood without to the number of fifteen hundred, not counting women and children, who are very numerous, the town being composed of five or six hundred fires.

The father spoke to all this gathering, and addressed them ten words by ten presents which he made them;* he explained to them the principal mysteries of our religion, and the end for which he had come to their country; and especially he preached to them Christ crucified, for it was the very eve of the great day on which he died on the cross for them, as well as for the rest of men. He then said mass.

Three days after, on Easter Sunday, things being arranged in the same manner as on Thursday, he celebrated the holy mysteries for the second time, and by these two sacrifices, the first ever offered there to God, he took possession of that land in the name of Jesus Christ, and gave this mission the name of the Immaculate Conception of the Blessed Virgin.

He was listened to with universal joy and approbation by all this people, who earnestly besought him to return as soon as possible among them, since his malady obliged him to leave them. The father, on his part, showed them the affection he bore them, his satisfaction at their conduct, and gave his word that he or some other of our fathers would return to continue this mission so happily begun. This promise he repeated again and again, on parting with them to begin his

---

* Words addressed to Indians, when not accompanied by a wampum belt, were considered unimportant; and the missionary who first announced the gospel in a village, always spoke by the belt of *the prayer,* which he held in his hand, and which remained to witness his words when the sound had died away.

journey. He set out amid such marks of friendship from these good people, that they escorted him with pomp more than thirty leagues of the way, contending with one another for the honor of carrying his little baggage.

SECTION II.

THE FATHER IS COMPELLED TO LEAVE HIS ILINOIS MISSION.—HIS LAST ILLNESS.—HIS PRECIOUS DEATH AMID THE FORESTS.

AFTER the Ilinois had taken leave of the father, filled with a great idea of the gospel, he continued his voyage, and soon after reached the Ilinois lake, on which he had nearly a hundred leagues to make by an unknown route, because he was obliged to take the southern [eastern] side of the lake, having gone thither by the northern [western]. His strength, however, failed so much, that his men despaired of being able to carry him alive to their journey's end; for, in fact, he became so weak and exhausted, that he could no longer help himself, nor even stir, and had to be handled and carried like a child.

He nevertheless maintained in this state an admirable equanimity, joy, and gentleness, consoling his beloved companions, and encouraging them to suffer courageously all the hardships of the way, assuring them that our Lord would not forsake them when he was gone. During this navigation he began to prepare more particularly for death, passing his time in colloquies with our Lord, with His holy mother, with his angel-guardian, or with all heaven. He was often heard pronouncing these words : " I believe that my Redeemer liveth," or, " Mary, mother of grace, mother of God, remember me." Besides a spiritual reading made for him every day, he toward the close asked them to read him his meditation on the preparation for death, which he carried about him : he recited his breviary every day; and although he was so low, that both sight and strength had greatly failed, he did not omit it till the last day of his life, when his companions induced him to cease, as it was shortening his days.

A week before his death, he had the precaution to bless some holy water, to serve him during the rest of his illness, in his agony, and at his burial, and he instructed his companions how to use it.

The eve of his death, which was a Friday, he told them, all radiant with joy, that it would take place on the morrow. During the whole day he conversed with them about the manner of his burial, the way in which he should be laid out, the place to be selected for his interment; he told them how to arrange his hands, feet, and face, and directed them to raise a cross over his grave. He even went so far as to enjoin them, only three hours before he expired, to take his chapel-bell, as soon as he was dead, and ring it while they carried him to the grave. Of all this he spoke so calmly and collectedly, that you would have thought that he spoke of the death and burial of another, and not of his own.

Thus did he speak with them as they sailed along the lake, till, perceiving the mouth of a river, with an eminence on the bank which he thought suited for his burial, he told them that it was the place of his last repose. They wished, however, to pass on, as the weather permitted it, and the day was not far advanced; but God raised a contrary wind, which obliged them to return and enter the river pointed out by Father Marquette.*

* A marginal note says, "This river now bears the father's name." It was indeed long called Marquette river, but from recent maps the name seems to

They then carried him ashore, kindled a little fire, and raised for him a wretched bark cabin, where they laid him as little uncomfortably as they could ; but they were so overcome by sadness, that, as they afterward said, they did not know what they were doing.

The father being thus stretched on the shore, like St. Francis Xavier, as he had always so ardently desired, and left alone amid those forests — for his companions were engaged in unloading — he had leisure to repeat all the acts in which he had employed himself during the preceding days.

When his dear companions afterward came up, all dejected, he consoled them, and gave them hopes that God would take care of them after his death in those new and unknown countries; he gave them his last instructions, thanked them for all the charity they had shown him during the voyage, begged their pardon for the trouble he had given them, and directed them also to ask pardon in his name of all our fathers and brothers in the Ottawa country, and then disposed them to receive the sacrament of penance, which he administered to them for the last time ; he also gave them a paper on which he had written all his faults since his last confession, to be given to his superior, to oblige him to pray more earnestly for him. In fine, he promised not to forget them in heaven, and as he was very kind-hearted, and knew them to be worn out with the toil of the preceding days, he bade them go and take a little rest, assuring them that his hour was not yet so near, but that he would wake them when it was time, as in fact he did, two or three hours after, calling them when about to enter his agony.

have been forgotten. Its Indian name is Notispescago, and according to others, Aniniondibeganining. It is a very small stream, not more than fifteen paces long, being the outlet of a small lake, as Charlevoix assures us.

When they came near he embraced them for the last time, while they melted in tears at his feet; he then asked for the holy water and his reliquary, and taking off his crucifix which he wore around his neck, he placed it in the hands of one, asking him to hold it constantly opposite him, raised before his eyes; then feeling that he had but a little time to live, he made a last effort, clasped his hands, and with his eyes fixed sweetly on his crucifix, he pronounced aloud his profession of faith, and thanked the Divine Majesty for the immense grace he did him in allowing him to die in the society of Jesus; to die in it as a missionary of Jesus Christ, and above all to die in it, as he had always asked, in a wretched cabin, amid the forests, destitute of all human aid.

On this he became silent, conversing inwardly with God; yet from time to time words escaped him: "Sustinuit anima mea in verba ejus," or "Mater Dei, memento mei," which were the last words he uttered before entering on his agony, which was very calm and gentle.

He had prayed his companions to remind him, when they saw him about to expire, to pronounce frequently the names of Jesus and Mary. When he could not do it himself, they did it for him; and when they thought him about to pass, one cried aloud Jesus Maria, which he several times repeated distinctly, and then, as if at those sacred names something had appeared to him, he suddenly raised his eyes above his crucifix, fixing them apparently on some object which he seemed to regard with pleasure, and thus with a countenance all radiant with smiles, he expired without a struggle, as gently as if he had sunk into a quiet sleep.

His two poor companions, after shedding many tears over his body, and having laid it out as he had directed, carried it devoutly to the grave, ringing the bell according to his injunction, and raised a large cross near it to serve as a mark for passers-by.

When they talked of embarking, one of them, who for several days had been overwhelmed with sadness, and so racked in body by acute pains that he could neither eat nor breathe without pain, resolved, while his companion was preparing all for embarkation, to go to the grave of his good father, and pray him to intercede for him with the glorious Virgin, as he had promised, not doubting but that he was already in heaven. He accordingly knelt down, said a short prayer, and having respectfully taken some earth from the grave, he put it on his breast, and the pain immediately ceased ; his sadness was changed into a joy, which continued during the rest of his voyage.

SECTION III.

WHAT OCCURRED IN THE TRANSPORT OF THE BONES OF THE LATE FATHER MARQUETTE, WHICH WERE TAKEN UP ON THE 19TH OF MAY, 1677, THE ANNIVERSARY OF HIS DEATH TWO YEARS BEFORE.—SKETCH OF HIS VIRTUES.

GOD did not choose to suffer so precious a deposite to remain unhonored and forgotten amid the woods. The Kiskakon Indians,* who, for the last ten years, publicly professed Christi-

---

* Of the Kiskakons little more is known than is here stated. They are, I think, first mentioned in a letter of F Allouez, in the *Relation* 1666–'67. The name Kiskakon given in this narrative, and the *Relation* of 1678–'79 is, I suppose, the longer name Kichkakoueiac of the *Relation* of 1672–'73, which places them at that time near Sault St. Mary's, the Hurons being then alone at Mackinac. The last *Relation* (1673–'79) states their number then at 1,300, all Christians; they subsequently appear in collision with the Iroquois, but are soon lost sight of; if they have disappeared from the nations, it was not in their infidelity; many, we may trust, were faithful to the graces they received, and if they have melted away before our encroachments, it is a reason why we should bless the men who sought to save their souls without caring whether a century later any

anity in which they were first instructed by Father Marquette, when stationed at Lapointe du Saint Esprit at the extremity of Lake Superior, were hunting last winter on the banks of Lake Ilinois; and as they were returning early in spring, they resolved to pass by the tomb of their good father, whom they tenderly loved; and God even gave them the thought of taking his remains and bringing them to our church at the mission of St. Ignatius, at Missilimakinac, where they reside.

They accordingly repaired to the spot and deliberated together, resolved to act with their father, as they usually do with those whom they respect; they accordingly opened the grave, unrolled the body, and though the flesh and intestines were all dried up, they found it whole without the skin being in any way injured. This did not prevent their dissecting it according to custom; they washed the bones, and dried them in the sun, then putting them neatly in a box of birch bark, they set out to bear them to the house of St. Ignatius.

The convoy consisted of nearly thirty canoes in excellent order; including even a good number of Iroquois who had joined our Algonquins to honor the ceremony. As they approached our house, Father Nouvel, who is superior, went to meet them with Father Pierson,* accompanied by all the French Indians of the place, and having caused the convoy to stop, made the ordinary interrogations to verify the fact, that the body which

would exist to show the endurance of their labors. It has been justly remarked of the catholic missions that, "they ended only with the extinction of the tribe."

* Father Nouvel was the Ottawa, and Father Pierson the Huron missionary. Each nation had its village apart, at a distance of three quarters of a league from each other. The church here spoken of was built apparently in 1674, while F. Marquette was there (*Rel.* 1672–'73, and 1673–'79); it lay nearest the Huron village, which Hennepin thus describes: "It is surrounded with palisades twenty-five feet high, and situated near a great point of land opposite the island of Missilimakinac."—*Description de la Louisiane*, p. 62.

they bore was really Father Marquette's. Then, before landing, he intoned the "De Profundis" in sight of the thirty canoes still on the water, and of all the people on the shores; after this the body was carried to the church, observing all that the ritual prescribes for such ceremonies. It remained exposed under a pall stretched as if over a coffin all that day, which was Whitsun-Monday, the 8th of June; and the next day, when all the funeral honors had been paid it, it was deposited in a little vault in the middle of the church, where he reposes as the guardian angel of our Ottawa missions. The Indians often come to pray on his tomb, and to say no more, a young woman of about nineteen or twenty, whom the late father had instructed and baptized last year, having fallen sick, asked Father Nouvel to bleed her, and give her some remedies; but in place of medicine he bade her go for three days and say a pater and ave on the tomb of Father Marquette. She did so, and before the third day, was entirely cured without bleeding or other remedies.

Father James Marquette, of the province of Champagne, died at the age of thirty-eight, of which he had spent twenty-one in the society, namely twelve in France, and nine in Canada. He was sent to the missions of the upper Algonquins, called Ottawas, and labored there with all the zeal that could be expected in a man who had taken St. Francis Xavier as the model of his life and death. He imitated that great saint, not only in the variety of the barbarous languages which he learned, but also by the vastness of his zeal which made him bear the faith to the extremity of this new world, nearly eight hundred leagues from here, in forests where the name of Jesus had never been announced.

He always begged of God to end his days in these toilsome missions, and to die amid the woods like his beloved St.

Francis Xavier, in utter want of everything. To attain this he daily employed the merits of Christ and the intercession of the Immaculate Virgin, for whom his devotion was equally rare and tender.

By such powerful mediators, he obtained what he so earnestly asked, since he had the happiness to die like the apostle of the Indies, in a wretched cabin on the banks of Lake Ilinois, forsaken by all.

We could say much of the rare virtues of this generous missionary, of his zeal which made him carry the faith so far, and announce the gospel to so many nations unknown to us; of his meekness which endeared him to every one, and which made him all to all—French with the French, Huron with the Hurons, Algonquin with the Algonquins; of his childlike candor in discovering his mind to his superiors, and even to all persons with an ingenuousness that gained all hearts, of his angelic purity and continual union with God.

But his predominant virtue was a most rare and singular devotion to the Blessed Virgin, and especially to the mystery of the Immaculate Conception; it was a pleasure to hear him preach or speak on this subject. Every conversation and letter of his contained something about the Blessed Virgin Immaculate, as he always styled her. From the age of nine, he fasted every Saturday; and from his most tender youth began to recite daily the little office of the Conception, and inspired all to adopt this devotion. For some months before his death, he daily recited, with his two men, a little chaplet of the Immaculate Conception, which he had arranged in this form; after the creed, they said one " Our Father and hail Mary," then four times these words : " Hail daughter of God the Father, hail mother of God the Son, hail spouse of the Holy Ghost, hail temple of the whole Trinity, by thy holy virginity and immaculate conception, O most pure Virgin, cleanse my flesh and my heart. In the name of the Father, and of the Son, and of the Holy Ghost," and last of all the "Glory be to the Father," &c., the whole being thrice repeated.

He never failed to say the mass of the Conception, or at least the collect, whenever he could; he thought of nothing else scarcely by night or by day, and to leave us an eternal mark of his sentiments, he gave the name of the Conception to the Ilinois mission.

So tender a devotion to the mother of God, deserved some singular grace, and she accordingly granted him the favor he had always asked, to die on a Saturday;* and his two companions had no doubt that she appeared to him at the hour of his death when, after pronouncing the names of Jesus and Mary, he suddenly raised his eyes above his crucifix, fixing them on an object which he regarded with such pleasure, and a joy that lit up his countenance; and they, from that moment, believed that he had surrendered his soul into the hands of his good mother.

One of the last letters which he wrote to the superior of the missions before his great voyage, will be a sufficient instance of his sentiments. It began thus :—

"The Blessed Virgin Immaculate has obtained for me the grace to arrive here in good health, and resolved to correspond to God's designs upon me, since he has destined me to the voyage to the south. I have no other thought than to do what God wills. I fear nothing; neither the Nadouessii, nor the meeting of nations alarms me. One of two things must come: either God will punish me for my crimes and omissions, or else he will share his cross with me (for I have not

---

* In the devotions of catholics, Saturday among the days of the week, like May among the months, is especially set apart to honor her whom Jesus loved and honored as a mother.

borne it yet since I have been in this country, though, perhaps, it has been obtained for me by the Blessed Virgin Immaculate), or perhaps death to cease to offend God. For this I will endeavor to hold myself ready, abandoning myself entirely in his hands. I pray your reverence not to forget me, and to obtain of God, that I may not remain ungrateful for the favors he heaps upon me."

There was found among his papers a book entitled, "The Conduct of God toward a Missionary," in which he shows the excellence of that vocation, the advantages for self-sanctification to be found in it, and the care which God takes of his gospel-laborers. This little work shows the spirit of God by which he was actuated.

NARRATIVE

OF

A VOYAGE MADE TO THE ILINOIS,

BY

*FATHER CLAUDE ALLOUEZ.**

SECTION I.

FATHER ALLOUEZ SETS OUT ON THE ICE.— A YOUNG MAN KILLED BY A BEAR.—VENGEANCE TAKEN.—VARIOUS CURIOSITIES ON THE WAY.

WHILE preparing for my departure, as the weather was not yet suitable, I made some visits in the bay where I baptized two sick adults, one of whom died next day; the other lived a month longer; he was a poor old man, who

---

* "Father Claude Allouez, has imperishably connected his name with the progress of discovery in the west," says Bancroft. Unhonored among us now, he was not inferior in zeal or ability to any of the great missionaries of his time. He is not, indeed, encircled with that halo of sanctity which characterizes the first Franciscan and Jesuit missionaries of New France, nor do his writings display the learning and refinement which show in some the greatness of their sacrifice; but, as a fearless and devoted missionary, one faithful to his high calling, a man of zeal and worth, he is entitled to every honor. No record tells us the time or place of his birth. We meet him first as a Jesuit, seeking a foreign mission. An entry in his journal has been preserved, in which, under the date of March 3d, 1657, he expresses his rapture on receiving permission to embark for Canada. That he was not led by any erroneous idea of the field which he solicited, we know by his own words. He sought only to labor and suffer; man can not command results, nor will his reward depend upon them. "To convert our barbarians, or savages, of Canada," says he, "we need work no miracle but that

being decrepit and half deaf, was the laughing stock and out-
cast of all, even of his children; but God did not cast him

of doing them good, and suffering without complaint, except to God, regarding
ourselves as useless servants."

He sailed from France with two lay brothers in the vessel which took out the
new governor Viscount d'Argenson, in 1658, and by the eleventh of July arrived
safely at Quebec. Selected for the Algonquin missions, he soon after began the
study of the Indian languages. In the following year he saw two of his order,
Garreau and Druilletes, embark for Lake Superior, where Father Jogues and
Father Raymbault had planted the cross seventeen years before, to continue the
interrupted work; but one was killed, the other abandoned near Montreal.
When made superior at Three-Rivers, in 1660, he saw his predecessor, the fearless René Menard, depart for a distant goal, to die amid the rocks and woods
of the Menominee, on his way to Green Bay. This field of toil and danger
was still the object of Allouez' desires. Destined to it in 1664, he reached Montreal, but the Ottawas had not come there as late as usual. He had now
to wait another year; but, with him, time rolled not away in idleness; a
thorough Algonquin, not unacquainted with Iroquois, objects of zeal were
everywhere to be found. On the 14th of May, 1665, he again left Quebec to
meet them; the "Angels of the upper Algonquins" at last arrive; for so in
his desire does he call the brutal men whose cruel treatment of the previous
missionaries would have appalled any heart not borne up by supernatural motives. On the 7th of August, the flotilla finally started, and Allouez, after much
suffering and ill-treatment, dauntlessly struggled on, and, by the first of September, was at Sault St. Mary's. Thrice had the Jesuits taken possession of that
spot in the name of catholicity; it was not now to be a permanent centre. He
did not stop here; he explored, in his frail canoe, the whole southern shore of
the vast upper lake, whose icy waters contrast so strangely with the fantastic
scenery of the shore, still marked by the traces of that terrible fire which shiv-
ered its crags into a thousand forms, and poured the molten copper over them as
if in mockery and sport. His first mission was at the Outchibouec (Ojibwa, or
Chippeway) village of Chegoimegon. Here, in October, rose his chapel, dedicated to the Holy Ghost. Some Hurons and the Algonquin converts of Menard
were already there; to increase the number of the faithful, Allouez entered the
arena to struggle till death, with the wild superstition of the Ottawa. Ten or
twelve lake tribes were assembled at once in council at the spot. Pottawatomies,
Sacs, Foxes, and even Ilinois, swelled the numbers of those who gathered around
that lone cross of the wilderness, with nations from the western sea, Dahcotahs,
Assiniboins and Winnebagoes, with their Tartar dialect and thought. To all
these he announced the intolerant faith of the cross, which required a total re-
nunciation of their traditions, an unreserved acceptance of its dogmas. Each
tribe departed with this first glimpse of truth, prepared to receive a clear
development as time went on. And now came tidings that touched the heart of
Allouez; on a lake north of Superior, were gathered some Nipissings, sad rem-
nants of a once powerful tribe, but now like the Huron, Christians and fugitives be-

out; he did him the grace to enrol him among his children by baptism, and to receive him into heaven, as I have every reason to believe.

fore the face of the Iroquois. Menard died while seeking the Huron; but unappalled by aught, Allouez hastened to their relief. Scarcely had he reached Chegoimegon again, in 1667, when a flotilla was about starting for Quebec; he embarked to secure companions, and explain to his superiors the vastness of the new field which he had seen, and of the still greater, but untried one which lay along the mighty "Mes-sipi." On the 4th of August he reached that city, the 6th embarked again for the west with the aid he needed. Father Louis Nicholas, and a lay brother set out with him. Once in the west, he resumed his toils, as though returned from a voyage of pleasure, and struggled on another year at the lake. Then joined by Marquette and later by Dablon, he hastened to a new field. He mounted Fox river and laid the foundation of the mission of St. Francis Xavier. In 1671, the great council of the French commander, with the Indians, required the presence of the missionaries, and especially of Allouez, at the Sault St. Mary's as interpreters. Nouvel was now superior of the western missions, and from him they received a new impulse. Of the three missionary stations now established, the Sault, Mackinaw, and Green Bay, the last was given to Allouez. In 1672, aided by F. André, he instructed the Foxes and Fire nation, and again ascended Fox River to Maskoutens to preach to the Maskoutens, Miamis, Kikapoos, and Ilinois, assembled there. As he descended, he threw down a rude, unshapely rock, honored at Kakaling by the adoration of the benighted Indian. The next year he was stationed at St. James, or Maskoutens, where he planted the cross as the limit of his discoveries and labors. They were not grateful for his toil, while superstition, and indifference almost neutralized his efforts. With the Fox and Pottawatomi, he was more successful. In the following years, he was assisted by F. Silvy and F. Bonneault, and met with greater consolations.

On the death of Marquette, he was appointed to the Ilinois mission, and we now publish for the first time, the account of his journey. This visit was in 1676.

Two years afterward, he repaired to it once more, and remained till the following year, when on learning the approach of La Salle, he retired, as that great traveller had conceived a strong prejudice against him, in consequence of some correspondence between him and his fellow missionary on the Seneca country, Father Garnier. La Mothe, La Salle's lieutenant, had even required the Seneca sachems to cause the latter to leave the lodge at a conference between them. Allouez cared not to meet, in anger, La Salle, whom he had doubtless known in France before, when he was a Jesuit like himself; he therefore returned to his missions in Wisconsin to wait till the mind of the gifted but irritable explorer should recover from its false impressions. Unfortunately it proved the reverse, if some accounts are to be credited; La Salle implicated him in some efforts made by the western traders to excite the Ilinois against him. To clear Father Allouez of this charge, we need no better proof than the friendly relations between him and Tonty, than whom there was surely no man more faithful to the interest and honor of La Salle. Allouez went to Ilinois again in 1684, with

In another visit which I made to the nation of the Outa-gamies (Foxes), I baptized six children almost all at the point of death. I was much consoled to see a marked change in the mind of these people; God visits them by his scourges to render them more docile to our instructions.

After these excursions, the time being proper for departing, I embarked about the close of October, 1676, in a canoe with two men to endeavor to go and winter with the Ilinois; but I had not got far when the ice prevented us, so early had the winter set in. This obliged us to lie to and wait till it was strong enough to bear us; and it was only in February that we undertook a very extraordinary kind of navigation, for instead of putting the canoe in the water, we put it on the ice, on which a favorable wind carried it along by sails, as if it was was on water. When the wind failed us, instead of paddles, we used ropes to drag it as horses do a carriage. Passing near the Poüteoütamis, I learned that a young man had been lately killed by the bears. I had previously baptized him at Lapointe du St. Esprit, and was acquainted with his parents; this obliged me to turn a little off my way to go and console them. They told me that the bears get fat in the fall and re-main so, and even grow fatter during the whole winter, al-though they do not eat as naturalists have remarked. They

Durantaye, when he probably remained for some time. He was there in 1687, when the survivors of La Salle's last expedition reached Fort St. Louis, in Ilinois, but left for Mackinaw on the arrival of F. Anastasius Douay, and M. Cavelier, in consequence of their false report that La Salle was still alive. Father Allouez, however, still clung to his beloved Ilinois mission, which events had thus strangely disturbed; and I am inclined to think, from a deed which fell into my hands, that he was at Fort St. Louis, in the winter of 1689. If so, it was his last visit. A letter dated in August, 1690, details the virtues of the great and holy missionary of the west. He had gone to receive the reward of his labors.

The authorities for his life are the superior's journal, the *Relations* from 1663–'64 to 1671–'72; *MS. Rel.* 1672–'73, 1673–'79, 1678; MSS. of a Jesuit, in 1690; Joutel and Tonty's journals published in *Hist. Coll. of Louisiana.*

hide in hollow trees, especially the females, to bring forth their young, or else they lie on fir branches which they tear off on purpose to make a bed on the snow, which they do not leave all winter, unless discovered by the hunters, and their dogs trained to this chase. This young man having discovered one hidden in some fir-branches, fired all the arrows of his quiver at him. The bear feeling himself wounded, but not mortally, rose, rushed upon him, clawed off his scalp, and tearing out his bowels, scattered him all in pieces around. I found his mother in deep affliction ; we offered up together prayers for the deceased, and though my presence had at first redoubled her grief, she wiped away her tears, saying for consolation: "Paulinus is dead; that good Paulinus whom thou didst always come to call to prayer."

Then to avenge, as they said, this murder, the relatives and friends of the deceased made war on the bears while they were good—that is, during the winter; for in summer they are lean, and so famished, that they eat even toads and snakes. The war was so vigorous, that in a little while they killed more than five hundred, which they shared with us, saying that God had given them into our hands, to make them atone for the death of this young man who had been so cruelly treated by one of their nation.

Twelve leagues from the Poûteaoûatami town we entered a very deep bay, whence we transported our canoe across the wood to the great lake of the Ilinois [Michigan]. This portage was a league and a half. On the eve of St. Joseph, the patron of all Canada, finding ourselves on the lake, we gave it the name of that great saint, and shall henceforth call it Lake St. Joseph. We accordingly embarked on the 23d of May, and had much to do with the ice, through which we had to break a passage. The water was so cold, that it froze on our oars, and on the side of the canoe which the sun did not reach.

It pleased God to deliver us from the danger we were in on landing, when a gust of wind drove the cakes of ice on one side of our canoe, and the other on the ice which was fast to the shore. Our great trouble was, that the rivers being still frozen, we could not enter them till the 3d of April. We consecrated that which we at last entered in holy week by planting a large cross on the shore, in order that the Indians, who go there in numbers to hunt—either in canoes on the lake, or on foot in the woods—might remember the instructions we had given them on that mystery, and that the sight of it might excite them to pray. The next day we saw a rock seven or eight feet out of water, and two or three fathoms around, and called it the Pitch rock. In fact, we saw the pitch running down in little drops on the side which was warmed by the sun. We gathered some, and found it good to pitch our canoes, and I even use it to seal my letters.* We also saw, the same day, another rock, a little smaller, part in and part out of water; the part washed by the water was of a very bright and clear red. Some days after, we saw a stream running from a hill, the waters of which seemed mineral; the sand is red, and the Indians said it came from a little lake where they have found pieces of copper.

We advanced coasting always along vast prairies that stretched away beyond our sight; from time to time we saw trees, but so ranged that they seemed planted designedly to form alleys more agreeable to the sight than those of orchards. The foot of these trees is often watered by little streams, where we saw herds of stags and does drinking and feeding quietly on the young grass. We followed these vast plains

---

* An American mineral, resembling asphaltum. It is of a brown color, inclining to black, and sometimes so liquid that it flows in a stream down the sides of this rock.—F.

for twenty leagues, and often said, " Benedicite opera Domini Domino."

After making seventy-six leagues on Lake St. Joseph, we at last entered the river which leads to the Ilinois. I here met eighty Indians of the country, by whom I was handsomely received. The chief advanced about thirty steps to meet me, holding in one hand a firebrand and in the other a feathered calumet. As he drew near, he raised it to my mouth, and himself lit the tobacco, which obliged me to pretend to smoke. He then led me into his cabin, and, giving me the most honorable place, addressed me thus :—

" Father! take pity on me : let me return with thee, to accompany thee and lead thee to my village ; my meeting with thee to-day will be fatal to me, unless I profit by it. Thou bearest to us the gospel and the prayer : if I lose the occasion of hearing thee, I shall be punished by the loss of my nephews, whom thou seest so numerous, but who will assuredly be defeated by the enemy. Embark, then, with us, that I may profit by thy coming into our land."

With these words he embarked at the same time as ourselves, and we soon after reached his village.

SECTION II.

FATHER ALLOUEZ ARRIVES AT THE ILINOIS TOWN.—DESCRIPTION OF IT AND THE COUNTRY.—THE FAITH PROCLAIMED TO ALL THESE NATIONS.

In spite of all our efforts to hasten on, it was the 27th of April, before I could reach Kachkachkia, a large Ilinois town.   I immediately entered the cabin where Father Marquette had lodged, and the sachems with all the people being assembled, I told them the object of my coming among them, namely, to preach to them the true, living, and immortal God, and his only Son, Jesus Christ.   They listened very attentively to my whole discourse, and thanked me for the trouble I took for their salvation.

I found this village much increased since last year.   It was before composed of only one nation, the Kachkachkia.   There are now eight; the first having called the others who dwelt in the neighborhood of the Missipi.   You could not easily form an idea of the number of Indians who compose this town ; they are lodged in three hundred and fifty-one cabins, easily counted, for they are mostly ranged on the banks of the river.

The place which they have selected for their abode is situated at 40° 42′ ; it has on one side a prairie of vast extent, and on the other an expanse of marsh which makes the air unhealthy, and often loaded with mists ; this causes much sickness and frequent thunder.   They, however, like this post, because from it they can easily discover their enemies.*

* This and the position assigned to the town of the Kaskaskias (40° 42′) would bring it near Rockfort, making allowance for the old latitude.   When Father Marquette first visited it, he found seventy-four cabins : this was in 1673.   The next year it had increased to five or six hundred fires, which, at the rate of four fires to a cabin, gives one hundred to one hundred and fifty cabins, with a population of two thousand men, besides women and children.   Father Allouez visiting it now in 1677, is very exact, and gives the number of cabins as three

These Indians are in character hardy, proud, and valiant. They are at war with eight or nine tribes; they do not use fire-arms, as they find them too awkward, and too slow; they carry them, however, when they march against nations unacquainted with their use, to terrify them by the noise, and thus rout them. They ordinarily carry only the war-club, bow, and a quiver full of arrows, which they discharge so adroitly and quickly, that men armed with guns, have hardly time to raise them to the shoulder. They also carry a large buckler made of skins of wild cattle; which is arrow-proof, and covers the whole body.

They have many wives, of whom they are extremely jealous, leaving them on the least suspicion. The women usually behave well, and are modestly dressed, though the men are not, having no shame of their nakedness.

They live on Indian corn, and other fruits of the earth, which they cultivate on the prairies, like other Indians. They eat fourteen kinds of roots which they find in the prairies; they made me eat them; I found them good and very sweet. They gather, on trees or plants, fruits of forty-two different kinds, which are excellent; they catch twenty-five kinds of fish, including eels. They hunt cattle, deer, turkeys, cats, a

hundred and fifty-one. In 1680, the Recollect Father Membré estimates the population of the great village at seven or eight thousand, in four or five hundred cabins — this did not include the Kaskaskias, whom he seems to place on the Chicago river. Hennepin, at the same time, estimates it at "four hundred and sixty cabins, made like long bowers, covered with double mats of flat rushes, so well sowed as to be impenetrable to wind, snow, and rain. Each cabin has four or five fires, and each fire one or two families."—(p. 137.) It would seem, then, that Bancroft rejects too lightly the estimate given by Father Rale, in the *Lettres Edifiantes*, where he estimates their number at three hundred cabins, each of four or five fires, and two families to a fire. When their decadence began, they disappeared with great rapidity. Charlevoix, in 1721, makes their number then to have been very inconsiderable, although he gives no estimate of the population of the Illinois, who still formed five distinct villages. At present, the remnant of the tribe does not comprise a hundred souls, yet all who remain are Christians.

kind of tiger, and other animals, of which they reckon twenty-two kinds, and forty kinds of game and birds. In the lower part of the river there are, I am told, salt springs, from which they make salt; I can not speak from my own experience. They assure me, too, that there are quarries near their town of slate as fine as ours. I have seen here, as in the Ottawa country, copper, found here as elsewhere, on the banks of the river in lumps. They tell me too, that there are rocks of pitch like that I saw on the banks of Lake St. Joseph. The Indians cut it and find silvery veins, which, when pounded, give a fine red paint. They also find other veins, from which the pitch runs; when thrown in the fire, it burns like ours.

This is all that I could remark in this country, during the short stay I made there. I will now tell what I did for Christianity.

As I had but little time to remain, having come only to acquire the necessary information for the perfect establishment of a mission, I immediately set to work to give all the instruction I could to these eight different nations, by whom, by the help of God, I made myself sufficiently understood.

I would go to the cabin of the chief of the particular tribe that I wished to instruct, and there preparing a little altar with my chapel ornaments, I exposed a crucifix, before which I explained the mysteries of our faith. I could not desire a greater number of auditors, nor a more favorable attention. They brought me their youngest children to be baptized, those older, to be instructed. They repeated themselves all the prayers that I taught them. In a word, after I had done the same in all the eight nations, I had the consolation of seeing Christ acknowledged by so many tribes, who needed only careful cultivation to become good Christians. This we hope to give hereafter, at leisure.

I laid the foundation of this mission by the baptism of thirty-five children, and a sick adult, who soon after died, with one of the infants, to go and take possession of heaven in the name of the whole nation. And we too, to take possession of these tribes in the name of Jesus Christ, on the 3d of May, the feast of the Holy Cross, erected in the midst of the town a cross twenty-five feet high, chanting the Vexilla Regis in the presence of a great number of Ilinois of all tribes, of whom I can say, in truth, that they did not take Jesus Christ crucified for a folly, nor for a scandal; on the contrary, they witnessed the ceremony with great respect, and heard all that I said on the mystery with admiration. The children even went to kiss the cross through devotion, and the old earnestly commended me to place it well so that it could not fall.

The time of my departure having come, I took leave of all these tribes, and left them in a great desire of seeing me as soon as possible, which I more willingly induced them to expect; as, on the one hand, I have reason to thank God for the little crosses he has afforded me in this voyage, and on the other, I see the harvest all ready and very abundant. The devil will, doubtless, oppose us, and perhaps will, for the purpose, use the war which the Iroquois seek to make on the Ilinois. I pray our Lord to avert it, that so fair a beginning be not entirely ruined.

"The next year, namely, 1678, Father Allouez set out to return to this mission, and to remain there two years in succession, to labor more solidly for the conversion of these tribes. We have since learned that the Iroquois made an incursion as far as there, but were beaten by the Ilinois. This will go far to enkindle the war between these nations, and do much to injure this mission, if God does not interpose."*

* The concluding paragraph of this narrative is in the handwriting of Father Claude Dablon, the superior of the missions at the time.

BIBLIOGRAPHICAL NOTICE

OF

THE "ETABLISSEMENT DE LA FOI,"

BY

FATHER CHRISTIAN LE CLERCQ, RECOLLECT.

THIS curious and now rare work is the source whence all the following narratives, except Hennepin's, are drawn. It was published at Paris, by Aimable Auroy, in 1691, with the following very comprehensive title: "First Establishment of the Faith in New France, containing the Publication of the Gospel, the History of the French Colonies, and the famous Discoveries from the Mouth of the St. Lawrence, Louisiana, and the River Colbert, to the Gulf of Mexico, accomplished under the Direction of the late Monsieur de la Salle, by Order of the King, with the Victories gained in Canada, by the Arms of his Majesty over the English and Iroquois, in 1690. Dedicated to M. de Comte de Frontenac, Governor and Lieutenant-General of New France, by Father Christian le Clercq, Recollect Missionary of the Province of St. Anthony of Padua, in Arthois, and Warden of the Recollects of Lens."

Of Father le Clercq, under whose name the work is thus published, we know little beyond what we glean from this work, and from his *Relation de Gaspesie*. He was a zealous and devout missionary on the wild coast of Gaspé, where he lived in most cordial and friendly relations with the neighboring Jesuit missionaries, especially with Father Bigot, who speaks of him in the highest terms, as le Clercq did of him and his labors. He was the first novice of the province to which he belonged, and one of the first religious sent by it to Canada, in 1675. After spending five years as missionary at Isle Percée and Gaspé, he returned to Europe, was concerned in the establishment of a church and mission at Montreal, resumed for a time his missionary career, and was subsequently employed as superior in France. His *Relation de Gaspesie* is a description of his own field and his own labors; the *Etablissement* assumes to be a general history of religion in Canada, and of La Salle's voyages, as tending to the establishment of missions. How far it realizes the promise of the title-page, we shall soon see.

Had this work been a mere satirical pamphlet, we could at once understand it, and give it its proper value; but in this light it can not be regarded; it contains much historical information, especially with respect to La Salle, being the first printed account of his voyage down the Mississippi, and his last fatal attempt. A striking feature in the work is its literary skepticism, as to a great mass of early works on Canada, and the similar doubts raised subsequently as to the Etablissement itself. Le Clercq, or the real author, doubts the authenticity of the *Relation* of 1626, ascribed to F. Charles Lalemant. The ground of this doubt is completely destroyed by the title of one of the chapters in Sagard's larger work; the doubt has, however, been raised within the last few years by men of research, though probably from want of a close study of the doubting humor of the author. Having thus thrown a slur on the first Relation, he next brings the whole forty volumes of Relations, from 1632 to 1672, into the same category, because, forsooth, from his high respect for the Jesuits, he can not believe they ever wrote them; and, finally, Father Marquette's published journal, which is, however, never ascribed to him, is treated as an imposture, and his voyage as pretended, on every possible occasion.

This wholesale skepticism almost entitles him to a place with the celebrated Father Hardouin, who believed all the Greek and Latin classics to be forgeries. In a work like this, intended to show the validity of Marquette's claim, we must examine these doubts, and the person who makes them. Joutel, who contradicts the Etablissement pointedly in several places, says that it was composed on false relations, and thus gives some force to a charge brought in 1697, by the strange Hennepin, who asserts broadly that the Etablissement was published by Father Valentine le Roux, under the borrowed name of le Clercq; and he charges that the so-called narrative of Membré in the work, is really a transcript of the journal of his great voyage down the Mississippi, a copy of which he had left in le Roux's hands at Quebec. At a still later date, when all had become calm, Charlevoix states it as a common impression that Frontenac himself had a considerable hand in it. When with all this we remember that the first published narrative of Tonty is regarded as spurious, and that Mr. Sparks has irrefragably shown Hennepin's later works to be mere romances and literary thefts; the whole series of works relative to La Salle seems drawn up or moulded to suit some party views, and to unravel the whole, we must examine what parties at the time agitated Canada. We find immediately that the civil and ecclesiastical authorities were then completely at variance, chiefly from two causes: The first was what may be called the brandy war, in which Bishop Laval seeing the injury done to the Indians by the sale of liquor, had pronounced ecclesiastical censures against those who carried on the nefarious traffic: his clergy, and especially the Jesuits, sided with him and his successor entirely on this point, as being better able from daily intercourse to see the ruin of the native tribes by the use of spirituous liquors. But if the ecclesiastical authorities pronounced censures, the civil officers were not slow in taking up most curious modes of revenge; and ridicule, above all, was brought to play upon their antagonists. So far had public opinion become vitiated, that in a memoir drawn up apparently by the intendant Duchesneau with regard to the Indian village of Caughnawaga, the writer addressing the French court, deemed it necessary to defend the Jesuit missionaries against the charge of preventing the erection of any tavern on their lands at Laprairie, in the vicinity of their Indian village! The only defence made is more curious; it admits the fact, but denies the necessity of taverns there, as Montreal was full of them. In this brandy war, the Jesuits being in charge of the missions, were chiefly attacked, and soon after a new charge was made against them personally. 2. Frontenac especially insisted that Indian villages apart would never result in civilizing the natives; his plan was a complete fusion of the two races, by bringing them into perfect contact. The missionaries convinced that Indians living among the whites were irrecoverably lost, adhered pertinaciously to their original system of separate villages and gradual advancement. Frontenac's theory is much upheld by the Etablissement, and many arguments are adduced in favor of this plan which is assumed to be that of the early Recollects; but he startles us not a little, and somewhat unseats our gravity, when he tells us that it had been carried out with perfect success in the neighboring English and Dutch colonies; though, unfortunately, he does not tell us what New York or New England half-breed village resulted from the union.

But to return to ancient politics. Religion was at that time upheld by popular opinion; a man in rank or office had to practise his religious duties; indeed, he never thought of not doing so. Now these duties in the catholic church are something very positive indeed, and many in Canada found themselves under ecclesiastical censures for trading in liquor with the Indians, and saw no other alternative but that of renouncing a lucrative traffic, unless, indeed they could find more lenient confessors. A party now called for the return of the Recollects as earnestly as they had opposed it, when they deemed them too expensive. Le Clercq states this ground of recall without a word of censure; the Recollects returned, became the fashionable confessors, and were stationed at trading points. In this way they became involved in existing disputes, and favored by and favoring Frontenac, found themselves arrayed in a manner against the rest of the clergy. A general charge made about the time seems to have been, that the Jesuits had really made no discoveries, and no progress in converting the natives. With this as a principle, it would not do to allow the discovery of the Mississippi to be ascribed wholly or in part to one of the missionaries of that society; hence a work dedicated to Frontenac must naturally be a eulogy of his ideas and his friends, and a well-directed attack on his enemies. It must be, and be expected to be, a party affair. When then we attack this work, it will be simply as to these matters; in an historical point of view, as faithful to the documents on which it professes to be founded, it has, I believe, never been called in question. It is a well-written history of the Recollect missions and La Salle's voyages, the rest is satire.

The work itself consists of three parts: the first in substance an abridgment of Sagard, for the first period of French rule in Canada, down to the capture of Quebec by 1629, contains some new facts derived from manuscripts, and especially from those of the great le Caron, the founder of the Huron missions. The English carried off both the Recollects and the Jesuits whom they had invited to aid them; but as the restoration of Canada was expected, both prepared for a speedy return. For some reason, however, the French government determined to send out another missionary body, and offered Canada to the Capuchins, like the Recollects, a branch of the great Franciscan order. The Capuchins, however, declined it, and recommended the Jesuits, who were accordingly sent, and the Recollects excluded. This was their first grief, and the volume before us details their unavailing efforts to return, and the suspicions entertained of opposition, or at least of lukewarmness, on the part of the Jesuits. They are, indeed, exculpated, but the charge is constantly renewed. With this on his heart, le Clercq proceeds to the second part, that of the Jesuit missions: and here he doubts the authenticity of all their Relations, and treats the missions they describe as chimerical. In this pretended account of the progress of Christianity during the period in question, there is no historical order preserved, no mention is made of the Huron missions, their rise and fall with the nation, and the death of the various missionaries whose last moments are a sufficient proof of their sincerity in the accounts which they had given. Of the Algonquin and Montagnais missions, and their almost entire destruction by sickness and war, no notice is taken; and what is said of the Iroquois is so garbled, that it were better unsaid.

No missionary ever could have written this part; or, if he did, he must be content to rank below Hennepin. One instance will show the spirit of this portion. Speaking of the mission in New-York, in 1655–'58, he mentions the fact that Menard, at Cayuga, baptized four hundred; and adds, "Christianity must have advanced each year by still more happy and multiplied progress, and *consequently all these people must be converted.*" Then, as he finds the mass of the Iroquois in 1690, as we find them in 1850, pagans, he concludes that the accounts of the missions are false. Now, in the first place, the period of missionary effort in New York embraces only the periods from 1655 to 1658, and from 1667 to 1685; in all, not more than twenty years, with a few visits at intervals before and after these dates; in 1690, there was no missionary in New York save Father Milet, who had just been dragged to Oneida as a prisoner taken at Fort Frontenac. And as to baptisms, no fact is more clearly stated in early writers, the Relations, and all others, than this, that the baptisms were chiefly those of dying children and adults. Among the Iroquois there were, indeed, children of Christian Hurons, who could be baptized in health, but only there. Hence the baptisms gave a very slight increase to the number of living neophytes, and in time of epidemics, a very great number might be baptized, and yet the church lose in point of numbers. To begin then by assuming that 400 baptisms gave as many living members, and that ten times as many gave 4,000 is a puerility in one who is not much acquainted with the matter, but a gross deceit in one who is.

The second part then is not to be considered as historical; it notices, indeed, the coming of the Ursuline and Hospital nuns, of the Sulpitians and the bishop; but even for these we must go elsewhere for a clear account.

The third part stands on a different footing; it is mainly historical, and though marked by the prevailing prejudice, and as we shall show by gross injustice to Marquette and Joliet, is, undoubtedly, the best account of La Salle's voyages, and, for some parts, the only one we have. It is, too, an account of the rise and progress of the second Recollect missions, in a very brief form, which, with the mass of manuscripts of the time, gives rich materials for Canadian history. All that relates to La Salle is given in the present volume, for the first time, we believe, in English. The remaining portion of Le Clercq is,

6

as the title states, an account of the defeat of the English at Quebec, in 1690, by Frontenac, who had returned the previous year.

Compelled by a love of truth to be somewhat severe on both le Clercq and Hennepin, we would by no means seem to reflect generally on the Recollects of Canada. The latter committed his forgeries when cast off by his province, the former was not, I believe, the author of the objectionable parts in the work that bears his name; that two hands were employed in it, will I think, appear to any one who will read it over attentively several times. That all the Recollects should have been at the time under some prejudice is natural, owing to their position, and allowance is made for that, as we must daily make for those who can not judge of an individual without some attack on the church to which he belongs. Fortunately for all, the Recollects were soon relieved from their false position by the settlement of the disputes, and without attempting new Indian missions, labored for the good of the colony with a zeal beyond all praise. Chosen almost always as chaplains to the troops and forts, they were to be found at every French post, and thus became the earliest pastors of some of our western towns. Like the Jesuits, they were a second time excluded from Canada by the English on their conquest in the last century, and the last survivor has long since descended to the grave. A few names, and a church that bears their name, are almost all that recall to the traveller the labors and merits of the children of St. Francis.

NARRATIVE

OF THE FIRST ATTEMPT BY

M. CAVELIER DE LA SALLE

TO

EXPLORE THE MISSISSIPPI.

DRAWN UP FROM THE MANUSCRIPTS OF FATHER ZENOBIUS MEMBRÉ, A
RECOLLECT BY FATHER CHRETIEN LECLERCQ.

THE Sieur Robert Cavelier de la Salle, a native of Rouen, of one of the most distinguished families there, a man of vast intellect, brought up for literary pursuits,* capable and learned in every branch, especially in mathematics, naturally

---

* La Salle, in early life, resolved to consecrate himself to God in a religious order, and entered the Society of Jesus. After passing ten years, however, teaching and studying in their colleges, he left them — for what reason is not now known — and came to Canada to build up his fortunes, for he had lost his inheritance by the unjust provisions of the French law. His previous seclusion from the world had, perhaps, but too well fitted him for conceiving vast projects, but totally disqualified him for their successful conduct; the minute details, the cautious choice of men, the constant superintendence required in a large establishment, were foreign to his character, and we shall, in the result, see in this the cause of all his misfortunes. Like many others, he thought of finding a way to China, and began some enterprise which resulted only in giving the name of Lachine to his trading-post near Montreal. The fur trade was the great means of wealth, and he next conceived the plan of a large trading monopoly on Lake Ontario, to be centred at Fort Frontenac; from that moment, however, he raised against him all the individual traders in the Indian country, and he was soon aware that this was no speedy road to wealth. His

enterprising, prudent, and moral, had been for some years in
Canada, and had already, under the administration of De
Courcelles and Talon, shown his great abilities for discoveries.
M. de Frontenac selected him to command Fort Frontenac,
where he was nearly a year, till coming to France in 1675, he
obtained of the court the government and property of the lake
and its dependencies, on condition of building there a regular
stone fort, clearing the ground, and making French and Indian villages, and of supporting there, at his own expense, a
sufficient garrison, and Recollect missionaries.

ideas now took a new turn, Joliet had returned to Canada, after exploring the
Mississippi with Marquette, far enough to verify the supposition that it emptied
into the gulf of Mexico. His accounts of the buffalo country, induced La Salle
to believe that a very lucrative trade in their skins and wool might be opened
directly between the buffalo plains and France by the Mississippi and gulf, without carrying them through Canada. To secure this was now his object. Joliet,
who seems not to have been favored, was rewarded with a grant, not on the river
he had explored, but at the other extreme of the French colony, the island of Anticosti, and La Salle, who had secured Frontenac's favor, obtained a royal patent,
such as he desired. It was, however, provided, "that he carry on no trade whatever with the Indians called Ottawas, and others who bring their beaver-skins
and other peltries to Montreal," while to him and his company, the privilege of
the trade in buffalo skins was granted.—(Vol. i., p. 35.) The private traders who
had already visited the Illinois country, considered his including it in his grant
as unjustifiable, and both in the west and at Quebec opposed him in every way,
monopolies having always been objects of dislike. A variety of circumstances
defeated his first plan in the Illinois country, in 1680, and no new discovery
having been made by himself or Hennepin, he abandoned his first plan of descending the Mississippi in a vessel, and sailing thence to the isles, and resolved to
examine the mouth in boats, and acquire such a knowledge of its position as
would enable him to reach it direct from France by sea. He accordingly sailed
down in 1682, and following the course of Marquette and Joliet, reached their
furthest station on the 3d of March, then passing on, explored the river to the
gulf, which he reached on the 9th of April, thus crowning the work of the
former explorers, and with Hennepin's voyage, tracing its whole course from the
falls of St. Anthony to the sea. In pursuance of his plan he returned to France,
and attempted to reach it by sea, but missed the mouth, and landing in Texas,
perished in an attempt to reach the Illinois country by land. As a great but un-
successful merchant, vast and enterprising in his plans, though unfitted by early
associations from achieving them, he presents one of the most striking examples
of calm and persevering courage amid difficulties and disasters. He rose above
every adversity, unshaken and undiscouraged, ever ready to make the worse the

Monsieur de la Salle returned to Canada and fulfilled these conditions completely ; a fort with four bastions was built at the entrance of the lake on the northern side at the end of a basin, where a considerable fleet of large vessels might be sheltered from the winds. This fort enclosed that built by Monsieur de Frontenac. He also gave us a piece of ground fifteen arpents in front, by twenty deep, the donation being accepted by Monsieur de Frontenac, syndic of our mission.

It would be difficult to detail the obstacles he had to encounter, raised against him daily in the execution of his plans, so that he found less opposition in the savage tribes whom he was always able to bring into his plans. Monsieur de Frontenac went up there every year, and care was taken to assemble there the chiefs and leading men of the Iroquois nations, great and small ; maintaining by this means alliance and commerce with them, and disposing them to embrace Christianity, which was the principal object of the new establishment.*

My design being to treat of the publication of the faith to that prodigious quantity of nations who are comprised in the dominions of the king, as his majesty has discovered them, we shall continue our subject by those which were made during the rest of the present epoch in all parts of New France.

While the reverend father Jesuits among the southern Iro-

---

better fortune.   His life by Sparks, is one of the most valuable contributions to the early history of America.

* Le Clercq, p. 119.   The subsequent pages, down to page 131, relate to the religious affairs of the colony.   The only reference to La Salle, is this on p. 127 : "Our reverend fathers having obtained of the king letters-patent for our establishments at Quebec, Isle Percée, and Fort Frontenac, they were registered at the sovereign council of Quebec, and Monsieur de la Salle built, at his own expense, a house on the land he had given us near the fort, in which a chapel was made.   A fine church was afterward added, adorned with paintings and necessary vestments — also, a regular house and appendages, completed by the exertions of Father Joseph Denis."

quois on the upper part of the river had the honor of bearing
the gospel to the nations bordering on those tribes; the peace
between the two crowns of France and England giving them
free access everywhere, without being traversed by the English, they announced the faith to the Etchemins, and other Indian nations that came to trade at Loup river, where the ordinary post of the mission was; our missions of St. John's
River, Beaubassin, Mizamichis, Nipisiguit, Ristigouche, and
Isle Percée, were similarly supported — we continued to labor
for the conversion of the Indians of those vast countries com-
prized under the name of Acadia, Cape Breton and the
great bay (gulf of St. Lawrence).

In the time of M. de Courcelles and Talon, the discoveries
were pushed toward the north bay (Hudson's), of which
something was known from two or three previous attempts.
The sieur de St. Simon was chosen for the expedition, with
the reverend father Albanes (Albanel), a Jesuit.   By the
maps of the country it is easy to see what difficulties had to
be surmounted, how much toil and hardship undergone, how
many falls and rapids to be passed, and portages made, to
reach by land these unknown parts and tribes, as far as Hudson's bay or strait.   M. de Frontenac was in Canada on the
return of the party in 1672.   This discovery thenceforward
enabled them to push the mission much further to the north,
and draw some elect from those distant nations to receive the
first rudiments of Christianity, until in 1686, the victorious
arms of the king, under the guidance of M. de Troye, D'Hi-
berville, Ste. Helaine, and a number of brave Canadians, by
order of the marquis d'Enonville, then governor-general of
the country, conquered those northern parts where, as the
French arms are still gloriously maintained, the zeal of the
Jesuit fathers is employed in publishing the gospel.

The unwearied charity of those illustrious missionaries advanced their labors with much more success during the present epoch, among the Ottawa nations, seconded by the great zeal of Frontenac's protection, and the ascendant which the wisdom of the governor had acquired over the savages. A magnificent church, furnished with the richest vestments, was built at the mission of St. Mary's of the sault; that of the bay of the Fetid (Green bay), and Michilimakinak island, were more and more increased by the gathering of Indian tribes. The missions around Lake Condé (Superior) further north, were also increased. This lake alone is one hundred and fifty miles long, sixty wide, and about five hundred in circuit, inhabited by different nations, whence we may form an idea of the labors of the missionaries in five or six establishments. Finally, in the last years of M. de Frontenac's first administration, Sieur du Luth, a man of talent and experience opened a way to the missionaries and the gospel in many different nations turning toward the north of that lake, where he even built a fort. He advanced as far as the lake of the Issati, called Lake Buade, from the family name of M. de Frontenac, planting the arms of his majesty in several nations on the right and left, where the missionaries still make every effort to introduce Christianity, the only fruit of which indeed consists in the baptism of some dying children, and in rendering adults inexcusable at God's judgment by the gospel preached to them.*

---

* The promise of a general account of discoveries made, and his praise of the Jesuit missionaries in the preceding pages, must excite contempt when we find them a mask for falsehood and concealment. Nothing here would lead the reader to suppose that Father Allouez and other missionaries had explored the country around Lake Superior for seven years prior to the coming of Frontenac; that an accurate map had been published by them, in 1672; that Father Marquette, after many disappointments, at last, with Joliet, descended the Mississippi far enough to be certain as to the sea into which it emptied. Yet the discoveries of Allouez

I shall hereafter limit myself to publish the great discoveries made by order of the king, under the command of M. de Frontenac and the direction of M. de la Salle, as being those which promised the greatest fruits for the establishment of the faith, if in course of time they are resumed and supported as they deserve.

The sieur de la Salle having completed the construction of Fort Frontenac, and greatly advanced the establishment of French and Indian settlements, was induced, by the report of many tribes, to believe that great progress could be made by pushing on the discoveries by the lakes into the river Mississipi, which he then supposed to empty into the Red sea (gulf of California).* He made a voyage to France in 1677,

and the map are in the Relations which he elsewhere ridicules; the voyage of Joliet he must have heard of during his residence in Canada, and known as well as Hennepin who refers to it in his first work, even if we are to suppose him never to have read the work of his fellow-missionary, or Thevenot's edition of Father Marquette's journal. In his eagerness to ascribe no discovery to the Jesuits, he actually sends Du Luth to Lake Issati before any of the missionaries. Was he there before Hennepin?

* This assertion seems perfectly gratuitous, and is not justified by the letters patent to La Salle. Joliet's return set the matter at rest, and left no doubt as to its emptying into the gulf. In this work, indeed, Marquette is never mentioned, and Joliet's voyage decried, if not denied; but in the first of the series of works on La Salle, Hennepin's "*Description de la Louisane*" (Paris, 1684), of which the printing was completed January 5th, 1683, that is but a few days after Membré's arrival with the account of La Salle's voyage, the prior voyage of Joliet is admitted, and La Salle's object thus stated: "Toward the end of the year 1678 (1677), the sieur de la Salle came to France to report to M. Colbert the execution of his orders; he then represented to him that Fort Frontenac gave him great opportunities for making discoveries with our Recollects; that his principal design in building the fort had been to continue these discoveries in rich, fertile, and temperate countries, where commerce in the skins and wool of the wild cattle, called by the Spaniards Cibola, might establish a great trade, and support powerful colonies; that, however, as it would be difficult to bring these buffalo-hides in canoes, he prayed M. Colbert to grant him a commission to go and discover the mouth of the great river Mechasipi, on which vessels might be built to come to France; and that, considering the great expense he had undergone in building and supporting Fort Frontenac, he would be pleased to grant him an exclusive privilege of trading in buffalo-skins, of which he brought one as a sample, and his request was granted."—P. 14.

and favored by letters from the count de Frontenac, obtained of the court necessary powers to undertake and carry out this great design at his own expense.

Furnished with these powers, he arrived in Canada toward the close of September, 1678, with the sieur de Tonty, an Italian gentleman, full of spirit and resolution, who afterward so courageously and faithfully seconded him in all his designs. He had also with him thirty men — pilots, sailors, carpenters, and other mechanics, with all things necessary for his expedition. Some Canadians having joined him, he sent all his party in advance to Fort Frontenac, where Father Gabriel de la Ribourde, and Father Luke Buisset were already, and where Fathers Louis Hennepin, Zenobius Membré, and Melithon Watteau, now repaired. They were all three missionaries of our province of St. Anthony of Padua, in Artois, as well as Father Luke Buisset, his majesty having honored the Recollects with the care of the spiritual direction of the expedition by express orders addressed to Father Valentine le Roux, commissary provincial, and superior of the mission. The sieur de la Salle soon followed them, the Almighty preserving him from many perils in that long voyage from Quebec, over falls and rapids to Fort Frontenac, where he arrived at last, much emaciated. Deriving new strength from his great courage, he issued all his orders and sent off his troop in a brigantine for Niagara with Father Louis, on the 18th of November.

The navigation, in which they had to encounter many dangers and even disasters crossing the great lake in so advanced a season, prevented their reaching Niagara river before the 5th of December. On the sixth, they entered the river, and the following days, by canoe and land, advanced to the spot where the sieur de la Salle intended to raise a fort, and build a bark above Niagara falls, whence the St. Lawrence (*Le Fleuve*) communicates with Lake Conty (Erie), and Lake Frontenac (Ontario), by the said falls and river, which is, as it were, the strait of communication.

A glance at the map will show that this project with that of Fort Frontenac, and the fort he was about to build at Niagara, might excite some jealousy among the Iroquois who dwell in the neighborhood of the great lake. The sieur de la Salle, with his usual address, met the principal chiefs of those tribes in conference, and gained them so completely that they not only agreed to it, but even offered to contribute with all their means to the execution of his design. This great concert lasted some time. The sieur de la Salle also sent many canoes to trade north and south of the lake among these tribes.

Meanwhile, as certain persons traversed with all their might the project of the sieur de la Salle, they insinuated feelings of distrust in the Seneca Iroquois as the fort building at Niagara began to advance, and they succeeded so well that the fort became an object of suspicion, and the works had to be suspended for a time, and he had to be satisfied with a house surrounded by palisades. The sieur de la Salle did not fail to give prompt orders; he made frequent voyages from Fort Frontenac to Niagara, during the winter on the ice, in the spring with vessels loaded with provisions. In all the opposition raised by those envious of him, fortune seemed to side with them against him; the pilot who directed one of his well-loaded barks, lost it on Lake Frontenac. When the snow began to melt, he sent fifteen of his men to trade on the lake in canoes, as far as the Ilinois to prepare him the way, till his barque building at Niagara was completed. It was perfectly ready in the month of August, 1679.

The father commissary had started some time before from Quebec for the fort, to give the orders incumbent on his office, and put in force those expedited in the month of July, by which Father Gabriel was named superior of the new expedition, to be accompanied by Father Louis Hennepin, Zenobius Membré, and Melithon Watteaux, the latter to remain at Niagara, and make it his mission, while Father Luke should remain at the fort.

The three former accordingly embarked on the 7th of August, with Monsieur de la Salle and his whole party in the vessel, which had been named the Griffin in honor of the arms of Monsieur de Frontenac. Father Melithon remained at the house at Niagara, with some laborers and clerks. The same day they sailed for Lake Conty, after passing contrary to all expectations the currents of the strait. This was due to the resolution and address of the sieur de la Salle, his men having before his arrival used every means to no purpose. It appeared a kind of marvel, considering the rapidity of the current in the strait, which neither man nor animal, nor any ordinary vessel can resist, much less ascend.

The map will show that from this place you sail up Lake Conty (Erie), to Lake Orleans (Huron), which terminates in Lake Dauphin (Michigan); these lakes being each a hundred, or a hundred and twenty leagues long, by forty or fifty wide, communicating with one another by easy channels and straits, which offer vessels a convenient and beautiful navigation. All these lakes are full of fish; the country is most finely situated, the soil temperate, being north and south, bordered by vast prairies, which terminate in hills covered with vines, fruit-trees, groves, and tall woods, all scattered here and there, so that one would think that the ancient Romans, princes and nobles would have made them as many villas. The soil is everywhere equally fertile.

The sieur de la Salle having entered Lake Conty on the 7th, crossed it in three days, and on the 10th reached the strait (Detroit), by which he entered Lake Orleans. The voyage was interrupted by a storm as violent as could be met in the open sea; our people lost all hope of escape; but a vow which they made to St. Anthony, of Padua, the patron of mariners, delivered them by a kind of miracle, so that, after long making head against the wind, the vessel on the 27th reached Missilimakinak, which is north of the strait, by which we go from Lake Orleans to Lake Dauphin.

No vessels had yet been seen sailing on the lakes; yet an enterprise which should have been sustained by all well-meaning persons, for the glory of God, and the service of the king, had produced precisely the opposite feelings and effects, which had been already communicated to the Hurons, the Outaoüats of the island and the neighboring nations, to make them ill affected. The sieur de la Salle even found here the fifteen men, whom he had sent in the spring, prejudiced against him, and seduced from his service; a part of his goods wasted, far from having proceeded to the Ilinois to trade according to their orders; the sieur de Tonty, who was at their head, having in vain made every effort to inspire them with fidelity.*

At last he weighed anchor on the 2d of September, and arrived pretty safely at the Bay of the Fetid (Green bay), at the entrance of Lake Dauphin, forty leagues from Missilimakinak. Would to God that the sieur de la Salle had continued his route in the vessel. His wisdom could not foresee the misfortunes which awaited him; he deemed proper to send it back by the same route to Niagara, with the furs al-

* La Salle's sending them was a violation of his patent.—See *Historical Collections of Louisiana*, vol. i., p. 85.

ready bought, in order to pay his creditors. He even left in it a part of his goods and implements, which were not easy to transport. The captain had orders to return with the vessel as soon as possible, and join us in the Ilinois.

Meanwhile, on the 18th of September, the sieur de la Salle with our fathers and seventeen men, continued their route in canoes by Lake Dauphin, from the Pouteotatamis to the mouth of the river of the Miamis (St. Joseph's), where they arrived on the first of November. This place had been appointed a rendezvous for twenty Frenchmen, who came by the opposite shore, and also for the sieur de Tonty, who had been sent by the sieur de la Salle to Missilimakinak on another expedition.

The sieur de la Salle built a fort there to protect his men and property against any attack of the Indians ; our religious soon had a bark cabin erected to serve as a chapel, where they exercised their ministry for French and Indians until the third of December, when leaving four men in the fort, they went in search of the portage which would bring them to the Seignelay (Ilinois), which descends to the Missisipi. They embarked on this river to the number of thirty or forty, by which after a hundred, or a hundred and twenty leagues sail, they arrived toward the close of December, at the largest Ilinois village, composed of about four or five hundred cabins, each of five or six families.

It is the custom of these tribes at harvest-time to put their Indian corn in caches, in order to keep it for summer, when meat easily spoils, and to go and pass the winter in hunting wild cattle and beaver, carrying very little grain. That of our people had run short, so that passing by the Ilinois village, they were obliged, there being no one there, to take some Indian corn. as much as they deemed necessary for their subsistence.

They left it on the 1st of January, 1680, and by the 4th, were thirty leagues lower down amid the Ilinois camp; they were encamped on both sides of the river, which is very narrow there, but soon after forms a lake about seven leagues long, and about one wide, called Pimiteoui, meaning in their language that there are plenty of fat beasts there. The sieur de la Salle estimated it at 33° 45´. It is remarkable, because the Ilinois river, which for several months in winter is frozen down to it, never is from this place to the mouth, although navigation is at times interrupted by accumulations of floating ice from above.

Our people had been assured that the Ilinois had been excited and prejudiced against them. Finding himself then in the midst of their camp, which lay on both sides of the river, at a narrow pass, where the current was hurrying on the canoes faster than they liked, the sieur de la Salle promptly put his men under arms, and ranged his canoes abreast so as to occupy the whole breadth of the river, the canoes nearest the two banks, in which were the sieur de Tonty, and the sieur de la Salle, were not more than half a pistol-shot from the shore. The Ilinois, who had not yet discovered the little flotilla ranged in battle order, were alarmed ; some ran to arms, others fled in incredible confusion. The sieur de la Salle had a calumet of peace, but would not show it, not liking to appear weak before them. As they were soon so near that they could understand each other, they asked our Frenchmen, who they were. They replied that they were French, still keeping their arms ready, and letting the current bear them down in order, because there was no landing place till below the camp.

The Indians alarmed and intimidated by this bold conduct (although they were several thousand against a handful), immediately presented three calumets; our people at the same time presented theirs, and their terror changing to joy, they conducted our party to their cabins, showed us a thousand civilities, and sent to call back those who had fled. They were told, that we came only to give them a knowledge of the true God, to defend them against their enemies, to bring them arms and other conveniences of life. Besides presents made them, they were paid for the Indian corn taken at their village; a close alliance was made with them, the rest of the day being spent in feasts and mutual greetings.

All the sieur de la Salle's intrepidity and skill were needed to keep the alliance intact, as Monsoela, one of the chiefs of the nation of Maskoutens came that very evening to traverse it. It was known that he was sent by others than those of his nation; he had even with him some Miamis, and young men bearing kettles, knives, axes, and other goods. He had been chosen for this embassy rather than a Miami chief, to give more plausibility to what he should say, the Ilinois not having been at war with the Maskoutens, as they had with the Miamis. He cabaled even the whole night, speaking of the sieur de la Salle as an intriguer, a friend of the Iroquois, coming to the Ilinois only to open the way to their enemies, who were coming on all sides with the French to destroy them; he made them presents of all that he had brought, and even told them that he came on behalf of several Frenchmen whom he named.

This council was held at night, the time chosen by the Indians to transact secret business. This embassador retired the same night, so that the next day the Ilinois chiefs were found completely changed, cold and distrustful, appearing even to plot against our Frenchmen, who were shaken by the change, but the sieur de la Salle, who had attached one of the chiefs to him particularly by some present, learned from him the subject of this change. His address soon dispelled all these suspicions, but did not prevent six of his men, already tampered with and prejudiced at Michilimakinak, from deserting that very day.

The sieur de la Salle not only reassured that nation, but found means in the sequel, to disabuse the Maskoutens and Miamis, and to form an alliance between them and the Ilinois which lasted as long as the sieur de la Salle was in the country.

With this assurance the little army, on the 14th of January, 1680, the floating ice from above having ceased, repaired to a little eminence, a site quite near the Ilinois camp where the Sieur de la Salle immediately set to work to build a fort, which he called Crèvecœur, on account of the many disappointments he had experienced, but which never shook his firm resolve. The fort was well advanced, and the little vessel already up to the string-piece by the first of March, when he resolved to proceed to Fort Frontenac. There were four or five hundred leagues to go by land, but not finding his brigantine, the Griffin, return, nor those he had sent on to meet her, and foreseeing the disastrous consequences of the probable loss of his vessel, his courage rose above the difficulties of so long and painful a journey.

As he had chosen Father Louis, and as the latter had offered to continue the discovery toward the north, by ascending the Missisipi, the sieur de la Salle reserving to himself its continuation in canoe by descending till he found the sea, Father Louis set out in canoe from Fort Crevecœur on the 29th of February, 1680, with two men well armed and equipped, who had besides twelve hundred livres in goods, which make a good passport. The enterprise was great and hardy, although it did not equal the great zeal of the intrepid missionary who undertook and continued it with all the firmness, constancy, and edification, which can be desired, amid inconceivable toils.

Although the discovery had already been pushed four or five hundred leagues into Louisiana,* from Fort Frontenac to Fort Crevecœur; this great march can be considered only as a prelude and preparation for enterprises still more vast, and an entrance to be made in countries still more advantageous.

I have hitherto given only a short abridgment of the Relations which Father Zenobius Membré gives of the commencement of this enterprise. Father Louis, whom we see starting for the upper Missisipi has published a description of the countries which he visited and into which he carried the gospel. I therefore refer my reader to it without repeating it here.† We have then only to describe what is most essential and important in this discovery conducted by the personal labors of the sieur de la Salle, in the subsequent years.

* In fact no discovery had been made; the Ilinois country was visited by traders before Marquette's second voyage to it, and was perfectly known; Allouez, too, was there shortly before this, as La Salle himself states.

† We prefer to interrupt Le Clercq's narrative here, and insert the account published by Father Louis Hennepin, in 1684.

BIBLIOGRAPHICAL NOTICE

OF

THE WORKS OF FATHER LOUIS HENNEPIN,

A RECOLLECT OF THE PROVINCE OF ST. ANTHONY, IN ARTOIS.

WE have already in the notice on Le Clercq alluded to the uncertainty which hangs around many of the works connected with the history of La Salle. In them, however, it was a question as to authorship, alterations made by publishers, or the influence of party spirit in the original writers; against Hennepin, however, there is a still heavier charge. A good man may be so blinded by party zeal as to be unjust to others, and be guilty of acts which he would personally shrink from doing, and in this case we must, to attain the truth, realize fully the position of the antagonistic parties at the time. Such is peculiarly the case with Le Clercq, as we have shown, and in judging the work, we have endeavored to go back to his own period.

The charge against Hennepin is, that he was vain, conceited, exaggerating, and even mendacious. To weigh so serious an accusation, we shall examine his several volumes, which, however, as will be seen, resolve themselves into two, published at an interval of fourteen years. It is the more necessary to enter into a full discussion of his merits as few works relative to America have been more widely spread than that of Hennepin. Published originally in French, it appeared subsequently in Dutch, English, Italian, and Spanish, and if I am not mistaken in German; and in a large class of writers is quoted with the commendation. It was, however, soon attacked. The editor of Joutel, in 1713, calls it in question; but he was too ignorant of Canadian history to give his charge any weight. Severer strictures were passed upon it by Harris, and by Kalm, the celebrated Swedish traveller. Harris says, in vol. ii., p. 850, "As to the accounts of La Hontan, and Father Hennepin, they have been formerly very much admired, yet we are now well satisfied that they are rather romances than relations, and that their authors had their particular schemes so much in view, that they have made no scruple of abusing the confidence of mankind." In this country, within the last few years a more thorough examination of authorities has consigned Hennepin,* La Hontan, and Lebeau, to that amiable class who seem to tell truth by accident and fiction by inclination. The works of Hennepin are, I. Description de la Louisiane, nouvellement découverte au su-doüest de la nouvelle France, par ordre du roy. Avec carte du pays, les moeurs et la manière de vivre des sauvages, dediée a sa Majesté, par le R. P. Louis Hen-

---

* N. A. Review for January, 1845, Spark's Life of La Salle.

nepin, Missionare Recollet et Notaire Apostolique, pp. 312, and 107 Paris. Auroy, 1684.

Charlevoix takes exception to the title of this work on the ground that he misapplies the name Louisiana, but in fact Illinois, from La Salle's time, was included under that name. The title is, however, false in the words "newly discovered to the southwest of Canada," as no new discovery had been made in that direction, and the whole volume can show nothing in the way of new exploration, beyond what had already been published in Europe, except of so much of the Mississippi as lies between the Wisconsin river and the falls of St. Anthony, which he was the first European to travel. But let us enter on the volume itself, which, apart from any intrinsic faults, possesses considerable value, as being the first published, and by far the fullest account of La Salle's first expedition. Such it pretends to be, and accordingly opens with an account of that adventurer's project of reaching China, his attempt with some Sulpitians, in 1669, and his establishment at Fort Frontenac. Hennepin introduces himself to us, for the first time, on page twelve, as having established a mission at that fort with Father Luke Buisset; then mentions Joliet's voyage down the Mississippi as far as the Illinois (Indians), which he represents as the work of La Salle's enemies. Then follow the latter's voyage to France, in 1677, his return the next year with an order for the author to accompany him in his discoveries, and his own voyage to Fort Frontenac, which he details as though it were his first trip to that place. At Fort Frontenac La Salle's expedition begins, and our author relates all that happened with great detail, and a vast profusion of nautical expressions, down to the building of Fort Crevecœur, and his own departure from it, February 29th, 1680. His journal from this point being given in the present volume, we need not analyze it further than to say, that being sent to explore the Illinois to its mouth, in the Mississippi (p. 184), he reached that point on the 8th of March (192), and after being detained there by floating ice till the 12th, continued his route, traversing and sounding the river. Then follows, not a journal of his voyage, but a geographical description of the upper Mississippi, from the Illinois river to Mille lake and the Sioux country. After this description, he resumes his journal and tells us (p. 206), that he was taken by the Indians on the eleventh of April, after having sailed two hundred leagues (p. 218), from the Illinois (Indians). He was taken by them to their villages, relieved by de Luth in July, and returned to Mackinaw by way of the Wisconsin and Green bay. Thence, in the spring, he proceeded to the Seneca country, Fort Frontenac and Montreal. His work contains, besides the journal given, only some account of the party he left at Fort Crevecœur, from letters he saw at Quebec, and of La Salle's descent to the gulf from others received by him in France. This is followed by an account of the manners of the savages (p. 107).

Taking this volume by itself, the reader is struck by the unclerical character of the writer, his intense vanity and fondness for exaggeration. The manner in which he rises in importance, is truly amusing; not only does he, to all appearance, make himself the superior of the little band of missionaries in La Salle's expedition, but even a kind of joint commander with La Salle himself. Take as a specimen the following passage, which we select the more readily, as it bears on his voyage to the Mississippi. Fort Crevecœur was almost built, the Dauphin had sent no tidings of her voyage, the men were discontented and mutinous, all was dark and gloomy around the exploring party in Illinois. "We must remark," says Hennepin, "that the winter in the Ilinois country is not longer than that in Provence; but, in 1679, the snow lasted more than twenty days, to the great astonishment of the Indians who had never seen so severe a winter, so that the *sieur de la Salle and I* beheld ourselves exposed to new hardships that will appear incredible to those who have no experience of great voyages and new discoveries. Fort Crèvecœur was almost completed, the wood was all prepared to finish the bark, but we had not cordage, nor sails, nor iron enough; we received no tidings of the bark we had left on Lake Dauphin, nor of those sent to find what had become of her; meanwhile the sieur de la Salle saw that summer was coming on, and that, if he waited some months in vain, *our* enterprise would be retarded one year, and perhaps two or three, because being so far from Canada, he could not regulate affairs, nor have the necessary articles forwarded.

In this extremity we both took a resolution as extraordinary as it was difficult to execute, I to go with two men in unknown countries where we are every moment in great danger of death, and he on foot to Fort Frontenac more than five hundred leagues distant. We were then at the close of winter, which had been, as we have said, as severe in America as in France; the ground was still covered with snow, which was neither melted nor able to bear a man in snowshoes. He had to carry the usual equipment in such cases, that is, a blanket, pot, axe, gun, powder, and lead, with dressed skins to make Indian shoes, which last only a day, French shoes being of no use in the western countries. Besides, he had to resolve to pierce through thickets, march through marshes and melting snow, sometimes waist high, for whole days, at times with nothing to eat, because he and his three companions could not carry provisions, being compelled to rely for subsistence on what they killed with their guns, and to expect to drink only the water they found on the way. Finally he was exposed every day, and especially every night, to be surprised by four or five nations at war with each other, with this difference that the nations through which he had to pass all know the French, while those where I was going had never seen Europeans. Yet all these difficulties did not astound him *any more than myself; our* only difficulty was to find some of *our* men stout enough to accompany us and prevent the rest already much shaken from deserting on our departure." This is a remarkable passage, and has struck almost every writer on La Salle as their accounts often seem inspired by this graphic sketch of Hennepin. It is more than we said at first: Hennepin is here even greater than La Salle in the resolution he took at this trying crisis. After this we expect to see the two commanders depart on their dangerous expeditions, we run over the succeeding pages, the highflown language cools down, and we come to some details of La Salle's appointment of Tonty to command, which, are followed by these matter-of-fact words, completely destroying the delusion created by the preceding passage.

"He begged me to take the trouble to go and discover in advance the route he would have to take as far as the river Colbert on his return from Canada, but as I had an abscess in my mouth which had suppurated constantly for a year and a half, *I showed my repugnance*, and told him that I needed to go back to Canada to have medical treatment. He replied, that if I refused this voyage,

he would write to my superiors that I would be the cause of the failure of our
new missions; the reverend father Gabriel de la Ribourde, who had been my
novice master, begged me to go, telling me, that if I died of that infirmity, God
would one day be glorified by my apostolic labors.   'True, my son,' said that
venerable old man, whose head was whitened with more than forty years' austere
penance, 'you will have many monsters to overcome, and precipices to pass, in
this enterprise which requires the strength of the most robust; you do not know
a word of the language of these tribes whom you are going to endeavor to gain
to God, but take courage, you will gain as many victories as you have combats.'
Considering that this father had at his age been ready to come to my aid in the
second year of our new discoveries, with the view of announcing Christ to unknown tribes, and that this old man was the only male descendant and heir of
his father's house, for he was a Burgundian of rank, I offered to make the
voyage and endeavor to make the acquaintance of the tribes among whom I
hoped soon to establish myself, and preach the faith.   The sieur de la Salle
showed me his satisfaction, gave me a calumet of peace, and a canoe with two
men, one of whom was called the Picard du Gay, who is now at Paris, and the
other, Michael Ako; the latter he intrusted with some merchandise fit to make
presents, and worth ten or twelve thousand livres; and to myself he gave ten
knives, twelve awls, a little roll of tobacco to give to the Indians, about two
pounds of white and black beads, a little package of needles, declaring that he
would have given me more, if he could.   In fact, he is quite liberal to his friends.
Having received the blessing of the reverend father Gabriel, and taken leave of
the sieur de la Salle, and embraced all the party who came down to see us off,
Father Gabriel concluding his adieu with the words, 'Viriliter age et confortetur
cor tuum,' we set out from Fort Crèvecœur on the 29th of February," &c.

Can anything be more striking than the difference of these two accounts; in
one he seems a leader, in the other, a reluctant member of the expedition?

But La Salle is not the only one sacrificed to his vanity.   Delivered by de
Luth from his Sioux captivity, he seems to lay that officer under great obligations to him, and disposes of him so summarily, that the name of de Luth, after
being only three times mentioned, disappears from his pages, and he seems to be
the commander of the united parties.   He passes by one Jesuit mission at Green-
bay without mentioning its existence, winters at another at Mackinaw, not only
without uttering a word to induce us to suppose a missionary there, but actually
using expressions which give us the idea that he was the only missionary to be
found in all those parts, to minister to the Christians and instruct the heathen.
When he leaves Mackinaw, in April, 1681, our Recollect rises still higher in importance; he is fired at the wrongs of an Ottawa chief, and apparently considering it beneath him to look for La Salle, or give him any account of the expedition on which he had been sent, proceeds to the Seneca country, convenes a
council, compels that haughty tribe to make amends to the injured Ottawa, and
returns to Fort Frontenac, after this somewhat curious proceeding in a good friar
who never meddled in civil affairs, *as some other people did.*   He crowns the whole
by telling us at the close of the volume, that La Salle descended to the gulf, "as *I
had made peace* with the nations of the north and northwest, five hundred leagues
up the river Colbert, who made war on the Ilinois and southern tribes."

This is enough to show to what extent even then he pushed his self-glorification. As to the object of his expedition, we are completely in the dark; we can not tell whether he was sent to explore the Illinois to its mouth, or to open intercourse with some tribe or tribes, where it was intended to begin a mission. At all events, he says nothing of having been sent up the Mississippi; but whatever was his mission, he seems to have so well avoided La Salle, that they never met again. Hennepin hastened back to France, and by the 3d of September, 1682, had the royal permission to print his work, which issued from the press on the 5th of January, 1683, though most copies have on the titlepage the date 1684. He was then for a time, it would seem, at Chateau Cambrensis, till ordered by his superiors to return to America; this he refused, and was in consequence compelled to leave France. Falling in with Mr. Blaithwait, secretary of war to William III., he passed to the service of the English king, as a Spanish subject, by permission of his own sovereign and his clerical superiors, as he avers. He assumed a lay dress in a convent at Antwerp, and proceeding to Utrecht, published in 1697, a new work entitled—

II. "Nouvelle description d'un très grand pays situé dans l'Amerique entre le nouveau Mexique et la mer glaciale," reprinted the next year as "Nouvelle Decouverte d'un pays plus grandque l'Europe," a translation of which appeared in England, in 1699, entitled: "A new discovery of a vast country in America, extending above four thousand miles between New France and New Mexico."

This work begins with his own personal history, and from it we derive the following data for a life of this worthy, should any one deem it worth while to attempt it. He was born at Ath, in Hainault, and feeling a strong inclination to retire from the world, entered the order of St. Francis. He was soon seized with a desire of rambling; and while studying Dutch at Ghent, was strongly tempted to go to the East Indies, but was appeased by a tour through the Franciscan convents of Italy and Germany, back to Hainault, where, for a whole year, he was compelled to discharge the ministry. This year of permanent residence in one spot seems to have been an epoch in his erratic life. He next roamed to Artois, thence set out to beg at Calais, returned by Dunkirk to Dies, and after sauntering through several Dutch towns, spent eight months at Maestricht, in the care of an hospital, where acquiring some military ardor, he was next an army chaplain at the battle of Senef (1674), immediately after which he was sent to Rochelle to embark for Canada. A convent life was, it is clear, irksome to him, and how little he was sensible of the dignity of the priesthood, either before God or man, we may judge by this extraordinary admission: "I used oftentimes to skulk behind the doors of victualling houses, to hear the seamen give an account of their adventures. . . . . This occupation was so agreeable to me, that [despite, he tells us, the nausea caused by their smoking] I spent whole days and nights at it without eating." Arrived in Canada, he preached the Advent and Lent to the hospital nuns at Quebec, being chosen by Bishop Laval, whose favor he had secured on the voyage by a display of zeal which by a train of incidents drew on him all La Salle's enmity. This brings him to 1676, when after rambling around Quebec, as far as Three-Rivers, he was sent to Fort Frontenac, with Father Buisset to direct the Indians gathered there. This now became the centre of new rambles, which he extended to the cantons of the

Five Nations, visiting Onondaga, Oneida, and the Mohawk, in the last of which
while entertained by the Jesuit missionary (probably Father Bruyas), he copied
his Iroquois dictionary, for in this work, as if to spite his former friends, he mentions those missionaries in several places with terms of praise.   He then visits
Albany, and though entreated by the Dutch to stay, returned to Fort Frontenac.
In 1678, he went down to Quebec, and soon after his arrival received orders to
join La Salle's expedition.   From this point his journal rolls on as in the "Description de la Louisiane," down to the 12th of March, 1680, till which day he
was detained by the floating ice, but here a new scene breaks on the startled
reader: Hennepin tells us, that he actually went down the Mississippi to the
gulf, but had not published the fact to avoid the hostility of La Salle.   Amazed at
so unexpected a revelation, we read on carefully, but find that he waited till the
twelfth, yet started on the eighth, being consequently in two places at once,
each moment during those four days; thus aided, he reached the mouth of the
Mississippi by the twenth-fifth, or at most, twenty-sixth of March, after celebrating, on the 23d of March, the festival of Easter which, unfortunately for his
accuracy, fell that year on the 21st of April, as he himself knew, for in his
former work (p. 242), he states that he reached the Issati village about Easter,
which, in his loose style, means some days after it.   But to return to his voyage
down, achieved in thirteen, or at most, eighteen days; he planted a cross and
wished to wait a few days to make observations, but his men refused, and he
was compelled to embark again.   They did wait, however, some days it seems,
for he started only on the first of April; by the twenty-fourth, he had reached
and left the Arkansas, as he tells us in two different places (pp. 129, 137), and
ascending toward the Illinois, advanced only by night for fear of a surprise by
the French of Fort Crèvecœur.   By the twelfth of the same month of April,
being twelve days before he reached the Arkansas, he was taken by the Sioux a
hundred and fifty leagues above the mouth of the Illinois, making all that distance from the gulf in eleven days, and the distance from the Arkansas, in considerably less than no time at all.

From this point, it continues with but occasional variations, as in the *Description de la Louisiane*, except that de Luth appears more frequently down to
their ascending the Wisconsin.

The second part, or second volume, contains an account of La Salle's last
voyage, in which Father Anastasius is frequently cited; the subsequent part,
from page 49 to 151, treats of the manners, and customs of the Indians, and
their conversion, and then follows an account of the capture of Quebec, in 1628,
by the English, and of the early Recollect missions.

Two things in this volume at once meet us, the horrible confusion of dates,
and the utter impossibility of performing the voyages in the times given.
These objections were made at the time, but were stoutly met by Hennepin, although the former seems not to have been much attended to by him.   He gives
us, however, a dissertation on the variation of the needle, and the difference of
time in Europe and America, which had confused him somewhat in his ideas,
and prevented his accuracy in that point.   As to the impracticability of the matter, he denies it, averring that he had time enough and to spare, as a bark canoe
can, if necessary, go ninety miles a day up stream!

But a heavier charge was made when his new work was compared to the *Etablissement de la Foi;* his new journal down was but a set of scraps from that of Father Membré, and the reader may verify the truth of this charge by examining the parallel passages given by the accurate and judicious Sparks, in his life of La Salle, or by comparing Membré's journal in this volume with the English Hennepin, or even with the abridgment of it in vol. i., of Historical Collections of Louisiana.   Hennepin admits the similarity, and accuses le Clercq or le Roux, whom he asserts to be the real author, of having published as Membré's, his, Hennepin's journal, which he had lent to le Roux, at Quebec.   Let us hear his own words : "But if I do not blame Father le Clercq for the honorable mention he makes of his relative (Membré), I think everybody will condemn him for his concealing the name of the author he has transcribed, and thereby attributing to himself (? Membré or le Clercq), the glory of my perilous voyage.   This piece of injustice is common enough in this age."

Sparks, who has the honor of having completely exposed Hennepin, and "the injustice common in that age," which induced Hennepin, le Clercq, Douay, Joutel, and others, to endeavor to rob Marquette of the glory due to his perilous voyage, shows this pretext of Hennepin to be groundless.   We might stop to examine it, if only here he had copied le Clercq; but, on examination, we find that almost all the additional matter in the *Nouvelle Decouverte* is drawn from the *Etablissement de la Foi,* and almost literally.   This is the case with the whole second part, where, though he cites Father Anastasius, he copies the remarks of the author of the *Etablissement.*   What relates to the Indians is full of extracts from the latter work, and the capture of Quebec, and the early missions are mere copies.   In the edition of 1720, which Charlevoix calls the second, and, perhaps, in some previous edition the amount of stolen matter is still larger; but some was of such a nature as to bring ecclesiastical censure on the work.   For, strange as it may seem, Hennepin residing unfrocked in Holland, the flatterer and pensioner of William III., seems to have remained a Catholic and Franciscan to the last; at least I have seen nothing to establish the contrary.   Had interest or ambition been his only motive, he would certainly have thrown off both titles at a time when the frenzy of religious animosity possessed the English public.

But while doing him this justice, that he does not seem to have been led by interest or ambition of place, while admitting that many of his descriptions are graphic, and to some extent reliable, we say all that can be said in his favor. Where in the main fact he is supported by others, we have followed him with caution in details, but we must admit that the charges brought against him are too well substantiated to allow us hesitate as to his character.

A question still remains as to what he really did do on leaving Fort Crève-cœur.   In his first work, as we have already remarked, he states that he was sent to explore the Illinois to its mouth, or to visit some tribes where a mission was to be established; and he tells us that he had some design of going down the Mississippi to the gulf, but he nowhere says that he ascended it before he was taken.   In the last, he was sent to the Mississippi, and the tribes on it to get the friendship of the nations inhabiting its banks, and as he tells us he went down.   In both, at a very late period, he tells us that La Salle promised to send him further supplies at the mouth of the Wisconsin.

In neither have we any journal of his voyage up the river; the geographical description is not that of a traveller ascending, as he describes first what he saw last; and though voyaging with Sioux, gives the Wisconsin the same name as Marquette, who reached it through the Outagamis. What then did he do between March 12th, and April 12th? This must remain a mystery. That he went down to the gulf, is too absurd to be received for a moment; that he went up is nowhere asserted by him, and is, I think, very doubtful. For my own part, I should rather believe that he was taken in an attempt to descend, or in some way acting contrary to the directions of La Salle. His evident avoiding of the latter is suspicious, and shows that he could not give a satisfactory account of his proceedings; for wintering at Mackinaw, he must have known that La Salle had passed out to rejoin them at Fort Crèvecœur, and that his own companions had been compelled to leave the fort, and were then at Green bay.* Then, too, as to his description of the upper Mississippi, I am inclined to think it due to de Luth, who, as le Clercq tells us, was the first to reach the lake of the Issatis, and open the way to the missionaries; this seems more probable as in his last work Hennepin attacks de Luth, and endeavors to destroy the credit, as though de Luth could and, perhaps, did tell another story. It will, therefore, be a matter of interest to learn whether any reports of his are still to be found, as the mere fact of Hennepin's attacking him gives them considerable value.

In the meantime Hennepin's account of the upper Mississippi must stand as first published, though we can not tell how much of it he really saw; standing on its own merits, it is an account which the first American explorers of the upper river compared as they went along, and found sufficiently accurate in one who could only guess at the various distances which he had to mention. As a valuable paper connected with the discoveries of the Mississippi, we insert it here, regretting our inability to give in justice a more flattering portrait of the writer.

* Hennepin left Mackinaw on Easter week, 1681 (April 6–13), and F. Membré arrived there on the 13th of June, and La Salle from Illinois, about the fifteenth. On Vol. I., p. 59, of this series, there is a typographical error Fete Dieu, in October, should be Octave of Corpus Christi, being that year June 13th.

NARRATIVE

OF THE VOYAGE

TO THE UPPER MISSISSIPPI,

BY

FATHER LOUIS HENNEPIN.

FROM HIS "DESCRIPTION DE LA LOUISIANE," PRINTED AT PARIS, IN 1683.

WE set out from Fort Crèvecœur the 29th of February, 1680, and toward evening, while descending the Seignelay [Ilinois], we met on the way several parties of Islinois* returning to their village in their periaguas or gondolas, loaded with meat. They would have obliged us to return, our two boatmen were even shaken, but as they would have had to pass by Fort Crèvecœur, where our Frenchmen would have stopped them, we pursued our way the next day, and my two men afterward confessed the design which they had entertained.†

---

* We have retained Hennepin's orthography of proper names throughout this narrative.

† Hennepin's party, according to his account, consisted of himself and two men, Anthony Auguelle, commonly called the Picard du Gay, and Michael Ako. The latter was intrusted by La Salle with the goods, and is probably the sieur Dacan of some other writers, as Mr. Sparks informs me, that he saw manuscripts in which it was written d'Acau. Hennepin in the preface to the first part of the English volume, charges La Salle with having maliciously caused the death of one of his two companions, meaning Ako, as he represents the other to be alive.

The river Seignelay on which we were sailing, is as deep and broad as the Seine, at Paris, and in two or three places widens out to a quarter of a league. It is lined with hills, whose sides are covered with fine large trees. Some of these hills are half a league apart, leaving between them a marshy strip often inundated, especially in the spring and fall, but producing, nevertheless, quite large trees. On ascending these hills, you discover prairies further than the eye can reach, studded at intervals, with groves of tall trees, apparently planted there intentionally. The current of the river is not perceptible, except in time of great rains ; it is at all times navigable for large barks about a hundred leagues, from its mouth to the Islinois village, whence its course almost always runs south by southwest.

On the 7th of March, we found, about two leagues from its mouth, a nation called Tamaroa, or Maroa, composed of two hundred familes. They would have taken us to their village west of the river Colbert (Mississippi), six or seven leagues below the mouth of the river Seignelay; but our two canoemen, in hopes of still greater gain, preferred to pass on, according to the advice I then gave them. These last Indians seeing that we carried iron and arms to their enemies, and unable to overtake us in their periaguas, which are wooden canoes, much heavier than our bark ones, which went much faster than their boats, despatched their young men after us by land, to pierce us with their arrows at some narrow part of the river, but in vain ; for soon after discovering the fire made by these warriors at their ambuscade, we crossed the river at once, and gaining the other side, encamped in an island, leaving our canoe loaded and our little dog to wake as, so as to embark with all speed, should the Indians attempt to surprise us by swimming across.

Soon after leaving these Indians, we came to the mouth of the River Seignelay, fifty leagues distant from Fort Crève-cœur, and about a hundred from the great Islinois village. It is between 36° and 37° N. latitude, and consequently one hundred and twenty or thirty leagues from the gulf of Mexico.

In the angle formed on the south by this river, at its mouth, is a flat precipitous rock, about forty feet high, very well suited for building a fort. On the northern side, opposite the rock, and on the west side beyond the river, are fields of black earth, the end of which you can not see, all ready for cultivation, which would be very advantageous for the existence of a colony.

The ice which floated down from the north kept us in this place till the 12th of March, when we continued our route, traversing the river and sounding on all sides to see whether it was navigable. There are, indeed, three islets in the middle, near the mouth of the river Seignelay, which stop the floating wood and trees from the north, and form several large sand-bars, yet the channels are deep enough, and there is sufficient water for barks; large flat-boats can pass there at all times.

The River Colbert runs south-southwest, and comes from the north and northwest; it runs between two chains of mountains, quite small here, which wind with the river, and in some places are pretty far from the banks, so that between the mountains and the river, there are large prairies, where you often see herds of wild cattle browsing. In other places these eminences leave semi-circular spots covered with grass or wood. Beyond these mountains you discover vast plains, but the more we approach the northern side ascending, the earth became apparently less fertile, and the woods less beautiful than in the Islinois country.

This great river is almost everywhere a short league in width, and in some place, two or three; it is divided by a number of islands covered with trees, interlaced with so many vines as to be almost impassable. It receives no considerable river on the western side except that of the Otontenta,* and another, St. Peter's,† which comes from the west northwest, seven or eight leagues from St. Anthony of Padua's falls.

On the eastern side you meet first an inconsiderable river (Rock river), and then further on another, called by the Indians Onisconsin, or Misconsin, which comes from the east and east-northeast. Sixty leagues up you leave it, and make a portage of half a league to reach the Bay of the Fetid (Puants) by another river which, near its course, meanders most curiously. It is almost as large as the river Seignelay, or Ilinois, and empties into the river Colbert, a hundred leagues above the river Seignelay.‡

* This would seem the Desmoines, the largest south of St. Peter's, but the Iowa is not much inferior, and would better suit his description as being near half way between the Illinois and Lake Pepin. The name, too, would induce us to put it higher, as he doubtless means the tribe called by Membré *Anthoutantas*, and by Marquette on his map, Otontanta, the same as the former, if *u* and *n* are transposed.

† The St. Peter's river flows through the centre of the Sioux territories, and is a magnificent river. It was visited by Le Sueur, the French geologist, as early as 1688 (*Hist. Coll. La.*, vol. iii.), and is very correctly described by him. It is remarkable for its mineral deposites, and the variety of clays found on its banks, which are employed by the Indians in painting their faces and bodies. Its waters are transparent, hence the Indian name of wate-paw-mené-saute, or clear water river. The Minokantongs, or people of the waters, are located about its mouth, and the Yengetongs, and the Sissitongs, inhabit the upper part of it (Schoolcraft); their principal traffic is in buffalo-robes. The numerical strength of the Sioux nation is now estimated at about twenty-two thousand.—F

‡ It must have been just here that he was taken by the Sioux, if he sailed up the Mississippi before his capture, for he had gone two hundred leagues after leaving the Illinois, who were one hundred leagues from the mouth of their river, and the other one hundred would bring him to the Wisconsin; though if he counts the hundred on the Illinois from the village proper, and not from the

Twenty-four leagues above, you come to the Black river called by the Nadouessious, or Islati Chabadeba, or Chabaaudeba, it seems quite inconsiderable. Thirty leagues higher up, you find the lake of Tears (Lake Pepin), which we so named, because some of the Indians who had taken us, wishing to kill us, wept the whole night, to induce the others to consent to our death. This lake which is formed by the River Colbert, is seven leagues long, and about four wide; there is no considerable current in the middle that we could perceive, but only at its entrance and exit.* Half a league below the lake of Tears, on the south side, is Buffalo river, full of turtles. It is so called by the Indians on account of the numbers of buffalo (*bœufs*) found there. We followed it for ten or twelve leagues; it empties impetuously into the river Colbert, but as you ascend it, it is constantly calm and free from rapids. It is skirted by mountains, far enough off at times to form prairies. The mouth is wooded both sides, and is full as large as that of the Seignelay.

Forty leagues above is a river full of rapids (St. Croix), by which, striking northwest, you can reach Lake Condé (Superior), that is, as far as Nimissakouat river,† which empties into the lake. This first river is called Tomb river, because the

camp, we must go thirty leagues further, above Black river. But if captured here, how could it have taken the Indians, rowing from morning till night, nineteen days to reach St. Anthony's falls?

* This beautiful sheet of water is an expansion of the Mississippi river, six miles below the Sioux village of Talangamanae, and one hundred below the falls of St. Anthony. It is indented with several bays and prominent points which serve to enhance the beauty of its scenery. A few miles below this lake, on the west bank of the Mississippi, are the remains of one of the most interesting and extensive of those ancient circumvallations, which are spread over the valley of the Mississippi. It was first described by Carver, in 1768.—F.

† This is probably the St. Louis which, on the map of the Jesuit Relation of 1670–'71 (Bancroft, vol. iii.), is marked as the way to the Sioux, sixty leagues west, being nearly the distance here given by Hennepin between Millelacs and Lake Superior.

Issati left there the body of one of their warriors, killed by a rattlesnake. According to their custom, I put a blanket on the grave, which act of humanity gained me much importance by the gratitude displayed by the deceased's countrymen, in a great banquet which they gave me in their country, and to which more than a hundred Indians were invited.

Continuing to ascend the Colbert ten or twelve leagues more, the navigation is interrupted by a fall, which I called St. Anthony of Padua's, in gratitude for the favors done me by the Almighty through the intercession of that great saint, whom we had chosen patron and protector of all our enterprises. This fall is forty or fifty feet high, divided in the middle by a rocky island of pyramidal form.* The high mountains which skirt the river Colbert last only as far as the river Onisconsin, about one hundred and twenty leagues; at this place it begins to flow from the west and northwest, without our having been able to learn from the Indians, who have ascended it very far, where it rises. They merely told us that twenty or thirty leagues below (dessous), there is a second fall, at the foot of which are some villages of the prairie people, called Thinthonha, who live there a part of the year. Eight leagues above St. Anthony of Padua's falls on the right, you find the Issati or Nadoussion river (Rum river), with a very narrow mouth, which you can ascend to the north for about seventy leagues to Lake Buade or Issati (Mille lake), where it rises. We called this St. Francis river. This

---

* These celebrated falls, now no longer beyond the pale of civilization, have been much better described by modern travellers. Schoolcraft places them fourteen miles below the confluence of the Mississawgaeigon, or Rum river. The village of St. Anthony with its schools and its churches now occupies the east bank of the river at the head of the cataract. The scenery is picturesque and beautiful, but presents none of that majesty and grandeur which belong to the cataract of Niagara. The Indian name of these falls in the Sioux language, is Owah-menah, or the falling water.—F.

last lake spreads out into great marshes, producing wild-rice, like many other places down to the extremity of the Bay of the Fetid. This kind of grain grows wild in marshy places : it resembles oats, but tastes better, and the stems are longer as well as the stalk. The Indians gather it when ripe. The women tie several stalks together with white wood bark to prevent its being all devoured by the flocks of duck and teal found there. The Indians lay in a stock for part of the year, to eat out of the hunting season.

Lake Buade, or Lake of the Issati (Mille lake), is about seventy leagues west of Lake Condé ; it is impossible to go from one to the other on account of the marshy and quaggy nature of the ground ; you might go, though with difficulty on the snow in snowshoes ; by water it is a hundred and fifty leagues, on account of the many detours to be made, and there are many portages. From Lake Condé, to go conveniently in canoe, you must pass by Tomb river, where we found only the bones of the Indian whom I mentioned above, the bears having eaten the flesh, and pulled up poles which the deceased's relatives had planted in form of a monument. One of our boatmen found a war-calumet beside the grave, and an earthen pot upset, in which the Indians had left fat buffalo meat, to assist the departed, as they say, in making his journey to the land of souls.

In the neighborhood of Lake Buade are many other lakes, whence issue several rivers, on the banks of which live the Issati, Nadouessans, Tinthonha (which means prairie-men), Chongaskethon, Dog, or Wolf tribe (for chonga among these nations means dog or wolf), and other tribes, all which we comprise under the name Nadonessiou. These Indians number eight or nine thousand warriors, very brave, great runners, and very good bowmen. It was by a part of these tribes

8

that I and our two canoemen were taken in the following way :—

We scrupulously said our morning and evening prayers every day on embarking, and the Angelus at noon, adding some paraphrases on the Response of St. Bonaventure in honor of St. Anthony of Padua. In this way we begged of God to meet these Indians by day, for when they discover people at night, they kill them as enemies, to rob those whom they murder secretly of some axes or knives which they value more than we do gold and silver; they even kill their own allies, when they can conceal their death, so as afterward to boast of having killed men, and so pass for soldiers.

We had considered the river Colbert with great pleasure, and without hinderance, to know whether it was navigable up and down : we were loaded with seven or eight large turkeys, which multiply of themselves in these parts. We wanted neither buffalo nor deer, nor beaver, nor fish, nor bear meat, for we killed those animals as they swam across the river.

Our prayers were heard when, on the 11th of April, 1680, about two o'clock in the afternoon, we suddenly perceived thirty-three bark canoes, manned by a hundred and twenty Indians, coming down with extraordinary speed, to make war on the Miamis, Islinois, and Maroa. These Indians surrounded us, and while at a distance, discharged some arrows at us ; but as they approached our canoe the old men seeing us with the calumet of peace in our hands, prevented the young men from killing us. These brutal men leaping from their canoes, some on land, others into the water with frightful cries and yells, approached us, and as we made no resistance, being only three against so great a number, one of them wrenched our calumet from our hands, while our canoe and theirs were tied to the shore. We first presented them a piece of French tobacco, better for smoking than theirs, and the eldest among them uttered the words Miamiha, Miamiha. As we did not understand their language, we took a little stick, and by signs which we made on the sand, showed them that their enemies, the Miamis whom they sought, had fled across the river Colbert to join the Islinois; when they saw themselves discovered and unable to surprise their enemies, three or four old men, laying their hands on my head, wept in a lugubrious tone. With a wretched handkerchief I had left, I wiped away their tears, but they would not smoke our peace-calumet. They made us cross the river with great cries, which all shouted together with tears in their eyes; they made us row before them, and we heard yells capable of striking the most resolute with terror. After landing our canoe and goods, part of which had been already taken, we made a fire to boil our kettle; we gave them two large wild turkeys that we had killed. These Indians having called an assembly to deliberate what they were to do with us; the two head-chiefs of the party approaching, showed us, by signs, that the warriors wished to tomahawk us. This compelled me to go to the war chiefs with one of my men, leaving the other by our property, and throw into their midst six axes, fifteen knives, and six fathom of our black tobacco, then bowing down my head, I showed them, with an axe, that they might kill us, if they thought proper. This present appeased many individual members, who gave us some beaver to eat, putting the three first morsels in our mouth according to the custom of the country, and blowing on the meat which was too hot, before putting their bark dish before us, to let us eat as we liked ; we spent the night in anxiety, because before retiring at night, they had returned us our peace-calumet.

Our two boatmen were, however, resolved to sell their lives dearly, and to resist if attacked ; their arms and swords were ready.   As for my own part, I determined to allow myself to be killed without any resistance, as I was going to announce to them a God, who had been falsely accused, unjustly condemned, and cruelly crucified, without showing the least aversion to those who put him to death. We watched in turn in our anxiety so as not to be surprised asleep.

In the morning, April 12th, one of their captains named Narrhetoba, with his face and bare body smeared with paint, asked me for our peace-calumet, filled it with tobacco of his country, made all his band smoke first, and then all the others who plotted our ruin.   He then gave us to understand that we must go with them to their country, and they all turned back with us ; having thus broken off their voyage, I was not sorry in this conjuncture to continue our discovery with these people.

But my greatest trouble was, that I found it difficult to say my office before these Indians, many seeing me move my lips said, in a fierce tone, Ouackanché ; and as we did not know a word of their language, we believed that they were angry at it.   Michael Ako, all out of countenance, told me, that if I continued to say my breviary we should all three be killed, and the Picard begged me at least to pray apart, so as not to provoke them.   I followed the latter's advice, but the more I concealed myself, the more I had the Indians at my heels, for when I entered the wood, they thought I was going to hide some goods under ground, so that I knew not on what side to turn to pray, for they never let me out of sight.   This obliged me to beg pardon of my two canoemen, assuring them that I could not dispense with saying my office, that if we were massacred for that, I would be the innocent

cause of their death, as well as of my own. By the word
Ouakanché, the Indians meant that the book I was reading
was a spirit; but by their gesture they nevertheless showed a
kind of aversion, so that to accustom them to it, I chanted the
litany of the Blessed Virgin in the canoe with my book open.
They thought that the breviary was a spirit which taught me
to sing for their diversion, for these people are naturally fond
of singing.

The outrages done us by these Indians during our whole
route was incredible, for seeing that our canoe was much
larger and more heavily laden than theirs (for they have only
a quiver full of arrows, a bow, and a wretched dressed skin,
to serve too as a blanket at night, for it was still pretty cold
at that season, always going north), and that we could not go
faster than they, they put some warriors with us to help us
row, to oblige us to follow them. These Indians sometimes
make thirty or forty leagues, when at war and pressed for
time, or anxious to surprise some enemy. Those who had
taken us were of various villages and of different opinions as
to us; we cabined every night by the young chief who had
asked for our peace-calumet, and put ourselves under his protection; but jealousy arose among these Indians, so that the
chief of the party named Aquipaguetin, one of whose sons
had been killed by the Miamis, seeing that he could not
avenge his death on that nation as he had wished, turned all
his rage on us. He wept through almost every night him he
had lost in war, to oblige those who had come out to avenge
him, to kill us and seize all we had, so as to be able to per-
sue his enemies; but those who liked European goods were
much disposed to preserve us, so as to attract other Frenchmen there and get iron, which is extremely precious in their
eyes; but of which they knew the great utility only when

they saw one of our French boatmen kill three or four bustards or turkeys at a single shot, while they can scarcely kill
only one with an arrow. In consequence, as we afterward
learned, that the words Manza Ouackangé, mean "iron that
has understanding," and so these nations call a gun which
breaks a man's bones, while their arrows only glance through
the flesh they pierce, rarely breaking the bones of those whom
they strike, and consequently producing wounds more easily
cured than those made by our European guns, which often
cripple those whom they wound.

We had some design of going to the mouth of the river
Colbert, which more probably empties into the gulf of Mexico
than into the Red sea ; but the tribes that seized us, gave us
no time to sail up and down the river.

We had made about two hundred leagues by water since
leaving the Islinois, and we sailed with the Indians who took
us during some nineteen days, sometimes north, sometimes
northwest, according to the direction which the river took.
By the estimate which we formed, during that time (depuis
cetemps là), we made about two hundred and fifty leagues,
or even more on Colbert river ; for these Indians row in
great force, from early in the morning till evening, scarcely
stopping to eat during the day. To oblige us to keep up with
them, they gave us every day four or five men to increase the
crew of our little vessel, which was much heavier than theirs.
Sometimes we cabined when it rained, and when the weather
was not bad, we slept on the ground without any shelter ; this
gave us all time to contemplate the stars and the moon when
it shone. Notwithstanding the fatigue of the day, the youngest of these Indian warriors danced the calumet to four or
or five of their chiefs till midnight, and the chief to whom
they went, sent a warrior of his family in due ceremony to

those who sang, to let them in turn smoke his war-calumet, which is distinguished from the peace-calumet by different feathers. The end of this kind of pandemonium was terminated every day by two of the youngest of those who had had relations killed in war; they took several arrows which they presented by the points all crossed to the chiefs, weeping bitterly; they gave them to them to kiss. Notwithstanding the force of their yelling, the fatigue of the day, the watching by night, the old men almost all awoke at daybreak for fear of being surprised by their enemies. As soon as dawn appeared one of them gave the cry, and in an instant all the warriors entered their bark canoes, some passing around the islands in the river to kill some beasts, while the most alert went by land, to discover whether any enemy's fire was to be seen. It was their custom always to take post on the point of some island for safety sake, as their enemies have only periaguas, wooden canoes, which can not go as fast as they do, on account of their weight. Only northern tribes have birch to make bark canoes; the southern tribes who have not that kind of tree, are deprived of this great convenience, which wonderfully facilitates the northern Indians in going from lake to lake, and by all rivers to attack their enemies, and even when discovered, they are safe if they can get into their canoes, for those who pursue them by land, or in periaguas, can not attack or pursue them quickly enough.

During one of these nineteen days of painful navigation, the chief of the party by name Aquipaguetin, resolved to halt about noon in a large prairie; having killed a very fat bear, he gave a feast to the chief men, and after the repast all the warriors began to dance. Their faces, and especially their bodies, were marked with various colors, each being distinguished by the figure of different animals, according to his particular taste or inclination; some having their hair short and full of bear oil, with white and red feathers; others besprinkled their heads with the down of birds which adhered to the oil. All danced, with their arms akimbo, and struck the ground with their feet so stoutly as to leave the imprint visible. While a son, master of ceremonies, gave each in turn the war-calumet to smoke, he wept bitterly. The father in a doleful voice, broken with sighs and sobs, with his whole body bathed in tears, sometimes addressed the warriors, sometimes came to me, and put his hands on my head, doing the same to our two Frenchmen, sometimes he raised his eyes to heaven and often uttered the word Louis, which means sun, complaining to that great luminary of the death of his son. As far as we could conjecture this ceremony tended only to our destruction; in fact, the course of time showed us that this Indian had often aimed at our life; but seeing the opposition made by the other chiefs who prevented it, he made us embark again, and employed other trickery to get by degrees the goods of our canoemen, not daring to take them openly, as he might have done, for fear of being accused by his own people of cowardice, which the bravest hold in horror.

This wily savage had the bones of some important deceased relative, which he preserved with great care in some skins dressed and adorned with several rows of black and red porcupine quills; from time to time he assembled his men to give it a smoke, and made us come several days in succession to cover the deceased's bones with goods, and by a present wipe away the tears he had shed for him, and for his own son killed by the Miamis. To appease this captious man, we threw on the bones several fathoms of French tobacco, axes, knives, beads, and some black and white wampum bracelets.

In this way the Indian stripped us under pretexts, which we could not reproach him with, as he declared that what he asked was only for the deceased, and to give the warriors. In fact, he distributed among them all that we gave him. By these feints he made us believe that being a chief, he took nothing for himself, but what we gave him of our own accord. We slept at the point of the lake of Tears, which we so called from the tears which this chief shed all night long, or by one of his sons, whom he caused to weep when tired himself, in order to excite his warriors to compassion, and oblige them to kill us and pursue their enemies to avenge his son's death

These Indians at times sent their fleetest by land to chase the buffalo on the water side; as these animals crossed the river, they sometimes killed forty or fifty, merely to take the tongue, and most delicate morsels, leaving the rest with which they would not burthen themselves, so as to go on more rapidly. We sometimes indeed eat good pieces, but without bread, wine, salt, or other seasoning. During our three years' travels we had lived in the same way, sometimes in plenty, at others compelled to pass twenty-four hours, and often more, without eating; because in these little bark canoes you can not take much of a load, and with every precaution you are, for most part of the time, deprived of all necessaries of life. If a religious in Europe underwent many hardships and labors, and abstinences like those we were often obliged to suffer in America, no other proof would be needed for his canonization. It is true that we do not always merit in such cases and suffer only because we can not help it.

During the night some old men came to weep piteously, often rubbing our arms and whole bodies with their hands, which they then put on our head. Besides being hindered from sleeping by these tears, I often did not know what to think, nor whether these Indians wept because some of their warriors would have killed us, or out of pure compassion at the ill treatment shown us.

On another occasion, Aquipaguetin relapsed into his bad humor: he had so gained most of the warriors, that one day when we were unable to encamp near our protector Narhetoba, we were obliged to go to the very end of the camp, the Indians declaring that this chief insisted positively on killing us. We accordingly drew from a box twenty knives and some tobacco, which we angrily flung down amid the malcontents; the wretch regarding all his soldiers one after another hesitated, asking their advice, either to refuse or take our present; and as we bowed our head and presented him with an axe to kill us, the young chief who was really or pretendedly our protector took us by the arm, and all in fury led us to his cabin. One of his brothers taking some arrows, broke them all in our presence, showing us by this action, that he prevented their killing us.

The next day they left us alone in our canoe, without putting in any Indians to help us, as they usually did; all remained behind us. After four or five leagues sail another chief came to us, made us disembark, and pulling up three little piles of grass, made us sit down; he then took a piece of cedar full of little round holes in one of which he put a stick, which he spun round between his two palms, and in this way made fire to light the tobacco in his great calumet. After weeping some time, and putting his hands on my head, he gave me his peace-calumet to smoke, and showed us that we should be in his country in six days.

Having arrived on the nineteenth day of our navigation five leagues below St. Anthony's falls, these Indians landed us in a bay and assembled to deliberate about us. They distributed us separately, and gave us to three heads of families in place of three of their children who had been killed in war. They first seized all our property, and broke our canoe to pieces, for fear we should return to their enemies. Their own they hid in some alders to use when going to hunt; and though we might easily have reached their country by water, they compelled us to go sixty leagues by land, forcing us to march from daybreak to two hours after nightfall, and to swim over many rivers, while these Indians, who are often of extraordinary height, carried *our* habit on their head; and our two boatmen, who were smaller than myself, on their shoulders, because they could not swim as I could. On leaving the water, which was often full of sharp ice, I could scarcely stand; our legs were all bloody from the ice which we broke as we advanced in lakes which we forded, and as we eat only once in twenty-four hours, some pieces of meat which these barbarians grudgingly gave us, I was so weak that I often lay down on the way, resolved to die there, rather than follow these Indians who marched on and continued their route with a celerity which surpasses the power of the Europeans. To oblige us to hasten on, they often set fire to the grass of the prairies where we were passing, so that we had to advance or burn. I had then a hat which I reserved to shield me from the burning rays of the sun in summer, but I often dropped it in the flames which we were obliged to cross.

As we approached their village, they divided among them all the merchandise of our two canoemen, and were near killing each other for our roll of French tobacco, which is very precious to these tribes, and more esteemed than gold among Europeans. The more humane showed by signs that they

would give many beaver-skins for what they took. The reason of the violence was, that this party was made up from
two different tribes, the more distant of whom, fearing lest
the others should retain all the goods in the first villages
which they would have to pass, wished to take their share in
advance. In fact, some time after they offered peltries in
part payment; but our boatmen would not receive them, until
they gave the full value of all that had been taken. And
in course of time I have no doubt they will give entire satisfaction to the French, whom they will endeavor to draw
among them to carry on trade.

These savages also took our brocade chasuble, and all the
articles of our portable chapel, except the chalice, which they
durst not touch; for seeing that glittering silver gilt, they closed
their eyes, saying that it was a spirit which would kill them.
They also broke a little box with lock and key, after telling
me, that if I did not break the lock, they would do so themselves with sharp stones; the reason of this violence was that
from time to time on the route, they could not open the box
to examine what was inside, having no idea of locks and
keys; besides, they did not care to carry the box, but only
the goods which were inside, and which they thought considerable, but they found only books and papers.

After five days' march by land, suffering hunger, thirst, and
outrages, marching all day long without rest, fording lakes
and rivers, we descried a number of women and children
coming to meet our little army. All the elders of this nation
assembled on our account, and as we saw cabins, and bundles
of straw hanging from the posts of them, to which these
savages bind those whom they take as slaves, and burn them;
and seeing that they made the Picard du Gay sing, as he
held and shook a gourd full of little round pebbles, while his

hair and face were filled with paint of different colors, and a tuft of white feathers attached to his head by the Indians, we not unreasonably thought that they wished to kill us, as they performed many ceremonies, usually practised, when they intend to burn their enemies. The worst of it was, too, that not one of us three could make himself understood by these Indians; nevertheless, after many vows, which every Christian would make in such straits, one of the principal Issati chiefs gave us his peace-calumet to smoke, and accepted the one we had brought. He then gave us some wild rice to eat, presenting it to us in large bark dishes, which the Indian women had seasoned with whortleberries, which are black grains which they dry in the sun in summer, and are as good as currants. After this feast, the best we had had for seven or eight days, the heads of families who had adopted us, instead of their sons killed in war, conducted us separately each to his village, marching through marshes knee deep in water, for a league, after which the five wives of the one who called me Mitchinchi, that is to say, his son, received us in three bark canoes, and took us a short league from our starting place to an island where their cabins were.

On our arrival, which was about Easter, April 21st, 1680,[*] one of these Indians who seemed to me decrepit, gave me a large calumet to smoke, and weeping bitterly, rubbed my head and arms, showing his compassion at seeing me so fatigued that two men were often obliged to give me their hands ·to help me to stand up. There was a bearskin near the fire, on which he rubbed my legs and the soles of my feet with wild-cat oil.

[*] This is somewhat vague; Easter Sunday, in 1680, fell on the 21st of April; he was taken on the 11th of April, travelled nineteen days in canoe, and five by land, which brings him to the 5th of May. He perceived this afterward, and in the English edition, he says, that he arrived some time in May; but he there falls into a worse error by putting Easter back to the 23d of March.

Aquipaguetin's son, who called me his brother, paraded about with our brocade chasuble on his bare back, having rolled up in it some dead man's bones, for whom these people had a great veneration. The priest's girdle made of red and white wool, with two tassels at the end, served him for suspenders, carrying thus in triumph what he called Pere Louis Chinnien, which means " the robe of him who is called the sun." After these Indians had used this chasuble to cover the bones of their dead, they presented it to some of their allies, tribes situated about five hundred leagues west of their country, who had sent them an embassy and danced the calumet.

The day after our arrival, Aquipaguetin, who was the head of a large family, covered me with a robe made of ten large dressed beaver-skins, trimmed with porcupine quills. This Indian showed me five or six of his wives, telling them, as I afterward learned, that they should in future regard me as one of their children. He set before me a bark dish full of fish, and ordered all those assembled, that each should call me by the name I was to have in the rank of our near relationship; and seeing that I could not rise from the ground but by the help of two others, he had a sweating cabin made, in which he made me enter naked with four Indians. This cabin he covered with buffalo-skins, and inside he put stones red to the middle. He made me a sign to do as the others before beginning to sweat, but I merely concealed my nakedness with a handkerchief. As soon as these Indians had several times breathed out quite violently, he began to sing in a thundering voice, the others seconded him, all putting their hands on me, and rubbing me, while they wept bitterly. I began to faint, but I came out, and could scarcely take my habit to put on. When he had made me sweat thus three times a week, I felt as strong as ever.

I often spent sad hours among these savages; for, besides their only giving me a little wild rice and smoked fish roes five or six times a week, which they boiled in earthen pots, Aquipaguetin took me to a neighboring island with his wives and children to till the ground, in order to sow some tobacco seed, and seeds of vegetables that I had brought, and which this Indian prized extremely.   Sometimes he assembled the elders of the village, in whose presence he asked me for a compass that I always had in my sleeve; seeing that I made the needle turn with a key, and believing justly that we Europeans went all over the habitable globe, guided by this instrument, this chief, who was very eloquent, persuaded his people that we were spirits, and capable of doing anything beyond their reach.   At the close of his address, which was very animated, all the old men wept over my head, admiring in me what they could not understand.   I had an iron pot with three lion-paw feet, which these Indians never dared touch, unless their hand was wrapped up in some robe.   The women hung it to the branch of a tree, not daring to enter the cabin where it was.   I was some time unable to make myself understood by these people, but feeling myself gnawed by hunger, I began to compile a dictionary of their language by means of their children, with whom I made myself familiar, in order to learn.

As soon as I could catch the word Taketchiabihen, which means in their language, "How do you call that," I became, in a little while, able to converse with them on familiar things. At first, indeed, to ask the word *run* in their language, I had to quicken my steps from one end of their large cabin to the other.   The chiefs of these savages seeing my desire to learn, often made me write, naming all the parts of the human body, and as I would not put on paper certain indelicate words, at which they do not blush, it afforded them an agreeable amusement. They often put me questions, but as I had to look at my paper, to answer them, they said to one another: "When we ask Pere Louis [for so they had heard our two Frenchmen call me], he does not answer us; but as soon as he has looked at what is white [for they have no word to say paper], he answers us, and tells us his thoughts; that white thing," said they, "must be a spirit which tells Pere Louis all we say." They concluded that our two Frenchmen were not as great as I, because they could not work like me on what was white. In consequence the Indians believed that I could do everything; when the rain fell in such quantities as to incommode them, or prevent their going to hunt, they told me to stop it; but I knew enough to answer them by pointing to the clouds, that he was great chief of heaven, was master of everything, and that they bid me to do, did not depend on me.

These Indians often asked me how many wives and children I had, and how old I was, that is, how many winters, for so these nations alway count. These men never illumined by the light of a faith were surprised at the answer I made them; for pointing to our two Frenchmen whom I had then gone to visit three leagues from our village, I told them that a man among us could have only one wife till death; that as for me, I had promised the Master of life to live as they saw me, and to come and live with them to teach them that he would have them be like the French; that this great Master of life had sent down fire from heaven, and destroyed a nation given to enormous crimes, like those committed among them. But that gross people till then, lawless and faithless, turned all I said into ridicule. "How," said they, "would you have those two men with thee have wives? Ours would not

live with them, for they have hair all over the face, and we
have none there or elsewhere." In fact, they were never better pleased with me, than when I was shaved ; and from a
complaisance certainly not criminal, I shaved every week.
All our kindred seeing that I wished to leave them, made a
packet of beaver-skins worth six hundred livres among the
French. These peltries they gave me to induce me to remain among them, to introduce me to strange nations that
were coming to visit them, and in restitution of what they had
robbed me of; but I refused these presents, telling them that
I had not come among them to gather beaver-skins, but only
to tell them the will of the great Master of life, and to live
wretchedly with them, after having left a most abundant country. "It is true," said they, "that we have no chase in this
part, and that thou sufferest, but wait till summer, then we
will go and kill buffalo in the warm country." I should have
been satisfied had they fed me as they did their children,
but they eat secretly at night unknown to me. Although
women are, for the most part, more kind and compassionate
than men, they gave what little fish they had to their children, regarding me as a slave made by their warriors in their
enemies' country, and they reasonably preferred their children's lives to mine.

There were some old men who often came to weep over
my head in a sighing voice, saying, "Son," or "Nephew, I
feel sorry to see thee without eating, and to learn how badly
our warriors treated thee on the way; they are young braves,
without sense, who would have killed thee, and have robbed
thee of all thou hast. Hadst thou wanted buffalo or beaver-
robes, we would wipe away thy tears, but thou wilt have
nothing of what we offer thee."

Ouasicoudé, that is, the Pierced-pine, the greatest of all the

9

Issati chiefs, being very indignant at those who had so mal-
treated us, said, in open council, that those who had robbed
us of all we had, were like hungry curs that stealthily snatch
a bit of meat from the bark dish, and then fly; so those who
had acted so toward us, deserved to be regarded as dogs,
since they insulted men who brought them iron and merchandise, which they had never had; that he would find
means to punish the one who had so outraged us. This is
what the brave chief showed to all his nation, as we shall see
hereafter.

As I often went to visit the cabins of these last nations, I
found a sick child, whose father's name was Mamenisi; having
a moral certainty of its death, I begged our two Frenchmen
to give me their advice, telling them I believed myself
obliged to baptize it. Michael Ako would not accompany
me, the Picard du Gay alone followed me to act as sponsor,
or rather as witness of the baptism.* I christened the child
Antoinette in honor of St. Anthony of Padua, as well as from
the Picard's name which was Anthony Auguelle. He was a
native of Amiens, and a nephew of Mr. de Cauroy, procurator-general of the Premonstratensians, both now at Paris.
Having poured natural water on the head of this Indian
child, and uttered these words: "Creature of God, I baptize
thee in the name of the Father, and of the Son, and of the
Holy Ghost," I took half an altar cloth which I had wrested
from the hands of an Indian who had stolen it from me, and
put it on the body of the baptized child; for as I could not
say mass for want of wine and vestments, this piece of linen
could not be put to a better use, than to enshroud the first
Christian child among these tribes. I do not know whether the

---

* This a curious affair, a missionary consulting two canoemen as to the expe-
diency of conferring a sacrament.

softness of the linen had refreshed her, but she was the next day smiling in her mother's arms, who believed that I had cured her child, but she died soon after to my great consolation.

During our stay among the Issati or Nadouessiou, we saw Indians who came as embassadors from about five hundred leagues to the west. They informed us that the Assenipoualacs* were then only seven or eight days distant to the northeast of us; all the other known tribes on the west and northwest inhabit immense plains and prairies abounding in buffalo and peltries, where they are sometimes obliged to make fires with buffalo dung for want of wood.

Three months after, all these nations assembled, and the chiefs having regulated the places for hunting the buffalo, they dispersed in several bands so as not to starve each other. Aquipaguetin, one of the chiefs who had adopted me as his son, wished to take me to the west with about two hundred families; I made answer that I awaited spirits (so they called Frenchmen), at the river Oüisconsin, which empties into the river Colbert, who were to join me to bring merchandise, and that if he went that way, I would continue with him; he would have gone but for those of his nation. In the beginning of July, 1680, we descended in canoe southward with the great chief named Ouasicoudé, that is to say, the Pierced-pine, with about eighty cabins, composed of more than a hundred and thirty families, and about two hundred and fifty warriors. Scarcely would the Indians give me a place in their little fleet, for they had only old canoes. They went four leagues lower down to get birch bark to make some more. Having made a hole in the ground to hide our silver chalice and our

* This name, Assenipoualak, has now been softened to Assiniboin; it is the Algonquin epithet for a large branch of the Dahcotah family, long hostile to the Sioux, written also simply Poualak.

papers till we returned from the hunt, and keeping only our
breviary, so as not to be loaded, I stood on the bank of a lake
formed by the river we had called St. Francis, and stretched
out my hand to the canoes as they rapidly passed in succession; our Frenchmen also had one for themselves, which the
Indians had given them; they would not take me in, Michael
Ako saying that he had taken me long enough to satisfy him.
I was hurt at this answer, seeing myself thus abandoned by
Christians, to whom I had always done good, as they both
often acknowledged; but God having never abandoned me
in that painful voyage, inspired two Indians to take me in
their little canoe, where I had no other employment than to
bale out with a little bark tray the water which entered by little
holes. This I did not do without getting all wet. This boat
might, indeed, be called a death-box, from its lightness and
fragility. These canoes do not generally weigh over fifty
pounds; the least motion of the body upsets them, unless you
are long habituated to that kind of navigation. On disem-
barking in the evening, the Picard, as an excuse, told me
that their canoe was half rotten, and that, had we been three
in it, we should have run a great risk of remaining on the
way. In spite of this excuse I told him, that being Christians, they should not act so, especially among Indians, more
than eight hundred leagues from the French settlements;
that if they were well received in this country, it was only
in consequence of my bleeding some asthmatic Indians, and
my giving them some orvietan and other remedies which I
kept in my sleeve, and by which I had saved the lives of
some Indians bit by rattlesnakes, and because I had neatly
made their tonsure, which Indian children wear to the age
of eighteen or twenty, but have no way of making except by
burning the hair with red-hot flat stones. I reminded them

that by my ingenuity I had gained the friendship of these people, who would have killed us or made us suffer more, had they not discovered about me those remedies which they prize, when they restore the sick to health. However, the Picard only, as he retired to his host's, apologised to me.

Four days after our departure for the buffalo hunt, we halted eight leagues above St. Anthony of Padua's falls on an eminence opposite the mouth of the river St. Francis; here the Indian women made their canoe frames while waiting for those who were to bring bark to make canoes. The young men went to hunt stag, deer, and beaver, but killed so few animals for such a large party, that we could very rarely get a bit of meat, having to put up with a broth once in every twenty-four hours. The Picard and myself went to look for haws, gooseberries, and little wild fruit, which often did us more harm than good; this obliged us to go alone, as Michael Ako refused, in a wretched canoe to Ouisconsin river, which was more than a hundred leagues off, to see whether the sieur de la Salle had sent to that place a reinforcement of men, with powder, lead, and other munitions, as he had promised us on our departure from the Islinois.*

The Indians would not have suffered this voyage, had not one of the three remained with them; they wished me to stay, but Michael Ako absolutely refused. Our whole stock was fifteen charges of powder, a gun, a wretched earthern pot which the Indians had given us, a knife, and a beaver-robe, to make a journey of two hundred leagues, thus abandoning ourselves to Providence. As we were making the portage of our canoe at St. Anthony of Padua's falls, we perceived five or six of our Indians who had taken the start;

---

* This is the first we hear of this promise, or of La Salle's having sent him to the Wisconsin, or given him a rendezvous there.

one of them was up in an oak opposite the great fall weeping bitterly, with a well-dressed beaver robe, whitened inside and trimmed with porcupine quills which he was offering as a sacrifice to the falls, which is in itself admirable and frightful. I heard him while shedding copious tears say as he spoke to the great cataract: "Thou who art a spirit, grant that our nation may pass her quietly without accident, may kill buffalo in abundance, conquer our enemies, and bring in slaves, some of whom we will put to death before thee; the Messenecqz (so they call the tribe named by the French Outouagamis), have killed our kindred, grant that we may avenge them." In fact, after the heat of the buffalo-hunt, they invaded their enemies, killed some, and brought others as slaves. If they succeed a single time, even after repeated failures, they adhere to their superstition. This robe offered in sacrifice served one of our Frenchmen, who took it as we returned.

A league below St. Anthony of Padua's falls, the Picard was obliged to land and get his powder-horn which he had left at the falls. On his return, I showed him a snake about six feet long crawling up a straight and precipitous mountain and which gradually gained on some swallows' nests to eat the young ones; at the foot of the mountain, we saw the feathers of those he had apparently eaten, and we pelted him down with stones.

As we descended the river Colbert, we found some of our Indians cabined in the islands, loaded with buffalo-meat, some of which they gave us. Two hours after landing, fifteen or sixteen warriors of the party whom we had left above St. Anthony of Padua's falls, entered tomahawk in hand, upset the cabins of those who had invited us, took all the meat and bear-oil that they found, and greased themselves from head to foot; we at first took them to be enemies, but one of those who called himself my uncle, told me, that having gone to the buffalo-hunt before the rest, contrary to the maxims of the country, they had a right to strip them, because they put the buffaloes to flight before the arrival of the mass of the nation.

During sixty leagues that we sailed down the river, we killed only one deer, swimming across, but the heat was so great that the meat spoiled in twenty-four hours. This made us look for turtles, which we found hard to take, as their hearing is acute, and the moment they hear the least noise, they jump quickly into the water. We, however, took one much larger than the rest, with a thinner shell and fatter meat. While I tried to cut off his head, he all but cut off one of my fingers. We had drawn one end of our canoe ashore, when a gust of wind drove it into the middle of the great river; the Picard had gone with the gun into the prairie to try and kill a buffalo; so I quickly pulled off our habit, and threw it on the turtle with some stones to prevent its escaping, and swam after our canoe which went very fast down stream, as the current there was very strong. Having reached it with much difficulty, I durst not get in for fear of upsetting it, so I either pushed it before me, or drew it after me, and so little by little reached the shore about one eighth of a league from the place where I had the turtle. The Picard finding only our habit, and not seeing the canoe, naturally believed that some Indian had killed me. He retired to the prairie to look all around whether there were no people there. Meanwhile I remounted the river with all diligence in the canoe, and had just put on my habit, when I saw more than sixty buffalo crossing the river to reach the south side; I pursued the animals, calling the Picard with all my might; he ran up at the noise and had time to enter the canoe, while the dog which had jumped into the water had driven them into an island. Having given them chase here, they were crossing back when he shot one, which was so heavy that we could get it ashore only in pieces, being obliged to cut the best morsels, while the rest was in the water. As it was almost two days since we had eaten, we made a fire with the drift-wood we found on the sand; and while the Picard was skinning the animal, I cooked the morsels of the fat meat in our little earthern pot; we then eat it so eagerly that we both fell sick, and had to stay two days in the island to recover. We could not take much of the meat, our canoe was so small, and besides the excessive heat spoiled it, so that we were all at once deprived of it, as it was full of worms; and when we embarked in the morning, we did not know what we would eat during the day. Never have we more admired God's providence than during this voyage, for we did not always find deer, and could not kill them when we would; but the eagles, which are very common in these vast countries, some-times dropped from their claws bream, or large carp, which they were carrying to their nests. Another time we found an otter on the bank of the river Colbert eating a large fish, which had, running from the head, a kind of paddle or beak, five fingers broad and a foot and a half long, which made our Picard say, that he thought he saw a devil in the paws of that otter: but his fright did not prevent our eating the mon-strous fish which we found very good.

While seeking the Ouisconsin river, Aquipaguetin, that savage father, whom I had left, and whom I believed more than two hundred leagues off, suddenly appeared with ten warriors, on the 11th of July, 1680. We believed that he was coming to kill us, because we had left him with the knowledge, indeed, of the other Indians, but against his will. He first gave us some wild-rice, and a slice of buffalo-meat to eat, and asked whether we had found the Frenchmen who were to bring us goods; but not being satisfied with what we said, he started before us, and went to Ouisconsin to try and carry off what he could from the French; this savage found none there, and rejoined us three days after. The Picard had gone in the prairie to hunt, and I was alone in a little cabin on the bank of the river, which I had made to screen us from the sun, with a blanket that an Indian had given me back. Aquipaguetin seeing me alone came up, tomahawk in hand: I laid hold of two pocket-pistols, which the Picard had got back from the Indians, and a knife, not intending to kill my pretended Indian father, but only to frighten him, and prevent his crushing me, in case he had that intention. Aquipaguetin reprimanded me for exposing myself thus to the insults of their enemies, saying that I should at least take the other shore to be more in safety. He wished to take me with him, telling me that he was with three hundred hunters, who killed more buffalo than those to whom I had abandoned myself. I would have done well to follow his advice, for the Picard and myself ascending the river almost eighty leagues way, ran great risk of perishing a thousand times.

We had only ten charges of powder which we were obliged to divide into twenty to kill wild-pigeons, or turtle-doves; but when these at last gave out we had recourse to three hooks, which we baited with bits of putrid barbels dropped by an eagle. For two whole days we took nothing, and were thus destitute of all support when, during night prayer, as we were repeating these words addressed to St. Anthony of Padua, " Pereunt pericula, cessat et necessitas," the Picard heard a noise, left his prayers, and ran to our hooks which he drew

from the waters with two barbels so large that I had to go
and help him. Without cleaning these monstrous fish we cut
them in pieces, and roasted them on the coals, our only little
earthen pot having been broken. Two hours after night, we
were joined by Mamenisi, the father of the little Indian girl
that I had baptized before she died ; he gave us plenty of
meat.

The next day the Indians whom we had left with Michael
Ako, came down from Buffalo river with their flotilla of
canoes loaded with meat. Aquipaguetin had, as he passed,
told how exposed the Picard and I were on our voyage, and
the Indian chiefs represented to us the cowardice of Michael
Ako, who had refused to undertake it, for fear of dying by
hunger. If I had not stopped him, the Picard would have
insulted him.

All the Indian women hid their stock of meat at the mouth
of Buffalo river, and in the islands, and we again went down
the Colbert about eighty leagues to hunt with this multitude
of canoes ; from time to time the Indians hid their canoes
on the banks of the river and in the islands; then struck in to
the prairies seven or eight leagues beyond the mountains,
where they took, at different times, a hundred and twenty
buffaloes. They always left some of their old men on the
tops of the mountains to be on the lookout for their enemies.
One day when I was dressing the foot of one who called himself my brother, and who had run a splinter deep into his
foot, an alarm was given in the camp, two hundred bowmen
ran out ; and that brave Indian, although I had just made a
deep incision in the sole of his foot to draw out the wood,
left me and ran even faster than the rest, not to be deprived
of the glory of fighting, but instead of enemies, they found
only a herd of about eighty stags, who took flight. The

wounded man could scarcely regain the camp. During this alarm, all the Indian women sang in a lugubrious tone. The Picard left me to join his host, and I remaining with one called Otchimbi, had to carry in the canoe an old Indian woman of over eighty. For all her great age, she threatened to strike with her paddle three children who troubled us in the middle of our canoe. The men treated me well enough, but as the meat was almost entirely at the disposal of the women, I was compelled, in order to get some, to make their children's tonsures, about as large as those of our religious, for these little savages wear them to the age of fifteen or sixteen, and their parents make them with red hot stones.

We had another alarm in our camp : the old men on duty on the top of the mountains announced that they saw two warriors in the distance ; all the bowmen hastened there with speed, each trying to outstrip the others ; but they brought back only two of their own women, who came to tell them that a party of their people were hunting at the extremity of Lake Condé (Superior), had found five spirits (so they call the French) ; who, by means of a slave, had expressed a wish to come on, knowing us to be among them, in order to find out whether we were English, Dutch, Spaniards, or Frenchmen being unable to understand by what roundabout we had reached those tribes.

On the 25th of July, 1680, as we were ascending the river Colbert after the buffalo-hunt, to the Indian villages we met the sieur de Luth, who came to the Nadouessious, with five French soldiers ; they joined us about two hundred and twenty leagues distant from the country of the Indians who had taken us ;* as we had some knowledge of their language,

---

* This would make his meeting with de Luth take place some time below the Illinois, according to his description of the river. In the English edition,

they begged us to accompany them to the villages of those
tribes, to which I readily agreed, knowing that these Frenchmen had not approached the sacraments for two years.   The
sieur de Luth, who acted as captain, seeing me tired of ton-
suring the children, and bleeding asthmatic old men to get a
mouthful of meat, told the Indians that I was his elder brother,
so that, having my subsistence secured, I labored only for the
salvation of these Indians.

We arrived at the villages of the Issati on the 14th of August, 1680.   I there found our chalice and books which I had
hidden in the ground; the tobacco which I had planted, had
been choked by the weeds; the turnips, cabbages, and other
vegetables were of extraordinary size.   The Indians durst not
eat them.   During our stay, they invited us to a feast where
there were more than a hundred and twenty men all naked.
The first chief, a relative of the one whose body I had covered
with a blanket, brought me a bark dish of food which he put
on a buffalo-robe, dressed, whitened, and trimmed with porcupine quills on one side, and the curly wool on the other.
He afterward put it on my head, saying: "He whose body
thou didst cover, covers thine; he has borne tidings of thee
to the land of souls.   Brave was thy act in his regard; all
the nation praises thee for it."   He then reproached the sieur
du Luth, for not having covered the deceased's body, as I did.
He replied that he covered only those of captains like himself; but the Indian answered, "Père Louis is a greater captain than thou for his robe (meaning our brocade chasuble),

doubtless, for good reasons, he says, *one* hundred and twenty which would bring
it just below the Wisconsin.   If de Luth came by way of Lake Superior, it is
not easy to see how he met them so far down, or how after descending the Mississippi he needed the aid of Hennepin in ascending.   This officer who figured
considerably in the affairs of Canada, was captain in the marines, and was commander of Fort Frontenac, in 1696.

which we have sent to our allies, who dwell three moons from this country, is more beautiful than that which thou wearest."

Toward the end of September, having no implements to begin an establishment, we resolved to tell these people, that for their benefit, we would have to return to the French settlements.* The grand chief of the Issati, or Nadouessiouz, consented, and traced in pencil on a paper I gave him, the route we should take for four hundred leagues. With this chart, we set out, eight Frenchmen, in two canoes, and descended the rivers St. Francis and Colbert. Two of our men took two beaver-robes at St. Anthony of Padua's falls, which the Indians had hung in sacrifice on the trees.

We stopped near Ouisconsin river to smoke some meat; three Indians coming from the nations we had left, told us that their great chief named Pierced-pine, having heard that one of the chiefs of the nation wished to pursue and kill us, had entered his cabin and tomahawked him, to prevent his pernicious design. We regaled these three Indians with meat, of which we were in no want then.

Two days after, we perceived an army of one hundred and forty canoes, filled with about two hundred and fifty warriors; we thought that those who brought the preceding news were spies, for instead of descending the river on leaving us, they ascended to tell their people; however, the chiefs of the little army visited us and treated us very kindly, and the same day descended the river as we did to the Ouisconsin. We found that river as wide as the Seignelay (Illinois), with a strong current. After sailing up sixty leagues, we came to a portage of half a league, which the Nadouessiouz chiefs had marked for us; we slept there to leave marks

* Here, *a la Hennepin*, de Luth is merged in the *we*.

and crosses on the trunks of the trees.* The next day we entered a river which winds wonderfully, for after six hours sailing, we found ourselves opposite the place where we started. One of our men wishing to kill a swan on the wing, capsized his canoe, fortunately not beyond his depth.

We passed four lakes, two pretty large, on the banks of which the Miamis formerly resided, we found Maskoutens, Kikapous, and Outaougamy there, who sow Indian corn for their subsistence. All this country is as fine as that of the Islinois.

We made a portage at a rapid called Kakalin, and after about four hundred leagues sail from our leaving the country of the Issati, and Nadouessiouz, we arrived safely at the extremity of the bay of the Fetid, where we found Frenchmen trading contrary to orders with the Indians. They had some little wine in a tin flagon, which enabled me to say mass; I had then only a chalice and altar stone; but Providence supplied me with vestments, for some Islinois flying from the tyranny of the Iroquois, who had destroyed a part of their nation, took the vestments of the chapel of Father Zenobius Membré, Recollect, who was with the Islinois in their flight. They gave me all they took, except the chalice, which they promised to give back in a few days for a present of tobacco.

I had not celebrated mass for over nine months for want of wine; I had still some hosts. We remained two days to rest, sing the Te Deum, high mass, and preach. All our Frenchmen went to confession and communion, to thank God for having preserved us amid so many wanderings and perils.

One of our Frenchmen gave a gun for a canoe larger than

* This was the same route that Marquette took going down. See his description. The Kakalin rapid had been previously visited and explored by Allouez, and mentioned in the *Rel.*, 1669–'70.

ours, with which, after sailing a hundred leagues, we reached Missilimackinac, where we were obliged to winter. To employ the time usefully, I preached every holyday, and on the Sundays of Advent and Lent.* The Ottawas and Hurons were often present, rather from curiosity than from any inclination to live according to the Christian maxims. These last Indians said, speaking of our discovery, that they were men, but that we Frenchmen were spirits, because, had they gone so far, the strange nations would have killed them, while we went fearlessly everywhere.

During the winter, we took whitefish in Lake Orleans (Huron), in twenty or twenty-two fathoms water. They served to season the Indian corn, which was our usual fare. Forty-two Frenchmen trading there with the Indians begged me to give them all the cord of St. Francis, which I readily did, making an exhortation at each ceremony.

We left Missilimackinac in Easter week, 1681, and were obliged to drag our provisions and canoes on the ice, more than ten leagues on Lake Orleans; having advanced far enough on this fresh-water sea, and the ice breaking, we embarked after Low Sunday, which we celebrated, having some little wine which a Frenchman had fortunately brought, and which served us quite well the rest of the voyage. After a hundred leagues on Lake Orleans, we passed the strait (Detroit), for thirty leagues and Lake St. Clare,† which is in the middle and entered Lake Conty, where we killed, with sword

---

* In the English edition he tells us that he enjoyed, during the winter, the hospitality of Father Pierson, a Jesuit and a fellow-townsmen of his own, whom he eulogizes there, but passes over in perfect silence here. What was his reason in each case? In neither he mentions the church at Green bay.

† This name is commonly written St. Clair, but this is incorrect; we should either retain the French form Claire, or take the English Clare. It received its name in honor of the founder of the Franciscan nuns, from the fact that La Salle reached it on the day consecrated to her.

and axe, more than thirty sturgeon which came to spawn on the banks of the lake. On the way we met an Ottawa chief called Talon, six persons of whose family had died of starvation, not having found a good fishery or hunting-ground. This Indian told us that the Iroquois had carried off a family of twelve belonging to his tribe, and begged us to deliver them, if yet alive.

We sailed along Lake Conty, and after a hundred and twenty leagues we passed the strait of the great falls of Niagara and Fort Conty, and entering Lake Frontenac, coasted along the southern shore. After thirty leagues from Lake Conty, we reached the great Seneca village about Whitsunday, 1681. We entered the Iroquois council and asked them, why they had enslaved twelve of our Ottawa allies, telling them that those whom they had taken, were children of the governor of the French, as well as the Iroquois, and that by this violence, they declared war on the French. To induce them to restore our allies, we gave them two belts of wampum.

The next day the Iroquois answered us by two belts, that the Ottawas had been carried off by some mad young warriors; that we might assure the governor of the French, that the Iroquois would hearken to him in all things; that they wished to live with Onontio like real children with their father (so they call the governor of Canada), and that they would restore those whom they had taken.

A chief named Teganeot, who spoke for his whole nation in all the councils, made me a present of otter and beaver-skins, to the value of over twenty-five crowns. I took it with one hand, and gave it with the other to his son, telling him that I gave it to him to buy goods of the other Frenchmen; that as for us, Barefeet, as the Iroquois called us, we would not take beaver or peltries ; but that I would report their friendly feeling to the governor of the French. This Iroquois chief was surprised at my refusing his present, and told his own people that the other French did not do so. We took leave of the chief men, and after sailing forty leagues on the lake, reached Fort Frontenac, where the dear Recollect Father Luke was greatly surprised to see me, as for two years it had been reported that the Indians had hung me with our Franciscan cord. All the inhabitants, French and Indians, whom we had gathered at Fort Frontenac, welcomed me with extraordinary joy at my return ; the Indians calling me Atkon, and putting their hand to their mouth, which means, Barefeet is a spirit to have travelled so far. At the mouth of Lake Frontenac the current is strong, and the more you descend the more it increases ; the rapids are frightful. In two days and a half we descended the river St. Lawrence so rapidly that we reached Montreal (sixty miles from the fort), where the count de Frontenac, governor-general of all New France then was. This governor received me as well as a man of his probity can receive a missionary. As he believed me killed by the Indians, he was for a time thunderstruck, believing me to be some other religious. He beheld me wasted, without a cloak, with a habit patched with pieces of buffalo-skin. He took me with him for twelve days to recover, and himself gave me the meat I was to eat, for fear I should fall sick by eating too much after so long a diet. I rendered him an exact account of my voyage, and represented to him the advantage of our discovery.*

---

* Of course the English edition says, nothing about this exact account, nor tells how he concealed the truth and avoided questions.

10

NARRATIVE

OF THE ADVENTURES OF

LA SALLE'S PARTY AT FORT CREVECŒUR, IN ILINOIS,

FROM FEBRUARY, 1680, TO JUNE, 1681, BY

*FATHER ZENOBIUS MEMBRÉ, RECOLLECT.**

FATHER LOUIS (HENNEPIN) having set out on the 29th of February, 1680, the sieur de la Salle left the sieur de Tonty as commander of Fort Crevecœur with ammunitions, and provisions, and peltries, to pay the workmen

* If the projects of La Salle had raised up against him pertinacious enemies, they nevertheless drew around him a few faithful and devoted friends, and none more conspicuous than the excellent missionary whose journals we here insert. The amiable Father Membré is the name under which all seem to delight in presenting him to us, so much were they touched by his goodness of heart. Were it prudent to credit Hennepin's last work for anything new, we might say, that Membré was born at Bapaume, a small fortified town, now in France, but then in the Spanish Netherlands, and that he was a cousin of Father Christian le Clercq, who published his journals in the "Etablissement de la Foi." It was probably on entering the Recollect convent in Artois, where he was the first novice in the new province of St. Anthony, that he assumed the name of Zenobius. With his cousin le Clercq, he was the first sent by that province to Canada where he arrived in 1675, from which time till that of his departure for Frontenac, in September, 1678, he was probably employed at the convent of Quebec, as his name does not appear in any of the neighboring parish registers examined to obtain his autograph. From Fort Frontenac he accompanied La Salle to Niagara, Mackinaw, and, at last, to Fort Crevecœur, in Illinois. Here he was left by that commander with Tonty and Father Gabriel de la Rebourde, with whom on the inroad of the Iroquois and flight of the Illinois, he endeavored to reach Green

as agreed, and merchandise to trade with and buy provisions
as we needed them, and having lastly given orders as to what
was to be done in his absence, set out with four Frenchmen
and an Indian on the 2d of March, 1680.   He arrived on
the 11th at the great Ilinois village where I then was, and
thence, after twenty-four hours' stay, he continued his route

Bay.   Father Gabriel perished on the way by the hand of the Kikapoos; the
survivors were hospitably received by the Jesuits at Green Bay, where they
wintered, and in the spring proceeded to Mackinaw with Father Enjalran.
Here La Salle soon joined them, and Membré, after a voyage to Fort Frontenac,
and probably to Montreal, with that commander in the spring of 1681, descended
the Mississippi with him to the gulf, and on their return proceeded at his request
to France in 1682, to lay before the government the result of the expedition.
He left a journal of his voyage at Quebec; but, as he declined communicating it
to the new governor, De la Barre, the latter, in his report to the home government, throws imputations on any account of the missionary, which must, however, be ascribed only to bias and dissatisfaction.   After fulfilling his mission at
court, Father Membré became warden of the recollects at Bapaume, and
remained so till he was appointed at La Salle's request, superior of the missionaries who were to accompany his expedition by sea.   Father Membré reached
Texas in safety, and though nearly drowned in the wreck of one of the vessels,
was left by La Salle in good health at Fort St. Louis, in January, 1687, intending
as soon as possible to begin a mission among the friendly Cenis, with Father
Maximus le Clercq.   The colony was, however, cut to pieces by the Indians, for,
when in 1689, a party of Spaniards set out to expel the French as intruders, all
was silent as they drew near; to their horror they found on reaching it nothing
but dead bodies within and without: priest and soldier, husband and wife, old
and young, lay dead before them, pierced with arrows, or crushed with clubs!
Touched with compassion, the Spaniards committed their remains to a common
grave, and retired.   Here Father Membré perished, but earth has no record
of the day.   He was not, apparently, a man of refined education, nor is this a
reproach, as his order was not intended to direct colleges and seats of learning,
but to preach to the poor and lowly.   But though his journal is often involved
and obscure, it bears intrinsic marks of fidelity, and shows him to have been
less prejudiced than many of his companions.   Fitted rather for the quiet direction of a simple flock, his zeal could not bear up against the hardships and bar-
renness of an Indian mission for which no previous training or associations had
fitted him, while his many wanderings tended still more to prevent his useful-
ness.   His only permanent mission was in Illinois, where he labored assiduously
with Father Gabriel from March to September, 1680, notwithstanding the repugnance which he felt for the ungrateful field.   They are, accordingly, after
the Jesuits, Marquette, and Allouez, the first missionaries of Illinois, and worthy
of a distinguished place in her annals, and of the noble eulogy of Mr. Sparks, on
the missionaries of New France.

on foot over the ice to Fort Frontenac. From our arrival at Fort Crévecœur on the 14th of January past, Father Gabriel, our superior, Father Louis, and myself, had raised a cabin in which we had established some little regularity, exercising our functions as missionaries to the French of our party, and the Ilinois Indians who came in crowds. As by the end of February I already knew a part of their language, because I spent the whole of the day in the Indian camp, which was but half a league off, our father superior appointed me to follow when they were about to return to their village. A chief named Oumahouha had adopted me as his son in the Indian fashion and M. de la Salle had made him presents to take care of me. Father Gabriel resolved to stay at the fort with the sieur de Tonty and the workmen; this had been, too, the request of the sieur de la Salle who hoped that by his credit and the apparent confidence of the people in him, he would be able to keep them in order, but God permitted that the good intentions in which the sieur de la Salle thought he left them, should not last long. On the thirteenth, he himself had met two of his men whom he had sent to Missilimakinac to meet his vessel, but who had got no tidings of it. He addressed them to the sieur de Tonty; but these evil disposed men caballed so well, that they excited suspicion and dissatisfaction in most of those there, so that almost all deserted, carrying off the ammunition, provisions, and all that was in the store. Two of them who were conducting Father Gabriel to the Ilinois village where M. de Tonty had come on a visit, abandoned the good father at night in the middle of the road, and spiked the guns of the sieur de Boisrondet, and the man called Lesperance, who were in the same canoe, but not in their plot. They informed the sieur de Tonty who, finding himself destitute of everything, sent four of those who remained by two different routes to inform the sieur de la Salle.

The perfidious wretches assembled at the fort which the sieur de la Salle had built at the mouth of the Myamis' river, demolished the fort, carried off all that was there, and as we learned some months after, went to Missilimackinac, where they seized the peltries belonging to the sieur de la Salle, and left in store there by him.

The only great Ilinois village being composed of seven or eight thousand souls, Father Gabriel and I had a sufficient field for the exercise of our zeal, besides the few French who soon after came there. There are, moreover, the Miamis situated southeast by south of the bottom of Lake Dauphin, on the borders of a pretty fine river, about fifteen leagues inland at 41° N.; the nation of the Maskoutens and Outagamies, who dwell at about 43° N., on the banks of the river called Melleoki (Milwauki), which empties into Lake Dauphin, very near their village; on the western side the Kikapous and the Ainoves (Iowas), who form two villages; west of these last, above the river Checagoumemant, the village of the Ilinois Cascaschia, situated west of the bottom of Lake Dauphin, a little southwest at about 41° N.; the Anthoutantas* and Maskoutens, Nadouessions, about one hundred and thirty leagues from the Ilinois, in three great villages built near a river which empties into the river Colbert on the west side, above that of the Ilinois, almost opposite the mouth of the Miskoncing in the same river. I might name here a number of other tribes, with whom we had intercourse, and to whom French coureurs-de-bois, or lawfully sent, rambled while I was with the Ilinois, under favor of our discovery.

The greater part of these tribes, and especially the Ilinois,

* The Otontantas of Marquette's real map.

with whom I have had intercourse, make their cabins of double mats of flat rushes sewed together. They are tall of stature, strong, and robust, and good archers; they had as yet, no firearms; we gave them some. They are, wandering, idle, fearful, and desolate, almost without respect for their chiefs, irritable, and thievish. Their villages are not enclosed with palisades, and being too cowardly to defend them, they take to flight at the first news of a hostile army. The richness and fertility of the country gives them fields everywhere. They have used iron implements and arms only since our arrival. Besides the bow, they use in war a kind of short pike, and wooden maces.* Hermaphrodites are numerous. They have many wives, and often take several sisters that they may agree better; and yet they are so jealous that they cut off their noses on the slightest suspicion. They are lewd, and even unnaturally so, having boys dressed as women, destined for infamous purposes. These boys are employed only in women's work, without taking part in the chase or war. They are very superstitious, although they have no religious worship. They are, besides, much given to play, like all the Indians in America, that I am able to know.†

As there are in their country many serpents, these Indians know herbs much superior to our orvietan and theriaque, for

---

* All agree in the great skill of the Illinois bowmen, and even as late as 1692–'3, when Rale was with them, they had not yet begun to use guns.

† Neither Marquette nor Allouez first, nor Membré and Douay, afterward, allude to the mode of burial among the Illinois, which is stated by F. Rale, and deserves to be mentioned. "Their custom," says he, "is not to bury the dead, but to wrap them in skins, and to attach them by the head and feet to the tops of trees." See his letter in Kip's "Jesuit Missions," p. 38. The use made of this trait by the French poets is familiar to the readers of Delille. On the whole however, the various descriptions of the Illinois and their country by Marquette, Allouez, Membré, Hennepin, Douay, Ioutel, Tonty, Rale, and Marest, are remarkably alike: all but those of the two last are contained in the present series of Hist. Collections, and these will be found in the translation of Mr. Kip, already cited.

after rubbing themselves with them, they can without fear play with the most venomous insects, and even put them some distance down their throat. They go perfectly naked in summer except the feet, which are covered with shoes of ox-hide, and in winter they protect themselves against the cold (which is piercing in these parts though of short duration), with skins which they dress and card very neatly.

Although we were almost destitute of succor, yet the sieur de Tonty never lost courage ; he kept up his position among the Ilinois either by inspiring them all the hopes which he built on the sieur de la Salle's return, or by instructing them in the use of firearms, and many arts in the European way. As during the following summer a rumor ran that the Myamis wished to move and join the Iroquois, he taught them how to defend themselves by palisades, and even made them erect a kind of little fort with intrenchments, so that, had they had a little more courage, I have no doubt they would have been in a position to sustain themselves.

Meanwhile, from the flight and desertion of our men about the middle of March to the month of September, Father Gabriel and I devoted ourselves constantly to the mission. An Ilinois named Asapista, with whom the sieur de la Salle had contracted friendship, adopted Father Gabriel as his son, so that that good father found in his cabin a subsistence in the Indian fashion. As wine failed us for the celebration of the divine mysteries, we found means, toward the close of August, to get wild grapes which began to ripen, and we made very good wine which served us to say mass till the second disaster, which happened a few days after. The clusters of these grapes are of prodigious size, of very agreeable taste, and have seeds larger than those of Europe.*

* In Brown's "History of American Trees," we fail to find any notice of the

With regard to conversions, I can not rely on any. During the whole time Father Gabriel unraveled their language a little, and I can say that I spoke so as to make myself understood by the Indians on all that I wished; but there is in these savages such an alienation from the faith, so brutal and narrow a mind, such corrupt and antichristian morals, that great time would be needed to hope for any fruit. It is, however, true that I found many of quite docile character. We baptized some dying children, and two or three dying persons who manifested proper dispositions. As these people are entirely material in their ideas, they would have submitted to baptism, had we liked, but without any knowledge of the sacrament. We found two who had joined us, and promised to follow us everywhere; we believed that they would keep their word, and that by this means we would insure their baptisms; but I afterward felt great scruples when I learned than an Indian named Chassagouaché, who had been baptized, had died in the hands of the medicine-men, abandoned to their superstitions, and consequently doubly a child of hell.

During the summer, we followed our Indians in their camps, and to the chase. I also made a voyage to the Myamis to learn something of their dispositions; thence I went to visit other villages of the Ilinois all, however, with no great success, finding only cause for chagrin at the deplorable state and blindness of these nations. It is such that I can not express it fully.

Thus far we enjoyed a pretty general peace, though mean-

early wine-making in the country by the catholic missionaries. They were certainly the first in the northern parts. Sagard, in his "History of Canada" (ch. 9), details the *modus operandi* of probably the first wine-making in the country. The Jesuit missionaries were afterward frequently compelled to do so, in order to say mass, as we find repeated allusions to it in the Relations from Maine to the Mississippi.

while, a cruel war, which we knew not, was machinating. While we were still at Fort Frontenac, the year before the sieur de la Salle learned that his enemies had, to baffle his designs, excited the Iroquois to resume their former hostilities against the Ilinois, which had been relinquished for several years. They sought too to draw the Myamis into the same war. This is a tribe which formerly dwelt beyond the Ilinois, as regards the Iroquois and Fort Frontenac. They had persuaded them to invite the Iroquois by an embassy to join them against their common enemy; those who came to treat of this affair with the Iroquois, brought letters from some ill-disposed Frenchmen who had correspondents in those tribes, for there were at that time many coureurs de bois.

The sieur de la Salle happened to be among the Senecas when this embassy arrived; the moment seemed unfavorable, and the embassadors were privately warned that they risked their lives, if they did not depart as soon as possible, the sieur de la Salle being a friend of the Ilinois. The Myamis, however, left his former country, and came and took up a position where he is now between the Iroquois and the Ilinois. This was afterward believed intentional, and we having to pass through both these nations suspected by each other, might become so to one of them who would then prevent our progress. Monsieur de la Salle, on his arrival at the Ilinois last year, made peace between the two nations; but as the Indians are very inconstant and faithless, the Iroquois and the Myamis afterward united against the Ilinois, by means which are differently related.

Be that as it may, about the 10th of September, in the present year, 1680, the Ilinois allies of Chaouenons (Shawnees), were warned by a Shawnee, who was returning home from an Ilinois voyage, but turned back to advise them, that he had discovered an Iroquois army, four or five hundred strong, who had already entered their territory. The scouts sent out by the Ilinois confirmed what the Shawnee had said, adding that the sieur de la Salle was there. For this there was no foundation, except that the Iroquois chief had a hat and a kind of vest. They at once talked of tomahawking us, but the sieur de Tonty undeceived them, and to show the falsity of the report, offered to go with the few men he had to fight the Iroquois with them. The Ilinois had already sent out to war the greater part of the young men, yet the next day they took the field against the enemy, whom the Myamis had reinforced with a great number of their warriors. This multitude terrified the Ilinois; nevertheless, they recovered a little at the solicitation of the sieur de Tonty and the French; they at first mingled and wrangled, but the sieur de Tonty having grounds to fear for the Ilinois who had almost no firearms, offered to put matters in negotiation, and to go to the Iroquois as a man of peace, bearing the calumet. The latter hoping to surprise the Ilinois, and seeing their hopes baffled by the state in which they found them resolved for battle, received without any demur a man who came with a calumet of peace, telling them, that the Ilinois were his brothers, friends of the French, and under the protection of Ononto, their common father. I was beside the sieur de Tonty, when an Iroquois, whom I had known in the Seneca village, recognised me. These proposals for peace did not, however, please some young men whose hands itched for fight; suddenly a volley of balls and arrows came whizzing around us, and a young Onondaga ran up with a drawn knife and struck M. de Tonty near the heart, the knife fortunately glancing off a rib. They immediately surrounded him, and wished to carry him off; but when, by his ears, which were not pierced, they saw that he was a Frenchman, one of the Iroquois chiefs asked loudly, what they had meant by striking a Frenchman in that way? that he must be spared, and drew forth a belt of wampum to stanch the blood, and make a plaster for the wound. Nevertheless a mad young Iroquois having hoisted the sieur de Tonty's hat on a gun to intimidate the Ilinois, the latter believing by this sign that Tonty was dead, we were all in danger of losing our heads ; but the Iroquois having told us to show ourselves and stop both armies, we did so. The Iroquois received the calumet and pretended to retire ; but scarcely had the Ilinois reached his village, when the Iroquois appeared on the opposite hills.

This movement obliged the sieur de Tonty and the chiefs of the nation to depute me to these savages to know their reason. This was not a very agreeable mission to a savage tribe, with arms in their hands, especially after the risk I had already run ; nevertheless, I made up my mind, and God preserved me from all harm. I spoke with them ; they treated me very kindly, and at last told me, that the reason of their approach was, that they had nothing to eat. I made my report to the Ilinois, who gave them their fill, and even offered to trade for beaver and other furs, very abundant in those parts. The Iroquois agreed, hostages were given and received, and I went with an Ilinois to the enemy's camp, where we slept. The Iroquois came in greater numbers into that of the Ilinois, and even advanced to their village, committing hostilities so far as to disinter the dead, and destroy their corn ; in a word, seeking a quarrel, under show of peace, they fortified themselves in the village. The Ilinois, on the first announcement of war, had made their families draw off behind a hill, to put them out of sight, and enable them to reach the Mississippi, so that the Iroquois found the village empty. The Ilinois warriors retired in troops on the hills, and even gradually dispersed, so that we seeing ourselves abandoned by our hosts, who no longer appeared in force, and left alone exposed to to the fury of a savage and victorious enemy, were not long in resolving to retreat. The reverend father Gabriel, the sieur de Tonty, the few French who were with us, and myself, began our march on the 18th of September, without provisions, food, or anything, in a wretched bark canoe, which breaking the next day, compelled us to land about noon to repair it. Father Gabriel seeing the place of our landing fit for walking in the prairies and hills with little groves, as if planted by hand, retired there to say his breviary while we were working at the canoe all the rest of the day. We were full eight leagues from the village ascending the river. Toward evening I went to look for the father seeing that he did not return; all our party did the same; we fired repeatedly, to direct him, but in vain; and as we had reason to fear the Iroquois during the night, we crossed to the other side of the river and lit up fires which were also useless. The next morning at daybreak, we returned to the same side where we were the day before, and remained till noon, making all possible search. We entered the wood, where we found several fresh trails, as well as in the prairie on the bank of the river. We followed them one by one without discovering anything, except that M. de Tonty had ground to believe and fear that some hostile parties were in ambush to cut us all off, for seeing us take flight, the savages had imagined that we declared for the Ilinois. I insisted on staying to wait for positive tidings; but the sieur de Tonty forced me to embark at three o'clock, maintaining that the father had been killed by the enemy, or else had walked on along the bank, so that following it constantly, we should at last infallibly meet him.

We got, however, no tidings of him, and the more we advanced, the more this affliction unmanned us, and we supported this remnant of a languishing life by the potatoes and garlick, and other roots, that we found by scraping the ground with our fingers.

We afterward learned that we should have expected him uselessly, as he had been killed soon after landing. The Kikapous, a little nation you may observe on the west, quite near the Winnebagoes, had sent some of their youth in war-parties against the Iroquois, but learning that the latter were attacking the Ilinois, the war-party came after them. Three braves who formed a kind of advanced guard having met the good father alone, although they knew that he was not an Iroquois, killed him for all that, cast his body into a hole, and carried off even his breviary, and diurnal, which soon after came to the hands of a Jesuit father. They carried off the scalp of this holy man, and vaunted of it in their village as an Iroquois scalp. Thus died this man of God by the hands of some mad youths. We can say of his body what the Scripture remarks of those whom the sanguinary Herod immolated to his fury, " Non erat qui sepileret." Surely he deserved a better fate, if, indeed, we can desire a happier one before God, than to die in the exercise of the apostolic functions, by the hands of nations to whom we are sent by God. He had not been merely a religious of common and ordinary virtue ; it is well known that he had in Canada, from 1670, maintained the same sanctity of life which he had shown in France as superior, inferior, and master of novices. He had for a long time in transports of fervor acknowledged to me the profound grief which he felt at the utter blindness of these people, and that he longed to be an anathema for their salvation. His death, I doubt not, has been precious before God, and will one day have its effect in the vocation of these people to the faith, when it shall please the Almighty to use his great mercy.*

We must admit that this good old man, quite extenuated like ourselves by want of everything, would not have been able to support the hardships we had to go through after that. The sieur de Tonty and de Boisrondet, and two other Frenchmen with myself, had still eighty leagues to make to the Pottawatamis. Our canoe often failed us, and leaked on all sides. After some days we had to leave it in the woods, and make the rest of our journey by land, walking barefooted over the snow and ice. I made shoes for my companions and myself, of Father Gabriel's cloak. As we had no compass, we frequently got lost, and found ourselves in the evening where we had started in the morning, with no other food than acorns and little roots. At last, after fifteen days' march, we killed a deer, which was a great help to us. The sieur de

---

* Of this estimable missionary, we know little but what was given in Hennepin. He was, we are assured, the last scion of a noble Burgundian house, who not only renounced his inheritance and the world, to enrol himself among the lowly children of St. Francis, but even when advanced in life, and honored with the first dignities of his order, sought the new and toilsome mission of Canada. He came out among the first Recollect fathers in the summer of 1670; and, on the return of the provincial, F. Allart to France, became commissary and first superior of the mission, as well as confessor to Frontenac. He restored such missions as circumstances enabled him to begin, and guided his little flock with such moderation and skill in the troublous times on which he had fallen that he acquired the veneration and respect of all parties. His moderation, was not, indeed, liked by all, and a few years after, F. Eustace Maupassant was sent out to succeed him, and the venerable Ribourde was sent as missionary to Fort Frontenac, but not before he had witnessed the consecration of their church at Quebec. He was subsequently joined by Buisset and Hennepin, and consulting his zeal rather than his age, embarked with La Salle. The date of his death is September 9, 1680; he was then in the seventieth year of his age, and had spent more than forty in the religious state, and, as master of novices, trained many to imitate his zeal and virtues. "This holy religious," with Membré, who was to perish in the same unknown way, are among the earliest missionaries of Illinois.

Boisrondet lost us, and for at least ten days, we thought him
dead.   As he had a tin cup, he melted it to make balls for
his gun, which had no flint.   By firing it with a coal, he
killed some turkeys, on which he lived during that time ; at
last we fortunately met at the Pottawatami village, where
their chief, Onanghissê, quite well known among those nations, welcomed us most cordially.   He used to say, that he
knew only three great captains, M. de Frontenac, M. de la
Salle, and himself.   This chief harangued all his people who
contributed to furnish us food.   Not one of us could stand for
weakness ; we were like skeletons, the sieur de Tonty extremely sick, but being a little recruited, I found some Indians going to the bay of the Fetid, where the Jesuits have a
house.*   I accordingly set out for it, and can not express the
hardships I had to undergo on the way.   The sieur de Tonty
followed us soon after with the rest.   We can not sufficiently
acknowledge the charity these good fathers displayed toward
us until the thaws began, when we set out with Father Enjalran in a canoe for Missilimakinac, hoping to find news there
from Canada.

From the Ilinois, we had always followed the route by
the north, had God permitted us to take that by the south of
Lake Dauphin, we should have met the sieur de la Salle who
was coming with well-furnished canoes from Fort Frontenac,
and had gone by the south to the Ilinois, where he expected

* This is more frank than Hennepin, who in his first edition mentions neither
those at Green Bay, nor those at Mackinaw, and would have us believe that he
was the only missionary to be found in these parts.   In his last edition he
acknowledges that he met his countryman, Father Pierson, at Mackinaw.   He
must have passed Green Bay a few days before the arrival of Membré, which was
about October 22, as Tonty seems to say (vol. i., p. 59), and Hennepin started
for Green Bay by the Wisconsin, in the close of September.   They failed to meet
at Mackinaw, also, for Hennepin left it at Easter, and Membré reached only on
the octave of Corpus Christi.   This will account for the silence of both as to
each other.

to find us with all his people in good order as he had left us, when he started in the preceding year (March 2d, 1680).

This he told us himself when he arrived at Missilimakinac, about the middle of June, when he found us a little restored from our sufferings. I leave you to conceive our mutual joy, damped, though it was, by the narrative he made us of all his misfortunes, and by that we made him of our tragical adventures. He told us, that after our departure from Fort Frontenac, they had excited his creditors before the time to seize his property and all his effects, on a rumor which had been spread, that he had been drowned with all his people. He told us that his ship, the Griffin, had perished in the lakes a few days after leaving the bay of the Fetid; that the captain, sailors, and more than ten thousand crowns in merchandise, had been lost and never heard of. He had sent little fleets of canoes to trade right and left on Lake Frontenac; but these wretches, he told us, had profited by the principal and the trade, without his being able to obtain any justice from those who should have rendered it, notwithstanding all the efforts made by M. de Frontenac, the governor in his favor; that to complete his misfortunes, a vessel coming from France with a cargo for his account, amounting to twenty-two thousand livres, had been wrecked on St. Peter's islands in the gulf of St. Lawrence; that canoes ascending from Montreal to Fort Frontenac loaded with goods, had been lost in the rapids; in a word, that except the count de Frontenac, all Canada seemed in league against his undertaking; the men he had brought from France had been seduced from him, some had run off with his goods to New York, and as regarded the Canadians who had joined him, means had been found to work upon them, and draw them from his interests.

11

Although he had left Fort Frontenac in his bark on the 23d of July, 1680, he was detained on the lake by head winds so that he could not reach the straits of lake de Conty till the close of August. All seemed to oppose his undertaking; embarking in the beginning of September, on Lake de Conty, he had been detained with M. de la Forrest, his lieutenant and all his men, at Missilimakinac, being unable to obtain corn for goods or money; but at last, as it was absolutely necessary, he was obliged, after three weeks' stay, to buy some for liquor, and in one day he got sixty sacks.

He left there the 4th of October, and on the 28th of November, reached the Myamis' river, where he left a ship-carpenter and some of his people; then pushing on, reached the Ilinois on the first of December. There he was greatly surprised to find their great village burnt and empty. The rest of the time was spent in a journey to the Myamis' river, where he went to join his men forty leagues from the Ilinois. Thence he passed to different tribes, among others to an Outagamis village, where he found some Ilinois, who related to him the unhappy occurrences of the preceding year.

He learned, moreover, that after our flight and departure, from the Ilinois, their warriors had returned from the Nadouessiouz, where they had been at war, and that there had been several engagements with equal loss on both sides, and that, at last, of the seventeen Ilinois villages, the greater part had retired beyond the river Colbert, among the Ozages, two hundred leagues from their country, where too a part of the Iroquois had pursued them.

At the same time the sieur de la Salle intrigued with the Ontagami chiefs, whom he drew into his interests and those of the Ilinois; thence he passed to the Myamis, whom he induced by presents and arguments to leave the Iroquois and

join the Ilinois ; he sent two of his men and two Abenaquis
to announce this to the Ilinois, and prevent new acts of hostility, and to recall the dispersed tribes. To strengthen both
more, he sent others with presents to the Shawnees to invite
them to come and join the Ilinois against the Iroquois, who
carried their wars even to them. All this had succeeded
when M. de la Salle left on the 22d of May, 1681, to return
to Missilimakinac, where he expected to find us. If we
wish to settle in these parts, and see the faith make any progress, it is absolutely necessary to maintain peace and union
among all these tribes, as well as among others more remote,
against the common enemy, that is the Iroquois, who never
makes a real peace with any whom he has once beaten, or
whom he hopes to overcome by the divisions which he art-
fully excites, so that we should be daily exposed to routs like
that to which we were subjected last year. M. de la Salle
convinced of this necessity, has since our return, purchased
the whole Ilinois country,* and has given cantons to the Shawnees, who there colonize in large families.

The sieur de la Salle related to us all his hardships and
voyages, as well as all his misfortunes, and learned from us
as many regarding him ; yet never did I remark in him the
least alteration, always maintaining his ordinary coolness and
self-possession. Any one but him would have renounced and
abandoned the enterprise ; but far from that, by a firmness
of mind, and an almost unequalled constancy, I saw him
more resolute than ever to continue his work, and to carry
out his discovery. We accordingly left for Fort Frontenac,
with his whole party to adopt new measures to resume and
complete our course with the help of Heaven, in which we put
all our trust.

* See his second patent in the Appendix.

NARRATIVE

OF

LA SALLE'S VOYAGE DOWN THE MISSISSIPPI,

BY

FATHER ZENOBIUS MEMBRÉ, RECOLLECT.

M. LA SALLE having arrived safely at the Miamies on the 3d of November, 1681, began with his ordinary activity and vast mind, to make all preparations for his departure. He selected twenty-three Frenchmen, and eighteen Mohegans and Abnakis,* all inured to war. The latter in-

---

* The Mohegans, whose name is generally translated by old French writers, who call them *"Loups,"* or "Wolves," were hereditary enemies of the Iroquois. They were known to the French as early as the time of Champlain, who calls them "Mayganathicoise." It is needless here to follow the varieties in orthography which it underwent. The Iroquois called them "Agotsagenens" (F. Jogues' MS.). Their relations with their European neighbors seem always to have been friendly, and they never apparently warred on either English, Dutch, or French, although their position between the Hudson and Connecticut exposed them to frequent occasions of trouble. Though never really the allies of the French, the hostility of the Iroquois to both brought them in contact, so that Mohegans frequently figure in small parties in French campaigns.

The Abnakis were a people of Maine, and like the Mohegans of the Algonquin family. They were originally allies of the English, who called them "Taranteens," but the unwise policy of the New England colonies compelled them to join the French. Their conversion to the catholic religion, which they still profess, tended still more to embitter the colonies against them, and long and bloody wars resulted, in which the Abnakis, forsaken by the French, were at last humbled. They now form about five villages in Maine and Canada.

sisted on taking along ten of their women to cook for them, as their custom is, while they were fishing or hunting. These women had three children, so that the whole party consisted of but fifty-four persons, including the sieur de Tonty and the sieur Dautray, son of the late sieur Bourdon, procurator-general of Quebec.

On the 21st of December, I embarked with the sieur de Tonty and a part of our people on Lake Dauphin (Michigan), to go toward the divine river, called by the Indians Checagou, in order to make necessary arrangements for our voyage. The sieur de la Salle joined us there with the rest of his troop on the 4th of January, 1682, and found that Tonty had had sleighs made to put all on and carry it over the Chicago which was frozen ; for though the winter in these parts is only two months long, it is notwithstanding very severe.

We had to make a portage to enter the Ilinois river, which we found also frozen ; we made it on the 27th of the same month, and dragging our canoes, baggage, and provisions, about eighty leagues on the river Seignelay (Ilinois), which runs into the river Colbert (Mississippi), we traversed the great Ilinois town without finding any one there, the Indians having gone to winter thirty leagues lower down on Lake Pimiteoui (Peoria), where Fort Crévecœur stands. We found it in a good state, and La Salle left his orders here. As from this spot navigation is open at all seasons, and free from ice, we embarked in our canoes, and on the 6th of February, reached the mouth of the river Seignelay, at 38° north. The floating ice on the river Colbert, at this place, kept us till the 13th of the same month, when we set out, and six leagues lower down, found the Ozage (Missouri) river, coming from the west. It is full as large as the river Colbert into which it empties troubling it so, that from the mouth of the Ozage the water is hardly drinkable. The Indians assure us that this river is formed by many others, and that they ascend it for ten or twelve days to a mountain where it rises; that beyond this mountain is the sea where they see great ships; that on the river are a great number of large villages, of many different nations; that there are arable and prairie-lands, and abundance of cattle and beaver. Although this river is very large, the Colbert does not seem augmented by it; but it pours in so much mud, that from its mouth the water of the great river, whose bed is also slimy, is more like clear mud than river water, without changing at all till it reaches the sea, a distance of more than three hundred leagues, although it receives seven large rivers, the water of which is very beautiful, and which are almost as large as the Mississippi.

On the 14th, six leagues further, we found on the east the village of the Tamaroas,* who had gone to the chase; we left there marks of our peaceful coming, and signs of our route, according to practice, in such voyages. We went slowly, because we were obliged to hunt and fish almost daily, not having been able to bring any provisions but Indian corn.

Forty leagues from Tamaroa is the river Oüabache (Ohio), where we stopped. From the mouth of this river you must advance forty-two leagues without stopping, because the banks are low and marshy, and full of thick foam, rushes and walnut trees.

On the 24th, those whom we sent to hunt all returned but Peter Prudhomme; the rest reported that they had seen an

---

* The Tamaroas or Maroas were an Illinois tribe, who long had their village in this quarter. After their conversion to Christianity, they and the Cahokias were under the spiritual guidance of the priests of the Seminary of Foreign Missions. At this period no missionary had reached them.

Indian trail, which made us suppose our Frenchman killed or taken. This induced the sieur de la Salle to throw up a fort and intrenchment, and to put some French and Indians on the trail. None relaxed their efforts till the first of March, when Gabriel Minime and two Mohegans took two of five Indians whom they discovered. They said, that they belonged to the Sicacha (Chickasaw) nation, and that their village was a day and a half off. After showing them every kindness, I set out with the sieur de la Salle and half our party to go there, in hopes of learning some news of Prud- homme ; but after having travelled the distance stated, we showed the Indians that we were displeased with their du- plicity ; they then told us frankly, that we were still three days off. (These Indians generally count ten or twelve leagues to a day.) We returned to the camp, and one of the Indians having offered to remain while the other carried the news to the village, La Salle gave him some goods, and he set out after giving us to understand that we should meet their nation on the bank of the river as we descended.

At last Prudhomme, who had been lost, was found on the ninth day, and brought back to the fort, so that we set out the next day, which was foggy. Having sailed forty leagues till the third of March, we heard drums beating and sasa- coüest (war cries) on our right. Perceiving that it was an Akansa village, the sieur de la Salle immediately passed over to the other side with all his force, and in less than an hour threw up a retrenched redoubt on a point, with pali- sades, and felled trees to prevent a surprise, and give the In- dians time to recover confidence. He then made some of his party advance on the bank of the river, and invite the Indians to come to us. The chiefs sent out a periagua (these are large wooden canoes, made of a hollow tree like little batteaux), which came within gun-shot. We offered them the calumet of peace, and two Indians advancing, by signs invited the French to come to them. On this the sieur de la Salle sent a Frenchman and two Abnakis, who were received and regaled with many tokens of friendship. Six of the principal men brought him back in the same periagua, and came into the redoubt where the sieur de la Salle made them presents of tobacco and some goods. On their side they gave us some slaves, and the most important chief invited us to go to the village to refresh ourselves, which we readily did.

All those of the village, except the women, who had at first taken flight, came to the bank of the river to receive us. Here they built us cabins, brought us wood to burn, and provisions in abundance. For three days they feasted us constantly; the women now returned, brought us Indian corn, beans, flour, and various kinds of fruits; and we, in return, made them other little presents, which they admired greatly.

These Indians do not resemble those at the north, who are all sad and severe in their temper; these are far better made, honest, liberal, and gay. Even the young are so modest, that though they had a great desire to see La Salle, they kept quietly at the doors not daring to come in.

We saw great numbers of domestic fowls, flocks of turkeys, tame bustards, many kinds of fruits, peaches already formed on the trees, although it was only the beginning of March.

On the 14th of the same month, the sieur de la Salle took possession of this country with great ceremony. He planted a cross, and set up the king's arms, at which the Indians showed a great joy. You can talk much to Indians by signs, and those with us managed to make themselves a little understood in their language. I took occasion to explain something of the truth of God, and the mysteries of our redemption, of which they saw the arms. During this time they showed that they relished what I said, by raising their eyes to heaven, and kneeling as if to adore. We also saw them rub their hands over their bodies after rubbing them over the cross. In fact, on our return from the sea, we found that they had surrounded the cross with a palisade. They finally gave us provisions and men, to conduct us, and serve as interpreters with the Taensa, their allies, who are eighty leagues distant from their village.

On the 17th we continued our route, and six leagues lower down we found another village of the same Akansa nation, and then another three leagues lower, the people of which were of the same kind, and received us most hospitably.* We gave them presents and tokens of our coming in peace and friendship.

On the 22d we reached the Taensa, who dwell around a

* Amid the conflict of names to be found in early narratives, it is a relief to meet so much uniformity relative to the Akansas. It is not, indeed, easy to recognise them in the Quigata, Quipana, Pacaha, or Cayas, of De Soto's expedition. Marquette, in his journal, first gives the name, "Akansea," which has remained to this day on his map. He gives near them the Papikaha, and Atotchasi. Father Membré here mentions three towns of the tribe, but does not name them. Tonty does, and has on the Mississippi the Kappas, and inland the Toyengan or Tongenga, the Toriman, and the Osotonoy or Assotoué. The latter is, indeed, his post, but, old deeds show a village lay opposite, which probably gave its name. On the next expedition, Father Anastasius writes Kappa, Doginga, Toriman, and Osotteoez, which Joutel repeats, changing Doginga to Tongenga, and Osotteoez to Otsotchové. In 1721, Father Charlevoix writes them the Kappas, Toremans, Topingas, and Sothouis, adding another tribe, the Ouyapes, though there were still but four villages. In 1729, Father Poisson places them all on the Arkansas—the Tourimans and Tongingas, nine leagues from the mouth by the lower branch, the Sauthouis three leagues further, and the Kappas still higher up.

The only material difference is in the Atotchasi, Otsotchové, Osotteoez, Ossotonoy, Assotoué, or Sothouis, in which, however, there is similarity enough to establish identity. They call themselves Oguapas, and never use the term "Arkansas."—(*Nuttal.*)

little lake formed in the land by the river Mississippi. They have eight villages. The walls of their houses are made of earth mixed with straw; the roof is of canes, which form a dome adorned with paintings; they have wooden beds, and much other furniture, and even ornaments in their temples, where they inter the bones of their chiefs. They are dressed in white blankets made of the bark of a tree which they spin; their chief is absolute, and disposes of all without consulting anybody. He is attended by slaves, as are all his family. Food is brought him outside his cabin; drink is given him in a particular cup, with much neatness. His wives and children are similarly treated, and the other Taensa address him with respect and ceremony.

The sieur de la Salle being fatigued and unable to go into the town, sent in the sieur de Tonty and myself with presents. The chief of this nation not content with sending him provisions and other presents, wished also to see him, and accordingly, two hours before the time a master of ceremonies came, followed by six men; he made them clear the way he was to pass, prepare a place, and cover it with a delicately-worked cane-mat. The chief who came some time after was dressed in a fine white cloth, or blanket. He was preceded by two men, carrying fans of white feathers. A third carried a copper plate, and a round one of the same metal, both highly polished. He maintained a very grave demeanor during this visit, which was, however, full of confidence and marks of friendship.

The whole country is covered with palm-trees, laurels of two kinds, plums, peaches, mulberry, apple, and pear trees of every kind. There are also five or six kinds of nut-trees, some of which bear nuts of extraordinary size. They also gave us several kinds of dried fruit to taste; we found them

large and good. They have also many other kinds of fruit-
trees which I never saw in Europe; but the season was too
early to allow us to see the fruit. We observed vines already
out of blossom. The mind and character of this people appeared on the whole docile and manageable, and even capable of reason. I made them understand all I wished about
our mysteries. They conceived pretty well the necessity of
a God, the creator and director of all, but attribute this divinity to the sun. Religion may be greatly advanced among
them, as well as among the Akansas, both these nations being
half civilized.

Our guides would go no further for fear of falling into the
hands of their enemies, for the people on one shore are generally enemies of those on the other. There are forty villages on the east, and thirty-four on the west, of all of which
we were told the names.

The 26th of March resuming our course, we perceived,
twelve leagues lower down, a periagua or wooden canoe, to
which the sieur de Tonty gave chase, till approaching
the shore, we perceived a great number of Indians. The
sieur de la Salle, with his usual precaution, turned to the opposite banks, and then sent the calumet of peace by the sieur
de Tonty. Some of the chief men crossed the river to come
to us as good friends. They were fishermen of the Nachié
tribe (Natchez), enemies of the Taensa. Although their village lay three leagues inland, the sieur de la Salle did not
hesitate to go there with a part of our force. We slept there,
and received as kindly a welcome as we could expect; the
sieur de la Salle, whose very air, engaging manners, and
skilful mind, command alike love and respect, so impressed
the heart of these Indians, that they did not know how to
treat us well enough. They would gladly have kept us with

them; and even in sign of their esteem, that night informed the Koroa,* their ally, whose chief and head men came the next day to the village, where they paid their obeisance to the king of the French, in the person of the sieur de la Salle, who was well able to exalt in every quarter the power and glory of his nation.

After having planted the king's arms under the cross, and made presents to the Nachié, we returned to the camp the next day with the head men of the town, and the Koroa chief, who accompanied us to his village, situated ten leagues below, on a beautiful eminence, surrounded on one side by fine corn lands, and on the other by beautiful prairies. This chief presented the sieur de la Salle with a calumet, and feasted him and all his party. We here, as elsewhere, made presents in return. They told us that we had still ten days to sail to the sea.

The Sicacha (Chickasaw) whom we had brought thus far, obtained leave to remain in the village, which we left on Easter Sunday, the 29th of March, after having celebrated the divine mysteries for the French, and fulfilled the duties of good Christians. For our Indians, though of the most advanced and best instructed, were not yet capable.

About six leagues below, the river divides into two arms, or channels, forming a great island, which must be more than sixty leagues long. We followed the channel on the right, although we had intended to take the other, but passed it in a fog without seeing it. We had a guide with us, who pointed it out by signs; but his canoe being then behind, those in it neglected when the Indian told them to overtake us, for we were considerably ahead. We were informed that, on the

* Marquette's map mentions this tribe as lying inland, on the western side. He writes it "Akoroa."

other channel, there are ten different nations, numerous, and well-disposed.

On the second of April, after having sailed forty leagues, we perceived some fishermen on the bank of the river; they took flight, and we immediately after heard sasacoüest, that is, war-cries, and beating of drums. It was the Quinipissa nation. Four Frenchmen were sent to offer them the calumet of peace, with orders not to fire; but they had to return in hot haste, because the Indians let fly a shower of arrows at them. Four of our Mohegans, who went soon after, met no better welcome. This obliged the sieur de la Salle to continue his route, till two leagues lower down, we entered a village of the Tangibao,* which had been recently sacked and plundered; we found there three cabins full of human bodies dead for fifteen or sixteen days.

At last, after a navigation of about forty leagues, we arrived, on the sixth of April, at a point where the river divides into three channels. The sieur de la Salle divided his party the next day into three bands, to go and explore them. He took the western, the sieur Dautray the southern, the sieur Tonty, whom I accompanied, the middle one. These three channels are beautiful and deep. The water is brackish; after advancing two leagues it became perfectly salt, and advancing on, we discovered the open sea, so that on the ninth of April, with all possible solemnity, we performed the ceremony of planting the cross and raising the arms of France. After we had chanted the hymn of the church, "Vexilla Regis," and the "Te Deum," the sieur de la Salle, in the name of his majesty, took possession of that river, of all rivers that enter it, and of all the country watered by them. An authentic act was drawn up, signed by all of us

---

* Called in act of possession, "Maheouala."

there, and amid a volley from all our muskets, a leaden plate inscribed with the arms of France, and the names of those who had just made the discovery, was deposited in the earth.* The sieur de la Salle, who always carried an astrolabe, took the latitude of the mouth. Although he kept to himself the exact point, we have learned that the river falls into the gulf of Mexico, between 27° and 28° north, and, as is thought, at the point where maps lay down the Rio Escondido. This mouth is about thirty leagues distant from the Rio Bravo, (Rio Grande), sixty from the Rio de Palmas, and ninety or a hundred leagues from the river Panuco (Tampico), where the nearest Spanish post on the coast is situated. We reckoned that Espiritu Santo bay (Appalachee Bay), lay northeast of the mouth. From the Ilinois' river, we always went south or southwest; the river winds a little, preserves to the sea its breadth of about a quarter of a league, is everywhere very deep, without banks, or any obstacle to navigation, although the contrary has been published.† This river is reckoned eight hundred leagues long; we travelled at least three hundred and fifty from the mouth of the river Seignelay.

We were out of provisions, and found only some dried meat at the mouth, which we took to appease our hunger; but soon after perceiving it to be human flesh, we left the rest to our Indians. It was very good and delicate. At last on the tenth of April, we began to remount the river, living only on potatoes and crocodiles (alligators). The country is so bordered with canes, and so low in this part, that we could not hunt, without a long halt. On the twelfth we slept at the

---

* See De la Salle's *procès verbal* of the taking possession of Louisiana, in the *Hist. Coll. of Louisiana*, vol. i., p. 45.

† We do not know to what Father Membré refers. Marquette's work makes no such assertion of the Mississippi. Hennepin, indeed, says that an Illinois had so stated before La Salle went down.—*Description de la Louisiane*, p. 177.

village of the Tangibao, and as the sieur de la Salle wished to have corn willingly or by force . . . Our Abnakis perceived, on the thirteenth, as we advanced, a great smoke near. We thought that this might be the Quinipissa, who had fired on us some days before; those whom we sent out to reconnoitre brought in four women of the nation, on the morning of the fourteenth, and we went and encamped opposite the village. After dinner some periaguas came toward us, to brave us; but the sieur de la Salle having advanced in person with the calumet of peace, on their refusal to receive it, a gun was fired which terrified these savages who had never seen fire-arms. They called it thunder, not understanding how a wooden stick could vomit fire, and kill people so far off without touching them. This obliged the Indians to take flight, although in great force, armed in their manner. At last the sieur de la Salle followed them to the other side, and put one woman on the shore with a present of axes, knives, and beads, giving her to understand that the other three should follow soon, if she brought some Indian corn. The next day a troop of Indians having appeared, the sieur de la Salle went to meet them, and concluded a peace, receiving and giving hostages. He then encamped near their village, and they brought us some little corn. We at last went up to the village, where these Indians had prepared us a feast in their fashion. They had notified their allies and neighbors, so that, when we went to enjoy the banquet in a large square, we saw a confused mass of armed savages arrive one after another. We were, however, welcomed by the chiefs, but having ground for suspicion, each kept his gun ready, and the Indians seeing it, durst not attack us.

The sieur de la Salle retired with all his people, and his hostages into his camp, and give up the Quinipissa women.

The next morning before daybreak, our sentinel reported that he heard a noise among the canes on the banks of the river. The sieur Dautray said that it was nothing; but the sieur de la Salle, always on the alert, having already heard noise, called to arms. As we instantly heard war-cries, and arrows were fired from quite near us, we kept up a brisk fire, although it began to rain. Day broke, and after two hours' fighting, and the loss of ten men killed on their side, and many wounded, they took to flight, without any of us having been injured. Our people wished to go and burn the village of these traitors; but the sieur de la Salle prudently wished only to make himself formidable to this nation, without exasperating it, in order to manage them in time of need. We, however, destroyed many of their canoes. They were near, but contented themselves with running away and shouting. Our Mohegans took only two scalps.

We set out then the evening of the same day, the eighthteenth of April, and arrived on the first of May, at the Koroa, after having suffered much from want of provisions. The Koroa had been notified by the Quinipissa, their allies, and had, with the intention of avenging them, assembled Indians of several villages, making a very numerous army, which appeared on the shores, and often approached us to reconnoitre. As this nation had contracted friendship with us on our voyage down, we were not a little surprised at the change; but they told us the reason, which obliged us to keep on our guard. The sieur de la Salle even advanced intrepidly, so that the Indians durst not undertake anything.

When we passed going down, we were pretty well provided with Indian corn, and had put a quantity in *cache*, pretty near their village. We found it in good condition; and having taken it up, continued our route; but were sur-

prised to see the Indian corn at this place, which, the twenty-
ninth of March, was just sprouting from the ground, already
fit to eat, and we then learned that it ripened in fifty days.
We also remarked other corn four inches above ground.

We set out then the same day, the first of May in the
evening, and after seeing several different nations on the following days, and renewed our alliance with the Taensa, who
received us perfectly well, we arrived at the Akansa where
we were similarly received. We left it on the eighteenth, the
sieur de la Salle went on with two canoes of our Mohegans and
pushed on to a hundred leagues below the river Seignelay,
where he fell sick. We joined him there with the rest of
the troop on the second of June. As his malady was dangerous, and brought him to extremity, unable to advance any
further, he was obliged to send forward the sieur de Tonty
for the Ilinois and Miamis, to take up our *caches*, and put
everything in order, appointing Tonty to command there.
But at last the malady of the sieur de la Salle, which lasted
forty days, during which I assisted him to my utmost, having
somewhat abated, we started at the close of July, by slow
journeys. At the end of September, we reached the Miami
river, where we learned of several military expeditions made
by the sieur de Tonty after he had left us. He had left the
sieur Dautray, and the sieur Cochois among the Miamis, and
other people among the Ilinois, with two hundred new cabins
of Indians, who were going to repeople that nation. The said
sieur de Tonty pushed on to Missilimakinac, to render an account, more at hand, of our discovery to the governor, the
count de Frontenac, on behalf of the sieur de la Salle, who
prepared to retrace his steps to the sea the next spring with
a larger force, and families to begin establishments.

The river Seignelay is very beautiful, especially below the

Ilinois (Indians), wide and deep, forming two lakes as far as the sea (*jusqu'a la mer*), edged with hills, covered with beautiful trees of all kinds, whence you discern vast prairies on which herds of wild-cattle pasture in confusion. The river often overflows, and renders the country around marshy, for twenty or thirty leagues from the sea.* The soil around is good, capable of producing all that can be desired for subsistence. We even found hemp there growing wild, much finer than that of Canada. The whole country on this river is charming in its aspect.

It is the same with what we have visited on the river Colbert. When you are twenty or thirty leagues below the Maroa, the banks are full of canes until you reach the sea, except in fifteen or twenty places where there are very pretty hills, and spacious, convenient, landing-places. The inundation does not extend far, and behind these drowned lands you see the finest country in the world. Our hunters, French and Indian, were delighted with it. For an extent of at least two hundred leagues in length, and as much in breadth, as we were told, there are vast fields of excellent land, diversified here and there with pleasing hills, lofty woods, groves through which you might ride on horseback, so clear and unobstructed are the paths. These little forests also line the rivers which intersect the country in various places, and which abound in fish. The crocodiles are dangerous here, so much so that in some parts no one would venture to expose himself, or even put his hand out of his canoe. The Indians told us that these animals often dragged in their people, where they could anywhere get hold of them.

The fields are full of all kinds of game, wild-cattle, stags,

* I can not see what he means by the term sea in these two places; unless in the former it means the mouth, and in the latter, the bed of the river.

does, deer, bears, turkeys, partridges, parrots, quails, wood-cock, wild-pigeons, and ring-doves. There are also beaver, otters, martens, till a hundred leagues below the Maroa, especially in the river of the Missouri, the Ouabache, that of the Chepousseau (the Cumberland?), which is opposite it, and on all the smaller ones in this part; but we could not learn that there were any beavers on this side toward the sea.

There are no wild beasts, formidable to man. That which is called Michybichy never attacks man, although it devours the strongest beasts; its head is like that of a lynx, though much larger; the body long and large like a deer's, but much more slender; the legs also shorter, the paws like those of a wild-cat, but much larger, with longer and stronger claws, which it uses to kill the beasts it would devour. It eats a little, then carries off the rest on its back, and hides it under some leaves, where ordinarily no other beast of prey touches it. Its skin and tail resemble those of a lion, to which it is inferior only in size.

The cattle of this country surpass ours in size; their head is monstrous, and their look frightful, on account of the long, black hair with which it is surrounded, and which hangs below the chin, and along the houghs of this animal. It has on the back a kind of upright crests (coste), of which that nearest the neck is longest, the others diminish gradually to the middle of the back. The hair is fine, and scarce inferior to wool. The Indians wear their skins which they dress very neatly with earth, which serves also for paint. These animals are easily approached, and never fly from you; they could be easily domesticated.

There is another little animal (the opposum) like a rat, though as large as a cat, with silvery hair sprinkled with black. The tail is bare, as thick as a large finger, and about a foot long; with this it suspends itself, when it is on the branches of trees. It has under the belly a kind of pouch, where it carries its young when pursued.

The Indians assured us that inland, toward the west, there are animals on which men ride, and which carry very heavy loads, they described them as horses, and showed us two feet which were actually hoofs of horses.

We observed everywhere wood of various kinds fit for every use; and among others the most beautiful cedars in the world, and another kind shedding an abundance of gum, as pleasant to burn as the best French pastilles. We also remarked everywhere, hemlocks, and many other pretty large trees with white bark. The cotton-wood trees are large; of these, the Indians dig out canoes forty or fifty feet long, and have sometimes fleets of a hundred and fifty below their villages. We saw every kind of tree fit for ship-building. There is also plenty of hemp for cordage, and tar might be made remarkably near the sea.

You meet prairies everywhere; sometimes of fifteen or twenty leagues front, and three or four deep, ready to receive the plough. The soil excellent, capable of supporting great colonies. Beans grow wild, and the stalk lasts several years, always bearing fruit; it is thicker than an arm, and runs up like ivy to the top of the highest trees. The peach-trees are quite like those of France, and very good; they are so loaded with fruit, that the Indians have to prop up those they cultivate in their clearings. There are whole forests of very fine mulberries, of which we ate the fruit from the month of May; many plum-trees and other fruit-trees, some known and others unknown in Europe; vines, pomegranates, and horse-chestnuts, are common. They raise three or four crops of corn a year. I have already stated that I saw some ripe, while more was sprouting.   Winter is known only by the rains.

We had not time to look for mines ; we only found coal in several places ; the Indians who had lead and copper wished to lead us to many places, whence they take it ; there are quarries of very fine stone, white and black marble, yet the Indians do not use it.

These tribes, though savage, seem generally of very good dispositions, affable, obliging, and docile.   They have no true idea of religion by a regular worship ; but we remarked some confused ideas, and a particular veneration they had for the sun, which they recognise as him who made and preserves all.   It is surprising how different their language is from that of tribes not ten leagues off ; they manage, however, to understand each ; and, besides, there is always some interpreter of one nation residing in another, when they are allies, and who acts as a kind of consul.   They are very different from our Canada Indians in their houses, dress, manners, inclinations, and customs, and even in the form of the head, for theirs is very flat.   They have large public squares, games, assemblies ; they seem lively and active ; their chiefs possess all the authority ; no one would dare pass between the chiefs and the cane-torch which burns in his cabin, and is carried before him when he goes out ; all make a circuit around it with some ceremony.   The chiefs have their valets and officers, who follow them and serve them everywhere.   They distribute their favors and presents at will.   In a word, we generally found them to be men.   We saw none who knew firearms, or even iron or steel articles, using stone knives and hatchets.   This was quite contrary to what had been told us, when we were assured that they traded with the Spaniards, who were said to be only twenty-five or thirty leagues off ;

they had axes, guns, and all commodities found in Europe.* We found, indeed, tribes that had bracelets of real pearls; but they pierce them when hot, and thus spoil them. Monsieur de la Salle brought some with him. The Indians told us that their warriors brought them from very far, in the direction of the sea, and receive them in exchange from some nations apparently on the Florida side.

There are many other things which our people observed on advancing a little into the country to hunt, or which we learned from the tribes, through whom we passed; but I should be tedious were I to detail them: and, besides, the particulars should be better known.

To conclude, our expedition of discovery was accomplished without having lost any of our men, French or Indian, and without anybody's being wounded, for which we were indebted to the protection of the Almighty, and the great cappacity of Monsieur de la Salle. I will say nothing here of conversions; formerly the apostles had but to enter a country, when on the first publication of the gospel, great conversions were seen. I am but a miserable sinner, infinitely destitute of the merits of the apostles; but we must also acknowledge that these miraculous ways of grace are not attached to the exercise of our ministry; God employs an ordinary and

---

* Here again it is difficult to decide whether he alludes to Marquette, or some other account that may have been given. Father Marquette found some guns rather for show than for use in the hands of the first Illinois party, west of the Mississippi, which Father Membré did not visit. He also met a tribe coming from the east to war on the Mississippi tribes, also supplied with firearms, these Father Membré did not meet. As to the Arkansas, Marquette states that he found among them knives, axes, and beads, bought from other Indian tribes on the east, and from the Illinois. Speaking of their trade, he makes no allusion to the Spaniards, although he must have supposed that the lower tribes traded with either Florida or Mexico. It is somewhat strange that Father Membré, who here seems to make light of Marquette's fear of being taken, and held a prisoner by the Spaniards, should have escaped only by a bloody death the detention to which the survivors of Fort St. Louis were subjected.

common way, following which I contented myself with announcing, as well as I could, the principal truths of Christianity to the nations I met. The Ilinois language served me about a hundred leagues down the river, and I made the rest understand by gestures and some term in their dialect which I insensibly picked up ; but I can not say that my little efforts produced certain fruits. With regard to these people, perhaps, some one by a secret effect of grace, has profited ; God only knows. All we have done has been to see the state of these tribes, and to open the way to the gospel and to missionaries ; having baptized only two infants, whom I saw struggling with death, and who, in fact, died in our presence.

ACCOUNT

OF

LA SALLE'S ATTEMPT TO REACH THE MISSISSIPPI BY SEA,

AND OF THE

ESTABLISHMENT OF A FRENCH COLONY IN ST. LOUIS BAY,

BY

FATHER CHRISTIAN LE CLERCQ.

THE first design of the sieur de la Salle had been to find the long-sought passage to the Pacific ocean, and although the river Colbert (Mississippi) does not lead to it, yet this great man had so much talent and courage, that he hoped to find it, if it were possible, as he would have done, had God spared his life.

The Ilinois territory, and vast countries around, being the centre of his discovery, he spent there the winter, summer, and beginning of autumn, 1683, in establishing his posts. He at last left Monsieur de Tonty, as commandant and resolved to return to France to render an account of his fulfilment of the royal orders. He reached Quebec early in November, and Rochelle, France, on the twenty-third of December.

His design was to go by sea to the mouth of the river Colbert, and there found powerful colonies under the good pleasure of the king. These proposals* were favorably received by Monsieur de Seignelay, minister and secretary of state, and superintendent of commerce and navigation in France. His majesty accepted them and condescended to favor the undertaking not only by new powers and commissions, which he conferred upon him, but also by the help of vessels, troops, and money, which his royal liberality furnished him.

The first care of the sieur de la Salle, after being invested with these powers, was to provide for the *spiritual*, to advance especially the glory of God in this enterprise. He turned to two different bodies of missionaries, in order to obtain men able to labor in the salvation of souls, and lay the foundations of Christianity in this savage land. He accordingly applied to Monsieur Tronçon, superior-general of the clergymen of the seminary of St. Sulpice, who willingly took part in the work of God, and appointed three of his ecclesiastics full of zeal, virtue, and capacity, to commence these new missions. They were Monsieur Cavelier, brother of the sieur de la Salle, Monsieur Chefdeville, his relative, and Monsieur de Maïulle,† all three priests.

As for nearly ten years the Recollects had endeavored to second the designs of the sieur de la Salle for the glory of God and the sanctification of souls throughout the vast countries of Louisiana, depending on him from Fort Frontenac, and had accompanied him on his expeditions, in which our Father Gabriel was killed, he made it an essential point to take some one of our fathers to labor in concert to establish the kingdom of God in these new countries. For this purpose, he applied to the Rev. Father Hyacinth le Febvre, who

* See M. de la Salle's Memoir in *Hist. Coll. of Louisiana*, vol. i., p. 25.

† Called by Joutel Dainmaville. See *Hist. Coll. of Louisiana*, vol. i., p.

had been twice provincial of our province of St. Anthony, in Artois, and was then, for the second time, provincial of that of St. Denis in France, who, wishing to second with all his power the pious intentions of the sieur de la Salle, granted him the religious he asked : namely, Father Zenobius Membré superior of the mission, and Fathers Maximus Le Clercq and Anastasius Douay, all three of our province of St. Anthony, the first having been for four years the inseparable companion of the sieur de la Salle during his discovery on land ; the second had served for five years with great edification in Canada, especially in the mission of the seven islands, and Anticosti. Father Dennis Morguet was added as a fourth priest; but that religious finding himself extremely sick on the third day after embarking, he was obliged to give up and return to his province.

The reverend father provincial had informed the Congregation de propagandâ fide, of this mission, to obtain necessary authority for the exercise of our ministry ; he received decrees in due form, which we will place at the end of the chapter, not to interrupt the reader's attention here. His holiness Innocent XI., added by an express brief, authentic powers, and permissions in twenty-six articles, as the holy see is accustomed to grant to missionaries whose remoteness makes it morally impossible to recur to the authority of the ordinary. It was granted against the opposition of the bishop of Quebec, Cardinal d'Estrées having shown that the distance from Quebec to the mouth of the river was more than eight or nine hundred leagues by land.*

The hopes that were then justly founded on this famous expedition, induced many young gentlemen to join the sieur de

---

* Similar opposition compelled the first Jesuits in Louisiana to leave soon after their arrival with Iberville.

la Salle as volunteers; he chose twelve who seemed most resolute; among them, the sieur de Morangé, and the sieur Cavelier, his nephews, the latter only fourteen years of age.

The little fleet was fitted out at Rochelle, to be composed of four vessels — the Joly, a royal ship, a frigate called the Belle, a storeship called the Aimable, and a ketch called the St. Francis. The royal vessel was commanded by Captain de Beaujeu, a Norman gentleman known for valor and experience, and his meritorious services; his lieutenant was M. le chevalier d'Aire, now captain in the navy, and son of the dean of the parliament of Metz. The sieur de Hamel, a young gentleman of Brouage, full of fire and courage, was ensign. Would to God the troops and the rest of the crew had been as well chosen! Those who were appointed, while M. de la Salle was at Paris, picked up a hundred and fifty soldiers, mere wretched beggars soliciting alms, many too deformed and unable to fire a musket. The sieur de la Salle had also given orders at Rochelle to engage three or four mechanics in each trade; the selection was, however, so bad, that when they came to the destination, and they were set to work, it was seen that they knew nothing at all. Eight or ten families of very good people presented themselves, and offered to go and begin the colonies. Their offer was accepted, and great advances made to them as well as to the artisans and soldiers.

All being ready, they sailed on the 24th of July, 1684. A storm which came on a few days later, obliged them to put in at Chef-de-Bois to repair one of their masts broken in the gale. They set sail again on the 1st of August, steering for St. Domingo; but a second storm overtook them, and dispersed them on the fourteenth of September, the Aimable and the Belle alone remaining together, reached Petit Goave in St. Domingo, where they fortunately found the Joly. The St. Francis being loaded with goods and effects, and unable to follow the others, had put in at Port de Paix, whence she sailed after the storm was over to join the fleet at the rendezvous; but as during the night, while quite calm, the captain and crew thinking themselves in safety, were perfectly off their guard, they were surprised by two Spanish periaguas, which took the ketch.

This was the first mishap which befell the voyage; a disaster which caused universal consternation in the party, and much grief to the sieur de la Salle, who was just recovering from a dangerous malady, which had brought him to the verge of the grave. They stayed, indeed, some time at St. Domingo, where they laid in provisions, a store of Indian corn, and of all kinds of domestic animals to stock the new country. M. de St. Laurent, governor-general of the Isles, Begon, intendant, and de Cussy, governor of St. Domingo, favored them in every way, and even restored the reciprocal understanding so necessary to succeed in such undertakings; but the soldiers, and most of the crew, having plunged into every kind of debauchery and intemperance, so common in those parts, were so ruined and contracted such dangerous disorders that some died in the island, and others never recovered.

The little fleet thus reduced to three vessels, weighed anchor November 25th, 1684, and pursued its way quite successfully along the Cayman isles, and passing by the Isle of Peace (pines), after anchoring there a day to take in water, reached Port San Antonio, on the island of Cuba, where the three ships immediately anchored. The beauty and allurement of the spot, and its advantageous position, induced them to stay and even land. For some unknown reason the Spaniards had abandoned their several kinds of provisions, and among the rest some Spanish wine, which they took, and after two days' repose, left to continue the voyage to the gulf of Mexico.

The sieur de la Salle, although very clear-headed, and not easily mislead, had, however, too easily believed the advice given him by some persons in St. Domingo ; he discovered, too late, that all the sailing directions given him were absolutely false ; the fear of being injured by northerly winds, said to be very frequent and dangerous at the entrance of the gulf, made them twice lie to, but the discernment and courage of the sieur de la Salle made them try the passage a third time, and they entered happily on the 1st of January, 1685, when Father Anastasius celebrated a solemn mass as a thanksgiving, after which, continuing the route, they arrived in fifteen days in sight of the coast of Florida, when a violent wind forced the Joly to stand off, the store-ship and frigate coasting along, the sieur de la Salle being anxious to follow the shore.

He had been persuaded at St. Domingo, that the gulf-stream ran with incredible rapidity toward the Bahama channel. This false advice set him entirely astray, for thinking himself much further north than he was, he not only passed Espiritu Santo bay (Appalachee) without recognising it, but even followed the coast far beyond the river Colbert, and would even have continued to follow it, had they not perceived by its turning south, and by the latitude, that they were more than forty or fifty leagues from the mouth, the more so, as the river, before emptying into the gulf, coasts along the shore of the gulf to the west, and as longitude is unknown to pilots, it proved that he had greatly passed his parallel lines.

The vessels at last, in the middle of February, met at Espiritu Santo bay, where there was an almost continual roadstead. They resolved to return whence they came, and advanced ten or twelve leagues to a bay which they called St. Louis bay (St. Bernard). As provisions began to fail, the soldiers had already landed, the sieur de la Salle explored and sounded the bay which is a league broad, with a good bottom. He thought that it might be the right arm of the river Colbert. He brought the frigate in without accident on the eighteenth of February; the channel is deep, so deep in fact, that even on the sand bar, which in a manner bars the entrance, there are twelve or fifteen feet of water at low tide.

The sieur de la Salle having ordered the captain of the store-ship not to enter without the pilot of the frigate, in whom he put all confidence, to unload his cannon and water into the boats to lighten his cargo, and lastly, to follow exactly the channel staked out; none of his orders were executed, and the faithless man, in spite of the advice given him by a sailor who was at the main-top, to keep off, drove his vessel on the shoals where he touched and stranded, so that it was impossible to get off.

La Salle was on the seashore when he saw this deplorable maneuvre, and was embarking to remedy it, when he saw a hundred or a hundred and twenty Indians come; he had to put all under arms, the roll of the drum put the savages to flight; he followed them, presented the calumet of peace, and conducted them to their camp, regaled them, and even made them presents; and the sieur de la Salle gained them so that an alliance was made with them; they brought meat to the camp the following days; he bought some of their canoes, and there was every reason to expect much from this necessary union.

Misfortune would have it that a bale of blanketing from

the wreck was thrown on shore; some days after a party
of Indians seized it, the sieur de la Salle ordered his men to
get it out of their hands peaceably; they did just the contrary; the commander presented his musket as if about to
fire; this so alarmed them, that they regarded us only as
enemies. Provoked to fury they assembled on the night
of the 6th and 7th of March, and finding the sentinel
asleep, poured in a destructive volley of arrows. Our men
ran to arms, the noise of musketry put them to flight, after
they had killed on the spot the sieurs Oris and Desloge, two
cadets volunteers, and dangerously wounded the sieur de
Moranger, lieutenant and nephew of the sieur de la Salle, and
the sieur Gaien, a volunteer. The next day they killed two
more of our men, whom they found sleeping on the shore.

Meanwhile, the store-ship remained more than three weeks
at the place of its wreck, without going to pieces, but full of
water; they saved all they could in periaguas and boats,
when a calm allowed them to reach it. One day Father Zenobius having passed in a boat, it was dashed to pieces against
the vessel by a sudden gust of wind. All quickly got on
board, but the good father who remained last to save the rest,
would have been drowned had not a sailor thrown him a
rope, with which he drew himself up as he was sinking.

At last Monsieur de Beaujeu sailed in the Joly with all
his party on the twelfth of March, to return to France,* and
the sieur de la Salle having thrown up a house with planks
and pieces of timber to put his men and goods in safety, left
a hundred men under the command of the sieur de Moranger,

---

* Le Clercq it will be observed, is silent as to the misunderstanding between
La Salle and Beaujeu, which is mentioned by others, and borne out by letters of
the latter. To him must in no small degree be ascribed the failure of La Salle's
attempt. For the detail of their disagreement see Sparks's excellent life of La
Salle, and Joutel's journal in Historical Collection of Louisiana.

and set out with fifty others; the sieur Cavelier and fathers Zenobius and Maximus intending to seek at the extremity of the bay, the mouth of the river, and a proper place to fix his colony.

The captain of the frigate had orders to sound the bay in boats, and to bring his vessel in as far as he could; he followed twelve leagues along the coast, which runs from southeast to northwest, and anchored opposite a point to which the sieur Hurier gave his name; he was appointed commander there; this post serving as a station between the naval camp, and the one the sieur de la Salle went, on the second of April, to form at the extremity of the bay, two leagues up a beautiful river called Cow river, from the great number of those wild animals, they found there. Our people were attacked there by a party of Indians, but repulsed them.

On the twenty-first, holy Saturday, the sieur de la Salle came to the naval camp, where the next day and the three following, those great festivals were celebrated with all possible solemnity, each one receiving his Creator. The following days all the effects, and generally all that could be of service to the camp of the sieur de la Salle, were transferred from those of the sieurs de Moranger and Hurier, which were destroyed. For a month the sieur de la Salle made them work in cultivating the ground; but neither the grain nor the vegetables sprouted, either because they were damaged by the salt water, or because, as was afterward remarked, it was not the right season. The fort which was built in an advantageous position, was soon in a state of defence, furnished with twelve pieces of cannon, and a magazine under ground, for fear of fire, in which all the effects were safely deposited. The maladies which the soldiers had contracted at St. Domingo, were visibly carrying them off, and

13

a hundred died in a few days, notwithstanding all the relief afforded by broths, preserves, treacle, and wine, which were given them.

On the 9th of August, 1685, three of our Frenchmen being at the chase which is plentiful in these parts, in all kinds of game and deer, were surrounded by several troops of armed savages, but our men putting themselves on the defensive, first killed the chief and scalped him; this spectacle terrified and scattered the enemy, who nevertheless, some time after, surprised and killed one of our Frenchmen.

On the thirteenth of October, the sieur de la Salle seeing himself constantly insulted by the savages, and wishing, moreover, to have some of their canoes by force or consent, as he could not do without them, resolved to make open war on them in order to bring them to an advantageous peace.

He set out with sixty men armed with wooden corslets to protect them against arrows, and arrived where they had gathered; in different engagements by day and night, he put some to flight, wounded several, killed some; others were taken, among the rest some children, one of whom a girl three or four years old was baptized and died some days after, as the first fruits of this mission, and a sure conquest sent to heaven. The colonists now built houses, and formed fields by clearing the ground, the grain sowed succeeding better than the first. They crossed to the other side of the bay in canoes, and found on a large river a plentiful chase, especially of cattle and turkeys. In the fort they raised all kinds of domestic animals, cows, hogs, and poultry, which multiplied greatly. Lastly, the execution done among the Indians had rendered the little colony somewhat more secure, when a new misfortune succeeded all the preceding.

The sieur de la Salle had ordered the captain of the frigate to sound the bay carefully as he advanced, and to recall all his men on board at nightfall; but this captain and six of his strongest, stoutest, and ablest men, charmed with the agreeableness of the season, and the beauty of the country, left their canoe and arms on the sand at low-water, and advanced a gun shot on the plain to be dry; here they fell asleep, and an Indian party espying them, surprised them, aided by their sleep and the darkness, massacred them cruelly, and destroyed their arms and canoe. This tragical adventure produced the greatest consternation in the camp.

After rendering the last honors to the murdered men, the sieur de la Salle leaving provisions for six months, set out with twenty men and his brother, the sieur Cavelier, to seek the mouth of the river (Mississippi) by land. The bay which he discovered to be in latitude 27° 45′ N., is the outlet of a great number of rivers, none of which, however, seemed large enough to be an arm of the river Colbert. The sieur de la Salle explored them in hope that a part of these rivers was formed further up by one of the branches of the said river; or, at least, that by traversing the country to some distance, he would make out the course of the Missisipi. He was longer absent than he had expected, being compelled to make rafts to cross the rivers, and to intrench himself every night to protect himself against attacks. The continual rains, too, formed ravines, and destroyed the roads. At last, on the 13th of February, 1686, he thought that he had found the river; he fortified himself there, left a part of his men, and with nine others continued to explore a most beautiful country, traversing a number of villages and nations, who treated him very kindly; at last, returning to find his people, he arrived at the general camp, on the 31st of May, charmed with the beauty and fertility of the fields, the incredible quantity of game of every kind, and the numerous tribes he had met on the way.

The Almighty was preparing him a still more sensible trial than the preceding, in the loss of the frigate, his only remaining vessel in which he hoped to coast along, and then pass to St. Domingo, to send news to France, and obtain new succor. This sad accident happened from want of precaution on the part of the pilot. All the goods were lost irrecoverably; the vessel struck on the shore, the sailors were drowned; the sieur de Chefdeville, the captain, and four others, with difficulty, escaped in a canoe which they found almost miraculously on the shore. They lost thirty-six barrels of flour, a quantity of wine, the trunks, clothes, linen, equipage, and most of the tools. We leave the reader to imagine the grief and affliction felt by the sieur de la Salle at an accident which completely ruined all his measures. His great courage even could not have borne him up, had not God aided his virtue by the help of extraordinary grace.

All these measures being thus disconcerted, and his affairs brought to extremes, he resolved to try to reach Canada by land; he returned some time after, and undertook a second in which he lost his life by the cruelty of his men, some of whom remaining faithful, continued their route and reached France, among the rest Father Anastasius Douay. Although the detail of his remarks was lost in his many wrecks, the following is an abridgment of what he could gather from them, with which, perhaps, the reader will be better pleased than if I gave it in my own style.

NARRATIVE

OF

LA SALLE'S ATTEMPT TO ASCEND THE MISSISSIPPI IN 1687,

BY

*FATHER ANASTASIUS DOUAY, RECOLLECT.**

THE sieur de la Salle seeing no other resource for his affairs, but to go by land to the Ilinois, to be able to give in France, tidings of his disasters, chose twenty of his best men, including Nika, one of our Shawnee Indians, who had constantly attended him from Canada to France, and from France to Mexico; Monsieur Cavelier, the sieur de Moranget and I also joined them for this great journey, for which we made no preparation but four pounds of powder, and four of lead, two axes, two dozen knives, as many awls, some beads, and two kettles. After celebrating the divine mysteries in

* Of Father Anastasius Douay we know little; Hennepin makes him a native of Quesnoy, in Hainault. He had never been in America before, but after being connected with La Salle's expedition, from 1684 to 1688, he reached France, as we shall see, in safety. He was, says Hennepin, vicar of the Recollects of Cambray, in 1697. Certain it is that he subsequently revisited America in 1699, with Iberville, but we can trace him no further. A man of observation and ability, he seems to have been quite sweeping in his charges, as we shall observe in the course of his narrative. The only point against him besides this, which was an excess of party feeling, was his share in the deception practised on Tonty.

the chapel of the fort, and invoking together the help of Heaven, we set out on the 22d of April, 1686, in a northeasterly direction.

On the third day we perceived in some of the finest plains in the world a number of people, some on foot, others on horseback; these came galloping toward us, booted and spurred, and seated on saddles. They invited us to their town, but as they were six leagues to the northwest, out of our route, we thanked them, after learning in conversation, that they had intercourse with the Spaniards. Continuing our march the rest of the day, we cabined at night in a little intrenched stockade fort, to be beyond reach of insult; this we always after practised with good results.

Setting out the next morning, we marched for two days through continual prairies to the river which we called Robek, meeting everywhere so prodigious a quantity of Cibola, or wild cattle, that the smallest herds seemed to us to contain two or three hundred. We killed nine or ten in a moment, and dried a part of the meat so as not to have to stop for five or six days. A league and a half further we met another and finer river, wider and deeper than the Seine at Paris, skirted by some of the finest trees in the world, set as regularly as though they had been planted by man. Among them were many mulberry and other fruit trees. On one side were prairies, on the other woods. We passed it on rafts, and called it La Maligne.

Passing through this beautiful country, its delightful fields, and prairies skirted with vines, fruit-trees, and groves, we, a few days after, reached a river which we called Hiens, after a German from Wittemburg, who got so fast in the mud that he could scarcely get out. One of our men, with an axe on his back, swam over to the other side, a second followed at once; they then cut down the largest trees, while others on our side did the same. These trees were cut so as to fall on each side into the river, where meeting, they formed a kind of bridge on which we easily passed. This invention we had recourse to more than thirty times in our journeys, finding it surer than the Cajeu, which is a kind of raft formed of many pieces, and branches tied together, on which we passed over, guiding it by a pole.

Here the sieur de la Salle changed his route from northeast to east, for reasons which he did not tell us, and which we could never discover.

After several days' march, in a pretty fine country, crossing ravines on rafts, we entered a much more agreeable and perfectly delightful territory, where we found a very numerous tribe who received us with all possible friendship, even the women coming to embrace our men. They made us sit down on well-made mats, at the upper end, near the chiefs, who presented us the calumet adorned with feathers of every hue, which we had to smoke in turn. They served up to us among other things a sagamity, made of a kind of root called Toqué, or Toquo. It is a shrub, like a kind of bramble without thorns, and has a very large root, which they wash and dry perfectly, after which it is pounded and reduced to powder in a mortar. The sagamity has a good taste, though astringent. These Indians presented us with some cattle-skins, very neatly dressed, to make shoes; we gave them in exchange beads, which they esteem highly. During our stay the sieur de la Salle so won them by his manners, and insinuated so much of the glory of our king, telling them that he was greater and higher than the sun, that they were all ravished with astonishment.

The sieur Cavelier and I endeavored here, as everywhere

else, to give them some first knowledge of the true God. This nation is call Biskatrongé, but we called them the nation of weepers,* and gave their beautiful river the same name, because at our arrival and entrance, they all began to weep bitterly for a good quarter of an hour. It is their custom when they see any who come from afar, because it reminds them of their deceased relatives whom they suppose on a long journey, from which they await their return. These good people, in conclusion, gave us guides, and we passed their river in their periaguas.

We crossed three or four others the following days, without any incident of note, except that our Shawnee, firing at a deer pretty near a large village, so terrified them all by the report that they took to flight. The sieur de la Salle put all under arms to enter the village, which consisted of three hundred cabins. We entered the largest, that of the chief, where we found his wife still, unable to fly from old age. The sieur de la Salle made her understand that we came as friends; three of her sons, brave warriors, observed at a distance what passed, and seeing us to be friendly, recalled all their people. We treated of peace, and the calumet was danced till evening, when the sieur de la Salle, not trusting them overmuch, went and encamped beyond the canes, so that, if the Indians approached by night, the noise of the canes would prevent our being surprised.

This showed his discernment and prudence, for during the night a band of warriors, armed with arrows, approached; but the sieur de la Salle, without leaving his intrenchment, threatened to thunder his guns; and in a word spoke so bold and firmly, that he obliged them to draw off. After

* Cabeza de Vaca from the same circumstance gives a similar name to a tribe in that quarter.

their retreat the night passed off quietly, and the next day after reciprocal marks of friendship, apparent at least on the side of the Indians, we pursued our route to five or six leagues beyond.   Here we were agreeably surprised to find a party of Indians come out to meet us, with ears of corn in their hands, and a polished, honest air.   They embraced us, inviting us most pressingly to go and visit their villages; the sieur de la Salle seeing their sincerity, agreed.   Among other things these Indians told us that they knew whites toward the west, a cruel, wicked nation, who depeopled the country around them.   (These were the Spaniards.)   We told them that we were at war with that people; when the news of this spread through the village called that of the Kironas, all vied with each other in welcoming us, pressing us to stay, and go to war with the Spaniards of Mexico.   We put them off with fair words, and made a strict alliance with them, promising to return with more numerous troops; then after many feasts and presents, they carried us over the river in periaguas.

As we constantly held on our way to the east, through beautiful prairies, a misfortune befell us after three days' march.   Our Indian hunter Nika suddenly cried out with all his might, "I am dead!"   We ran up and learned that he had been cruelly bitten by a snake; this accident stopped us for several days.   We gave him some orvietan, and applied viper's salt on the wound after scarifying it to let out the poison and tainted blood; he was at last saved.

Some days after we had many other alarms.   Having reached a large and rapid river, which we were told ran to the sea, and which we called Misfortune* river, we made a raft to cross; the sieur de la Salle and Cavelier with a part

---

* This river differs from the *Maligne*, and is supposed to be the Colorado of Texas.

of our people got on ; but scarcely had they got into the current, when by its violence it carried them off with incredible
rapidity, so that they disappeared almost instantly. I remained ashore with a part of our men : our hunter was absent,
having been lost for some days. It was a moment of extreme
anguish for us all, who despaired of ever again seeing our
guardian-angel, the sieur de la Salle. God vouchsafed to inspire me constantly with courage, and I cheered up those
who remained as well as I could. The whole day was spent
in tears and weeping, when at nightfall we saw on the opposite brink La Salle with all his party. We now learned that
by an interposition of Providence, the raft had been stopped
by a large tree floating in the middle of the river. This gave
them a chance to make an effort and get out of the current,
which would otherwise have carried them out to sea. One
of his men sprang into the water to catch the branch of a tree,
and then was unable to get back to the raft. He was a Breton named Rut; but he soon after appeared on our side,
having swam ashore.

The night was spent in anxiety, thinking how we should
find means to pass to the other side to join the sieur de la
Salle. We had not eaten all day, but Providence provided
for us by letting two eaglets fall from a cedar-tree; we were
ten at this meal.

The next day we had to pass; the sieur de la Salle advised
us to make a raft of canes; the sieur Moranget and I, with
three others, led the way, not without danger, for we went
under every moment, and I was obliged to put *our* breviary
in *our** cowl, because it got wet in the sleeve. The sieur

* The Franciscans were founded at a time when commerce was taking gigantic steps, and men all became inflamed with desires of rapidly acquiring wealth.
St. Francis arose to counteract this spirit so fatal to real Christianity in the
heart. Example is the easiest mode of teaching, and his poor friars rejecting

de la Salle sent two men to swim out and help us push the canes on, and they brought us safely in. Those who remained on the other side did not at all like risking it, but they had to do it at last, on our making show of packing up and continuing our march without them; they then crossed at less hazard than we.

The whole troop except the hunter being now assembled, we for two days traversed a thick cane-brake, the sieur de la Salle cutting his way with two axes, and the others in like manner to break the canes. At last, on the third day, our hunter Nika came in loaded with three dried deer, and another just killed. The sieur de la Salle ordered a discharge of several guns to show our joy.

Still marching east, we entered countries still finer than those we had passed, and found tribes that had nothing barbarous but the name; among others we met a very honest Indian returning from the chase with his wife and family. He presented the sieur de la Salle with one of his horses and some meat, invited him and all his party to his cabin; and to induce us, left his wife, family, and game, as a pledge, while he hastened to the village to announce our coming. Our hunter and a servant of the sieur de la Salle accompanied him, so that two days after they returned to us with two horses loaded with provisions, and several chiefs followed by warriors very neatly attired in dressed skins adorned with feathers. They came on bearing the calumet ceremoniously, and met us three leagues from the village; the sieur de la Salle was received as if in triumph, and lodged in the great chief's cabin. There was a great concourse of people; the young men being drawn out and under arms, relieving one

the word *mine*, showed in their whole deportment that contempt of wealth and property, which seemed a comment on the words, "Blessed are the poor in spirit."

another night and day, and besides loading us with presents and all kinds of provisions. Nevertheless, the sieur de la Salle fearing lest some of his party might go after the women, encamped three leagues from the village. Here we remained three or four days, and bought horses and all that we needed.

This village, that of the Cœnis, is one of the largest and most populous that I have seen in America. It is, at least, twenty leagues long, not that it is constantly inhabited, but in hamlets of ten or twelve cabins, forming cantons each with a different name. Their cabins are fine, forty or fifty feet high, of the shape of bee-hives. Trees are planted in the ground, and united above by the branches, which are covered with grass. The beds are ranged around the cabin, three or four feet from the ground ; the fire is in the middle, each cabin holding two families.

We found among the Cœnis many things which undoubtedly came from the Spaniards, such as dollars, and other pieces of money, silver spoons, lace of every kind, clothes and horses. We saw, among other things, a bull from Rome, exempting the Spaniards in Mexico from fasting during summer. Horses are common, they gave them to us for an axe ; one Cœnis offered me one for our cowl, to which he took a fancy.

They have intercourse with the Spaniards through the Choümans, their allies, who are always at war with New Spain. The sieur de la Salle made them draw on bark a map of their country, of that of their neighbors, and of the river Colbert, or Mississippi, with which they are acquainted. They reckoned themselves six days' journey from the Spaniards, of whom they gave us so natural a description, that we no longer had any doubts on the point, although the Spaniards had not yet undertaken to come to their villages, their warriors merely joining the Choümans to go war on New Mexico. The sieur de la Salle, who perfectly understood the art of gaining the Indians of all nations, filled these with admiration at every moment. Among other things he told them, that the chief of the French was the greatest chief in the world, as high as the sun, and as far above the Spaniard as the sun is above the earth. On his recounting the victories of our monarch, they burst into exclamations, putting their hand on their mouth as a mark of astonishment. I found them very docile and tractable, and they seized well enough what we told them of the truth of a God.

There were then some Choümans embassadors among them, who came to visit us; I was agreeably surprised to see them make the sign of the cross, kneel, clasp their hands, raise them from time to time to heaven. They also kissed my habit, and gave me to understand that men dressed like us instructed tribes in their vicinity, who were only two days' march from the Spaniards, where our religious had large churches, in which all assembled to pray. They expressed very naturally the ceremonies of mass, one of them sketched me a painting that he had seen of a great lady, who was weeping because her son was upon a cross. He told us that the Spaniards butchered the Indians cruelly, and finally that if we would go with them, or give them guns, they could easily conquer them, because they were a cowardly race, who had no courage, and made people walk before them with a fan to refresh them in hot weather.

After remaining here four or five days to recruit, we pursued our route through the Nassonis, crossing a large river which intersects the great Cœnis village. These two nations are allies, and have nearly the same character and customs.

Four or five leagues from there, we had the mortification

to see that four of our men had deserted under cover of night, and retired to the Nassonis; and, to complete our chagrin, the sieur de la Salle and his nephew, the sieur de Moranget, were attacked with a violent fever, which brought them to extremity. Their illness was long, and obliged us to make a long stay at this place, for when the fever, after frequent relapses, left them at last, they required a long time to recover entirely.

The length of this sickness disconcerted all our measures, and was eventually the cause of the last misfortunes which befell us. It kept us back more than two months, during which we had to live as we could; our powder began to run out; we had not advanced more than a hundred and fifty leagues in a straight line, and some of our people had deserted. In so distressing a crisis the sieur de la Salle resolved to retrace his steps to Fort Louis; all agreed and we straightway resumed our route, during which nothing happened worth note; but that, as we repassed the Maligne, one of our men was carried off with his raft by a crocodile of prodigious length and bulk.

After a good month's march, in which our horses did us good service, we reached the camp on the 17th of October, in the same year, 1686, where we were welcomed with all imaginable cordiality; but, after all, with feelings tinged alike with joy and sadness, as each related the tragical adventures which had befallen both since we had parted.

It would be difficult to find in history courage more intrepid or more invincible than that of the sieur de la Salle; in adversity he was never cast down, and always hoped with the help of Heaven to succeed in his enterprises, despite all the obstacles that rose against it.

He remained two months and a half at Saint Louis bay,

and we visited together all the rivers which empty into it. To my own knowledge, I am sure that there are more than fifty, all navigable, coming from the west and northwest; the place where the fort stands is somewhat sandy; everywhere else the ground is good. On every side we saw prairies on which the grass is, at all seasons of the year, higher than wheat with us. Every two or three leagues is a river skirted with oaks, thorn, mulberry, and other trees. This kind of country is uniform till within two days' march of the Spaniards.

The fort is built on a little eminence which runs north and south; it has the sea on the southwest, vast prairies to the west, and on the southwest two small lakes, and woods a league in circuit; a river flows at its foot. The neighboring nations are the Quoaquis, who raise Indian corn, and have horses cheap, the Bahamos, and the Quinets, wandering tribes with whom we are at war. During this time, the sieur de la Salle forgot nothing to console his little infant colony, in which the families began to increase by births. He advanced greatly the clearing of land, and the erection of buildings; the sieur de Chefdeville, priest, the sieur Cavelier, and we three Recollects, laboring in concert for the edification of the French, and of some Indian families who withdrew from the neighboring nations to join us. During all this time the sieur de la Salle did his utmost to render the Indians less hostile; peace with them being of the utmost consequence for the establishment of the colony.

At last Monsieur de la Salle resolved to resume his Ilinois voyage, so necessary for his plans; he made an address full of eloquence, with that engaging way so natural to him; the whole colony was present, and were almost moved to tears, persuaded of the necessity of his voyage, and the uprightness

of his intentions.   Would to God that all had persevered in
these sentiments !   He completed the fortification of a great
enclosure, encircling all the habitations and the fort, after
which he chose twenty men, the sieur Cavelier, his brother,
the sieurs Moranget and Cavelier, his nephews, with the
sieur Joutel,* pilot and myself.   After public prayers we set
out on the 7th of January, 1687.†

* Joutel was not in the previous excursion of the Cenis, of which the missionary's is the only account.

† The fate of the party left in the fort is involved in some obscurity; it is certain that they were killed by the Indians.   The period of this disaster seems to
have been some time after La Salle's departure.   The Spanish account of the
fate of La Salle's colony in Texas, from the Ensayo Cronologico of Barcia
(p. 294), is as follows:—

In the month of January, 1689, Don Alonso de Leon set out from the province of
Quaguila (Coahuila), with some horses, marching north of the sea, crossing great
mountains, and the river which runs near Valladolid, and those of Sauceda, Nasas,
Salinas, the river Florido, and others, to Caovil, a Spanish town in New Mexico,
which is also called Calhuila; he then turned to his right, and crossing the Rio
Bravo (which is also called Del Norte, or Rio Verde, and rises in the lake of the
Canibas) below Fort St. John, he entered the province of the Quelanhubeches
and Bahamos Indians, and in the interior of the country, came in his opinion to
the bay, called St. Bernard's; it had many estuaries and several large rivers
flowed into it.   The French called it St. Louis Bay.   He arrived at the fort which
Robert de la Salle had built with palisades, and ship timbers: he reconnoitred
it, and found nothing there but the dead bodies of some foreigners, inside and
outside the fort, killed by arrows and blows, and eighteen iron cannon on navy
gun carriages.

The destruction he witnessed excited his greatest compassion, and, as the
novelty of Don Alonso's squadron had congregated many Indians, he asked them
the motive of that deed, but the Indians, who had perpetrated it, pretended not
to understand his signs, and showed by others that, if any one knew the whole
matter, it would be five companions of the deceased, who were sick, in the
province of the Tejas, a hundred leagues distant; that they would go and inform
them; and although Don Alonso ascertained that the Indians of the neighborhood had conspired and put to death all the French, reserving only two children,
burning the powder, destroying the arms, and carrying off all they could, and
then celebrating the victory in all their towns with great feastings and dances
they constantly denied having any hand in the slaughter.

Such was the end of Fort St. Louis, which cost the unhappy Robert de la Salle
so much toil and anxiety.   Don Alonso could not then ascertain whether there
had been any motive for this cruelty, beyond the hatred of the Indians, or whether the French had given any cause; nor did he deem it prudent to examine the

The very first day we met an army of Bahamos going to war with the Erigoanna; the sieur de la Salle made an al-

Indians more closely, as he saw by their looks that, were he not accompanied by so well-appointed and well-armed a body of cavalry, prepared to meet them, they would have closed the tragedy with the Spaniards.

At the close of May Tonty knew it, being then one day's march from the Palaquesones: he states that the French of Fort St. Louis, being unable to keep together, had either mixed with the Indians, or started for French posts, and that, without examining further, he returned to Illinois.

In order to deliver the five Frenchmen who were among the Tejas, Don Alonso accepted the proposal made to inform them. He accordingly wrote to them in French, by means of an interpreter, telling them, with many kind expressions, that, having heard of the shipwreck, and peril of their companions, he had come by order of the viceroy of New Spain, to deliver them from the slavery of those savages, and save their lives; that he regretted extremely his having known the misfortune of their companions so late, as to have been unable to come more speedily, and prevent the murders which the Indians had perpetrated on them; that if they chose to come to him, he would free them, and treat them as became a Christian and a gentleman.

Four Indians carried this letter, and during the few days that it took them to return, Don Alonso ordered the French to be buried; this the Spaniards did, weeping over this catastrophe, and misfortune, and praying most earnestly for the salvation of their souls. This shows how ill-informed he was, who edited Joutel's account of La Salle's voyage, when he says, at the end, that when La Salle's death was known by the Spaniards, they sent a party who carried off the garrison of Fort St. Louis, and then put them to death, thus defrauding Don Alonso and his soldiers of the meed their piety deserved, by so ungrateful and notorious a falsehood.

The Indians arrived, with letter, in the province where the five Frenchmen were; when they had read it, their opinions as to it were divided. Three said that they could not believe that the Indians had killed their companions, and destroyed the fort; that it must have been the Spaniards, who now called them to do the same with them. "For why," they added, "can we expect a better fate, did we come into this country to do them any good? If they do not treat us as usurpers of territories they have occupied this many years, for having come now, without any ground, to despoil them and excite the Indians, by peace and war, against them, endeavoring to make them out horrible and abominable, by pretending cruelties, inventing tyrannies, and describing slaughters that never took place, at least they will treat us as robbers and pirates."

James Grollet, and John Larchevêque, of Bordeaux, endeavored to moderate their comrades' fears, saying that, "if the Spaniards had killed the French, the Indians of the country put to flight will relate the story, and will not confirm the bearers of the letter, and its contents; that they did not, and could not have anything to do with usurpation of countries, nor piracies, as a body of soldiers coming with their officers, would always go where their king sends them, and that the greatest evil would be, that they would be sent prisoners to Mexico.

14

liance with them.   He wished also to treat with the Quinets, who fled at our approach ; but having overtaken them by means of our horses, we treated them so kindly that they promised an inviolable peace.

The fourth day, three leagues further to the northeast, we came to the first Cane river.   Our route lay through prairies, with scattered groves ; the soil is so good that the grass grows ten or twelve feet high.   There are on this river many populous villages ; we visited only the Quaras and the Anachoremas.

In the same direction, three leagues further, we came to the second Cane river, inhabited by different tribes ; here we found fields of hemp.

And how much better," said they, "live among Christians, even as slaves, than among these savages, exposed to the whim of their cruelty, and risking, or abandoning their salvation.   If we were to invite the Spaniards, and they came under assurance of life, would we butcher them, without their giving fresh cause for their destruction ?   No.   Why then should we presume that their feelings will be unlike ours ?"   Finding, however, that the more they argued, the more obstinate the others became, Grollet and Larchevêque came with the four Indians without any suspicion.

They all reached Don Alonso, who ordered the Indians to be rewarded for their diligence, and the two Frenchmen to be supplied with necessary food and clothing.   Following his instructions, he questioned them on different points, and taking them into his company, returned to Quaguila by May without meeting any accident on the way.

He informed the viceroy of all that he had seen, observed, or discovered, and sent him Grollet and Larchevêque, directing those who conducted them to treat them well.   They arrived and delivered the viceroy the letters of Don Alonso. Before interrogating the Frenchmen at all, he summoned Don Andres de Pes, as a person so well informed in the matter, and then, in the presence of both the Frenchmen, stated La Salle's voyage in search of the mouth of the river Mississippi, his landing in St. Bernard's Bay, the building of the fort, the reason of their being among the Tejas, and other matters.

By the letters and statements made by Don Alonso, and the information elsewhere acquired, they saw the great injury to be done to New Spain by this project of the French, already, though unsuccessfully, attempted.   The viceroy asked Don Andres de Pes to go to Spain, to represent the danger, and the great advantage of fortifying Pensacola.   Don Andres, having obtained the necessary instructions, set out with the two Frenchmen, and embarking at Vera Cruz, reached Cadiz safely on the 9th of December.

Five leagues further, we passed the Sandy river, so called from the sandy strip along it, though all the rest is good land and vast prairies.

We marched seven or eight leagues to Robec river, passing through prairies, and over three or four rivers, a league from one another.   Robec river has many populous villages, where the people have a language so guttural, that it would require a long time to form ourselves to it.   They are at war with the Spaniards, and pressed us earnestly to join their warriors; but there was no hope of keeping us.   We stayed, however, five or six days with them, endeavoring to gain them by presents and Christian instruction, a thing they do not get from the Spaniards.

Continuing our route, we crossed great prairies to the Maligne.   This deep river, where one of our men had been devoured by a crocodile, comes from a great distance, and is inhabited by forty populous villages, which compose a nation called the Quanoatinno; they make war on the Spaniards, and lord it over the neighboring tribes.   We visited some of these villages;* they are a good people, but always savage, the cruelty of the Spaniards rendering them still more fierce. As they found us of a more tractable nature, they were charmed with our nation; but after these mutual presents, we had to part.   They gave us horses cheap, and carried us over their river in hide canoes.

In the same direction, after four leagues of similar land, extremely fertile, we crossed Hiens river on rafts; then turning north-northeast, we had to cross a number of little rivers and ravines, navigable in winter and spring.   The land is diversified with prairies, hills, and numerous springs.   Here we

---

* Joutel says they merely heard of the Canohatino, and calls them afterward enemies of the Cenis.

found three large villages, the Taraha, Tyakappan, and Palona, who have horses. Some leagues further on, we came to the Palaquesson* composed of ten villages, allies of the Spaniards.

After having passed these nations, the most disheartening of all our misfortunes overtook us. It was the murder of Monsieur de la Salle, of the sieur de Moranget, and of some others. Our prudent commander finding himself in a country full of game, after all the party had recruited and lived for several days on every kind of good meat, sent the sieur Moranget, his lackey Saget, and seven or eight of his people, to a place where our hunter, the Shawnee Nika, had left a quantity of buffalo meat (bœuf) to dry, so as not to be obliged to stop so often to hunt.

The wisdom of Monsieur de la Salle had not been able to foresee the plot which some of his people would make to slay his nephew, as they suddenly resolved to do, and actually did on the 17th of March, by a blow of an axe, dealt by one whom charity does not permit me to name (Liotot). They also killed the valet of the sieur de la Salle, and the Indian Nika, who, at the risk of his life, had supported them for more than three years. The sieur de Moranget lingered for about two hours, giving every mark of a death precious in the sight of God, pardoning his murderers, and embracing them; and making acts of sorrow and contrition, as they themselves assured us, after they recovered from their unhappy blindness. He was a perfectly honest man, and a good Christian, confessing every week or fortnight on our march. I have every reason to hope that God has shown him mercy.

The wretches resolved not to stop here; and not satisfied

---

* According to Joutel, *Hist. Coll. of Louisiana*, vol. i., p. 147. Palaquechaune was an Indian, whose tribe were allies of the Cenis, and who knew the Choumans, the friends of the Spaniards.

with this murder, formed a design of attempting their commander's life, as they had reason to fear his resentment and chastisement. We were full two leagues off; the sieur de la Salle, troubled at the delay of the sieur de Moranget and his people, from whom he had been separated now for two or three days, began to fear that they had been surprised by the Indians. Asking me to accompany him, he took two Indians and set out. All the way he conversed with me of matters of piety, grace, and predestination; expatiating on all his obligations to God for having saved him from so many dangers during the last twenty years that he had traversed America. He seemed to me peculiarly penetrated with a sense of God's benefits to him. Suddenly I saw him plunged into a deep melancholy, for which he himself could not account; he was so troubled that I did not know him any longer; as this state was far from being usual, I roused him from his lethargy. Two leagues after we found the bloody cravat of his lackey; he perceived two eagles flying over his head, and at the same time discovered some of his people on the edge of the river, which he approached, asking them what had become of his nephew. They answered us in broken words, showing us where we should find him. We proceeded some steps along the bank to the fatal spot, where two of these murderers were hidden in the grass, one on each side with guns cocked; one missed Monsieur de la Salle, the one firing at the same time shot him in the head; he died an hour after, on the 19th of March, 1687.

I expected the same fate, but this danger did not occupy my thoughts, penetrated with grief at so cruel a spectacle, I saw him fall a step from me, with his face all full of blood; I watered it with my tears, exhorting him, to the best of my power, to die well. He had confessed and fulfilled his

devotions just before we started ; he had still time to recapit-
ulate a part of his life, and I gave him absolution. During
his last moments he elicited all the acts of a good Christian,
grasping my hand at every word I suggested, and especially
at that of pardoning his enemies.   Meanwhile his murderers,
as much alarmed as I, began to strike their breasts, and de-
test their blindness.   I could not leave the spot when he had
expired without having buried him as well as I could, after
which I raised a cross over his grave.*

Thus died our wise commander, constant in adversity, intrepid, generous, engaging, dexterous, skilful, capable of
everything. He who for twenty years had softened the fierce
temper of countless savage tribes, was massacred by the
hands of his own domestics, whom he had loaded with caresses. He died in the prime of life, in the midst of his course
and labors, without having seen their success.

Occupied with these thoughts, which he had himself a
thousand times suggested to us, while relating the events of
the new discoveries, I unceasingly adored the inscrutable designs of God in this conduct of his providence, uncertain still
what fate he reserved for us, as our desperadoes plotted nothing less than our destruction. We at last entered the place
where Monsieur Cavelier was ; the assassins entered the cabin
unceremoniously, and seized all that was there. I had arrived a moment before them ; I had no need to speak, for as
soon as he beheld my countenance all bathed in tears, the
sieur Cavelier exclaimed aloud, " Ah ! my poor brother is
dead !"   This holy ecclesiastic, whose virtue has been so
often tried in the apostolic labors of Canada, fell at once on
his knees, his nephew, the sieur Cavelier, myself, and some

---

* This and the circumstances of Moranget's death, are denied by Joutel in
Hist. Coll. of Louisiana, vol. i.

others did the same, to prepare to die the same death, but the wretches touched by some sentiments of compassion at the sight of the venerable old man, and besides half penitent for the murders they had committed, resolved to spare us, on condition that we should never return to France ; but as they were still undecided, and many of them wished to return home, we heard them often say, that they must get rid of us ; that otherwise we would accuse them before the tribunals, if we once had them in the kingdom.

They elected as chief the murderer of the sieur de la Salle (Duhaut), and, at last, after many deliberations, resolved to push on to that famous nation of the Cœnis. Accordingly, after marching together for several days, crossing rivers and rivers, everywhere treated by these wretches as servants, having nothing but what they left, we reached the tribe without accident.

Meanwhile the justice of God accomplished the punishment of these men, in default of human justice. Jealousy and desire of command arose between Hiens and the sieur de la Salle's murderer ; each one of the guilty band sided on one side or the other. We had passed the Cœnis, after some stay there, and were already at the Nassonis, where the four deserters, whom I mentioned in the first expedition, rejoined us. On the eve of Ascension seeing all together, and our wretches resolved to kill each other, I made them an exhortation on the festival, at which they seemed affected, and resolved to confess ; but this did not last. Those who most regretted the murder of their commander and leader, had sided with Hiens who, seizing his opportunity two days' after, sought to punish crime by crime. In our presence he shot the murderer of La Salle through the heart with a pistol ; he died on the spot, unshriven, unable even to utter the names of Jesus and Mary. Another who was with Hiens, shot the murderer of the sieur de Moranget (Liotot), in the side with a musket-ball. He had time to confess, after which a Frenchman fired a blank cartridge at his head ; his hair, and then his shirt, and clothes, took fire and wrapped him in flames, and in this torment he expired. The third author of the plot and murder fled ; Hiens wished to make way with him, and thus completely avenge the death of the sieur de la Salle, but the sieur Joutel conciliated them, and it stopped there.*

By this means Hiens remained chief of the wretched band; we had to return to the Cœnis where they had resolved to settle, not daring to return to France for fear of punishment.

A Cœnis army was ready to march against the Kanoatino, a hostile tribe, cruel to their enemies, whom they boil alive; the Cœnis took our Frenchmen with them, after which Hiens pressed us strongly to remain with them, but we would not consent. Six of us, all French, accordingly set out from the Cœnis, among whom were the sieurs Cavelier, uncle and nephew, and the sieur Joutel. They gave us each a horse, powder and lead, and some goods to pay our way. We stopped at the Nassonis to celebrate the octave of Corpus Christi. They spoke to us daily of the cruelty of the Spaniards to the Americans, and told us that twenty Indian nations were going to war against the Spaniards, inviting us to join them, as we would do more with our guns than all their braves with their warclubs and arrows ; but we had very different designs. We only took occasion to tell them that we came on behalf of God to instruct them in the truth and save

* This was Larcheveque, *Hist. Coll. of Louisiana*, vol. i., p. 158. With Grollet who had deserted from La Salle on his first excursion, he surrendered to a Spanish party under Don Alonzo de Leon. See extract from the Ensayo Cronologico.

their souls. In this we spent ten or twelve days, till the 3d of June, the feast of St. Anthony of Padua whom the sieur de la Salle had taken as patron of his enterprise.

Having received two Indians to guide us, we continued our way north-northeast, through the finest country in the world ; we passed four large rivers and many ravines, inhabited by many different nations ; we reconnoitred the Haquis on the east, the Nabiri, and Naansi, all numerous tribes at war with the Cœnis, and at last, on the 23d of June, we approached the Cadodacchos.* One of our Indians went on to announce our coming ; the chiefs and youth whom we met a league from the village, received us with the calumet, which they gave us to smoke ; some led our horses by the bridle, others as it were, carried us in triumph, taking us for spirits and people of another world.

All the village being assembled, the women, as is their wont, washed our head and feet with warm water, and then placed us on a platform covered with a very neat, white mat ; then followed banquets, calumet-dances, and other public re-joicings, day and night. The people knew the Europeans only by report ; like other tribes through which we had passed, they have some very confused ideas of religion and adore the sun ; their gala dresses bear two painted suns ; on the rest of the body are representations of buffalo, stags, ser-pents, and other animals. This afforded us an opportunity to

* These were, doubtless, the Caddoes, a tribe which is not yet extinct. Ac-cording to Joutel, *Hist. Coll. of Louisiana*, vol. i., p. 168, the tribe consisted of four allied villages, Assony, Nathosos, Nachitos, and Cadodaquio. Tonty de-scribes them as forming three villages, Cadodaquis, Nachitoches, and Nasoui, all on the Red river, and speaking the same language. Two of these tribes, the Nasoui and Nachitoches bear a strong resemblance to the tribes found by Mus-coso, the successor of De Soto, in the same vicinity, and called by Biedma, Nis-sione (*Hist. Coll. of Louisiana*, vol. iii., p. 107), and by the gentleman of Elvas, Nissoone and Naquiscoza, while the Daycao, as their river is called, is not incom-patible with Cado-Daquio.—*Hist. Coll. of Louisiana*, vol. iii., p. 201.

give them some lessons on the knowledge of the true God, and on our principal mysteries.

At this place it pleased God to traverse us by a tragical accident. The sieur de Marne, in spite of all that we could say, went to bathe on the evening of the 24th, the younger sieur Cavelier accompanied him to the river side, quite near the village; de Marne sprang into the water and instantly disappeared. It was an abyss where he was in a moment swallowed up. A few hours after his body was recovered and brought to the chief's cabin; all the village mourned his death with all ceremony; the chief's wife herself neatly wound him in a beautiful cloth, while the young men dug the grave which I blessed the next day, when we buried him with all possible solemnity. The Indians admired our ceremonies, from which we took occasion to give them some instruction during the week that we remained in this fatal place. Our friend was interred on an eminence near the village, and his tomb surrounded by a palisade, surmounted by a large cross, which we got the Indians to raise, after which we started on the 2d of July.

This tribe is on the banks of a large river, on which lie three more famous nations, the Natchoos, the Natchites, the Ouidiches, where we were very hospitably received. From the Cœnis river, where we began to find beaver and otter, they became very plentiful as we advanced. At the Ouidiches, we met three warriors of two tribes called the Cahinnio and the Mentous, twenty-five leagues further east-northeast, who had seen Frenchmen. They offered to guide us there, and on our way we passed four rivers on rafts. We were received with the calumet of peace, and every mark of joy and esteem.* Many of these Indians spoke to us of a great

---

* Joutel calls this village Cahaynahoua. See Joutel's journal published in French's Historical Collections of Louisiana, vol. i., pp. 85–193.

captain, who had only one arm (this was Monsieur de Tonty), whom they had seen, and who told them that a greater captain than he would pass through their village ; this was Monsieur de la Salle.

The chief lodged us in his cabin, from which he made his family retire. We were here regaled for several days on every kind of meat ; there was even a public feast, where the calumet was danced for twenty-four hours, with songs made for the occasion, which the chief intoned with all his might, treating us as people of the sun, who came to defend them from their enemies by the noise of our thunder. Amidst these rejoicings the younger Cavelier fired his pistol three times, crying "Vive le roi," which the Indians repeated loudly, adding, "Vive le soleil." These Indians have prodigious quantities of beaver and otter skins, which could be easily transported by a river near the village ; they wished to load our horses with them, but we refused, to show our disin terestedness ; we made them presents of axes and knives, and set out with two Cahinnio to act as guides, after having received embassies from the Analao and Tanico, and other tribes to the northwest and southeast. It was delightful to traverse for several days the finest country, intersected by many rivers, prairies, little woods, and vine-clad hills. Among others, we passed four large navigable rivers, and at last, after a march of about sixty leagues, we reached the Osotteoez, who dwell on a great river which comes from the northwest, skirted by the finest woods in the world. Beaver and otter-skins, and all kinds of peltries, are so abundant there, that being of no value they burn them in heaps. This is the famous river of the Achansa, who here form several villages. At this point we began to know where we were, and finding a large cross, bearing below the royal arms, with a French-

looking house, our people discharged their guns; two Frenchmen at once came forth, and the one in command, by name
Coutûre, told us that the sieur de Tonty had stationed them
there to serve as an intermediate station to the sieur de la
Salle, to maintain the alliance with those tribes, and to shield
them against attacks by the Iroquois. We visited three of
these villages, the Torimans, the Doginga, and the Kappa;
everywhere we had feasts, harangues, calumet-dances, with
every mark of joy; we lodged at the French house, where
the two gentlemen treated us with all desirable hospitality,
putting all at our disposal. Whenever any affairs are to be
decided among these nations, they never give their resolution
on the spot; they assemble the chiefs and old men, and deliberate on the point in question. We had asked a periagua
and Indians to ascend the river Colbert, and thence to push
on to the Ilinois by the river Seignelay, offering to leave them
our horses, powder, and lead; when the council was held, it
was said that they would grant us the periagua, and four Indians to be selected, one from each tribe, in token of a more
strict alliance. This was faithfully executed, so that we dismissed our Cahinnio with presents, which perfectly satisfied
them.

At last, after some time stay, we embarked on the 1st of
August, 1687, on the river Colbert, which we crossed the
same day in our periagua forty feet long; but as the current
is strong, we all landed to make the rest of our journey on
foot, having left our ˙horses and equipage at the Akansa.
There remained in the canoe only the sieur Cavelier whose
age, joined to the hardships he had already undergone on the
way, did not permit him to accomplish on foot the rest of our
course (at least four hundred leagues), to the Ilinois. One
Indian was in the canoe to perch it along, one of his com-

rades relieving him from time to time. As for the rest of us, we used the periagua only when necessary to cross some dangerous passages or rivers. All this was not without much suffering; for the excessive heat of the season, the burning sand, the broiling sun, heightened by a want of provisions for several days, gave us enough to endure.

We had already travelled two hundred and fifty leagues across the country from St. Louis bay, viz.: one hundred leagues to the Cœnis (sixty north-northeast, the last forty east-northeast); from the Cœnis to the Nassonis, twenty-five to the east-northeast; from the Nassonis to the Cadodacchos, forty to the north-northeast; from the Cadodacchos to the Cahinnio and Mentous, twenty-five to the east-northeast; from the Cahinnio to the Akansa, sixty to the east-northeast.

We then continued our route, ascending the river through the same places which the sieur de la Salle had previously passed when he made his first discovery, of which I have heard him frequently speak, except that we went to the Sicacha, where he had not been. The principal village is twenty-five leagues east of the Akansa. This nation is very numerous; they count at least four thousand warriors, have an abundance of every kind of peltry. The chiefs came several times to offer us the calumet, wishing to form an alliance with the French and put themselves under their protection, offering even to come and dwell on the river Oüabache (Ohio) to be nearer to us.

This famous river is full as large as the river Colbert, receiving a quantity of others by which you can enter it. The mouth, where it empties into the river Colbert, is two hundred leagues from the Akansa, according to the estimate of the sieur de la Salle, as he often told me; or two hundred and fifty, according to Monsieur de Tonty, and those who accompanied him in his second voyage to the sea, not that it is that distance in a straight line across the prairies, but following the river which makes great turns, and winds a great deal, for by land it would not be more than five days' good march.

We crossed the Oüabache then on the 26th of August, and found it full sixty leagues to the mouth of the river Ilinois, still ascending the Colbert. About six leagues above this mouth, there is on the northwest the famous river of the Massourites or Osages, at least as large as the river into which it empties; it is formed by a number of other known rivers, everywhere navigable, and inhabited by many populous tribes; as the Panimaha who had but one chief and twenty-two villages, the least of which has two hundred cabins; the Paneassa, the Pana, the Paneloga, and the Matotantes, each of which, separately, is not inferior to the Panimaha. They include also the Osages who have seventeen villages on a river of their name, which empties into that of the Massou-rites, to which the maps have also extended the name of Osages. The Akansas were formerly stationed on the upper part of one of these rivers, but the Iroquois drove them out by cruel wars some years ago, so that they, with some Osage villages, were obliged to drop down and settle on the river which now bears their name, and of which I have spoken.

About midway between the river Oüabache and that of the Massourites is Cape St. Anthony. It was to this place only and not further that the sieur Joliet descended in 1673; they were there taken, with their whole party, by the Mansopela. These Indians having told them that they would be killed if they went further; they turned back, not having descended lower than thirty or forty leagues below the mouth of the Ilinois' river.

I had brought with me the printed book of this pretended

discovery, and I remarked all along my route that there was not a word of truth in it.   It is said that he went as far as the Akansa, and that he was obliged to return for fear of being taken by the Spaniards ; and yet the Akansa assured us that they had never seen any Europeans before Monsieur de la Salle.   It is said that they saw painted monsters that the boldest would have difficulty to look at, and that there was something supernatural about them.   This frightful monster is a horse painted on a rock with matachia,* and some other wild beasts made by the Indians.   It is said that they can not be reached, and yet I touched them without difficulty. The truth is that the Miamis, pursued by the Matsigamea, having been drowned in the river, the Indians ever since that time present tobacco to these grotesque figures whenever they pass, in order to appease the manitou.

I would not be inclined to think that the sieur Joliet avowed the printed account of that discovery which is not, in fact, under his name, and was not published till after the first discovery made by the sieur de la Salle.   It would be easy to show that it was printed only on false memoirs, which the author, who had never been on the spot, might have followed in good faith.†

* An old term for paint used by the Indians.

† In this short passage a heavy charge is brought against the narrative of Father Marquette, although it is amusing to see how they all, in denying it, seem to have dreaded to mention his name, as though his injured spirit would have been evoked by the word.

As Father Anastasius says expressly, that there is not a word of truth in it, we may examine the grounds which he adduces.

1st. It was not published till after the discovery made by La Salle.   This is incorrect.   Thevenot published Marquette's journal from a mutilated copy, in 1681, and La Salle reached the mouth of the Mississippi only in April, 1682, while his discovery was not known in France before January, 1683.

2d. The Arkansas said that they had never seen any European before La Salle.   Making every allowance for the difficulty of conversing with a tribe whose language was utterly unknown to him, and admitting the fact, it remains

At last, on the 5th of September, we arrived at the mouth of the Ilinois' river, whence they reckon at least a hundred leagues to Fort Crevecœur, the whole route presenting a very easy navigation. A Shawnee named Turpin, having per-

to show that the Arkansas whom he met, were the same as those visited by Marquette. This does not appear to be certain, as they were on different sides of the Mississippi.

3d. The painted rock, of which he exaggerates and refutes Marquette's account. Now, though Father Anastasius had the book of the pretended discovery in his hand, he did not read it carefully. Marquette describes a rock above the mouth of the Missouri, Anastasius saw another below the mouth, and half way between it and the Ohio, and, as it did not answer Marquette's account, there is not a word of truth in his book! Joutel, whose work appeared only in 1713, avoid this difficulty, whether conscious of Douay's error, we do not know. From the words of Father Anastasius, I am inclined to think, that they never saw Marquette's rock; but deceived by Thevenot's map which gives a figure and the word Manitou at the place below the Missouri, which Marquette mentions as the demon of the Illinois, mistook it for the painted rock. Here as Father Anastasius tells, some Indians actually perished, and their countrymen supposing them engulfed by some demon, propagated the belief in the existence of one there. This worshipping of rapids was common, and several cases are mentioned in the narratives of the time. As to the exaggerations made of Marquette's account, a moment's examination will show that he represented the figures he saw as terrible to superstitious Indians, and so high up on the rock that it was not easy to get up there to paint them. His estimate of the skill displayed is, indeed, too high; but there is nothing, beyond this, strange in his account.

4th. Last of all, comes his positive assertion that Marquette and Joliet went only as far as Cape St. Anthony, thirty or forty leagues below the mouth of the Illinois. For this he gives no authority; but it may be inferred that he found the Mansopelas there, and from his little knowledge of the Indians, concluded that being there, in 1687, they must have been there in 1673, and consequently, that Marquette went no further.

Enough, however, is here admitted to convict the author of the Etablissement de la Foi of injustice to Marquette, whom he never names, but who, even by their own statements, descended the Mississippi to the Mansopelas, many years before La Salle's expedition. Yet in the previous part of the work no mention at all is made of this voyage, and no opportunity passed to treat it as pretended in the accounts of their own.

Joutel, whose narrative was published subsequently to this, mentions (See *Hist. Coll. of Louisiana*, vol. i., p. 182) Father Marquette, and though he saw nothing extraordinary in the painted figures, does not make any of the charges here brought by his companion on the voyage whom he contradicts directly on two other points.

ceived us from his village, ran on to the fort to carry the
news to the sieur de Belle Fontaine, the commander, who
would not credit it; we followed close on the Indian, and
entered the fort on the 14th of September. We were conducted to the chapel where the Te Deum was chanted in
thanksgiving, amid the noise and volleys of the French and
Indians who were immediately put under arms. The sieur
de Tonty, the governor of the fort, had gone to the Iroquois
to conciliate the minds of those Indians, we, nevertheless, received a very cordial welcome; the commandant neglecting
nothing to show his joy at our arrival, to console us in our
misfortunes, and restore us after our hardships.

Although the season was advanced, we had, nevertheless,
set out in hopes of reaching Quebec soon enough to sail to
France; but head-winds having detained us a fortnight at
the entrance of Lake Dauphin, we had to give it over and winter at the fort, which we made a mission till the spring of 1688.

The sieur de Tonty arrived there at the beginning of winter with several Frenchmen; this made our stay much more
agreeable, as this brave gentleman was always inseparably
attached to the interests of the sieur de la Salle, whose la-
mentable fate we concealed from him, it being our duty to
give the first news to the court.

He told us that, at the same time that we were seeking the
river Missisipi by sea, he had made a second voyage, descending the river with some French and Indians to the
mouth, hoping to find us there; that he remained there a
week, visited all the remarkable points, and remarked that
there was a very fine port with a beautiful entrance, and wide
channel; and, also, places fit for building forts, and not at
all inundated as he had supposed, when he descended the
first time with the sieur de la Salle; adding, that the lower
15

river is habitable and even inhabited by Indian villages ; that ships can ascend the river a hundred leagues above the gulf ; that, besides the tribes which he had discovered when descending the first time, he had seen several others on the second, as the Picheno, the Ozanbogus, the Tangibao, the Otonnica, the Mausopelea, the Mouisa, and many others which I do not remember.

Our conversations together confirmed me in the opinion of the sieur de la Salle, that St. Louis bay could not be more than forty or fifty leagues from the mouth of one of the arms of the river Colbert in a straight line, for though we struck that river only at the Akansa, it was because we took the Ilinois route across the country, God having led us through these parts to enable us to discover all those tribes which dwell there.

I had remarked one hundred and ten populous nations on my route, not including a great many others of which I heard in those through which we passed, who knew them either in war, or in trade. The greatest part of these tribes are unknown to Europeans.

These are the finest and most fertile countries in the world ; the soil, which there produces two crops of every kind of grain a year, being ready to receive the plough. From time to time there are vast prairies where the grass is ten or twelve feet high at all seasons ; at every little distance there are rivers entering larger ones, everywhere navigable, and free from rapids. On these rivers are forests full of every kind of trees, so distributed that you can everywhere ride through on horseback.

The chase is so abundant and easy, especially for wild-cattle, that herds of thousands are discovered ; there are deer and other animals of the stag kind in numbers, as well as turkeys, bustards, partridges, parrots, rabbits, and hares. Poultry are common there, and produce at all seasons, and swine several times a year, as we observed at the settlement where we left more than two hundred.

The rivers are unusually abundant in all kinds of fish, so much so that we took them at the foot of the fort with our hands, without basket or net. Our people one day took away from the Indians a fish-head which was alone a load for a man. No settler arriving in the country will not find at first enough to support plenteously a large family, or will not, in two years time be more at his ease than in any place in Europe. I have already remarked that horses for every use are there very common, the Indians thinking themselves well paid when they get an axe for a horse.

The commerce might be very great there in peltries, tobacco, and cotton. Hemp grows very fine; and as the fields are full of mulberry-trees which also line the rivers, silk might be raised in abundance. Sugar-canes would succeed there well, and could be easily got by trade with the West Indies, as the Europeans nations have done in Terra-firma, where they are neighbors to Louisiana.* Besides, the great

---

* These observations from which Coxe (*Hist. Coll. of Louisiana*, vol. iii., pp. 262–'65), doubtless, took a hint, entitle Father Douay to the credit of pointing out sources of wealth to Louisiana. Cotton and sugar are already staple products, and silk may soon be. The valley of the Mississippi owes the introduction of the sugar-cane to the Catholic missionaries, for the Jesuits brought in some plants from which the colony was supplied, after they had shown in their gardens at New Orleans how successfully it could be raised. The same missionaries were also the first to raise wheat in Illinois, and engage others to do so; as one of their lay-brothers was the first to work the copper-mine of Lake Superior, to make articles for the church of Sault St. Mary's. In the east they deserve no less a place even in commercial history; they not only called the attention of New York to her salt-springs, and brought about a commercial intercourse between the French of Canada, and the English and Dutch in their colonies, but, by showing the identity of our ginseng with that of Tartary, enabled France for some time to carry on a very lucrative trade with China.

quantity of wool which the cattle of the country are loaded, the vast prairies everywhere afford means of raising flocks of sheep, which produce twice a year.

The various accidents that befell us, prevented our searching for the treasures of this country: we found lead quite pure, and copper ready to work. The Indians told us that there were rivers where silver mines are found: others wished to conduct us to a country known to the Spaniards, abounding in gold and silver mines. There are also some villages where the inhabitants have pearls, which they go to seek on the seacoast and find, they say, in oysters.

We found few nations within a hundred and fifty or two hundred leagues of the sea, who are not prejudiced against the Spaniards on account of their great cruelty. These tribes are all populous; and there is one which, in war, would furnish as many as five thousand men.

The shortness of our stay among these tribes gave us no time to lay solid foundations of Christianity; but we remarked good dispositions for the faith; they are docile, charitable, susceptible of good impressions; there is even some government and subordination, savage though it always be. By the help of God, religion might make progress there. The sun is their divinity, and they offer it in sacrifice the best of their chase in the chief's cabin. They pray for half an hour, especially at sunrise; they send him the first whiff of their pipes, and then send one to each of the four cardinal points.

I left St. Louis bay on the second voyage to remain among the Cœnis and begin a mission there. Here Father Zenobius was to join me, to visit the neighboring tribes while awaiting from France a greater number of gospel laborers, but the melancholy death of the sieur de la Salle having compelled me to proceed, Father Zenobius no doubt went there to meet me, and is, perhaps, there yet with Father Maximus (le Clercq), having left M. de Chefdeville at the mission in the fort, to which he was destined at our departure. There were there nine or ten French families, and, besides, several of our people had gone to get and had actually married Indian women to multiply the colony. What has befallen them since, I do not know.

This, adds le Clercq, is a faithful extract of what Father Anastasius could remember of his toilsome voyage. He left the Ilinois in the spring of 1688, with M. Cavelier, his nephew, the sieur Joūstel, and an Indian now domiciled near Versailles. They arrived at Quebec on the 27th of July, and sailed for France on the 20th of August, where, God enabling them to be still together, after having passed through so many perils, they presented on account of all to the late marquis of Seignelay.

RECIT

DES VOYAGES ET DES DECOUVERTES

DU

P. JACQUES MARQUETTE,

DE LA COMPAGNIE DE JESUS EN L'ANNEE 1673, ET AUX SUIVANTES.

CHAPITRE IER.

Du Premier Voyage qu'a fait le P. Marquette vers le Nouveau Mexique et comment s'en est formé le dessein.

IL y avoit longtemps que le Pere premeditoit cette entreprise, porté d'un tres ardent desir d'estendre le Royaume de J. Ch. et de le faire connoistre et adorer par tous les peuples de ce pays. Il se voioit comme a la porte de ces nouvelles nations, lorsque des l'année 1670, il travailloit en la mission de lapointe du St. Esprit qui est a l'extremité du lac Superieur aux Outaoüacs, il voioit mesme quelquefois plusieurs de ces nouveaux peuples, desquels il prenoit toutes les connoissances quil pouvoit, c'est ce qui luy a fait faire plusieurs efforts pour commencer cette entreprise, mais tousiour inutilement, et mesme il avoit perdu l'esperance d'en venir about lorsque Dieu luy en fit naistre cette occasion.

En l'année 1673, M. Le Comte de Frontenac nostre gouverneur, et M. Talon alors nostre Intendant, connoissant l'importance de cette découverte, soit pour chercher un passage d'icy jusqu'a la mer de la Chine, par la riviere qui se décharge a la mer Vermeille au Californie, soit qu'on voulu s'asseurer de ce qu'on a dit du depuis, touchant les 2 Royaumes de Theguaïo et de Quivira, limitrophes du Canada, ou l'on tient que les mines d'or sont abondantes, ces Messieurs, dis-ie, nommerent en mesme temps pour cette entreprise le sieur Jolyet quils jugerent tres propres pour un si grand dessein, estant bien aise que le P. Marquette fut de le partie.

Il ne se tromperent pas dans le choix quils firent du sieur Jolyet, car c'estoit un jeune homme natif de ce pays, qui a pour un tel dessein tous les advantages qu'on peut souhaiter : Il a l'experience et la Connoissance des Langues du Pays des Outaoüacs, ou il a passé plusieurs années, il a la conduitte et la sagesse qui sont les principales parties pour faire reussir un voyage egalement dangereux et difficile.   Enfin il a le courage pour ne rien apprehender, ou tout est a craindre, aussi a-t-il remply l'attente qu'on avoit de luy, et si apres avoir passé mille sortes de dangers, il ne fut venu malheureusement faire nauffrage auport, son canot ayant tourné au dessoubs du Sault de St. Loüys proche de Montreal, ou il a perdu et ses hommes et ses papiers, et d'ou il n'a eschapé que par une espece de miracle, il ne lassoit rien a souhaiter au succez de son voyage.

SECTION I.

Depart du P. Jacques Marquette pour la découverte de la grande Riviere appellée par les sauvages Missisipi qai conduit au Nouveau Mexique.

LE jour de l'Immaculée Conception de la Ste. Vierge, que javois tousjour invoqué depuisque je suis en ce pays des Outaoüacs, pour obtenir de Dieu la grace de pouvoir visiter les nations qui sont sur la riviere de Missis-pi, fut justement celuy auquel arriva M. Jollyet avec les ordres de M. le comte de Frontenac nostre gouverneur et de M. Talon nostre Intendant, pour faire avec moy cette découverte. Je fus d'autant plus ravy de cette bonne nouvelle, que je voiois que mes desseins alloient étre accomplis et que je me trouvois dans une heureuse nécessité d'exposer ma vie pour le salut de tous ces peuples et particulierement pour les Ilinois qui m'avoient prié avec beaucoup d'instance lorsque j'estois a la pointe du St. Esprit de leur porter chez eux la parole de Dieu.

Nous ne fusmes pas long temps a preparer tout nostre equippage quoyque nous nous engageassions en un voyage dont nous ne pouvions pas prevoir la durée ; du Bled d'Inde avec quelque viande boucanée furent toutes nos provisions, avec lesquelles nous nous embarquam-

mes sur 2 canots d'écorce, M.Jollyet et moy avec 5 hommes, bien
resolus a tout faire et a tout souffrir pour une si glorieuse enterprise.

Ce fut donc le 17e jour de May, 1673, que nous partîmes de la
mission de St. Ignace a Michilimackinac, ou j'estois pour lors ; la
joye que nous avions d'étre choisis pour cette expedition animoit nos
courages et nous rendoit agreables les peines que nous avions a
ramer depuis le matin jusqu'au soir ; et parceque nous allions chercher des pays inconnus, nous apportammes toutes les precautions
que nous pûmes, affinque si nostre entreprise estoit hazardeuse elle
ne fut pas temeraire ; pour ce sujet nous primes toutes les connoissances que nous pûmes des sauvages qui avoient frequenté ces endroicts là et mesme nous tracâmes sur leur raport une carte de tout
ce nouveau pays, nous y fîmes marquer les rivieres sur lesquelles
nous devions naviger, les noms des peuples et des lieux par lesquels
nous devions passer, le cours de la grande riviere, et quels rund
devent nous devions tenir quand nous y serions.

Surtout je mis nostre voyage soubs la protection de la Ste. Vierge
Immaculée, luy promettant que si elle nous faisoit la grace de découvrir la grande riviere, je luy donnerois le nom de la Conception
et que je ferois aussi porter ce nom a la premiere mission que
j'établyrois chez ces nouveaux peuples, ce que j'ay fait de vray chez
les Ilinois.

SECTION II.

Le Pere visite en passant les Peuples de la folle avoine ; Ce que c'est que cette
folle avoine.   Il entre dans la baye des Puants, quelques particularitez de cette
baye, il arrive a la nation du feu.

AVEC toutes ces precautions nous faisons joüer joyeusement les
avirons, sur une partie du Lac Huron, et celuy des Ilinois, et dans la
baye des Puans.

Le premiere nation que nous rencontrâmes, fut celle de la folle
avoine. l'entray dans leur riviere pour aller visiter ces peuples aus
quels nous avons presché l'Evangile depuis plusieurs années, aussi
se trouve-t-il parmy eux plusieurs bons Chrestiens.

La folle avoine dont ils portent le nom, parcequelle se trouve sur
leurs terres est une sorte d'herbe qui croit naturellement dans les

petites rivieres dont le fond est de vase, est dans les lieux mares-
ageux ; elle est bien semblable a la folle avoine qui croit parmy nos
bleds.   Les epics sont sur des tuyeaux noüés d'espace en espace, ils
sortent de l'eau vers le mois de juin et vont tousjour montant jusqu'-
acequils surnagent de deux pieds environ ; Le grain n'est pas plus
gros que celuy de nos avoines, mais il est une fois plus long, aussi la
farine en est elle bien plus abondante.   Voicy comme les sauvages
la cueillent et la preparent pour la manger.   Dans le mois de Septembre qui est le tems propre pour cette recolte, ils vont en canot au
travers de ces champs de folle avoine, ils en secoüent les espics de
part et d'autre dans le canot, a mesure qu'ils avancent ; le grain
tombe aisément sil est meur, et en peu de temps ils en font leur provision.   Mais pour le nettoyer de la paille et le depouiller d'une
pellicule dans laquelle il est enfermé, ils le mettent sécher a la
fumée, sur un gril de bois soubs lequel ils entretiennent un petit feu,
pendant quelques jours, et lorsque l'avoine est bien seche, ils la
mettent dans une Peau en forme de pouche, laquelle ils enfoncent
dans un trou fait a ce dessein en terre, puis ils la pillent avec les
pieds, tant et si fortement que le grain s'estant separé de la paille,
ils le vannent tres aisément, apres quoy ils le pillent pour le reduire
en farine ; or mesme sans etre pillé ils le font cuire dans l'eau,
qu'ils assaisonnent avec de la graisse et de cette façon on trouve la
folle avoine presque aussi delicate, qu'est le ris, quand on n'y met
pas de meilleur assaisonnement.

Je racontay a ces peuples de la folle avoine, le dessein que j'avois
d'aller découvrir ces nations esloignées pour les pouvoir instruire
des mysteres de nostre Ste. Religion : ils en furent extremement
surpris, et firent tous leur possible pour m'en dissüader ; ils me
representerent que je rencontrerois des Nations qui ne pardonnent
jamais aux estrangers ausquels ils cassent la teste sans aucun sujet ;
que la guerre qui estoit allumée entre divers peuples qui estoient sur
nostre Route nous exposoit a un autre danger manifeste d'estre tuéz
par les bandes de guerriers qui sont tousjours en campagne ; que la
grande riviere est tres dangereuse, quand on n'en scait pas les
Endroicts difficiles, qu'elle estoit pleine de monstres effroyables, qui
devoroient les hommes et les canots tout ensemble ; qu'il y a mesme
un démon qu'on entend de fort loing qui en ferme le passage et qui
abysme ceux qui osent en approcher, enfin que les chaleurs sont si
excessives en ces pays la qu'elles nous causeroient la mort infaillible-
ment.

Je les remerciay de ces bons advis qu'ils me donnoît, mais je leur dis que je ne pouvois pas les suivre, puisqu'il s'agissoit du salut des ames pour lesquelles je serois ravy de donner ma vie, que je me moquois de ce demon pretendu, que nous nous deffenderions bien de ces monstres marins, et qu'au reste nous nous tienderions sur nos gardes pour eviter les autres dangers dont ils nous menaçoient. Apres les avoir fait prier Dieu et leur avoir donné quelque Instruction, je me separay d'eux, et nous estant embarquez sur nos canots nous arrivâmes peu de temps apres dans le fond de la Baye des Puantz, ou nos Peres travaillent utilement a la conversion de ces peuples, en ayant baptisé plus de deux mille depuis qu'ils y sont.

Cette baye porte un nom qui n'a pas une si mauvaise signification en la langue des sauvages, car ils l'appellent plustost la baye sallée que la Baye des Puans, quoyque parmy eux ce soit presque le mesme, et c'est aussi le nom qu'ils donnent a la mer ; cequi nous a fait faire de tres exactes recherches pour découvrir s'il n'y avoit pas en ces quartiers quelques fontaines d'eau sallée, comme il y en a parmy les hiroquois ; mais nous n'en avons pas trouvé nous jugeons donc qu'on luy a donné ce nom a cause de quantité de vase et de Boüe, qui s'y rencontre, d'ou s'eslevent continuellement de meschantes vapeurs qui y causent les plus grands et les plus continuels Tonnerres, que j'aye iamais entendu.

La Baye a environ trente lieües de profondeur et huict de large en son commencement ; elle va tousjour se retrécissant jusques dans le fond, ou il est aisé de remarquer la marée qui a son flux et reflux reglé presque comme celuy de la Mer.   Ce n'est pas icy le lieu d'examiner si ce sont des vrayes marées ; si elles sont causées par les vents ou par quelqu'autre principe ; s'il y a des vents qui sont les avant-coureurs de la Lune et attachez a sa suitte, lesquels par consequent agitent le lac et luy donnent comme son flux et reflux toutes les fois que la Lune monte sur l'horison.   Ce que je peux dire de certain est que quand l'eau est bien calme, on la voit aisément monter et descendre suivant le cours de la lune, quoyque je ne nie pas que ce mouvement ne puisse estre causé par les ventz qui sont bien éloignez et qui pesant sur le milieu du lac font que les bords croissent et décroissent de la façon qui paroit a nos yeux.

Nous quittâmes cette baye pour entrer dans la riviere qui s'y décharge ; elle est tres belle en son embouchure et coule doucement ; elle est pleine d'outardes, de Canards, de cercelles et d'autres oyseaux qui y sont attirez par la folle avoine, dont ils sont fort frians, mais quand on a un peu avancé dans cette riviere, on la trouve tres difficile, tant a cause des courants que des Roches affilées, qui couppent les canots et les pieds de ceux qui sont obligés de les traisner, surtout quand les eaux sont basses. Nous franchîmes pourtant heureusement ces rapides et en approchant de Machkoutens, le nation du feu, jeu la curiosité de boire des eaux mineralles de la riviere qui n'est pas loing de cette bourgade, je pris aussi le temps de reconnoistre un simple qu'un sauvage qui en scait le secret a enseigné au P. Alloües avec beaucoup de ceremonies. Sa racine sert contre la morsure des serpents, Dieu ayant voulu donner ce remede contre un venin qui est tres frequent en ces pays. Elle est fort chaude, et elle a un gout de poudre quand on l'escrase sous la dent; il faut la mascher et la mettre sur la piquurre du serpent, qui en a une si grande horreur, qu'il s'enfuit mesme de celuy, qui s'en est frotté, elle produit plusieurs tiges, hautes d'un pied, dont la feuille est un peu longue et la fleur blanche et beaucoup semblable a la giroflée. J'en mis dans mon canot pour l'examiner a loisir pendant que nous avancions tousjour vers Maskoutens, ou nous arrivâmes le 7 de Juin.

SECTION III.

Description de la Bourgade de Maskoutens, Cequi s'y passa entre le Pere et les sauvages ; Les François commencent d'entrer dans un Pays nouveau et inconnu et arrivent a Missispi.

Nous voicy rendus a Maskoutens. Ce mot en Algonquin peut signifier, nation du feu; aussi est ce le nom qu'on luy a donné. C'est ici le terme des découvertes qu'ont fait les François, car ils n'ont point encore passé plus avant.

Ce Bourg est composé de trois sortes de Nations qui s'y sont ramassées, des Miamis, des Maskoutens, et des Kikabous. Les premiers sont les plus civils, les plus liberaux, et les mieux faitz ; ils portent deux longues moustaches sur les oreilles, qui leur donnent bonne grace, ils passent pour les guerriers, et font rarement des parties sans succez ; ils sont fort dociles, ils escoutent paisiblement ce qu'on leur dit et ont paru si avides d'entendre le P. Alloües quand il les instruisoit, qu'ils luy donnoient peu de repos, mesme pendant la nuict. Les Maskoutens et les Kikabous sont plus grossiers et semblent etre des paysantz en comparaison des autres. Comme les Escorces a faire des cabannes sont rares en ce pays la, ils se servent de joncs qui leur tiennent lieu de murailles et de couvertures, mais qui ne les deffendant pas beaucoup des vents, et bien moins des pluyes quand elles tombent en abondance. La commodité de ces sortes de cabannes est qu'ils les mettent en pacquetz et les portent aisement ou ils veulent pendant le temps de leur chasse.

Lorsque je les visitay, je fus extremément consolé de veoir une belle croix plantée au milieu du bourg et ornée de plusieurs peaux blanches, de ceintures rouges d'arcs et de fléches que ces bonnes gens avoient offertz au grand Manitou (c'est le nom qu'ils donnent a Dieu), pour le remercier de ce qu'il avoit eu pitié d'eux pendant l'hyver, leur donnant une chasse abondante, lorsqu'ils apprendoient le plus la famine.

Je pris plaisir de veoir la situation de cette bourgade, elle est belle et bien divertissante ; car d'une eminence, sur laquelle elle est placée, on découvre de toutes parts des prairies a perte de veüe, partagées par des bocages ou par des bois de haute futaye. La terre y est tres bonne et rend beaucoup de bled d'inde ; les sauvages ramassent quantité de prunes et de raisins, dont on pourroit faire beaucoup de vin si l'on vouloit.

Nous ne fûmes pas plustost arrivez que nous assemblâmes les anciens M. Joclyet et moy, il leur dit qu'il estoit envoyé de la part de monsr. nostre gouverneur pour découvrir de nouveaux pays et moi de la part de Dieu pour les esclairer des lumieres du St. Evangile ; qu'au reste le maistre souverain de nos vies vouloit estre connu de toutes les nations, et que pour obeir a ses volontés, je ne craignois pas la mort a la quelle je m'exposois dans des voyages si perilleux ; que nous avions besoin de deux guides pour nous mettre dans nostre route ; nous leur fîmes un present, en les priant de nous les accorder, ce qu'ils firent tres civilement et mesme voulurent aussi nous parler par un present qui fut une nate pour nous servir de lit pendant tout nostre voyage.

Le lendemain qui fut le dixieme de Juin, deux Miamis qu'on nous donna pour guides s'embarquerent avec nous, a la veue d'un grand monde qui ne pouvoit assez s'estonner de veoir sept françois, seuls et dans deux canotz oser entreprendre une expedition si extresordinaire et si hazardeuse.

Nous scavions qu'a trois lieüs de Maskoutens estoit une riviere qui se décharge dans Missispi ; nous scavions encor que le rund de vent que nous devions tenir pour y arriver estoit l'ouest soroüest, mais le chemin est partagé de tant de marais et de petitz lacs, qu'il est aisé de s'y égarer d'autant plus que la riviere qui y méne est si chargée de folle avoine, qu'on a peine a en reconnoistre le canal ; c'est en quoy nous avions bien besoin de nos deux guides, aussi nous conduisirent ils heureusement jusqua un portage de 2,700 pas et nous aiderent a transporter nos canotz pour entrer dans cette riviere, apres quoy ils s'en retournerent nous laissant seuls en ce pays inconnu, entre les mains de la providence.

Nous quittons donc les eaux qui vont jusqua Quebeq a 400 ou 500 lieues d'icy pour prendre celles qui nous conduiront desormais dans les terres estrangeres. Avant que de nous y embarquer, nous commençâmes tous ensemble une nouvelle devotion a la Ste. Vierge Immaculée que nous pratiquâmes tous les jours, luy addressant des prieres particulieres pour mettre sous sa protection et nos personnes et le succez de nostre voyage et apres nous estre encouragés les uns les autres nous montons en canot.

La riviere sur laquelle nous nous embarquâmes s'appelle Mesxousing. Elle est fort large, son fond est du sable, qui fait diverses battures lesquelles rendent cette navigation tres difficile ; elle est pleine d'isles couvertes de vignes ; sur les bords paroissent de bonnes terres, entremeslées de bois, de prairies et de costeaux, on y voit des chesnes, des noiers, des bois blancs et une autre espece d'arbres, dontz les branches sont armées de longues espines. Nous n'avons vu ni gibier ni poisson, mais bien des chevreuils et des vaches en assez grande quantité. Nostre route estoit au suroüest et apres avoir navigé environ 30 lieües, nous apperceûmes un endroit qui avoit toutes les apparences de mine de fer, et de fait un de nous qui en a veu autrefois assure que celle que nous avons trouvé est fort bonne et tres abondante ; elle est couverte de trois pieds de bonne terre, assez proche d'une chaine de rocher, dont le bas est plein de fort beau bois. Apres 40 lieües sur cette mesme route nous arrivons a l'embouchure de nostre riviere et nous trouvant a 42 degrez et demy d'eslevation, nous entrons heureusement dans Misissipi le 17e Juin avec une joye que je ne peux pas expliquer.

SECTION IV.

De la grande Rivicre appelée Missisipi, ses plus notables particularités.—De divers animaux et particulierement les Pisikious ou bœufs sauvages, leur figure et leur naturel.—Des premiers villages des Ilinois ou les François arrivent.

Nous voyla donc sur cette riviere si renommée dont iay taché d'en remarquer attentivement toutes les singularités ; la riviere de Missisipi tire son origine de divers lacs qui sont dans le pays des peuples du nord ; elle est estroitte a sa décharge de Miskous. Son courant qui porte du costé du sud est lent et paisible. A la droitte on voist une grande chaisne de montagnes fort hautes et a la gauche de belles terres ; elle est coupée d'isles en divers endroictz. En sondant nous avons trouvés dix brasses d'eau, sa largeur est fort inegale, elle a quelquefois trois quartz de lieües, et quelquefois elle se rétressit jusqua trois arpens. Nous suivons doucement son cours, qui va au sud et au sudest jusqu'aux 42 degrés d'elevation. C'est icy que nous nous appercevons bien qu'elle a tout changé de face. Il n'y a presque plus de bois ny de montagnes, les isles sont plus belles et couvertes de plus beaux arbres ; nous ne voions que des chevreils et des vaches, des outardes et des cygnes sans aisles, parcequ'ils quittent leurs plumes en ce pays. Nous rencontrons de temps en temps des poissons monstrueux, un desquels donna si rudement contre nostre canot, que je crû que c'estoit un gros arbre qui l'alloit mettre en piéces. Une autrefois nous apperceûmes sur l'eau un monstre qui avoit une teste de tigre, le nez pointu comme celuy d'un chat sauvage, avec la barbe et des oreilles droittes élevées en haut, la teste estoit grize et le col tout noir, nous n'en vismes pas davantage. Quand nous avons jetté nos retz a l'eau nous avons pris des esturgeons et une espece de poisson fort extresordinaire, il ressemble a la truitte avec cette difference, qu'il a la gueule plus grande, il a proche du nez (qui est plus petit aussi bien que les yeux) une grande areste, comme un bust de femme, large de trois doigts, long d'une coudée, aubout de laquelle est un rond large comme la main, Cela l'oblige souvent en saultant hors de l'eau de tomber en derriere. Estant descendus jusqua 41 degrés 28 minuittes suivant le mesme rund, nous trouvons que les cocs d'inde ont pris la place du gibier et les pisikious ou bœufs sauvages celles des autres bestes.

Nous les appelons bœufs sauvages parcequ'ils sont bien semblables a nos bœufs domestiques, ils ne sont pas plus longs, mais ils sont pres d'une fois plus gros et plus corpulentz ; nos gens en ayant tué un, trois personnes avoient bien de la peine a le remüer. Ils ont la teste forte grosse, le front plat et large d'un pied et demy entre les cornes qui sont entierement semblables a celles de nos bœufs, mais elles sont noires et beaucoup plus grande. Ils ont sous le col comme une grande falle, qui pend en bas et sur le dos une bosse assez élevée. Toute la teste, la col et une partie des espaules sont couvertz d'un grand crin comme celuy des chevaux, c'est une hûre longue d'un pied, qui les rend hideux et leur tombant sur les yeux les empéche de voire devant eux. Le reste du corps est revetu d'un gros poil frisé a peu pres come celuy de nos moutons, mais bien plus fort et plus espais, il tombe en esté et la peau devient douce comme du velours. C'est pourlors que les sauvages les employent pour s'en faire de belles Robbes qu'ils peignent de diverses couleurs ; la chair et la graisse des pisikious est excellente et fait le meilleur mets des festins. Aureste ils sont tres méchants et il ne se passent point d'année qu'ils ne tuent quelque sauvage ; quand on vient les attaquer, ils prennent s'ils peuvent un homme avec leurs cornes, l'enlevent en l'air, puis ils le jettent contre terre, le foulent des pieds et le tuent. Si on tire de loing sur eux ou de l'arc au du fusil, il faut si tost apres le coup se jetter a terre et se cacher dans l'herbe, car s'ils apercoivent celuy qui a tiré, ils courent apres et le vont attaquer. Comme ils ont les pieds gros et assez courtz, ils ne vont pas bien viste pour l'ordinaire, si ce n'est lorsqu'ils sont irritez. Ils sont espars dans les prairies comme des troupeaux ; j'en ay veu une bande de 400.

Nous avancons tousjours mais comme nous ne sçavions pas où nous allions ayant fait deia plus de cent lieües sans avoir rien découvert que des bestes et des oyseaux nous nous tenons bien sur nos gardes ; c'est pourquoy nous ne faisons qu'un petit feu a terre sur le soir pour preparer nos repas et apres soûper nous nous en eloignons le plus que nous pouvons et nous allons passer la nuict dans nos canotz que nous tenons a l'ancre sur la riviere assez loing des bords ; ce qui n'empeche pas que quelqu'un denous ne soit tousjour en sentinelle de peur de surprise, Allant par le sud et le sud suroüest nous nous trouvons a la hauteur de 41 degrez et jusqua 40 degrez quelques minutes en partie par sudest et en partie par le suroüest apres avoir avancé plus de 60 lieües depuis nostre entrée dans la Riviere sans rien découvrir.

Enfin le 25e Juin nous aperceûmes sur le bord de l'eau des pistes d'hommes, et un petit sentier assez battu, qui entroit dans une belle prairie. Nous nous arrestâmes pour l'examiner, et jugeant que cestoit un chemin qui conduisoit a quelque village de sauvages, nous prîmes resolution de l'aller reconnoistre : nous laissons donc nos deux canotz sous la garde de nos gens, leur recommandant bien de ne se pas laisser surprendre, apres quoy M. Jollyet et moy entreprîmes cette découverte assez hazardeuse pour deux hommes seuls qui s'exposent a la discretion d'un peuple barbare et inconnu. Nous suivons en silence ce petit sentier et apres avoir fait environ 2 lieües, nous découvrîmes un village sur le bord d'une riviere, et deux autres sur un costeau escarté du premier d'une demi lieüe Ce fut pour lors que nous nous recommandâmes, a Dieu de bon cœur et ayant imploré son secours nous passâmes outre sans être découverts et nous vinsmes si pres que nous entendions mesme parler les sauvages. Nous crûmes donc qu'il estoit temps de nous découvrir, ce que nous fismes par un cry que nous poussâmes de toutes nos forces, en nous arrestant sans plus avancer. A ce cry les sauvages sortent promptement de leurs cabanes et nous ayant probablement reconnus pour françois, surtout voyant une robe noire, ou du moins n'ayant aucun suject de deffiance, puisque nous n'estions que deux hommes, et que nous les avions advertis de nostre arrivée, ils députerent quatre vieilliards, pour nous venir parler, dontz deux portoient des pipes a prendre du tabac, bien ornées et empanachées de divers plumages, ils marchoient a petit pas, et élevant leurs pipes vers le soleil, ils sembloient luy presenter a fumer, sans neamoins dire aucun mot. Ils furent assez long temps a faire le peu de chemin depuis leur village jusqu'a nous. Enfin nous ayant abordés, ils s'arresterent pour nous considerer avec attention ; je me rassuray, voyant ces ceremonies, que ne se font parmy eux qu'entre amys, et bien plus quand je les vis couvertz d'estoffe, jugeant par la qu'ils estoient de nos alliez. Je leur parlay donc le premier et je leur demanday, qui ils estoient, ils me répondirent qu'ils estoient Ilinois et pour marque de paix ils nous presenterent leur pipe pour petuner, ensuitte ils nous inviterent d'entrer dans leur village, où tout le peuple nous attendoit avec impatience. Ces pipes a prendre du tabac s'appellent en ce pays des calumetz ; ce mot sy est mis tellement en usage, que pour estre entendu je seray obligé de m'en servir ayant a en parler bien des fois.

16

SECTION V.

Comment les Ilinois reccurent le Pere dans leur Bourgade.

A LA porte de la cabane où nous devions estie receus, estoit un vielliard qui nous attendoit dans une posture assez surprenante, qui est la ceremonie qu'ils gardent quand ils recoivent des estrangers. Cet homme estoit debout et tout nud, tenant ses mains estendus et levées vers le soleil, comme s'il eut voulu se deffendre de ses rayons, lesquels neamoins passoient sur son visage entre ses doigts ; quand nous fusmes proches de luy, il nous fit ce compliment ; que le soleil est beau, françois, quand tu nous viens visiter, tout nostre bourg t'attend, et tu entreras en paix dans toute nos cabanes. Cela dit, il nous introduisit, dans la sienne, où il y avoit une foule de monde qui nous devoroit des yeux, qui cependant gardoit un profond silence, on entendoit neamoins ces paroles qu'on nous addressoit de temps en temps et d'une voix basse, que voyla qui est bien, mes freres, de ce que vous nous visitez.

Apres que nous eusmes pris place, on nous fit la civilité ordinaire du pays, qui est de nous presenter le calumet ; il ne faut pas le refuser, si on ne veut passer pour ennemy, ou du moins pour incivil, pourveu qu'on fasse semblant de fumer, c'est assez ; pendant que tous les anciens petunoient apres nous pour nous honorer, on vient nous inviter de la part du grande capitaine de tous les Ilinois de nous transporter en sa Bourgade, ou il vouloit tenir conseil avec nous. Nous y allâmes en bonne compagnie, car tous ces peuples, qui n'avoient jamais veu de françois chez eux ne se lassoient point de nous regarder, ils se couchoient sur l'herbe le long des chemins, ils nous devançoient, puis ils retournoient sur leurs pas pour nous venir voir encor. Tout cela se faisoit sans bruit et avec les marques d'un grand respect qu'ils avoient pour nous.

Estant arrivez au Bourg du grand Capitaine, nous le vismes a l'entrée de sa cabanne, au milieu de deux vielliards, tout trois debout et nud tenant leur calumet tourné vers le soleil, il nous harangua en peu de motz, nous félicitant de nostre arrivée, il nous présenta ensuitte son calumet et nous fit fumer, en mesme temps que nous entrions dans sa cabanne, où nous receumes toutes leurs caresses ordinaires.

Voyant tout le monde assemblé et dans le silence, je leur parlay par quatre presents que je leur fis, par le premier je leur disois que nous marchions en paix pour visiter les nations qui s'etoient sur la riviere jusqu'a la mer ; par le second je leur declaray que Dieu qui les a créés avoit pitié d'eux, puisqu'apres tant de temps qu'ils l'ont ignoré, il vouloit se faire connoistre a tous ces peuples, que jéstois envoyé de sa part pour ce dessein, que c'estoit a eux a le reconnoistre et a luy obeir, Par le troisiéme que le grand capitaine des françois leur faisoit sçavoir que c'estoit luy qui mettoit la paix partout et qui avoit dompté l'Iroquois. Enfin par le quatriéme nous les prions de nous donner toutes les connoissances qu'ils avoient de la mer, et des nations par lesquelles nous devions passer pour y arriver.

Quand jeu finy mon discour, le capitaine se leva, et tenant le main sur la teste d'un petit esclave qu'il nous vouloit donner il par la ainsi. Ie te remercie Robe Noire, et toy françois (s'addressant a M. Jollyet), de ce que vous prenez tant de peine pour nous venir visiter, jamais la terre n'a esté si belle ny le soleil si éclatant qu'aujourdhui ; jamais notre riviere n'a esté si calme, n'y si nette de rochers que vos canotz ont enlevées en passant, jamais nostre petun n'a eu si bon gout, n'y nos bleds n'ont paru si beau que nous les voions maintenant. Voicy mon fils que je te donne pour te faire connoistre mon cœur, je te prie d'avoir pitié de moy et de toute ma nation, c'est toy qui connoist le grand Genie qui nous a tous faits, c'est toy qui luy parle et quy escoute sa parole, demande luy qu'il me donne la vie et la santé et vient demeurer avec nous, pour nous le faire connoistre. Cela dit il mit le petit esclave proche de nous, et nous fit un second present, qui estoit un calumet tout mysterieux, dont ils font plus d'estat que d'un esclave ; il nous témoignoit par ce present l'estime qu'il faisoit de monsieur nostre gouverneur, sur le recit que nous luy en avions fait ; et pour un troisieme il nous prioit de la part de toute sa nation, de ne pas passer oultre, a cause des grands dangers où nous nous exposions.

Je répondis que je ne craignois point la mort, et que je n'estimois point de plus grand bonheur que de perdre la vie pour la gloire de Celuy que a tout fait. C'est ce que ces pauvres peuples ne peuvent comprendre.

Le conseil fut suivy d'un grand festin qui consistoit en quatre metz, qui'l fallut prendre avec toutes leurs façons, le premier service fut un grand plat de bois plein de sagamité, c'est-a-dire de farine de bled d'inde qu'on fait boüillur avec de l'eau qu'on assaisonne de graisse.

Le maistre des ceremonies avec une cuillier pleine de sagamité me la presenta a la bouche par trois ou 4 fois, comme on feroit a un petit enfant, il fit le mesme a M. Jollyet. Pour second mets il fit paroistre un second plat où il y avoit trois poissons, il en prit quelques morceaux pour en oster les arestes, et ayant soufflé dessus pour les rafraichir, il nous les mit a la bouche, comme l'on donneroit la beschée a un oyseau. On apporte pour troisiéme service un grand chien, qu on venoit de tuer, mais ayant appris que nous n'en mangions point, on le retira de devant nous. Enfin le 4e fut une piéce de bœuf sauvage, dont on nous mit a la bouche les morceaux les plus gras.

Apres ce festin il fallut aller visiter tout le village, qui est bien composé de 300 cabannes. Pendant que nous marchions par les rues, un orateur haranguoit continuellement pour obliger tout le monde a nous voir, sans nous estre importuns ; on nous presentoit partout des ceintures, des jartieres et autres ouvrages faits de poil d'ours et de bœuf et teins en rouge, en jaune, et en gris, ce sont toutes les raretez qu'ils ont ; commes elles ne sont pas bien considerbles, nous ne nous en chargeames point.

Nous couchâmes dans la cabane du capitaine etle lendemain nous prismes congé de luy, promettant de repasser par son bourg dans quatre lunes. Il nous conduisit jusqua nos canotz avec pres de 600 personnes qui nous vîrent embarquer, nous donnant toutes les marques qu'ils pouvoient de la joye que notre visite leur avoit causée. Je m'engageay en mon particulier, en leur disant adieu que je vien drois l'an prochain demeurer avec eux pour les instruire. Mais avant que de quitter le pays des Ilinois, il est bon que je rapporte ce que j'ay reconnu de leurs coustûmes et façons de faire.

SECTION VI.

Du naturel des Ilinois, de leurs mœurs, et de leurs coustumes, de l'estime qu'ils ont pour le Calumet ou pipe a prendre du Tabac et de la danse qu'ils font en son honneur.

Qui dit Ilinois, c'est comme qui diroit en leur langue les hommes, comme si les autres sauvages, aupres d'eux ne passoient que pour des bestes, aussi faut il advoüer qu'ils ont un air d'humanité que nous n'avons pas remarqué dans les autres nations que nous avons veües sur nostre route. Le peu de séjour que jay fait parmy eux ne m'a pas permis de prendre toutes les connoissances que j'aurois souhaité ; de toutes leurs façons de faire voicy ce que j'en ay remarqué.

Ils sont divisés en plusieures bourgades dont quelquesunes sont assés éloignées de celle dont nous parlons qui s'appelle Peoüarea, c'est ce qui met de la difference en leur langue, laquelle universalle-ment tient de l'allegonquin de sorte que nous nous entendions facile-ment les uns les autres. Leur naturel est doux et traitable, nous l'avons experimenté dans la reception qu'il nous ont faitte. Ils ont plusieures femmes dont ils sont extremement jaloux, ils les veillent avec un grand soin et ils leur couppent le nez ou les oreilles quand elles ne sont pas sages, j'en ay veu plusieures qui portoient les marques de leurs désordres. Ils ont le corps bien fait, ils sont lestes et fort adroits a tirer de l'arc et de la flèche. Ils se servent aussi des fusils qu'ils acheptent des sauvages nos alliés qui ont commerce avec nos françois ; ils en usent particulierement pour donner l'épouvante par le bruit et par la fumée a leurs ennemys qui n'en n'ont point l'usage et n'en ont jamais veu pour estre trop éloigné vers le couchant. Ils sont belliqueux et se rendent redoutables aux peuples éloignés du sud et de l'oüest, où ils vent faire des esclaves, desquels ils se ser-vent pour trafiquer, les vendant cherement a d'autres nations, pour d'autres marchandises. Ces sauvages si éloignes chez qui ils vont en guerre n'ont aucune connoissance d'Europeans ; ils ne savent ce que c'est ny de fer ny de cuivre et n'ont que des couteaux de pierre. Quand les Illinois partent pour aller on guerre, il faut que tout le bourg en soit adverty par le grand cry qu'ils font a la porte de leurs cabanes, le soir et le matin avant que de partir. Les capi-

taines se distinguent des soldats par des escharpes rouges qu'ils portent, elles sont faittes de crin d'ours et du poil de bœufs sauvages
avec assez d'industrie ; ils se peignent le visage d'un rouge de sanguine, dont ily a grande quantité a quelques journées du bourg.   Ils
vivent de chasse qui est abondante en ce pays et de bled d'inde dont
ils font tousjour une bonne recolte, aussi n'ont ils jamais souffert de
famine, ils sement aussi des febves et des melons qui sont excel-
lentz, surtout ceux qui ont la graine rouge, leurs citrouilles ne sont
pas des meilleures, ils les font secher au soleil pour les manger
pendant l'hyver et le primptemps.   Leur cabanes sont fort grandes,
elles sont couvertes et paveés de nattes faittes de joncs : ils trouvent
toutes leur vaiselle dans le bois et leurs cuilliers dans la teste de
bœufs dont ils savent si bien accommoder le crane qu'ils s'en servent
pour manger aisément leur sagamité.

Ils sont liberaux dans leurs maladies, et croyent que les medica-
mens qu'on leur donne, operent a proportion des presents qu'ils
auront fais au médecin.   Ils n'ont que des peaux pour habitz, les
femmes sont tousjours vestües fort modestement et dans une grande
bien seance au lieu que les hommes ne se mettent pas en peine de
se couvrir.   Je ne scais par quelle superstition quelques Ilinois,
aussi bien que quelques Nadoüessi, estant encore jeunes prennent
l'habit des femmes qu'ils gardent toute leur vie.   Il y a du mystere ;
car il ne se marient jamais, et font gloire de s'abaisser a faire tout
ce que font les femmes ; ils vont pourtant en guerre, mais ils ne
peuvent se servir que de la massüe, et non pas de l'arc ny de la
flèche qui sont les armes propres des hommes, ils assistent a toutes
les jongleries et aux danses solemnelles qui se font a l'honneur du
calumet, ils y chantent mais ils n'y peuvent pas danser, ils sont ap-
pellés aux conseils, ou l'on ne peut rien decider sans leurs advis ;
enfin par le profession qu'ils font d'une vie extresordinaire, ils passent pour des manitous, c'est-adire pour des Genies ou des personnes
de consequence.

Il ne reste plus qu'a parler du calumet.   Il n'est rien parmy eux ny
de plus mysterieux ny de plus recommandable, on ne rend pas tant
d'honneur aux couronnes et aux sceptres des Roys qu'ils luy en rendent ; il semble estre le dieu de la paix et de la guerre, l'arbitre de la
vie et de la mort. C'est assez de le porter sur soy et de le faire voir pour
marcher en assurance au milieu des ennemys, qui dans le fort du combat mettent bas les armes quand on le montre.   C'est pour cela que les
Ilinois m'en donnerent un pour me servir de sauvegarde parmy toutes

les nations, parlesquelles je devois passer dans mon voyage. Il y a un calumet pour la paix et un pour la guerre, qui ne sont distingué que par la couleur des plumages dontz ils sont ornés. (Le Rouge est marque de guerre), ils s'en servent encor pour terminer leur differ ents, pour affermir leurs alliances et pour parler aux estrangers.* Il est composé d'une pierre rouge polie comme du marbre et percée d'une telle façon qu'un bout sert a recevoir le tabac et l'autre s'enclave dans le manche, qui est un baston de deux pieds de long, gros comme une canne ordinaire et percée par le milieu ; il est embelly de la teste et du col de divers oyseaux, dont le plumage est très beau ; ils y ajoutent aussi de grandes plumes rouges, vertes et d'autres couleurs, dont il est tout empanaché ; ils en font estat particulierement, parcequ'ils le regardent comme le calumet du soleil ; et de fait ils le luy presentent pour fumer quand ils veulent obtenir du calme, ou de la pluye ou du beau temps. Ils font scrupule de se baigner au commencement de l'Esté, ou de manger des fruits nouveaux qu'apres l'avoir dancé. En voicy la façon.

La danse du calumet, qui est fort celebre parmy ces peuples, ne se fait que pour des sujets considerables ; quelque fois c'est pour affermir la paix ou se reünir pour quelque grande guerre ; c'est d'autres fois pour une rejoüissance publique, tantost on en fait honneur a une nation qu'on invite d'y assister, tantost ils sen servent a la reception de quelque personne considerable comme s'ils vouloient luy donner le divertissement du Bal ou de la Comede ; l'hyver la ceremonie se fait dans une cabane, l'Esté c'est en raze campagne. La place étant choisie, on l'environne tout a l'entour d'arbres pour mettre tout le monde a l'ombre de leurs feüillages, pour se défendre des chaleurs du soleil ; on étend une grande natte de joncs peinte de diverses couleurs au milieu de la place ; elle sert comme de tapis pour mettre dessus avec honneur le Dieu de celuy qui fait la Dance ; car chacun a le sien, qu'ils appellent leur manitou, c'est un serpent ou un oyseau, ou chose semblable qu'ils ont resvé en dormant et en qui ils mettent tout leur confiance pour le succez deleur guerre, de leur pesche et de leur chasse ; pres de ce manitou et a sa droite, on met le calumet en l'honneur de qui se fait la feste et tout a l'entour on fait comme une trophée et on éstend les armes dont se servent les guerriers de ces nations, sçavoir la massüe, la hache d arme, l'arc, le carquois et les fleches.

* From this to the next star is from Thevenot.

Les choses estant ainsi disposées et l'heure de la dance approchant, ceux qui sont nommez pour chanter prennent la place la plus honorable sous les feüillages ; ce sont les hommes et les femmes qui ont les plus belles voix, et qui s'accordent parfaitement bien ensemble ; tout le monde vient ensuitte se placer en rond sous les branches, mais chacun en arrivant doit salüer le manitou, ce qu'il fait en petunant et jettant de sa bouche la fumée sur luy comme s'il luy presentoit de l'encens ; chacun va d'abord avec respect prendre le calumet et le soutenant des deux mains, il le fait dancer en cadence, s'accordant bien avec l'air des chansons ; il luy fait faire des figures bien differentes, tantost il le fait voir a toute l'assemblée se tournant de coté et d'autre ; apres cela, celuy qui doit commencer la dance paroist au miliéu de l'assemblée et va d'abord et tantost il le presente au soleil, comme s'il le vouloit faire fumer, tantost il l'incline vers la terre, d'autrefois il luy estend les aisles comme pour voler, d'autres fois il l'approche de la bouche des assistans, afinqu'ils fument, le tout en cadence, et c'est comme la premiere scene du Ballet.

La seconde consiste en un combat qui se fait au son d'une espece de tambour, qui succede aux chansons, ou mesme qui s'y joignant s'accordent fort bien ensemble ; le Danseur fait signe a quelque guerrier de venir prendre les armes qui sont sur la natte et l'invite a se battre au son des tambours ; celuyci s'approche, prend l'arc et la fleche, avec la hache d'armes et commence le düel contre l'autre, qui n'a point d'autre defense que le calumet. Ce spectacle est fort agreable, surtout les faisant tousjours en cadence, car l'un attaque, l'autre se defend, l'un porte des coups, l'autre les pare, l'un fuit, l'autre le poursuit et puis celuy qui fuyoit tourne visage et fait füyr son ennemy, ce qui se passe si bien par mesure et a pas comptez et au son reglé des voix et des tambours, que cela pourroit passer pour une assez belle entrée de Ballet en France.

La troisieme scene consiste en un grand discours que fait celuy qui tient le calumet, car le combat estant fini sans sang repandu, il raconte les batailles o'u il s'est trouvé, les victoires qu'il a remportées, il nomme les nations, les lieux et les captifs qu'il a faitz, et pour recompense celuy qui preside a la danse luy fait present d'une belle robe de castor ou de quelque autre chose et l'ayant receu il va presenter le calumet a un autre, celuyci a un troisieme, et ainsi de tous les autres, jusqu'aceque tous ayant fait leur devoir, le President fait present du calumet mesme a la nation qui a esté invitée a cette ceremonie, pour marque de la paix eternelle qui sera entre les deux peuples.

Voicy quelqu'une des chansons qu'ils ont coustume de chanter, ils leur donnent un certain tour qu'on ne peut assez exprimer par la notte, qui neamoins en fait toute la grace.

"Ninahani, ninahani, ninahani, naniongo."

SECTION VII.

Nous prenons congé de nos Ilinois sur la fin de Juin vers les trois heures apres midy, nous nous embarquons a laveüe de tous ces peuples qui admiroient nos petits canotz, n'en ayant jamais veu de semblables.

Nous descendons suivant le courant de la riviére appellée Pekitanoüi, qui se decharge dans Missisipi venant du Nordoüest, de la quelle j'ay quelque chose de considerable à dire apres que j'auray raconté ce que j'ay remarqué sur cette riviere.* Passant proche des rochers assez hautz qui bordent la riviere j'apperceu un simple qui m'a paru fort extraordinaire. La racine est semblable a des petitz naveaux attachez les uns aux autres par des petitz filetz qui ont le gout de carote ; de cette racine sort une feuille large comme la main, espaisses d'un demi doigt avec des taches au milieu ; de cette feuille naissent d'autres feuilles resemblables aux plaques qui servent de flambeaux dans nos sales et chasque feuille porte cinq ou six fleurs jaunes en forme de clochettes.

Nous trouvâmes quantité de meures aussi grosses que celle de France, et un petit fruict que nous prismes d'abord pour des olives, mais il avoit le gout d'orange et un aultre fruict gros comme un œuf de poule, nous le fendismes en deux et parurent deux separations, dans chasqu'une desquelles il y a 8 ou 10 fruicts enchasséz, ils ont la figure d'amande et sont fort bons quand ils sont meurs ; l'arbre neamoins qui les porte a tres mauvaise odeur et sa feuille ressemble a celle de noyer, il se trouve aussi dans les prairies un fruit semblable a des noisettes mais plus tendre : les feuilles sont fort grandes et viennent d'une tige au bout de laquelle est une teste semblable a celle d'un tournesol, dans laquelle toutes ces noisettes sont proprement arrangées, elles sont fort bonnes et cuites et crues.

Comme nous cottoions des rochers affreux pour leur haulteur et pour leur longeur, nous vismes sur un de ses rochers deux monstres en peinture qui nous firent peur d'abord et sur lesquels les sauvages les plus hardys n'osent pas arrester longtemps les yeux ; ils sont gros comme un veau ; ils ont des cornes en teste commes des chevreils ; un regard affreux, des yeux rouges, une barbe comme d'un tygre, la face a quelque chose de l'homme, le corps couvert d'écailles et la queüe si longue qu'elle fait tout le tour du corps passant par dessus la teste et retournant entre les jambes elle se termine en queue de poisson. Le vert le rouge et le noirastre sont les trois couleurs qui le composent ; au reste ces 2 monstres sont si bien peint que nous ne pouvons pas croire qu'aucun sauvage en soit l'autheur, puisqueles bons peintres en France auroient peine a si bien faire, venque d'ailleurs ils sont si hauts sur le rocher qu'il est difficile d'y atteindre commodément pour les peindre. Voicy apeupres la figure de ces monstres comme nous l'avons contretirée.

Comme nous entretenions sur ces monstres, voguant paisiblement dans une belle eau claire et dormante nous entendisme le bruit d'un rapide, dans lequel nous allions tomber. Je n'ay rien veu de plus affreux, un ambaras de gros arbres entiers, de branches, d'isletz flotans, sortoit de l'embouchure de la riviere Pekitanoüi avec tant d'impetuosité qu'on ne pouvoit s'exposer a passer au travers sans grand danger. L'agitation estoit telle que l'eau en estoit toute boueuse et ne pouvoit s'épurer. Pekitanoüi est une riviere considerable qui venant d'assez loing du costé du noroüest, se décharge dans Missisipi, plusieurs Bourgades de sauvages sont placées le long de cette riviere et jespere par son moyen faire la découverte de la mer Vermeille ou de Californie.

Nous jugeons bien par le rund de vent que tient Missisippi, si elle continue dans la mesme route, qu'elle a sa décharge dans le golphe mexique ; il seroit bien advantageux de trouver celle qui conduit a la mer du sud, vers la Californie et c'est comme j'ay dit ce que j'espere de rencontrer par Pekitanoui, suivant le rapport que m'en ont fait les sauvages, desquels j'ay appris qu'en refoulant cette riviere pendant 5 ou 6 journées on trouve une belle prairie de 20 ou 30 lieües de long, il faut la traverser allant au noroüest, elle se termine a une autre petite riviere, sur laquelle on peut s'embarquer, n'étant pas bien difficile de transporter les canotz par un si beau pays telle qu'est cette prairie. Cette 2de riviere a son cours vers le souroüest pendant 10 ou 15 lieües, apres quoy elle entre dans un petit lac, que est la source d'une autre riviere profonde, laquelle va au couchant, ou elle se jette dans la mer. Je ne doubte presque point que ce ne soit la Mer Vermeille.

et je ne désespere pas d'en faire un jour la découverte, si Dieu m'en fait la grace et me donne la santé affin de pouvoir publier l'Evangile a tous les peuples de ce nouveau monde, qui ont croupi si longtemps dans les tenebres de l'infidelité.

Reprenons nostre route apres nous estre eschapé comme nous avons pû de ce dangereux rapide causé par l'ambaras dont j'ay parlé.

SECTION VIII.

Des nouveaux pays que le Pere découvre.—Diverses particularités.—Rencontre de quelques sauvages : premieres nouvelles de la Mer et des Europeans.—Grand danger evité par le moyen du calumet.

Apres avoir fait environ 20 lieües droit au sud et un peu moins au sudest nous nous trouvons a une riviere nommée Ouabonkigou dont l'embouchure est par les 36 degrez d'élevation. Avant que d'y arriver nous passons par un lieu redoutable aux sauvages parcequ'ils estiment qu'il y a un manitou, c'est a dire un demon qui devore les passans et c'est de quoy nous menaçoient les sauvages qui nous vouloient détourner de nostre enterprise. Voicy ce demon, c'est une petite anse de rochers haulte de 20 pieds ou se dégorge tout le courant de la riviere lequel estant repoussé contre celuy qui le suit et arresté par une isle qui est proche, est contraint de passer par un petit canal, ce qui ne se fait pas sans un furieux combat de toutes ces eaux qui rebroussent les uns sur autres et sans un grand tintamarre qui donne de la terreur a des sauvages qui craignent tout, mais cela ne nous empéche point de passer et d'arriver a 8ab8kig8. Cette riviere vient des terres du levant où sont les peuples qu'on appelle Chaoüanons, en si grand nombre, qu'en un quartier on compte jusqua 23 villages et 15 en un aultre, assez proches les uns des aultres ; ils ne sont nullement guerriers, et ce sont les peuples que les Iroquois vont chercher si loing pour leur faire la guerre sans aucun sujet, et parceque ces pauvres gens ne scavent pas se deffendre, ils se laissent prendre et emmener comme des trouppeaux, et tout innocents qu'ils sont, ils ne laissant pas de ressentir quelque fois la barbarie des Iroquois qui les bruslent cruellement.

Une peu au dessus de cette riviere dont ie viens de parler sont des falaises ou nos françois ont apperceu une mine de fer, qu'ils

jugent tres abondante, il y en a plusieures veines et un lit d'un pied
de hauteur ; on en voit de gros morceaux liez avec des cailloux.   Il
s'y trouve d'une terre grasse de trois sortes de couleurs, de pourpre
de violet et des Rouges.   L'eau dans laquelle on la lave prend la
couleur de sang.   Il y a aussi d'un sable rouge fort pesant.   J'en mis
sur un aviron qui en prit la couleur si fortement, que l'eau ne la pût
effacer pendant 15 jours que je m'en servois pour nager.

C'est icy que nous commencons a voir des cannes ou gros roseaux
qui sont sur le bord de la riviere, elles ont un vert fort agreable, tous
les nœuds sont couronnéz de feüilles longues, estroittes et pointües,
elles sont fort hautes et en si grande quantité que les bœufs sauvages
ont peine de les forcer.

Jus lu'a present nous n'avions point estéz incommodés des maringouins, mais nous entrons comme dans leur pays.   Voicy ce que font
les sauvages de ces quartiers pour s'en deffendre ; ils clevent un eschaffault dont le plancher n'est fait que de perches, et par consequent
est percó a jour affinque la fumée du feu qu'ils font dessous passe
au travers et chasse ces petitz animaux qui ne la peuvent supporter,
on se couche sur les perches au dessus desquelles sont des escorces
estendües contre la pluye.   Cet eschaffault leur sert encor contre
les chaleurs excessives et insupportables de ce pays, car on s'y
met a l'ombre a l'estage d'en bas et on s'y garantit des rayons du
soleil, prenant le frais du vent qui passe librement autravers de cet
eschaffault.

Dans le mesme dessein nous fusmes contraints de faire sur l'eau
une espece de cabane avec nos voiles pour nous mettre a couvert et
des maringouins et des rayons du soleil, comme nous nous laissons
aller en cet estat au gré de l'eau, nous apperceumes a terre des
sauvages armez de fusilz avec lesquels ils nous attendoient.   Je leur
presentay d'abord mon calumet empanaché, pendant que nos françois
se mettent en deffense, et attendoient a tirer, que les sauvages ;
eussent fait la premiere décharge, je leur parlay en Huron, mais ils
me repondirent par un mot qui me sembloit nous declarer la guerre,
ils avoient neamoins autant de peur que nous, et ceque nous prenions
pour signal de guerre, estoit une invitation qu'ils nous faisoit de
nous approcher, pour nous donner a manger, nous débarquons donc
et nous entrons dans leur cabanes où ils nous presente du bœuf
sauvage et de l'huile d'ours, avec des prunes blanches qui sont tres
excellentes.   Ils ont des fusils, des haches, des houes, des cousteaux, de la rassade, des bouteilles de verre double ou ils mettent leur

poudre, ils ont les cheveux longs et se marquent par le corps a la façon des hiroquois, les femmes sont coiffés et vestües a la façon des huronnes, ils nous assurerent qu'ils n'y avoit plus que dix journées jusquâ la mer, qu'ils acheptoient les estoffes et toutes autres marchandises des Europeans qui estoient du costé de l'Est, que ces Europeans avoient des chapeletz et des images, qu'ils joüoient des instrumentz, qu'il y en avoit qui estoient faitz comme moy et qu'ils en estoient bien receu ; cependant je ne vis personne qui me parut avoir receu aucune instruction pour la foy, le leurs en donnay ceque je pûs avec quelques medailles.

Ces nouvelles animerent nos courages et nous firent prendre l'aviron avec une nouvelle ardeur.   Nous avançons donc et nous ne voions plus tant de prairies parceque les 2 costéz de la riviere sont bordéz de hauts bois.   Les cottonniers, les ormes et les boisblancs y sont admirables pour leur haulteur et leur grosseur.   La grande quantité de bœufs sauvages que nous entendions meugler nous fait croire que les prairies sont proches, nous voions aussi des cailles le bord de l'eau, nous avons tué un petit perroquet qui avoit la moitié de la teste rouge, l'autre et le col jaune et tout le corps vert. Nous estions descendus proche des 33 degrez d'eslevation ayant presque tousjour esté vers le sud, quand nous apperceumes un village sur le bord de l'eau nommé Mitchigamea.   Nous eusmes recours a nostre Patronne et a nostre conductrice la Ste. Vierge Immaculée, et nous avions bien besoin de son assistance, car nous entendismes de loing les sauvages qui s'animoient au combat par leurs crys continuels, ils estoient armés d'arcs, de flêches, de haches, de massües et de boucliers, ils se mirent en estat de nous attaquer par terre et par eau, une partie s'embarque dans de grands canotz de bois, les uns pour monter la riviere, les autres pour la descendre, affin de nous coupper chemin, et nous envelopper de tous costez ; ceux qui estoient a terre alloient et venoient comme pour commencer l'attaque. De fait de jeûnes hommes se jetterent a l'eau, pour venire saiser de mon canot, mais le courant les ayant contraint de reprendre terre, un d'eux nous jetta sa massüe qui passa par dessus nous sans nous frapper ; j'avois beau montrer le calumet, et leur faire signe par gestes que nous ne venions pas en guerre, l'alarme continuoit tousjour et l'on se preparoit déia a nous percer de flêches de toutes parts, quand Dieu toucha soûdainement le cœur des vieillards qui estoient sur le bord de l'eau sans doubte par la veüe de nostre calumet qu'ils n'avoient pas bien reconnu de loing, mais comme je ne cessois de le faire paroistre, ils en furent touchez, arresterent l'ardeur de leur jeunesse et mesme deux de ces anciens ayant jettez dans nostre canot comme a nos pieds leurs arcs et leurs carquois pour nous mettre en asseurance, ils y entrerent et nous firent approcher de terre, ou nous debarquâmes non pas sans crainte de nostre part. Il fallut au commencement parler par gestes, parceque personne n'entendoit rien des six langues que je scavois, il se trouva enfin un vieilliard qui parloit un peu l'Ilinois.

Nous leurs fîmes paroistre par nos presens que nous allions a la mer, ils entendirent bien ce que nous leur voulions dire, mais je ne scay s'ils conçeurent ce que je leurs dis de Dieu et des choses de leur salut, c'est une semence jettée en terre qui fructifira en son temps. Nous n'eusmes point d'autre réponse si non que nous apprendrions tout ce que nous desirions d'un aultre grand village nommé Akamsea qui n'estoit qu'a 8 ou 10 lieües plus bas, ils nous presenterent de la sagamité et du poisson et nous passâmes la nuict chez eux avec assez d'inquiétude.

SECTION IX.

Reception qu'on fait aux François dans la derniere des Bourgades qu'ils ont veües.—Les mœurs et façons de faire de ces sauvages.—Raisons pour ne pas passer outre.

Nous embarquâmes le lendemain de grand matin avec nostre interprette; un canot ou estoient dix sauvages alloit un peu devant nous, estant arrivés a une demie lieüe des Akamsea, nous vismes paroistre deux canotz qui venoient au devant de nous; celuy qui y commandoit estoit debout tenant en main le calumet avec lequel il faisoit plusieurs gestes selon le coustume du pays, il vint nous joindre en chantant assez agreablement et nous donna a fumer, apres quoy il nous presenta de la sagamité et du pain fait de bled d'inde, dont nous mangeammes un peu, ensuitte il prit le devant nous ayant fait signe de venir doucement apres luy; on nous avoit preparé une place sous l'eschaffault du chef des guerriers, elle estoit propre et tapissée de belles nattes de jonc, sur lesquelles on nous fit asseoir, ayant autour de nous les anciens, qui estoient plus proches, apres les guerriers et enfin tout le peuple en foule. Nous trouvâmes l'a par bonheur un

jeûne homme qui entendoit l'Ilinois beaucoup mieux que l'Interprette
que nous avions amené de Mitchigamea, ce fut par son moyen que je
parlay d'abord a toute cette assemblée par les presens ordinaires ; ils
admiroient ce que je leur disois de Dieu et des mysteres de nostre
Ste foy, ils faisoient paroistre un grand desir de me retenir avec eux
pour les pouvoir instruire.

Nous leurs demandâmes ensuitte ce qu'ils scavoient de la mer ;
ils nous répondirent que nous n'en estions qu'a dix journées, nous
aurions pû faire ce chemin en 5 jours, qu'ils ne connoissoient pas les
nations qui l'habitoient a cause que leurs ennemys les empéchoient
d'avoir commerce avec ces Europeans, que les haches, cousteaux, et
rassade que nous voions leur estoient vendües en partie par des nations de l'Est et en partie par une bourgade d'Ilinois placée a l'oüest
a quattro journées de la, que ces sauvages que nous avons rencontrés
qui avoient des fusils estoient leurs ennemys, lesquels leur fermoient
le passage de la mer et les empéchoient d'avoir connoissance des
Europeans et d'avoir avec eux aucun commerce ; qu'au reste nous
nous exposions beaucoup de passer plus oultre a cause des courses
continuelles que leurs ennemys font sur la riviere, qui ayant des fusils
et estant fort agguerris, nous ne pouvions pas sans un danger evident
avancer sur cette riviere qu'ils occupent continuellement.

Pendant cet entretien on nous apportoit continuellement à manger
dans de grands platz de bois, tantost de la sagamité, tantost du bled
entier, tantost d'un morceau de chien, toute la journée se passa en
festins.

Ces peuples sont assez officieux et liberaux de ce qu'ils ont, mais
ils sont miserables pour le vivre, nosant aller a la chasse des bœufs
sauvages a cause de leurs ennemys, ils est vray qu'ils ont le bled
d'inde en abondance, qu'ils sement en toute saison, nous en visme
en mesme temps qui estoit en maturité, d'autre qui ne faisoit que
pousser et d'autre qui estoit en laict, de sorte qu'ils sement trois fois
l'an. Ils le font cuire dans de grands potz de terre qui sont fort bien
faits ; ils ont aussi des assiétes de terres cuitte dontz ils se servent
a divers usages. Les hommes vont nuds, portent les cheveux
courtz, ont le nez percé d'ou pend de la rassade aussi bien que de
leurs oreilles. Les femmes sont vestüés de meschantes peaux,
noüent leurs cheveux en deux tresses, qu'elles jettent derriere les
oreilles, et n'ont aucune rareté pour se parer. Leurs festins se font
sans aucune ceremonie, ils presentent aux invitez de grands platz
dontz chascun mange a discretion, et se donnent les restes les uns

aux aultres. Leur langue est extremement difficile et je ne pouvois venir about d'en prononcer quelques motz, quelque effort que je pusse faire. Leurs cabanes qui sont faittes d'escorce, sont longues et larges, ils couchent aux deux bouts elevez de deux pieds de terre, ils y gardent leur bled dans de grands panniers faits de cannes, ou dans des gourdes grosses comme des demy bariques. Ils ne scavent ce que c'est que le castor, leurs richesses consistent en peaux de bœufs sauvages, ils ne voient jamais de neige chez eux et ne connoissent l'hyver que par les pluyes qui y tombent plus souvent qu'en esté; nous n'y avons pas mangé de fruictz que des melons d'eau. S'ils scavoient cultiver leur terre ils en auroient de toutes les sortes.

Le soir les anciens firent un conseil secret dans le dessein que quelque'uns avoient de nous casser la teste pour nous piller, mais le chef rompit toutes ces menées. Nous ayant envoyé querir, pour marque de parfaitte assurance, il dansa le calumet devant nous, de la façon, que jay descript cy dessus, et pour nous oster toute crainte, il m'en fit present.

Nous fismes M. Jolliet et moy un aultre conseil, pour deliberer sur ce que nous avions a faire, si nous pousserions oultre o'u si nous nous contenterions de la découverte que nous avions faite. Apres avoir attentivement consideré que nous n'estions pas loing du golphe mexique, dont le bassin estant a la haulteur de 31 degrez 60 minutes (*sic*), et nous nous trouvant a 33 degrez 40 minutes nous ne pouvions pas en estre eloignes plus de 2 ou 3 journées, qui indubitablement la riviere Missisipi avoit sa décharge dans la floride ou golphe Mexique, n'on pas du costé de l'est dans la Virginie, dont le bord de la mer est a 34 degrez que nous avons passéz sans neamoins estre encor arrivés a la mer; non pas aussi du costé de l'oüest a la Californie, parceque nous devions pour cela avoir nostre route a l'oüest ou a l'oüest soroüest et nous l'avons tousjour en au sud. Nous considerâmes de plus que nous nous exposions a perdre le fruict de ce voyage duquel nous ne pourrions pas donner aucune connoissance, si nous allions nous jetter entre les mains des Espagnols qui sans doubte nous auroient du moins retenus captifs. En oultre nous voyions bien que nous n'estions pas en estat de resister a des sauvages alliés des Europeans, nombreux et expertz a tirer du fusil qui infestoient continuelment le bas de cette riviere. Enfin nous avions pris toutes les connoissances qu'on peut souhaiter dans cette découverte. Toutes ces raisons firent conclure pour le retour, que nous declarames aux sauvages et pour lequel nous nous preparâmes apres un jour de repos.

SECTION X.

Retour du Pere et des François.——Bapteme d'un enfant moribond.

APRES un mois de navigation en descendant sur Missisipi depuis le 42ᵈ degré jusqu'au 34ᵉ et plus, et apres avoir publié l'Evangile, autant que j'ay pû, aux nations que j'ay rencontrées nous partons le 17ᵉ Juillet du village des Akensea pour retourner sur nos pas. Nous remontons donc a Missisipi qui nous donne bien de la peine a refouler ses courans, il est vray que nous le quittons vers les 38ᵉ degré pour entrer dans une aultre riviere qui nous abbrege de beaucoup le chemin et nous conduit avec peu de peine dans le lac des Ilinois.

Nous n'avons rien veu de semblable a cette riviere ou nous entrons pour la bonté des terres, des prairies, des bois, des bœufs, des cerfs, des chevreux, des chatz sauvages, des outardes, de cygnes, des canards, des perroquetz et mesme des castors, il y a quantité de petitz lacs et de petites rivieres. Celle sur laquelle nous navigeons est large, profonde, paisible pendant 65 lieües le primptemps et une partie de l'esté, on ne fait de transport que pendant une demy lieüe. Nous y trouvames une bourgade d'Ilinois nommé Kaskaskia composée de 74 cabanes, ils nous y ont tres bien receus et m'ont obligé de leur promettre que je retournerois pour les instruire. Un de chefs de cette nation avec sa jeunesse nous est venu conduire jusu'au lac des Ilinois, d'ou enfin nous nous sommes rendus dans la baye des Puantz sur la fin de Septembre, d'ou nous estions partes vers le commencement de Juin.

Quand tout ce voyage n'auroit causé que le salut d'une ame, j'estimerois toutes mes peines bien recompensées, et c'est ce que j'ay sujet de presumer, car lorsque je retournois nous passames par les Ilinois de Pe8area, je fus trois jours a publier la foy dans toutes leurs cabanes, apres quoy comme nous nous embarquions, on m'apporte au bord de l'eau un enfant moribond que je baptisay un peu avant qu'il mourut par une providence admirable pour le salut de cette ame innocente.

17

UNFINISHED LETTER OF FATHER MARQUETTE

TO FATHER CLAUDE DABLON, SUPERIOR OF THE MISSIONS,

CONTAINING A

JOURNAL OF HIS LAST VISIT TO THE ILINOIS.

MON REVEREND PERE—
          Pax X¹:—

AYANT eté contraint de demeurer a St. François tout l'esté a cause de quelque incommodité. En ayant esté guery dez le mois de Septembre j'y attendois l'arrivée de nos gens au retour de la bas pour sçavoir ce qu ie ferois pour mon hyvernement ; lesquels m'apporterent les ordres pour mon voyage a la mission de le Conception des Ilinois. Ayant satisfait aux sentiments de V. R. pour les copies de mon iournal touchant la Riviere de Missisipi je partis avec Pierre Porteret et Jacque ——, le 25 Oct., 1674, sur les midy le vent nous contraignit de coucher a la sortie de la riviere ou les P8te8atamis s'assembloient, les anciens n'ayant pas voulu qu'on allast du costez des Ilinois, de peur que la jeunesse amassant des robbes avec les marchandises qu'ils ont apportez de la bas, et chassant au castor ne voulut descendre le printemps qu'ils croient avoir suiet de craindre les Nad8essi.

26 Oct. Passant au village nous n'y trouvasmes plus que deux cabannes qui partoient pour aller hyverner a la Gasparde, nous apprismes que 5 canots de P8te8atamis et 4 d'Ilinois estoient partis pour aller aux Kaskaskia.

27. Nous fusmes arrestez le matin par la pluye, nous eusmes beau temps et calme l'apresdisnée que nous rencontrasmes dans l'ance a l'esturgeon les sauvages qui marchoient devant nous.

28. On arrive au portage, un canot qui avoit pris le devant est cause (que) qu'on ne tue point de gibier ; nous commençons notre portage et allons coucher de l'autre bord, ou le mauvais temps nous fist bien de la peine. Pierre n'arrive qu'a une heure de nuit s'esgarant par d'un sentier ou il n'avoit iamais esté, apres la pluye et la tonnerre, il tombe de la neige.

29. Ayant este contraint de changer de cabannage, on continue de porter les paquets, le portage a pres d'une lieüe et assez incommode en plusieurs endroits, les Ilinois s'estant assembles le soir dans notre cabanne demandent qu'on ne les quitte pas, comme nous pouvions avoir besoin d'eux et qu'ils connoissent mieux le lac que nous, on leur promet.

30. Les femmes Ilinoises achevent le matin notre portage ; on est arreste par le vent, il n'y a point de bestes.

31. On parte par un assez beau temps et l'on vieut coucher a une petite riviere. Le chemin de l'ance a l'esturgeon par terre est tres difficile, nous n'en marchions pas loing l'automne passée, lorsque nous entrasmes dans le bois.

Nov. 1. Ayant dit la Ste. Messe on vient coucher dans une riviere, d'ou l'on va aux P8te8atamis par un beau chemin. Chachag8essi8 Ilinois fort considere parmy sa nation, a raison en partie qu'il se mesle des affaires de la traitte arrive la nuit avec un chevreux sur son dos, dont il nous fait part.

2. La Ste. Messe dit, nous marchons toute la iournée par un fort beau temps, on tüe deux chats qui n'ont quasi que de la graisse.

3. Comme i'estois par terre marchant sur le beau sable tout le bordde l'eau estoit d'herbes semblables a celle qu'on pesche aux retz St. Ignace, mais ne pouvant passer une riviere, nos gens y entrent pour m'embarquer, mais on n'en put sorter a cause de la lame, tous les autres canots passent a la reserve d'un seul qui vient avec nous.

4. On est arreste. Ily a apparence qu'il y a quelque isle au large le gibier y passant le soir.

5. Nous eusmes assez de peine de sorter de la riviere sur le midy'on trouva les sauvages dans une riviere, ou ie pris occasion d'instruire les Ilinois, a raison d'un festin que Na8asking8e venoit de faire a une peau de loup.

6. On fist une belle iournée, les sauvages estant a la chasse découvrirent quelques pistes d'hommes ce qui oblige d'arrester le lendemain.

9. On mit a terre sur les 2 heures a cause d'un beau cabannage,

ou l'on fust arreste 5 iours, a cause de la grande agitation du lac sans aucun vent, ensuitte par la neige, qui fust le lendemain fondüe par le soleil et un vent du large.

15. Apres avoir fait assez de chemin on cabanne dans un bel endroit ou l'on est arreste 3 iours Pierre raccommode le fusil d'un sauvage, neige tombe la nuit et fonde le iour.

20. On couche aux ecors assez mal cabannez les sauvages demeurent derriere durant qu'on est arreste du vent 2 iours et demy Pierre allant dans le bois trouve la prairie a 20 lieües du portage, il passe aussi sur un beau canal comme en voute, haut de la hauteur d'un homme, ou il y avoit un pied d'eau.

23. Estant embarque sur le midy nous eusmes assez de peine de gagner une riviere, le froid commença par l'est et plus d'un pied de neige couvrit la terre qui est tousiours depuis demeure ou fust arreste la 3 iours durant lesquels Pierre tua un chevreux, 3 outardes, et 3 cocqs d'inde, qui estoient fort bons, les autres passerent iusques aux prairies, un sauvage ayant descouvert quelques cabannes nous vint trouver, Jacques y alla le lendemain avec luy, 2 chasseurs me vinrent aussi voir, c'estoient des Mask8tens au nombre de 8 ou 9 cabannes, lesquelles s'estoient separez les uns des autres pour pouvoir vivre, avec des fatigues presque impossibles a des françois ils marchent tout l'hyver, dans des chemins tres difficiles, les terres estant pleines de ruisseaux, de petits lacs et de marests, ils sont tres mal cabannez, et mangent ou ieusnent selon les lieux ou ils se rencontrent ; estant arrestez par le vent nous remarquasmes qu'il y avoit de grandes battures au large ou la lame brisoient continuellement ; ce fust la que ie sentis quelques atteintes d'un flux de ventre.

27. Nous eusmes assez de peine de sortir de la riviere et ayant fait environ 3 lieües nous trouvasmes les sauvages qui avoient tuez des bœufs et 3 Ilinois qui estoient venu du village, nous fusmes arrestez la d'un vent de terre, des lames prodigieuses qui venoient du large, et du froid.

Decembre 1. On devance les sauvages pour pouvoir dire la Ste. Messe.

3. Ayant dit la Ste. Messe, estant embarque nous fusmes contraint de gagner une pointe pour pouvoir mettre a terre a cause des bourguignons.

4. Nous partismes heureusement pour venir a la riviere du portage qui estoit gelee d'un demy pied, ou il y avoit plus de neige que partout ailleurs, comme aussi plus de pistes de bestes et de cocqs d'In-

de. La navigation du lac est assez belle d'un portage a l'autre, n'y ayant aucune traverse a faire et pouvant mettre a terre partout, moyennant qu'on ne soit point opiniastre a vouloir marcher dans les lames et de grand vent. Les terres qui le bordent ne valent rien, excepte quand on est aux prairies, on trouve 8 ou 10 rivieres assez belles, la chasse du chevreux est tres belle a mesure qu'on s'esloigne des P8te8atamis.

12. Comme on commençoit hir a traisner pour approcher du portage les Ilinois ayant quittez les P8te8atamis arriverent avec bien de la peine. Nous ne pusmes dire la Ste. Messe le iour de la Conception a cause du mauvais temps et du froid, durant notre seiour a l'entrée de la riviere Pierre et Jacques tuerent 3 bœufs et 4 chevreux dont un courut assez loing ayant le cœur coupe en 2 on se contente de tuer 3 ou 4 cocqs d'inde de plusieurs qui venoient autour de notre cabanne, parcequ'ils mouroient quasi de faim ; Jacques apporta un perdrix qu'il avoit tuez, semblable en tout a celles de France, excepte qu'elle avoit comme deux aislerons de 3 ou 4 aisles longues d'un doigt proche de la teste, dont elles couvrent les 2 costez du col ou il n'y a point de plume.

14. Estant cabannez proche le portage a 2 lieues dans la riviere nous resolusmes d'hyverner la, estant dans l'impossibilite de passer outre, estant trop embarasse, et mon incommodite ne me permettant pas de beaucoup fatiguer. Plusieurs Ilinois passerent hier pour aller porter leur pelleterie a Na8asking8e, ausquels on donne un bœufs et un chevreux que Jacque avoit tué le iour auparavant ie ne pense pas avoir veu de sauvage plus affamé de petun François qu'eux, ils vinrent ietter a nos pieds des castors pour en avoir quelque bout mais nour leur rendismes en leur en donnant quelque pipe, parceque nous n'avions pas encore conclu si nous passerions outre.

15. Chachag8essi8 et les autres Ilinois nous quitterent pour aller trouver leur gens, et leur donner les marchandises qu'ils avoient apportez pour avoir leur robbes en quoy ils se gouvernent comme des traitteurs et ne donnent guere plus que les François ; ie les instruisis avant leur depart, remettant au printemps de tenir conseil quand ie serois au village ; ils nous traitterent 3 belles robbes de bœuf pour une coudee de petun, lesquelles, nous ont beaucoup servi cet hyver, estant ainsi desbarassez, nous dismes la Messe de la Conception ; depuis le 14 mon incommodite se tourna en flux de sang.

30. Jacque arriva du village des Ilinois qui n'estoit qu'a six lieues d'icy ou ils avoient faim le froid et la neige les empeschant de chas-

ser, quelques uns ayant adverti la Toupine et le chirurgien que nous estions icy et ne pouvant quitter leur cabanne avoient tellement donnez la peur aux sauvages croyant que nous aurions faim demeurant icy que Jacque eust bien de la peine d'empescher 15 jeunes gens de venir pour emporter toute nostie affaire.

Janvier 16, 1675. Aussitot que les 2 françois sceurent que mon mal mempeschoit dàller chez eux le chirurgien vint icy avec un sauvage pour nous apporter des bluets et du bled ; ils ne sont que 18 lieües d'icy dans un beau lieu de chasse, pour les bœufs et les chevreux et les cocqs d'inde qui y sont excellents, ills avoient aussi amassez des vivres en nous attendant ; et avoient fait entendre aux sauvages que leur cabanne estoit a la Robbe noire, et on peut dire qu'ils ont fait et dit tout ce qu'on peut attendre d'eux : le chirurgien ayant icy seiourne pour faire ses devotions : j'envoiay Jacque avec luy pour dire aux Ilinois qui estoient proche de la., que mon incommodite m'empeschoit de les aller voir et que iaurois mesme de la peine d'yaller le printemps si elle continuoit.

24. Jacque retourna, avec un sac de bled et d'autres rafraichissement que les François luy avoient donnez pour moy : il apporta aussi les langues et de la viande de deux bœufs qu'un sauvage et luy avoient tuez proche d'icy ; mais toutes les bestes se sentent de mauvais temps.

26. 3 Ilinois nous apporterent de la part des Anciens 2 sacs de bled, de la viande seche, des citrouilles et 12 castors, 1°, pour me faire une natte, 2°, pour me demander de la poudre, 3°, pour que nous n'eussions faim, 4°, pour avoir quelque peu de marchandises ; ie leur repondis 1nt, que i'estois venu pour les instruire, en leur parlant de la priere, &c. 2nt, que ie ne leur donnerois point de poudre, puisque nous taschions de mettre partout la paix, et que ie ne voulois qu'ils commençassent la guerre avec les Miamis. 3nt, que nous n'apprehendions point le faim. 4nt, que iencouragerois les françcois a leur apporter des marchandises, et qu'il falloit qu'ils satisfissent ceux qui estoient chez eux pour la rassade qu'on leur avoit pris, dez que le chirurgien fust party pour venir icy. Comme ils estoient venus de 20 lieüs, pour les payer de leur peine et de ce qu'ils m'avoient apportez ie leur donnay une hache, 2 couteaux, 3 iambettes, 10 brasses de rassade et 2 mirouirs doubles, et leur disant qui ie tascherois d'aller au village seulement pour quelques iours si mon incommodite continuoit, ils me dirent de prendre courage de demeurer et de mourir daus leur pays et qu'on leur avoit dit que i'y resterois pour longtemps.

Fevrier 9. Depuis que nous nous sommes addressez a la Ste. Vierge Immaculée que nous avons commencez une neufvaine par une messe a laquelle Pierre et Jacque qui font tout ce qu'ils peuvent pour me soulager, ont communies pour demander a Dieu la sante, mon flux de sang m'a quitte, il ne me reste qu'un foiblesse d'estomac, ie commence a meporter beaucoup mieux et a reprendre mes forces : il ne cabanne d'Ilinois qui s'estoit rangee proche de nous depuis un mois une partie out repris le chemin des P8t et quelques uns sont encore au bord du lac ou ils attendent que la navigation soit libre, ils emportent des lettres pour nos P. P. de St. François.

20. Nous avons eu le temps de remarquer les mareez qui viennent du lac lesquels haussent et baissent plusieurs fois par iour et quoyqu'il n'y paraisse aucune abry dans le lac, on a veu les glaces aller contre le vent, ces mareez nous rendoient l'eau bonne ou mauvaisse parceque celle qui vient d'en hault coule des prairies et de petits ruisseaux, lestchevreux qui sont enquantite vers le bord du lac sont si maigres qu'on a este contraint d'en laisser quelques uns de ce qu'on avoit tuez.

Mars 23. On tue plusieurs perdrix dont il n'y a que les mals qui ayant des aislerons au col, les femelles u'en ayant point, ces perdrix sont assez bonnes mais non pas comme celle de France.

30. Le vent de nord ayant empesche le degeal jusques au 25 de Mars il commença par un vent de sud, dez le lendemain le gibier commença de paroistre, on tua 30 tourtres que ie trouvay meilleures que celles de la bas, mais plus petites, tant les vieilles que les ieunes ; le 28 les glaces se rompirent et s'arresterent au dessus de nous, le 29 les eaux crurent si fort que nous n'eusmes que le temps de descabanner au plutot, mettre nos affaires sur des arbres et tascher de chercher a coucher sur quelque but l'eau nous gagnant presque toute la nuit, mais ayant un peu gele et estant diminue comme nous estions aupres de nos paquets, la digue vient de se rompre et les glaces a s'escouler et parceque les eaux remontent desia nous allons nous embarquer pour continuer notre route.

La Ste. Vierge Immaculee a pris un tel soin de nous durant notre hyvernement que rien ne nous a mauque pour les vivres, ayant encore un grand sac de bled de reste, de la viande et de la graisse ; nous avons aussi vescu fort doucement, mon mal ne m'ayant point empesche de dire la Ste. Messe tous les iours ; nous n'avons point pu garder du caresme que les Vendredys et samedys.

31. Estant hier party nous fismes 3 lieües dans la riviere en re-

montant sans trouver aucun portage, on traisna peut estre environ un demy arpant outre cette descharge, la riviere en a une autre par ou nous debvons descendre. Il n'y a que les terres bien hautes qui ne soient point inondeez, celle ou nous sommes a cru plus de 12 pieds a-ce fut d'icy que nous commençasmes notre portage ily a 18 mois ; les outardes et les canards passent continuellement ; on s'est contente de 7, les glaces qui derivent encore nous font icy demeureur ne sachant pas en quel estat est le bas de la riviere.

Avril 1. Comme ie ne scais point encore si ie demeureray cet este au village ou non a cause de mon flux de ventre, nous laissons icy une partie de ce dont nous pouvons nous passer et surtout un sac de bled, tandis qu'un grand vent de sud nous arreste, nous esperons aller demain ou sont les François, distant de 15 lieues d'icy.

6. Les grands vents et le froid nous empeschent de marcher. Les deux lacs par ou nous avons passez sont plains d'outardes, d'oyes, de canards, de grues et d'autres gibiers que nous ne connoissons point. Les rapides sont assez dangereux en quelques endroits, nous venons de rencontrer le chirurgien avec un sauvage qui montoit avec une canottee de pelleterie, mais le froid estant trop grand pour des personnes qui sont obligez de traisner les canots dans l'eau, il vient de faire cache de son castor et retourne demain au village avec nous. Si les François ont des robbes de ce pays icy, ils ne les desrobbent pas tant les fatigues sont grands pour les en tirer.

LA SALLE'S PATENT OF NOBILITY.

(Paris Doc. in Secy's. Office, Albany, vol. ii. pp. 8–11,)

Données à Compeigne le 13 May, 1675.

LOUIS, par la grace de Dieu Roy de France et de Navarre, à tous presens et à venir salut. Les Roys nos predecesseurs ayant toujours estimé que l'honneur etait le plus puissant motif pour porter leurs sujets aux généreuses actions, ils ont pris soin de reconnaitre par des marques d'honneur ceux qu'une vertu extraordinaire en avait rendu dignes, et comme nous sommes informés des bonnes actions que font journellement les peuples de Canada, soit en reduisant ou disciplinant les sauvages, soit en se defendant contre leurs frequentes insultes, et celles de Iroquois et enfin en meprisant les plus grands perils pour étendre jusques au bout de ce nouveau monde, nostre nom et nostre empire, nous avons estimé qu'il estait de nostre justice de distinguer par des recompences d'honneur ceux qui se sont le plus signaléz pour exciter les autres à meriter de semblables graces, à ces causes, desirant traiter favorablement nostre cher et bien aimé Robert Cavelier sieur de la Salle pour le bon et louable rapport qui nous a été fait des bonnes actions qu'il a faite dans le pays de Canada où il s'est estably depuis quelques années et pour autres considerations à ce nous mouvans, et de notre grace speciale, pleine puissance, et autorité royale, nous avons annobly, et par ces presentes signées de nostre main annoblissons, et decorons du titre et qualité de noblesse le d. Sr. Cavalier, ensemble sa femme et enfans posterité et lignée tant males que femelles nés et à naitre en loyal mariage ; Voulons et nous plait qu'en tous actes tant en jugement que dehors ils soient tenus, censés et reputés nobles portant la qualite d'escuyer, et puissant parvenir à tous degrès de chevallerie et de gendarmerie, acquerir, tenir, et posséder toutes sortes de fiefs et seigneuries et heritages nobles de quelque titre et qualité qu'ils soient, et qu'ils jouissent de tous honneurs, autorités, prerogatives, préeminences, privileges, franchises, exemptions et immunités, dont jouissent et ont accoutumé de jouir et user les autres nobles de nostre Royaume et de porter telles armes qu'elles sont cy empraintes, sans ce que pour ce le dit Robert Cavelier soit tenu nous payer, ny à nos successeurs Roys, aucune finance ni indemnité, dont à quelque somme qu'elles se puissent monter, nous l'avons dechargé, et déchargeons et lui avons fait et faisons don par cesdites presentes, le tout par les causes et raisons portées en l'arrest de notre concil de cejourdhui donné nous y etant dont copie demeurera cy attachée sous le contreséil de nostre chancellerie. Si donnouns en mandement a nos aimés et feaux con^{ers} les gens tenants nostre cour de parlement de Paris, chambre des comptes, cour des aydes au dit lieu que ces presentes lettres d' annoblissement ils ayent à registrer, et du contenu en icelles faire souffrir et laisser jouir et user le dit Robert Cavelier, ses Enfans et posterité nés et à naître en loyal mariage, pleinement, paisiblement et perpetuellement, cessant et faisant cesser tous troubles et empeschemens nonobstant tous Edits et declarations, arrests, reglemens, et autres choses à ce contraries, aux quels nous avons derogé et derogons par ces presente car tel est notre plaisir. Et afin que ce soit chose ferme stable et à toujours, nous y avons fait mettre nostre scèl. Donne à compeigne le 13 May, l'an de grace mil six cens soixante quinze, et de nostre regne le trentetroisieme.

LA SALLE'S SECOND COMMISSION.

(Same vol., p. 275.)

À Versailles, le 14 Avril, 1684.

Louis, par la grace de Dieu Roy de France et de Nauarre, Salut. Ayant resolu de faire quelques entreprises dans l'Amerique Septentrionale pour assujetir sons nostre domination plusieurs nations sauvages, et leur porter les lumières de la foy et de l'evangile, nous avons cru que nous ne pouvions faire un meilleur choix que du sieur de la Salle, pour commander en nostre nom tous les Français et sauvages qu'il employera pour l'execution des ordres dont nous l'avons chargé. A ces causes, et autres à ce nous mouvans, et étant d'ailleurs bien informéz de son affection et de sa fidelité à nostre service, Nous avons le d. Sr. de la Salle commis et ordonné, commettons et ordonnons par ces presentes signées de nostre main, pour sous nostre autorité commander tant dans les pays qui seront assujettis de nouveau sous nostre domination dans l'Amerique Septentrionale, depuis le fort St. Louis sur la Riviere des Illinois jusques à la Nouvelle Biscaye, qu'aux François et sauvages qu'il employera dans les entreprises dont nous l'avons chargé, les faire vivre en union et concorde les uns avec les autres, contenir les gens de guerre en bon ordre et police, suivant nos Reglement, établir des Gouverneurs et commandans par^ers dans les lieux qu'il jugera à propos, jusques à cesqu' autrement par nous en ait été ordonné, maintenir le commerce et traffic, generalement faire et exercer tout ce qui pourra étre du fait de commandant pour nous esd. pays, et en jouir aux pouvoirs, honneurs, autorités, libertés, prerogatives prééminences, franchises, libertés, gages, droits, finites, proffits, revenues, et emolumens, tant qu'il nous plaira.

De ce faire vous avons donné et donnons pouvoir par ces d. presentes par lesquelles mandons à tous nos d. sujets et gens de guerre de vous reconnoistre, obeir, et entendre en choses concernant le present pouvoir. Car tel est nostre plaisir.

En temoin dequoi nous avons fait mettre nostre scel secret á ces d. presentes. Données à Versailles, le 14 Avril, 1684.

COMPARATIVE TABLE

Of the Names on the Map published by Thevenot, as Marquette's, and on his Real Map annexed.

Thevenot.	Marquette.	Usual Form.
Mouingwena	Moingwena	Moingonan
Pe-wanea	Pe-warea	Pe-oria
Tillini-wek	Ilinois	Alliniwek and Illinois
Missi-ousing	Miscousing	Wisconsin
Cach-ouach-wia	Kachkaskia	Kaskaskia
Manoutensac	Maskoutens	
Kamissi	Kanza	
Autrechaha	Ouchage	Osage
Ou-missouri	We-messouret	Missouri
Ahiahichi	Aiaichi	Ayiches
Tamisa	Tanik-wa	Tonica
Matoua	Matora	
Ototchassi	Atotchasi	Southouis
Monsouperea	Monsoupelea	
Wabouquigou	Wabous-quigou	Wabash
Kakinouba	Kakinonba	? Kanawha

The following names are on Marquette alone : —

Pahoutet		
Maha		Omaha
Pana		
Otontanta	Anthoutanta (Le Clercq)	
Akoroa	Koroa	
Papikaha		? Quapaw
Apistonga		
Maroa		Tamaroa

The following are on Thevenot alone : —

Kithigami, Minonk, Aganahali, Wabunghiharea, Taharea.

It will be observed that on the real map the part of Michigan then unexplored, is dotted only, and that the Mississippi descends only to Akansea, the limit of his discovery.

THE END.

POETICAL WORKS OF FITZ-GREENE HALLECK.

New and only Complete Edition, containing several New Poems, together with many now first collected.   One vol., 12mo., price one dollar.

"Halleck is one of the brightest stars in our American literature, and his name is like a household word wherever the English language is spoken."—*Albany Express.*

"To the numerous admirers of Mr. Halleck, this will be a welcome book; for it is a characteristic desire in human nature to have the productions of our favorite authors in an elegant and substantial form."—*Christian Freeman.*

"Mr. Halleck never appeared in a neater dress, and few poets ever deserved a better one."—*Christian Intelligencer.*

"There are few poems to be found, in any language, that surpass, in beauty of thought and structure, some of these."—*Boston Commonwealth.*

LILLIAN, AND OTHER POEMS.

By WINTHROP MACKWORTH PRAED.   Now first Collected.   One Vol., 12mo. Price One Dollar.

"A timely publication is this volume. A more charming companion (in the shape of a book) can scarcely be found for the summer holydays."—*New York Tribune.*

"They are amusing sketches, gay and sprightly in their character, exhibiting great facility of composition, and considerable powers of satire."—*Hartford Courant.*

"There is a brilliant play of fancy in 'Lillian,' and a moving tenderness in 'Josephine,' for which it would be hard to find equals. We welcome this first collected edition of his works."—*Albany Express.*

"As a writer of *vers de societe* he is pronounced to be without an equal among English authors."—*Syracuse Daily Journal.*

"The author of this volume was one of the most fluent and versatile English poets that have shone in the literary world within the last century. His versification is astonishingly easy and airy, and his imagery not less wonderfully graceful and aerial."—*Albany State Register.*

LAYS OF THE SCOTTISH CAVALIERS.

By WILLIAM E. AYTOUN, Professor of Literature and Belles-Lettres in the University of Edinburgh, and Editor of Blackwood's Magazine.   One vol., 12mo., price one dollar.

"Since Lockhart and Macauley's ballads, we have had no metrical work to be compared in spirit, vigor, and rhythm with this. These ballads imbody and embalm the chief historical incidents of Scottish history—literally in 'thoughts that breathe and words that burn.' They are full of lyric energy graphic description, and genuine feeling."—*Home Journal.*

"The fine ballad of 'Montrose' in this collection is alone worth the price of the book."—*Boston Transcript.*

"These strains belong to stirring and pathetic events, and until poetic descriptions of them shall be disregarded, we think Mr. Aytoun's productions well calculated to maintain a favorite place in public estimation."—*Literary Gazette.*

"Chosen from the ample range of Scottish history, clear in feeling, simple and direct in expression, and happily varied and variable in measure, they will, we are confident, outlive many, if not all, of his more pretensious and ornamented contemporaries."—*Literary World.*

THE BOOK OF BALLADS.

By BON GAULTIER.   One volume. 12mo., price, seventy-five cents.

"Here is a book for everybody who loves classic fun. It is made up of ballads of all sorts, each a capital parody upon the style of some one of the best lyric writers of the time from the thundering versification of Lockhart and Macaulay to the sweetest and simplest strains of Wordsworth and Tennyson. The author is one of the first scholars, and one of the most finished writers of the day, and this production is but the frolic of his genius in play-time."—*Courier & Enquirer.*

"We do not know to whom belongs this *nom de plume*, but he is certainly a humorist of no common power."—*Providence Journal.*

"Bon Gaultier's Book of Ballads, is simply the wittiest and best thing of the kind since the Rejected Addresses. Its parodies of Lockhart (in the Spanish Ballads), of Tennyson (his lovely sing-song puerilities), of Macaulay (the sounding Roman strain), of Moses (the 'puff poetical'), are with a dozen others, in various ways, any of them equal to the famous Crabbe, and Scott, and Coleridge of the reascending Drury-Lane."—*Literary World.*

LYRA, AND OTHER POEMS.

By ALICE CAREY. In one volume. 12mo, cloth, price 75 cts.

"Whether poetry be defined as the rhythmical creation of beauty, as passion or eloquence in harmonious numbers, or as thought and feeling manifested by processes of the imagination, Alice Carey is incontestably and incomparably the first living American poetess—fresh, indigenous, national—rich beyond precedent in suitably and sensuous imagery—of the finest and highest qualities of feeling and such powers of creation as the Almighty has seen fit to bestow but rarely or in far-separated countries."—*Boston Transcript.*

"The genuine inspiration of poetic feeling, . . . replete with tenderness and beauty, earnestness and truthful simplicity, and all the attributes of a powerful imagination and vivid fancy. We know of no superior to Miss Carey among the female authors of this country."—*N. Y. Journal of Commerce.*

"Alice Carey's book is full of beautiful thoughts; there is draught after draught of pure pleasure for the lover of sweet, tender fancies, and imagery which captivates while it enforces truth."—*New York Courier and Inquirer.*

"'Lyra and other Poems,' just published by Redfield, attracts everywhere, a remarkable degree of attention. A dozen of the leading journals, and many eminent critics, have pronounced the authoress the greatest poetess living."—*New York Mirror.*

CLOVERNOOK;

Or, Recollections of our Neighborhood in the West. By ALICE CAREY. Illustrated by DARLEY. One vol., 12mo, price $1.00. (Fourth edition.)

"In this volume there is a freshness which perpetually charms the reader. You seem to be made free of western homes at once."—*Old Colony Memorial.*

"They bear the true stamp of genius—simple natural, truthful—and evince a keen sense of the humor and pathos, of the comedy and tragedy, of life in the country."—*J. G. Whittier.*

"Alice Carey has perhaps the strongest imagination among the women of this country. Her writings will live longer than those of any other woman among us."—*American Whig Review.*

"Miss Carey's sketches are remarkably fresh and exquisite in delicacy, humor, and pathos. She is booked for immortality."—*Home Journal.*

DREAM-LAND BY DAY-LIGHT.

A Panorama of Romance. By CAROLINE CHESEBRO'. Illustrated by DARLEY. One vol., 12mo., price $1.25. (Second edition.)

"We find in this volume unmistakeable evidences of originality of mind, an almost superfluous depth of reflection for the department of composition to which it is devoted. a rare facility in seizing the multiform aspects of nature, and a still rarer power of giving them the form and hue of imagination, without destroying their identity."—*Harper's Magazine.*

"These simple and beautiful stories are all highly endued with an exquisite perception of natural beauty, with which is combined an appreciative sense of its relation to the highest moral emotions."—*Albany State Register.*

"Gladly do we greet this floweret in the field of our literature, for it is fragrant with sweet and bright with hues that mark it to be of Heaven's own planting."—*Courier and Enquirer.*

"There is a depth of sentiment and feeling not ordinarily met with, and some of the noblest faculties and affections of man's nature are depicted and illustrated by the skilful pen of the authoress."—*Churchman.*

ISA, A PILGRIMAGE.

By CAROLINE CHESEBRO'. One volume, 12mo, price, $1.00. Second edition.

"The Pilgrimage is fraught throughout with scenes of thrilling interest—romantic, yet possessing a naturalness that seems to stamp them as real; the style is flowing and easy, chaste and beautiful."—*Troy Daily Times.*

"Miss Chesebro' is evidently a *thinker*—she skims not the mere surface of life, but plunges boldly into the hidden mysteries of the spirit, by which she is warranted in making her startling revelations of human passion."—*Christian Freeman.*

"There comes out in this book the evidence of an inventive mind, a cultivated taste, an exquisite sensibility, and a deep knowledge of human nature."—*Albany Argus.*

"There is no one who will doubt that this is a courageous and ablework, displaying genius and depth of feeling, and striking at a high and noble aim."—*N. Y. Evangelist.*

"There is a fine vein of tenderness running through the story, which is peculiarly one of passion and sentiment."—*Arthur's Home Gazette.*

LADIES OF THE COVENANT:

Memoirs of Distinguished Scottish Female Characters, embracing the Period of the Covenant and the Persecution. By Rev. James Anderson. One vol., 12mo, price $1.25.

"It is written with great spirit and a hearty sympathy, and abounds in incidents of more than a romantic interest, while the type of piety it discloses is the noblest and most elevated."—*N. Y. Evangelist.*

"It is a record which, while it confers honor on the sex, will elevate the heart, and strengthen it to the better performances of every duty."—*Religious Herald. (Va.)*

"It is a book of great attractiveness, having not only the freshness of novelty, but every element of historical interest."—*Courier & Enquirer.*

"The author delineates with great fidelity the struggles and sufferings of the noble female worthies of Scotland in the cause of civil and religious liberty. It is refreshing to read these actual and heroic lives of Christian women in both the higher and lower walks of life."—*Prairie Herald.*

CHARACTERS IN THE GOSPEL,

Illustrating Phases of Character at the Present Day. By Rev. E. H. Chapin, One vol., 12mo., price 50 cents. (Second edition.)

"As we read his pages, the reformer, the sensualist, the skeptic, the man of the world, the seeker, the sister of charity and of faith, stand out from the Scriptures, and join themselves with our own living world."—*Christian Enquirer.*

"Mr. Chapin has an easy, graceful style, neatly touching the outlines of his pictures, and giving great consistency and beauty to the whole. The reader will find admirable descriptions, some most wholesome lessons, and a fine spirit."—*New York Evangelist.*

"The work is done with a skilful hand, and in a style attractive and impressive. The book furnishes not only agreeable, but very useful and instructive reading."—*Boston Traveller.*

"We commend this volume to those who imagine that the teachings of the pulpit are nothing if not dull. Its brilliant vivacity of style forms an admirable combination with its soundness of thought and depth of feeling."—*Tribune.*

LECTURES AND MISCELLANIES.

By Henry James.   One vol., 12mo., cloth, price $1.25.

"A series of essays by one of the most generous thinkers and sincere lovers of truth in the country. He looks at society from an independent point of view, and with the noblest and most intelligent sympathy."—*Home Journal.*

"This is the production of a mind richly endowed of a very peculiar mould. All will concede to him the merit of a vigorous and brilliant intellect."—*Albany Argus.*

"A perusal of the essays leads us to *think*, not merely because of the ideas which they contain, but more because the ideas are earnestly put forth, and the subjects discussed are interesting and important to every one."—*Worcester National Ægis.*

"They have attracted much attention both here and in Europe, where the author is considered as holding a distinctive and prominent position in the school of modern philosophy."—*Albany Atlas.*

"The writer wields a masterly and accurate pen, and his style is good."—*Boston Olive Branch.*

"It will have many readers, and almost as many admirers."—*N. Y. Times.*

THE STUDY OF WORDS.

By Archdeacon Richard C. Trench.   One vol., 12mo., price 75 cts.

"He discourses in a truly learned and lively manner upon the original unity of language, and the origin, derivation, and history of words, with their morality and separate spheres of meaning."—*Evening Post.*

"This is a noble tribute to the divine faculty of speech. Popularly written, exact in its learning, and poetic in its vision, it is a book at once for the scholar and the general reader."—*N. Y. Evangelist.*

"It is one of the most striking and original publications of the day, with nothing of hardness, dullness, or dryness about it, but altogether fresh, lively, and entertaining."—*Boston Evening Traveller.*

"This volume will be found exceedingly useful, not alone for what it teaches, but as a stimulus to thought and study, and opening wide a suggestive field for pleasing and beneficial investigation."—*Troy Daily Times.*

THE WORKS OF EDGAR ALLAN POE.

Complete in Three Volumes, with a Portrait; a Memoir by James Russell Lowell, and an Introductory Essay by N. P. Willis. Edited by Rufus W. Griswold, D. D. 12mo, price $4.00.

"Poe's writings are distinguished for vigorous and minute analysis, and the skill with which he has employed the strange fascination of mystery and terror. There is an air of reality in all his narrations—a dwelling upon particulars, and a faculty of interesting you in them, such as is possessed by few writers except those who are giving their own individual experiences."—*Philadelphia Ledger.*

"We need not say that these volumes will be found rich in intellectual excitements, and abounding in remarkable specimens of vigorous, beautiful, and highly suggestive composition; they are all that remains to us of a man whose uncommon genius it would be folly to deny."—*N. Y. Tribune.*

"Mr. Poe's intellectual character—his genius—is stamped upon all his productions, and we shall place these, his works, in the library among those books not to be parted with."—*N. Y. Com. Advert'r.*

"We feel, however, that these productions will live. They bear the stamp of true genius; and if their reputation begins with a 'fit audience though few,' the circle will be constantly widening, and they will retain a prominent place in our literature."—*Rev. Dr. Kip.*

TALES AND TRADITIONS OF HUNGARY.

By THERESA PULSZKY, with a Portrait of the Author. One vol., price $1.25.

The above contains, in addition to the English publication, a NEW PREFACE, and TALES, now first printed from the manuscript of the Author, who has a direct interest in the publication.

"Strikingly illustrative of the manners and customs that have prevailed in different periods of her history, it is written with graceful yet dignified freedom."—*Albany Argus.*

"The stories are of a wild and fanciful character, which will cause them to be read with interest by all, while they really throw light upon the early history and manners of Hungary."—*Albany Express.*

"Some of them are exceedingly beautiful, and indicate the character and habits of thought of the people better than anything we have seen."—*N. O. Journal and Courier.*

"This work claims more attention than is ordinarily given to books of its class. The tales contain highly suggestive illustrations of national literature and character."—*London Examiner.*

THE CAVALIERS OF ENGLAND;

Or, the Times of the Revolutions of 1642 and 1688. By HENRY WILLIAM HERBERT. One vol., 12mo, price $1.25.

"They are graphic stories, and in the highest degree attractive to the imagination as well as instructive, and can not fail to be popular."—*Commercial.*

"These tales are written in the popular author's best style, and give us a vivid and thrilling idea of the customs and influences of the chivalrous age."—*Christian Freeman.*

"His narrative is always full of great interest; his descriptive powers are of an uncommon order; the romance of history loses nothing at his hands; he paints with the power, vigor, and effect of a master."—*The Times.*

"They bring the past days of old England vividly before the reader, and impress upon the mind with indelible force, the living images of the puritans as well as the cavaliers, whose earnest character and noble deeds lend such a lively interest to the legends of the times in which they lived and fought, loved and hated, prayed and revelled."—*Newark Daily.*

THE KNIGHTS OF ENGLAND, FRANCE, AND SCOTLAND.

By HENRY WILLIAM HERBERT. One vol., 12mo, price $1.25.

"They are partly the romance of history and partly fiction, forming, when blended, portraitures valuable from the correct drawing of the times they illustrate, and interesting from their romance."—*Albany Knickerbocker.*

"They are spirit-stirring productions, which will be read and admired by all who are pleased with historical tales written in a vigorous, bold, and dashing style."—*Boston Journal.*

"These legends of love and chivalry contain some of the finest tales which the graphic and powerful pen of Herbert has yet given to the lighter literature of the day."—*Detroit Free Press.*

"Mr. Herbert has a quick and accurate eye for the picturesque features of the romantic past. He pursues the study of history with the soul of the poet, and skilfully availing himself of the most striking traditions and incidents, has produced a series of fascinating portraitures. Whoever would obtain a vivid idea of the social and domestic traits of France and Great Britain in the olden time, should not fail to read the life-life descriptions of this volume."—*Harper's Magazine.*

NAPIER'S PENINSULAR WAR.

History of the War in the Peninsula, and in the South of France, from the Year 1807 to 1814. By W. F. P. NAPIER, C. B., Col. 43d Reg., &c. Complete in one vol., 8vo, price $3.00.

"Napier's history is regarded by the critics as one of the best narratives that has recently been written. His style is direct, forcible, and impetuous, carrying the reader along often in spite of himself, through scenes of the most stirring interest and adventures full of excitement."—*Evening Mirror.*

"The Literature of War has not received a more valuable augmentation this century than Col. Napier's justly celebrated work. Though a gallant combatant in the field, he is an impartial historian."—*Tribune.*

"Napier's History, in addition to its superior literary merits, and truthful fidelity, presents strong claims upon the attention of all American citizens; because the author is a large-souled philanthropist and an inflexible enemy to ecclesiastical tyranny and secular despots."—*Post.*

"The excellency of Napier's History results from the writer's happy talent for impetuous, straightforward, soul-stirring narrative and picturing forth of characters. The military manœuvre, march, and fiery onset, the whole whirlwind vicissitudes of the desperate fight, he describes with dramatic force."—*Merchants' Magazine.*

GRISCOM ON VENTILATION.

The Uses and Abuses of Air: showing its Influence in Sustaining Life, and Producing Disease, with Remarks on the Ventilation of Houses, and the best Methods of Securing a Pure and Wholesome Atmosphere inside of Dwellings, Churches, Shops, &c. By JOHN H. GRISCOM, M. D. One vol. 12mo, $1.00.

"This comprehensive treatise should be read by all who wish to secure health, and especially by those constructing churches, lecture-rooms, school-houses, &c.—It is undoubted, that many diseases are created and spread in consequence of the little attention paid to proper ventilation. Dr. G. writes knowingly and plainly upon this all-important topic."—*Newark Advertiser.*

"The whole book is a complete manual of the subject of which it treats; and we venture to say that the builder or contriver of a dwelling, school-house, church, theatre, ship, or steamboat, who neglects to inform himself of the momentous truths it asserts, commits virtually a crime against society and his fellow-creatures."—*N. Y. Metropolis.*

"When shall we learn to estimate at their proper value, pure water and pure air, which God provided for man before he made man, and a very long time before he permitted the existence of a doctor? We commend the Uses and Abuses of Air to our readers, assuring them that they will find it to contain directions for the ventilation of dwellings, which every one who values health and comfort should put in practice."—*N. Y. Dispatch.*

BRONCHITIS, AND KINDRED DISEASES.

In language adapted to common readers. By W. W. HALL, M. D. One vol. 12 mo, price $1.00.

"It is written in a plain, direct, common-sense style, and is free from the quackery which marks many of the popular medical books of the day. It will prove useful to those who need it."—*Ch. Herald.*

"Those who are clergymen, or who are preparing for the sacred calling, and public speakers generally, should not fail of securing this work."—*Ch. Ambassador.*

"It is full of hints on the nature of the vital organs, and does away with much superstitious dread in regard to consumption."—*Greene County Whig.*

"This work gives some valuable instruction in regard to food and hygienic influences."—*Nashua Oasis.*

REICHENBACH ON DYNAMICS.

Physico-Physiological Researches on the Dynamics of Magnetism, Electricity, Heat, Light, Crystallization, and Chemism, in their relation to Vital Force: By Baron CHARLES VON REICHENBACH. With the Addition of a Preface and Critical Notes, by JOHN ASHBURNER, M. D. With all the Plates. In one Volume, 12mo, 456 pp. Price, $1.25.

"This book is a valuable addition to scientific knowledge upon subjects that have been involved in obscurity and mysticism. Charlatans have so long availed themselves of a slight knowledge of the phenomena of magnetism for mercenary purposes, that discredit has been thrown upon the whole subject, and men of science have been deterred from pursuing, or at least from publishing their researches. The work before us gives the result of a vast number of experiments conducted with great philosophical acumen, testing the truth of both modern theories and ancient superstitions. Phenomena attributed in past ages to a supernatural agency, and by the superficial skepticism of later times dismissed as mere impostures, are in many instances traced with great clearness to natural and explicable causes. It requires, and is eminently worthy of an attentive perusal."—*City Item.*

CONTEMPORARY BIOGRAPHY.

MEN OF THE TIME
OR SKETCHES OF LIVING NOTABLES,

AUTHORS   ENGINEERS   of   PHILANTHROPISTS
ARCHITECTS   JOURNALISTS   PREACHERS
ARTISTS   MINISTERS   SAVANS
COMPOSERS   MONARCHS   STATESMEN
DEMAGOGUES   NOVELISTS   TRAVELLERS
DIVINES   POLITICIANS   VOYAGERS
DRAMATISTS   POETS   WARRIORS

In One Vol., 12mo, containing nearly Nine Hundred Biographical Sketches,
PRICE $1.50.

"I am glad to learn that you are publishing this work. It is precisely that kind of information that every public and intelligent man desires to see, especially in reference to the distinguished men of Europe, but which I have found it extremely difficult to obtain."—*Extract from a Letter of the President of the United States to the publisher.*

"It forms a valuable manual for reference, especially in the American department, which we can not well do without; we commend it to the attention of our 'reading public.'"—*Tribune.*

"It is a book of reference which every newspaper reader should have at his elbow—as indispensable as a map or a dictionary—and from which the best-informed will derive instruction and pleasure."—*Evangelist.*

"This book therefore fills a place in literature; and once published, we do not see how any one could do without it."—*Albany Express.*

"It is evidently compiled with great care and labor, and every possible means seems to have been used to secure the highest degree of correctness. It contains a great deal of valuable information, and is admirable as a book of reference."—*Albany Argus.*

"For a book of reference, this volume will recommend itself as an invaluable companion in the library, office, and studio."—*Northern Budget.*

"We know of no more valuable book to authors, editors, statesmen, and all who would be 'up with the time,' than this."—*Spirit of the Times.*

"Men of all nations, creeds and parties, appear to be treated in a kindly spirit. The work will be found a useful supplement to the ordinary biographical dictionaries."—*Commercial Advertiser.*

"The value of such a work can scarcely be over-estimated. To the statesman and philanthropist, as well as the scholar and business man, it will be found of great convenience as a reference book, and must soon be considered as indispensable to a library as Webster's Dictionary."—*Lockport Courier.*

"It is a living, breathing epitome of the day, a directory to that wide phantasmagoria we call the world."—*Wall Street Journal.*

THE MASTER BUILDER;

Or, Life in the City.   By DAY KELLOGG LEE, author of "Summerfield, or Life on the Farm." One vol., 12mo, price $1.00.

"He is a powerful and graphic writer, and from what we have seen of the pages of the 'Master Builder,' it is a romance of excellent aim and success."—*State Register.*

"The 'Master Builder' is the master production. It is romance into which is instilled the reality of life; and incentives are put forth to noble exertion and virtue. The story is pleasing—almost fascinating; the moral is pure and undefiled."—*Daily Times.*

"Its descriptions are, many of them, strikingly beautiful; commingling in good proportions, the witty, the grotesque, the pathetic, and the heroic. It may be read with profit as well as pleasure."—*Argus.*

"The work will commend itself to the masses, depicting as it does most graphically the struggles and privations which await the unknown and uncared-for Mechanic in his journey through life. It is what might be called a romance, but not of love, jealousy and revenge order."—*Lockport Courier.*

HAGAR, A STORY OF TO-DAY.

By ALICE CAREY, author of "Clovernook," "Lyra, and Other Poems," &c. One vol., 12mo, price $1.00.

"'Hagar' is destined to have a great run among the readers of romantic fiction; in its kind, it is the book of the season; and it has the merit of conveying, with a fearful impressiveness, a lesson in morals as just and as striking as the speculation and tendencies of the time have made it necessary."—*Home Journal.*

"The story is written in a beautiful style, and is worthy of being read in every well-regulated domestic circle, for while it calls up the finer feelings of the soul, it guides the reader to the superior blessings of a reliance on Divine Providence."—*Brooklyn Journal.*

SORCERY AND MAGIC;

Narratives of Sorcery and Magic, from the most authentic Sources. By THOMAS WRIGHT, A. M. &c. One vol., 12mo, price 1.25.

"We have no hesitation in pronouncing this one of the most interesting works which has for a long time issued from the press."—*Albany Express.*

"The narratives are intensely interesting, and the more so, as they are evidently written by a man whose object is simply to tell the truth, and who is not himself bewitched by any favorite theory."—*New York Recorder.*

"The range of information in the book is extraordinarily wide, and it is popularly set forth throughout, without a touch of pedantry or a dull page."—*Examiner.*

"Mr. Wright must have devoted much reading and research to produce so comprehensive a view of sorcery and magic, not only in England and Scotland, but in France, Spain, Italy, Germany, Sweden, and New England."—*Literary Gazette.*

THE NIGHT-SIDE OF NATURE:

Or Ghosts and Ghost-Seers. By CATHERINE CROWE. One vol., 12mo.

"This book treats of allegorical dreams, presentiments, trances, apparitions, troubled spirits, haunted houses, etc., and will be read with interest by many because it comes from a source laying claim to considerable talent, and is written by one who really believes all she says, and urges her reasonings with a good deal of earnestness."—*Albany Argus.*

"This queer volume has excited considerable attention in England. It is not a catchpenny affair, but is an intelligent inquiry into the asserted facts respecting ghosts and apparitions, and a psychological discussion upon the reasonableness of a belief in their existence."—*Boston Post*

"This is not only a curious but also a very able work. It is one of the most interesting books of the season—albeit the reader's hair will occasionally rise on end as he turns over the pages, especially if he reads alone far into the night."—*Zion's Herald.*

THE CELESTIAL TELEGRAPH:

Or, Secrets of the World to Come, revealed through Magnetism; wherein the Existence, the Form, and the Occupations of the Soul, after its Separation from the Body, are proved by Many Years' Experiments, by the Means of eight Ecstatic Somnambulists, who had eighty Perceptions of thirty-six Deceased Persons of various Conditions. A description of them, their Conversation, etc., with Proofs of their Existence in the Spiritual World. By L. ALPH. CAHAGNET. In one volume, 12mo, 410 pp. Price $1.25.

"Mr. Cahagnet has certainly placed the human race under a vast debt of obligation to himself, by the vast amount of information vouchsafed respecting our hereafter. What we have read in this volume has exceedingly interested us in many ways and for many reasons—chiefly, perhaps, because we have perused it as we would any other able work of fiction. As a work of imagination, it is almost incomparable. Some of the revelations are as marvellous and interesting as those, or that, of Poe's M. Valdemar. We commend this work to lovers of the wild and incredible in romance."—*Ontario Repository.*

STILLING'S PNEUMATOLOGY.

Theory of Pneumatology; in Reply to the Question, What ought to be believed or disbelieved concerning Presentiments, Visions, and Apparitions, according to Nature, Reason, and Scripture. By Doct. JOHANN HEINRICH JUNG-STILLING. Translated from the German, with copious Notes, by SAMUEL JACKSON. Edited by Rev. GEORGE BUSH. In one vol., 12mo, 300 pp. Price $1.

"We have in the course of the discussion, a philosophical account of the magnetic influence, as showing the influence of mind upon mind, as well as of various other analogous subjects. The array of facts brought forward by the author is curious, and the work will interest any one who is engaged in studying the different phases of the human mind."—*State Register.*